Global Eating Disorder

"Global Eating Disorder is one of the most comprehensive and practical analyses of what will soon become dysfunctional in our global industrialized food system given the challenges ahead of us -- end of cheap energy, depleting natural resources and impacts of climate change. This is a must read for anyone interested in getting a head start preparing for the changes ahead."
–*Frederick Kirschenmann, author of Cultivating an Ecological Conscience: Essays From a Farmer Philosopher.*

"The food in your fridge is just the tip of the iceberg. Gunnar Rundgren takes you behind the scene of global food production and shows you who pulls the strings in the agricultural system. He doesn't mince his words but offers crystal clear argumentation why things are going wrong in the food chain. After reading this book you will think twice how to fill your shopping basket. A must read for all who want to catch a glimpse of the future of our food!"
–*Franz Fischler, President of the European Forum Alpbach and former EU Commissioner for Agriculture and Fisheries.*

"Rundgren's book has global reach and vision, and deserves a global audience."
–*Frederick Kaufman, food journalist and author of Bet the Farm.*

Global Eating Disorder

Gunnar Rundgren

Dear Rob,
Keep up your good work.
See pages 334-336 for the end result of the interview. Hopefully the rest is also intresta

R

Gunnar

Regeneration, Uppsala, Sweden
regeneratpublisher@gmail.com

First English edition, rev 27 November 2014

Front cover photo: Ann-Helen Meyer von Bremen
Back cover author photo: Ylva Andersson

ISBN: 9198089242
ISBN-13: 978-9198089240
Regeneration, Uppsala, Sweden

Table of Contents

An appetizer

A few years ago, I spent a few weeks in Samoa, a paradisiacal Pacific island country. Some things struck me there. One is the traditional villages which have a special building style, with open *fales*. They are, in effect, houses without walls, where life goes on for all to see. The village and the extended family have very strong positions. Land is mostly communal and leaders of the extended families, *the mathai*, assign land to family members. They have a proverb: 'the man who sells family land will not live to an old age – devils will bring about his early death'. Samoa's soils are volcanic, rich but extremely rocky and for generations Samoans have been growing coconuts, breadfruit, taro and bananas and a number of other fruits. Farmers make their choices of how and what to produce based on tradition, local resources, and the needs of the community and family. Coconuts were an important export crop for a while, but lately the plantations have been neglected. I assume they can no longer compete with palm oil from Malaysia and Indonesia. Most products are not sold in the market but are distributed within the families and villages; the meat is mostly consumed at big parties or given away. Traditionally pigs played a big role, and they are still quite important. I visited an agriculture fair where each village brought roasted piglets as tribute to the gathered dignitaries. Behind the stage, these piglets were being distributed to visitors. A vivid example of traditional ways of building community.

I was part of a World Bank team assisting the government in the development of a program to increase the competitiveness of the agriculture sector, to be financed by credit that would be repaid in a distant future. My role was to look into the opportunities for commercial organic production. Commercializing production would mean that farmers sell their produce in 'the market' to earn more money. But it also would mean farmers using more inputs – that they generally need to buy – including credit, fertilizers, irrigation and advisory and business planning services. In this way they could increase productivity and their incomes. That is the idea at least.

Part of the price to be paid for this is increased risk. But there is more: when traditional farming systems are brought into the market economy, the change is more than just technical or economic. The whole village social context is disrupted, reducing the role of the village and the extended family. When visiting farms, I realized that many farm families seemed to be happy with their way of life. When I asked directly what they would like for their business, they came up with nothing related to increased production, higher income and the like. There were few incentives for individuals to invest in commercial production as the benefits will be shared by so many. The very rocky soils make mechanization virtually impossible, so it is unlikely that Samoans can ever be competitive in commercially cultivating any annual crops. One of the few larger scale farmers I visited had bought soil and put a thick layer of topsoil on his land to cover the stones.

In personal terms the job on Samoa was very rewarding. Professionally, as a consultant it contributed to my growing uneasiness of being asked to recruit farmers into the global market economy, and leading them and their country into debt. At the end of the day, I found it hard to wholeheartedly recommend commercialization as the best solution for Samoan farmers and communities, not even commercial organic production. I suspect that the World Bank will no longer want my services, and even less so after reading this book.

- 1 -
The menu

food (n.)

Old English foda "food, nourishment; fuel," also figurative, from Proto-Germanic *fodon (cf. Gothic fodeins), from Germanic root *fod-, equivalent of PIE *pa- "to tend, keep, pasture, to protect, to guard, to feed" (cf. Greek pateisthai "to feed;" Latin pabulum "food, fodder," panis "bread," pasci "to feed," pascare "to graze, pasture, feed," pastor "shepherd," literally "feeder;" Avestan pitu- "food;" Old Church Slavonic pasti "feed cattle, pasture;" Russian pishcha "food") (http://www.etymonline.com)

We stayed overnight in Dodson, Montana in a charming Bed and Breakfast owned and managed by Sandra Calk. At breakfast we got a peep view into her fridge. There were fruit and vegetables, cheeses, juices, marmalade, honey pickles, condiments and everlasting tortillas. There were eggs and rhubarb from a neighbor but nothing else was from close by, the regular milk came from Texas, and the vanilla scented one from Idaho. Even most of the meat products did not come from Montana, despite the state having millions of cattle grazing its green rolling hills; Montana has more cows than people. Montana cattle are finished in huge feed lot operations in Colorado, Nebraska or Texas where they are fed on maize[a] from the fertile Corn Belt of the United States.

This snapshot of Sandra's fridge is a mirror of the global food and agriculture system. The example is in no way extreme. In most parts of the industrial and urbanized world, people hardly eat anything that comes from close by. Consumption has no direct link to local agriculture which is organized in the same way as modern assembly lines,

---

[a] In this book 'maize' is used for what in North America mostly is referred to as 'corn'.

with parts being delivered from all over the globe to be assembled as a Gorby's pizza, a McDonald's hamburger or a Ben and Jerry's ice cream. Indonesian consumers munched a stunning 14 billion packages of instant wheat noodles in 2012.[1] What is strange about that? Indonesia produces no wheat at all – what has become a national dish is based on a raw material that is completely imported.[2]

When anthropologists describe some preliterate society, the conditions of food production and its role in society usually forms a central part of the narrative. Taboos, gender roles, power, ownership are all linked to food. We often fail to realize that food is also ubiquitous in our modern society, not only providing nutrition, but also a strong determinant of most aspects of the economy, society and culture. Regardless of which models or epochs we look at, our relationship with food is one of the main shapers of human society. Many people say, or think, that industrialism has made us less dependent on nature and on farming. But, that is an illusion caused by human beings living further away from nature. Although we get our electricity via cables and petrol from tubes at filling stations we are no less dependent on nature for energy than a hunter sitting around the campfire or the farmer putting another log on her hearth. Nor are we any less dependent on farming than our ancestors; almost all our food comes from farms.

In farming, a few species of plants and animals are chosen and preferred over others. These species are evolutionary partners of the human species. We nurture and protect these faithful symbionts from other threats, at the price of ultimately eating them. They are almost an integral part of our species, and certainly our society, as it is today, couldn't exist without them. Neither would they exist without us, at least not on the scale they do now. Cows, sheep and goats would not cover one quarter of the planet's surface if we hadn't put them to work for us. Maize owes us as much as we owe maize. We have chosen a few species, and then selected and developed the more valuable traits in those species to create special varieties and breeds. Animals are bred to produce the most valuable product – whether it is meat, milk, fur or wool. We have selected plants with bigger, or more, seeds or more of an edible root, or a less bitter taste. This, in turn, has made plants and animals more dependent on human beings and the farmscape, as they would not otherwise survive outside of its boundaries.

The basis for farming, the collection of solar energy via a few selected plants, mainly grains, has been the basis for human civilizations for more than five thousand years, and this is likely to remain the case. Despite the break neck speed of change of human society, there has been almost no change in the fundamental biological basis for our food production. The total biological production per hectare remains much the same, but we take a greater and greater share of that production, by transforming grains to have fewer roots and straw and more kernel and by exterminating weeds, insects and wildlife in the fields.

Globally our farming system is based on a few grains, root crops and oil crops supplemented with animals, most of them known and used for centuries. Almost no new plants or animals have been domesticated in the last centuries. The balance between the staples has changed and instead of being bound to one or two staples, (bread and milk in the Swedish case, rice for many Asians) we can now eat rice, pasta, potatoes, cornflakes, meat, milk, cheese etc. Increasingly we eat fast and processed foods. Yet, these processed foods, to a very large extent, contain the same staples. The difference between food and fast-food is not so much a difference in raw materials, but in the process of making and preparing them.

Despite a doubling of population between 1960 and 2000, the nutritional status of the world's population has improved considerably in this time. The farmers of the world have reasons to be proud of their accomplishment. But it has come at a price. For most of its history, farming has been based on sustenance, reproduction, improving and building up capital in the soil, in the livestock or in physical assets. It was also the bearer of culture and society at large. But today, in many regions, food production is exceeding environmental limits or is close to doing so. The use of nitrogen and phosphorus fertilizers has passed the limits for a biosphere in balance. Our whole food system contributes at least one third of man-made total greenhouse gas emissions and agriculture is the single largest driver of biodiversity loss. The extraction of water for irrigation exceeds the regeneration of water sources in many parts of the world. Pesticides cause a major loss of biodiversity and hundreds of thousands of direct deaths among farmers and farm workers. Nobody really knows how they affect other aspects of our health. Taken together these factors (and others not mentioned here), could compromise the capacity of the earth to produce food in the future. The farming system is also socially and economically unsustainable.

There is growing concern over future food production and increasing competition for resources in the food, energy and water nexus are reflected in a new interest for investment in land and water. "I cannot farm myself out of this water problem," says Mark Shannon, a farmer who in 2010 had to let his land in the San Joaquin valley be converted into a solar power field.[3] This is a vivid illustration of the shortage of resources that will be a permanent feature in the future, and how land, water and energy interplay. Shortage of one can partly be compensated with another, but what happens if all of them are scarce? We see today that the market does not distribute scarce resources to those who are poor: if resources become scarcer the poor will be further disenfranchised. In more extreme cases the rich will drive their cars with fuels made from food crops that the poor cannot afford to buy and lack the resources to produce themselves.

Our industrial society is based on linear thinking and processes. We bring together certain inputs, process them and create a saleable product, the output. This is in contrast to how nature works, where matter and substances circulate or flow back and forth. This is why our industrial society creates problems such pollution, climate change and dead seas. The straight rows of endless monocultures in Mato Grosso are reflected in the aisles of the supermarket and the lanes of the highways full of lorries bringing goods into them and cars transporting food to people's homes. But the food system is a life support system and should be based on the principles of living systems, not on the perceived efficiency of the industrial model. Linear thinking and linear processes are fundamentally at odds with the cycles of nature and, ultimately, nature still rules.

Efficiency is a one of those misleading words that obscure reality. Nature is not efficient in our limited way of using the word. It is both abundant and contains a lot of redundancy. A tobacco plant can have several hundred thousand seeds, which would be enough to plant a hundred hectares of tobacco. One ejaculation of human sperm could in theory suffice for more than a year of global births. Natural systems have huge buffering capacities which make them resilient. In old times, societies stored grain and other key resources over years to ensure their survival. People often took it rather easy at work, the hours worked were often long, but the pace was slow and saints' days and festivals were abundant. A cow lived for fifteen or twenty years. Through competition and markets[a], these kinds of practices are too costly and have become seen as inefficient. The store of global food is just enough for a couple of months; we work hard, in systems that monitor our every movement and the poor cows only usually reach four years before they are sent to slaughter and replaced by younger and more efficient cows. We squander the capital of nature for short term gains. In what sense is this efficient?

---

[a] In short, I use the term 'the market' to describe 'the market economy', 'the market system' or 'the globalized capitalist market built on endless competition'.

In many countries, there is a lack of trust in the food industry's commitment to providing healthy and sound food and a desire to support local farms. Repeated food scandals and absurd transportation of food adds to this. There are valid concerns for what happens to our food if it is allowed to be fully subject to the logic of the market, where profit and unlimited competition rule. Interestingly, this lack of confidence in the global trading system's ability to work well for food is widespread and can even be found among countries that are otherwise committed to global free trade. During the food price hike of 2008, several food-importing countries made bilateral agreements with food-producing countries to safeguard their supplies of food. Some went a step further and initiated large-scale projects to produce food in other countries. Some food exporting countries banned exports to ensure that they would have sufficient food for their own population. And, in the wake of the financial crisis, community food production and self-sufficiency is on the increase.

It is no longer very controversial to question the direction our food system has taken. Twenty years ago there were only a few isolated dissenting voices but today competent expert bodies, such as the European Union's Standing Committee on Agricultural Research, and the International Assessment of Agricultural Knowledge, Science and Technology for Development, clarify that 'business as usual is not an option'. We simply have to find new ways, whether we want to or not. But we will only be able to find new ways if we understand the factors that determine how we farm, what we grow and what we eat. Most of the mainstream commentaries focus on the technical aspects of food production and farming, such as use of genetically modified organisms and chemical fertilizers, and their benefits and drawbacks. But these technical aspects of farming are only part of the problem, or part of the solution. The food system is a socio-economic system and needs to be viewed as such.

There are three megatrends that have shaped our food system over the last centuries: 1) the commercialization of the entire food system, 2) the use of energy and applied technology (be it in the form of machinery or nitrogen fertilizers) to replace animate labor and processes, and 3) demographic changes, such as population growth, demographic transition and urbanization, and the related lifestyle changes. These three megatrends are mutually reinforcing. Any of them alone would not produce the changes that can be observed today. For example, the application of energy and mechanization in farming, in particular the use of fossil fuels, has increased productivity per agriculture worker by between fifty and two hundred times, which meant that the share of population engaged in farming dropped tremendously. The use of nitrogen fertilizers (produced with huge energy investments) has been a major driver for the increase of crop yields per area unit. Without fossil fuels, globalization and massive urbanization could not have happened. And without urbanization there would be little development of markets for agriculture products. Similarly, without commercialization of farming there would be little incentive to mechanize and use chemical fertilizers, as both pre-suppose market driven farming.

The existence of markets in most human societies for some thousand years or longer is not at all the same as the existence of a 'market economy' and even less a globalized capitalist market economy. As farmers become integrated into the market economy, they no longer reproduce and regenerate their production system. They buy their seeds and breeds in the market; they feel that they don't have to take care of the reproduction of the soil, because they can compensate for this by buying chemical fertilizers in sacks. They don't have to take care of the balance between nature and what humans take away. Land, water and forests have been gradually transformed from commons to tradable commodities. The time perspective of farmers in my native Scandinavia has, until very recently, been intergenerational, some refer it to as 'glacial time.' The sustainable regeneration of productive forces, including labor and the knowledge needed, was engraved in the memes of those farming societies. This is in absolute contrast to the entrepreneurial approach farmers are encouraged to apply today. 'Farming as a business' is a code word for farming now from Narvik to Cape Town, from Alaska to the Tierra del Fuego and from Vladivostok to Tasmania. The market, initially just a tool for distributing surpluses, has become the conductor of the whole food system, from farm to fork. The commercialization of farming also leads us to view land, water, nature as private property and the life of the land, our symbionts, as commodities. The divide between society, culture, the economy and nature that we currently experience is a divide alien to farming, and can never be sustainable. If the transition from hunting to farming was the First Fall of Man, farming as a business is the Second Fall.

In most human societies the distribution of the most important foods was done outside the market and was strictly regulated. Gifts, taxes, rents, tribute and sharing were important channels for food distribution. We can still see in times of disaster, war or disturbance that societies rapidly shun the market as the main mechanism for distribution, and public or community control over food are the preferred ways of ensuring proper (that means somewhat equal) sharing. Cooking and eating were for a long time mostly social activities done within the household or in the community, with the work being done without pay and for no costs. Gradually, cooking and eating have become commercialized and acquired a total different meaning and role in society.[a] It is this process that is the real tragedy for food, and makes a large contribution to obesity because when food is a commodity its main purpose is to be consumed.

Food production is still not a limiting factor for human expansion. Starvation and malnutrition are symptoms of an unfair and unequal society rather than signs of overpopulation, and should be tackled as such. Access to food should be an inalienable right. This is actually already agreed by world leaders in the Universal Declaration of Human Rights. An equitable world will have the potential to feed everybody. It will certainly ensure that the food is distributed more fairly among the world's population. Nevertheless, there are biological limits for food production. The space used for farming cannot be expanded much; however, the yields per area unit can be increased and production systems can be changed to produce more food.

The challenge of feeding a growing population is formidable, but managing the planet's ecosystem is an even bigger challenge. Considering that farmed landscapes dominate more than half of the terrestrial area of the Earth, and even a bigger share of its biological production, it is clear that the way we farm has an enormous impact on the planet's ecosystems; that human agricultural ecosystems must be seen as planetary ecosystems. Yet, the food and farming system is increasingly managed by signals from 'the market', which do not include the signals from these ecosystems: of the species threatened by extinction and the loss of biodiversity, of pollution and of greenhouse gas emissions. The market signals also don't include the feelings of the animals brutalized in our service. The system is simply not geared towards stewardship of the planet and living beings but to the maximization of marketable output and profit.

Some efforts are being made to correct this, by payments for environmental services and some regulations on harmful practices, such as animal welfare regulations and the prohibition of particularly lethal pesticides. Overall, these have a minimal impact and are insufficient to encourage farmers and consumers to adopt behaviors that foster planetary stewardship. The Earth is our common home and respon-

---

[a] Interestingly enough, food recipes have not (yet) been subject to intellectual property rights – and this certainly doesn't seem to decrease innovations in cooking.

sibility and should be managed as such. Markets, in their various forms, are systems developed to organize the distribution of products between humans, and they only partially fulfill that function. There is no reason whatsoever for believing that a market is a good tool for regulating our relationship with the rose, the eagle or the water in the ocean. Instead of trying to squeeze more of the commons into the market, we should re-balance food towards public goods. In this way eco-system services and food production can be balanced within the same framework.

The rethinking of food as a right, of farming as a management system of the planet and the food system as a commons will lead us to develop new institutions that complement the roles of the market and the state. This does not rule out markets as one of several mechanisms for food distribution, but it rejects market hegemony over our food supplies, and the doctrine that market forces are the best way of allocating food-producing resources such as land, water, knowledge and seeds. This sounds very revolutionary. Perhaps it is. But it is not a completely either-or question. Even where market forces prevail, there are many aspects of food and farming which are not left to the vagaries of the market. Food and farming remain, together with energy, labor and housing, one of the most regulated parts of the economy, even before we consider all the cultural norms surrounding them. Even if many of the regulations are unnecessary and many of the subsidies are silly, there are there for a reason; a recognition that the free market doesn't work. Or rather that it does indeed work as it should, but we don't like the result of its workings.

We might believe that we chose to eat a certain food, but that is an erroneous starting point for a conversation about which foods we eat and which we should eat. Our palates have been shaped over centuries to like some things and dislike others. The mere difference in local foods and food preferences is proof not of how different from each other we are, but how well we adapt to what is available. For the large part of human existence, we have eaten the stuff that was locally available. If we were Inuit we liked caribou and whale meat and fat, if we were Swedes we liked herring and cheese; Bantu people like cassava and goat stew. Our habits have been dictated by what produce and which food technologies were available. Fermentation, drying, freezing, curing, have all played different roles in different countries. If you lived in the humid tropics, your culture would never developed a prosciutto ham, as the conditions for making the ham do not exist in such a climate. The availability of fats and fuels determine your favorite style of frying or roasting or if you mostly eat food boiled in water.

Today, our food choices are by and large determined by the economy instead of ecology. For sure, when standing in front of a supermarket shelf, or sitting at a table reading a restaurant menu, there are many choices. But before we face all those choices a number of people have made the selection for us to choose from. And they in turn have chosen from other people's choices. Governments and agri-business are 'choice architects' and their decisions shape what consumers can and cannot buy. The modern food system is simultaneously moving towards uniformity and diversity. Globalization gives many people access to many more kinds of foods than before, but at the same time the differences between regional cuisines are diminishing. We are easily duped by the bright colors of marketing messages and wrapping. A supermarket may carry some 50,000 food items, but a very large part of them are variations made out of the 'Big Five' – wheat, maize, palm oil, sugar and soybeans – and they are produced by a handful large companies, which source the raw materials from a few selected key locations.

Cheap food allows people to eat meat, fresh vegetables and fruits all year round, something most people could only dream of a few generations back – and something many people in the world can only still dream of. People live longer, are taller, and are generally healthier than in the agrarian societies of the 18th and 19th centuries. But the current food system has also produced obesity, allergies and other diseases, while at the same time destroying the environment. Food is cheap, too cheap, because we have externalized many of the costs of producing and consuming it. We let someone else – nature, other people, future generations, tax payers – foot the bill for climate change, for the loss of biodiversity, for eutrophication, for nitrates and pesticides in our groundwaters or even for losing the water or the soil altogether. Farmers using nitrogen fertilizers create costs for society at large that are on par with the economic benefits for them. But as long as the cost for this is not included in the cost for food it makes economic sense to use massive amounts of ammonium nitrate than to farm in an organic way. European chickens or Chinese pigs are, to a very large extent, fed soy protein from Latin America, much of it from the Cerrado, the Amazon or the Pampa, landscapes which are razed and raped by agro-business. The extinction of species and the greenhouse gas emissions caused by this are also not included in the price of chicken breast or the pulled pork. We can no longer afford cheap food.

We have to bite the bullet; the food system is not a *smorgasbord* where we can pick out the bits we like and keep those we don't like. There is no way to produce good artisanal foods and biologically diverse landscapes for the masses in a containerized, standardized and monopolistic food system. It is hard to see that one can combine animal welfare with the view of animals as commodities, instead we should see them as our symbionts and companions, for which we have responsibility. There are also ample opportunities to produce more foods with regenerative methods, such as organic farming. The 'problem', if you so wish, is that it will cost us more in terms of the share of population engaged in food production. This in turn affects how many people can be engaged in producing iPhones and cars and serving us coffee. By and large, I think such a shift will only be good for society, culture and nature.

"We can never do merely one thing" is a basic tenet of ecology ascribed to the ecologist Garret Hardin. It applies not only to ecology but to any system. It is certainly true when we talk about food and farming. Few things are so interconnected with each other and the rest of society and nature. And that is one of the key things I hope readers will get from this book. I hope it will contribute to a deeper understanding of the interactions between farming, food, landscapes, culture and economy. The food system, the farms and what we eat are part of an economic, political, cultural and social system, and without understanding how that system shapes farming and food, efforts to change any of them in a profound way, will be in vain. This is also reflected in the last part of the book where I discuss the way ahead, the alternatives. I don't offer any silver bullet but advocate a mix of a 'mice in the basement' strategy, political action and new ethics.

Often when I hold a lecture the organizers ask me to "give them hope, things they can do here and now to make a difference". This idea is based on the premise that people are 'empowered' by a message that gives them three (or five) points they can take home with them that can make a difference. And as things should be easy and 'actionable' it comes down to individual choices. In most cases those choices are about consumption. I always refuse to give those three or five points. Personally, I always buy organic foods and, professionally, I was the founder of one of the most successful organic labeling programs in the world (Krav in Sweden). I do think we have the moral obligation, as consumers, to buy humane, organic or fairly traded goods. But as commendable as it is, this falls blatantly short of changing the rules of the game. Telling consumers that they will change the world or eradicate poverty by shopping is to deceive them.

We need to build new relationships in the food system, new relationships that can gradually take over most of the food system. Those relationships should be based on food and farming as joint common activities. There should not be 'producers' and 'consumers', but co-production. The farming technologies themselves should also

be reoriented to the regeneration of resources, meaning and relationships. Consumption as a separate category should wither and we
would cook and eat in harmony with production. There will most
likely be markets in the future, but not 'the market' that we know
today, the globalized market with unlimited competition. Political
actions, of many kinds, are needed. Some should be oriented to limit
the harm produced by the current system, such as bans on pesticides
and harmful practices or reallocating resources. Others should target
the development of alternatives. This can range from re-allocating
research funds from industrial farming models to regenerative
farming, to revising tax codes to stimulate the numbers of people
engaged in farming and facilitating emerging new economic relations.

Finally, it is about us as human beings. Are we ready for the great
leap into an unknown future, based on new insights and a new balance
between matter and soul, between restless improvements and innovation and a simpler life in nature? Do we prefer the sterile and cheap,
ready to eat, meal wrapped in plastic from the supermarket over the
earthy smells and tastes of nature, combined with more sweat and toil?
In the long term I don't think we have a lot of choice. An increasing
scarcity of key resources will make the choice for us. But the ride will
be easier if we halt the depletion of resources and of nature and build a
regenerative food system now, before we are faced with the possibility
of worrying whether we will get any food at all before going to bed.

I will tell the story in four parts. First, the *Starters*, the history: how
agriculture and food developed over millennia. The second part, *Primi*,
has five case studies representing critical parts of our food and farming
system. These are grains, grazing animals, sugar, fat and chicken.
Taken together, these products represent much of our food system.
Third, in *Secondi*, I dive deeper into many of the complex problems and
challenges of the current food system. In the penultimate part, *Desserts*,
I point towards the future. In *Digestive*, I provide background
information on some of the calculations I have made.

You do not have to be a keen reader to understand the points I will
make. You can do an experiment at home yourself. Prepare a village
chicken and buy a fried industrial chicken. Buy a salad with green
house grown, drip-fed tomatoes and lettuce and another with tomatoes and green leaves grown outdoors in real soil, picked when ripe.
For the modern meal buy white bread in a plastic bag from the supermarket, for the other one use home baked bread from old cereal
varieties. When you eat, close your eyes; think about the history of
those foods, where they came from, how they have emerged and how

they reached your plate, what they tell. But most of all: how they *smell, taste and feel*. This will give a sensory experience of what I will try to say. But eating is also a good opportunity for a good conversation, so I hope you will be motivated to invite others to join your experimental meal.

Part I: Starters

The soldier's fare

500 g bread
150 g meat
200 g crushed oats
Beer, salt and butter

Mix it as you like and eat when you have a break.

The daily ration for a soldier in the Swedish army in 1635.[4] Without beer and butter it gives 2,500 calories – depending on the kind of meat.

2

Let there be light

"Go left!"
"Go right!"
The two synthetic voices talk the same language, Dutch, but they have different opinions on which way to turn at the junction. I am with two representatives of the Grodan company to visit Pudu Peppers in Roermond, a Dutch town close to the German border. The lack of agreement between the GPSs seems like a forewarning of the dangers of depending too much on modern technology. But I shouldn't worry.

Finally, we find our way and Ad Grubbers welcomes us in a very humble office to the hypermodern greenhouse he owns with his brother, where they produce some twenty five million yellow and red sweet peppers per year from 145,000 square meters. I am visiting the place to see a living example of state of the art intensive production, not one of those fancy things on the drawing boards or in investment prospectuses for startups. It provides a starting point for describing what farming is about. The temperature, humidity and water are controlled meticulously. There is no soil; instead the peppers grow in slabs of mineral wool made from molten rock, the same itchy stuff that is used for isolation. These are essentially a medium for the roots to grow; produced at 1,500 degrees C they are totally sterile, free from bacteria, fungi or weeds. Small seedlings, also in mini rock wool pots are bought from specialized nurseries, using strictly controlled seeds from one of the huge seed companies. Biological control methods, using natural enemies and pesticides are occasionally used against pests and disease.

The twelve essential nutrients, the building blocks of all plants, (nitrogen, iron, potash, manganese, phosphorous, boron, calcium, zinc, magnesium, copper, sulfur and molybdenum) are supplied by Yara, a Norwegian fertilizer giant. They are mixed to exact proportions and supplied via drip irrigation. Surplus water is drained, sterilized with UV light, and brought back into the process. The water itself comes from a well, the rainwater that falls on the glass is drained away, as its quality is too inconsistent to use in this scientifically managed production system. Even the air is enriched by the artificial addition of carbon dioxide. Doubling the concentration of carbon dioxide to 800 ppm can increase growth by some twenty-five percent.

The end result is that Pudu Peppers produce some 30 kg – or approximately 175 peppers – per square meter. This is about ten times as much as the average yield in China, the biggest producer of peppers in the world. In all its extremes, Pudu Peppers gives us an idea what farming is about. Control. Control of all the critical factors for growth; the soil, the water, the temperature, the air itself, nutrients and all other organisms that can influence a crop, either positively or negatively. There are many more things to say about Pudu Peppers, for example that they use natural gas with an energy content of one liter of oil equivalent to produce one kg peppers. I will say more about the enterprise later but for now it serves as an illumination of the fundaments of farming.

One of the few things Pudu Peppers don't control is the light. Artificial light is expensive and its use is limited to special crops and to the production of marijuana. It all starts with light. Sunlight is transformed into chemical energy, that is used to 'fuel' us, through a process called photosynthesis that occurs in the green leaves. Approximately 5 kWh (4,300 cal) of energy per square meter reaches the earth as solar radiation per day (in Chicago it is above 6 kWh in July but just 1.5 kWh in December[5]). This is more energy than in one person's daily food. But less than one percent of this energy is locked by plants as chemical energy, the rest is reflected, transformed to heat or used to evaporate water.[6] If one calculates backwards from the crops actually harvested, we find that the energy in harvested products represents only 0.4% of the solar energy that reaches the fields. Of this 0.4%, only 61% is actually used. Thus, in reality we use only around 0.25% of the solar energy reaching the ground.[7] Despite all the efforts in farming, and the tremendous progress in seed breeding, the basic energy-transformation efficiency has not improved; the efficiency of the green leaves in converting sunlight to calories has not improved, not even modern genetic engineering has ventured into this.[8]

For the benefit of readers who are not so conversant with farming, here is a crash course. Let's start with the seed. The seed contains all the genetic material and the capacity to initiate the process of reproducing and producing life. The seeds are selected to have the right properties. Seeds need to be stored from one season to another. In order to germinate, they need to be planted, sown in the soil. In nature seeds normally fall onto the ground and germinate there. This can also be done with farm seeds, but the conditions on the surface of the soil can be difficult. It might be too dry, so the seed doesn't germinate, or birds or rats may eat the seeds which are easy to spot on the surface. By putting the seeds in the soil they get enough moisture for germination and some protection – but at the same time they may be prone to fungal disease. Before sowing farmers prepare the land by tilling and harrowing the land so the seeds can be mixed into the upper layer of soil. In many cases, there is a need to roll the soil after sowing so that the soil is firm against the seed.

Farmers also often plow the land before sowing. Plowing involves turning over the top few inches of soil. It incorporates the residue of the previous crop into the soil for decomposition, prevents it getting entangled in the machinery used for sowing and cultivation and buries weeds and weed seeds at a depth where most of them will rot and die. The soil is loosened and water can percolate more easily. Better aeration helps decompose organic matter, the nutrients from which may become available for subsequent crops, or be washed away. In parts of the world people without machinery do the same but using a hoe or sometimes a spade. In some parts of the world farmers use direct-sowing machinery, which can be used to sow in unplowed land. This is known as no-till farming and is mostly combined with the use of weed-killers, herbicides, to control weeds. Before the land is prepared, fertilizers or manure is spread on the ground to provide nutrients for the crop. If the land is too acid, which is harmful for many plants, lime can be spread every five years or so.

After sowing the main job is normally weed control. This can be done manually, mechanically or with chemicals (herbicides). Small grains (wheat, oats, rye, barley and sorghum) are sown very densely and there is often no direct weed control or only use of herbicides during the growing season. Crops such as maize and potatoes are grown in rows and the land between the rows is kept free from weeds by hoeing and sometimes with herbicides. Farmers use a multitude of methods to control pests and diseases; these include crop rotations, companion cropping and hand picking but, more often today, using pesticides. Depending on crop and climate, the field can be irrigated by flooding (particularly for rice), open row irrigation, central pivot irrigation or drip irrigation methods. Some crops get one or more extra doses of fertilizer during the growing season.

If all goes well, the main work comes with harvesting the crops. Potatoes are dug up by hand or by machine and many vegetables and fruits are harvested by hand, even in rich countries where there are often ingenious transport solutions, such as conveyors, that make the work easier. In the old times, grain was often cut and bound to sheaves for drying and later threshing (which is the separation of the grain from the straw and the chaff). Today, combine harvesters do this in one single process.

The system of farming itself is often based on crop rotations, i.e. that crops follow each other in each field according to a certain order, so that the same crop is only grown in the same field every fourth to seventh year. In other systems farmers have mixed crops in the same field; these systems are known as polycultures. If the system includes trees or bushes it is often called agroforestry, and if the emphasis is on creating perennial systems it can be called permaculture. Many industrial farming systems are based on mono-cultures, where the same crop is grown year after year with no or little variation.

Farming means selecting a few species from in the environment, and giving them preferential treatment by providing them with more space and nurturing them. And, even for those plants that are selected, we favor the parts that are useful for us, i.e. we favor the grain over the straw and roots and we favor the meat of a chicken over its bones, which is the reason why many broilers cannot even walk properly. In this way, we can use a higher proportion of the biological production from a farmed system than from a 'wild' system.

In essence the primary biological production, the energy trans-formed by the plants through photosynthesis, is more or less the same for a farmed system as for a wild system. Compare a pasture that is established in place of a rainforest or a field that forms when a swamp is drained. In both cases, the biological production is likely to be higher in the original, natural, system than in the farmed system. Biological production is mostly increased by bringing external resources into the system. For example, when irrigation is introduced into drylands or when greenhouses are heated in a cool climate or when nutrients are brought from outside the system, productivity can increase greatly.

Farming has developed differently in different places. The emergence of different farming systems can be easily understood by looking at the conditions under which they developed.

The forest was burning and the area was in a smoky haze when I visited Pedro in the mid 1990s. It was ironic that my eyes were running and I was coughing from the smoke, there in the Amazon, the lungs of the world. Pedro, a young, soot-covered farmer, and the other farmers were clearing land for farming at the edge of the mighty forest, a few hours from Tarapoto in Peru. This was the first time I had visited a farmer practicing swiddening, or slash and burn agriculture. I'd arrived with the idea that swiddening was a primitive method used only by ignorant farmers. I had this image from my school days, the media and from my own love of forests. Clearly, it must be wrong to burn a forest just to grow crops for a few years. After this visit to Pedro, several other farm visits and a good deal of reading, I realized I was wrong. Partly, at least. Swiddening is a method of farming that is rational from the perspective of the farmer. It is also environmentally benign if practiced to a limited extent. Fire is part of nature, and pristine forests have burnt naturally. Human use of fire has shaped many of the most impressive landscapes in the world, including the savannah and the prairies as well as most forest landscapes. However, when population grows, or forest resources dwindle, what was once a good practice becomes a damaging one.

It is easy to understand why farmers like this way of farming. The only land preparation needed after swiddening is to use a stick to make a hole where seeds are dropped. The few weeds that grew there before are not serious competitors to the chosen crop as they are not adapted to an open landscape. There are no, or very few, seeds of the aggressive weeds that are everlasting companions of, and a curse to, farming; the pressure from pests is also low. Many nutrients are released, partly from the ashes of burnt wood and foliage, and partly through decomposition of dying roots in the soil. Swiddening thus clears the land, prepares it for sowing, regulates weeds, pests and diseases, and supplies nutrients, all with a minimal input of labor, making labor productivity very high. But the benefits decrease over time so new land has to be cleared by burning while the farmed land is left to regenerate.

Big rivers flowing through dry plains gave rise to unique possibilities for farming. Because the plains were dry, they had little forest, and because the plains were around the rivers, they were easily flooded. When this happened the land was covered by fertile mud. This meant that two of the most labor-intensive parts of farming – soil preparation and application of fertilizers – were done by nature. Although simplifying somewhat all that was left to do was to just sow and weed. Having water easily available, it was not a big step to later develop irrigation. Fertile flood plains have been the cradle for most successful and some of the most durable civilizations. Still today some of these flood plains continue to provide billions of us with food. In other cases the flood plains have become salinized or have turned into swamps as a result of mismanagement or our lack of understanding of the basics of the complicated set of new technologies which constitute agriculture, a technology that humans are still busy refining and understanding.

The distinction between foraging and domestication is not always clear cut, this is particularly clear when it comes to pastoralism.

Humans certainly manipulated the movements of herds as part of their hunting methods. They burned the forest to drive animals, but also to create an open and accessible landscape with a lot of grass – and ease of hunt. For example, Native Americans managed the prairie as 'a game farm' for bison and the forests were managed to stimulate the presence of trees such as chestnuts and oaks and be good habitat for elk and deer.[9] Many assume that cattle, goats, sheep and camels were domesticated by a process where agrarian societies captured individual animals for keeping. Others think that it is more likely that these kinds of herd animals were domesticated in a gradual process of hunters managing the herds they hunted. Both processes might have occurred in different places.[10] I believe that the domestication of our common herd animals such as cattle and sheep most likely emerged through gradual management and co-evolution with wild herds rather than through domestication of individual wild animals.

In some tropical parts of the world a farming system known as forest gardens has developed. This is a polyculture of forest plants and garden crops, sometimes in conjunction with long cycles of swiddening. The Maya developed this system to a very high level using raised beds watered by clay lined canals. There seems to have been a long cycle involving open fields, orchard gardens and closed canopy forest, which were also used to grow many useful crops. Forest garden systems still exist in Sri Lanka, India, Indonesia, the Pacific and many parts of Africa.[11] In Europe a mixed farming system emerged.

We cannot discuss agriculture or food in isolation from the landscape and nature where it takes place. In many 'marginal' areas – areas where climate or soil are harsh, such as drylands, steep land, mountains, swamps and tundra – farmed systems are often not very productive. More than two hundred and fifty years ago Carl Linnaeus, the founder of modern biological classification, noted that the 'Swedish' settlers had a miserable life – and couldn't pay any taxes – in the mountains whereas the non-farming, reindeer-keeping Sami people did well under the same conditions. And this is not restricted to cold areas. The livestock expert R. N. B. Kay says that humans over the centuries have made clumsy attempts to introduce domestic species of plants or animals into marginal, arid regions resulting in catastrophic collapses of the ecosystem. He found that the East African acacia savannah and bushland can carry roughly five times more biomass of wild animals than of our domesticated symbionts.[12]

Nature is based on cycles of various kinds. What is waste for one organism is food for another; nothing is unused. There are quick cycles, such as when an animal is eating and drinking, when much of what was taken in is soon let out again, and this feeds other organisms. There are also very slow and long cycles, such as the formation of rocks and their subsequent weathering. A particularly important cycle is the formation and erosion of topsoil (i.e. the rich soil that is the basis for farming). Both processes are natural; erosion can be slow or very rapid (as in landslides), whereas soil formation is mostly very slow, except in cases of dramatic flooding; the landslide that causes rapid erosion can lead to soil formation downstream. Other important cycles are the carbon, water, nitrogen and phosphorus cycles and the climate. The weather is the eternal topic of discussion in farming communities. Agriculture interacts, influences, and is influenced by, most of these cycles. These cycles and the local conditions determine which crops will be grown, which animals will be kept, and how they will be kept. Ultimately they have determined which food we have eaten.

3

From foragers to farming civilizations

In May and June, fishing is good in the lakes. In early July, the wild strawberries make my mouth water. In August, the chanterelles are ripe, as are the blueberries and cloudberries. A month later, other mushrooms and the lingonberry (cowberry) abound. When frost bites in fall, there is plenty of game in the forest that can be hunted, elk, deer and hares etc. I take a lot of pleasure in collecting wild things: it is not only a pleasure to be out in the wild, but the taste of these foraged crops and animals is generally far superior to that of cultivated plants or the tame animals we rear. They are also 'for free', even if such a statement neglects the considerable time and effort I have to expend to capture them. If counting the time spent and assign a typical labor cost to them, they are no longer cheap. This is why the only people who pick berries to sell in the Swedish forests today are migrants who work under conditions that, from a Swedish perspective, are deplorable, although they are apparently good enough to make them return every season, from as far away as Thailand.

Many believe that forager societies (I prefer this term to hunters and gatherers) were characterized by misery and starvation, but the opposite seems to be true.[13] Most hunters and gatherers ate well and they also worked little, much less than the farmers and laborers who succeeded them. And, their societies appear to have been more egalitarian than those which followed; there were no classes, economic specialization, private property or slavery. In some ways, the hunter and gatherer societies seem to have been a secure and rather pleasant way of life, although most of us today would certainly not voluntarily swap our lifestyles for such a way of life. And, it is not at all possible to feed a human population of 7 billion on wild resources alone. Our ancestors developed ways to support bigger populations by controlling more and more factors of biological production; they developed farming or agriculture.

Agriculture developed some 12,000 years ago through the gradual domestication of plants and animals. It is mostly assumed that farming developed independently in eight areas: the Fertile Crescent (West

Asia); South China, North China, New Guinea, Sub-Saharan Africa; the South Central Andes; Central Mexico and Eastern North America. The first animal to be domesticated was the dog, but that was probably before any farming, or livestock husbandry took place. Sheep and goats were tamed some 11,000 years ago, pigs 9000 years ago and cows 8000 years ago. Turkeys were domesticated in what is Mexico today and hens in India. Wheat, rye, beans and peas were grown in West Asia; buckwheat, soya, onion and eggplant in East Asia; sorghum, cotton, okra and banana in Africa; bananas, taro, coconuts, squash, rice and sweet potatoes in South East Asia; and chili, potato, tomato, peanuts and pineapple in the Americas.[14]

There are no strong reasons to believe that human beings were forced to farm in order to feed an increasingly hungry population. It was rather improved methods of hunting and fishing or life in particularly rich border zones, such as an oasis or coastal flats, which enabled people to settle in certain places. The Norte Chico settlements just north of today's Lima in Peru are an interesting, and perhaps odd example. These are more than 5000 years old, the oldest known civilization in the Americas. The Carla-Supe people who lived there were ostensibly engaged in farming. But they did not grow staple foods; instead they grew cotton and gourds, needed primarily for their extensive fishing. The cotton was used to make nets and lines, while the gourds were used as floats.[15]

The first farmers could not feed themselves from farming alone to begin with; if they had tried, they would have starved to death. On the contrary, farming was almost certainly developed by settled people who still got most of their food through the old ways of hunting and gathering. They farmed certain crops that were uncommon and difficult to find, such as medicinal herbs, or crops that they fancied a lot, more like gardening. In Mesoamerica, domestication of maize, beans and pepper can be traced back ten thousand years, but it was not until five thousand years later that domesticated plants and animals dominated the food system, a clear indication that a foraging culture can be competitive with farming, even under conditions which are conducive to farming.[16] As settled populations grew, farming changed from being an opportunity to a necessity.

There is not a straight-forward dividing line to be drawn between foraging and farming societies. Some foragers manipulated their environment a lot in order to 'produce' more of the kind of animals that humans like (such as bison) and less of those that humans don't like (wolves and tigers). Some dropped nuts in fertile soils to have more nuts to collect, or cleared the bush that threatened to crowd out that mouth-watering herb. Some had a tame dog as part of the hunting party. In North America before colonization, many native cultures successfully 'improved the wilderness' as an ecological strategy. The Kumeyaay in California planted cacti, created groves of wild oaks and pines and regularly burned the *chaparral* (shrublands) to improve the browsing for deer. On the Australian continent people developed 'fire-stick farming' primarily for small-game hunting. The fires created a high diversity of successional habitats, which, in turn, led to a better food supply.[17] The extensive use of fire for hunting or other landscape manipulation also contributed to the emergence of farming by stimulating the kind of pioneer annual crops which still today dominate farming as well as the grasses which formed the basis for livestock production. Most grasses are very resistant to fire, so burning favors grassland over other vegetation. A study of foraging cultures that still exist today concludes that "many of the wild foods are actively managed, suggesting there is a false dichotomy around ideas of the agricultural and the wild: hunter–gatherers and foragers farm and manage their environments, and cultivators use many wild plants and animals."[18]

There is no doubt about that farming has taken over from foraging and hunting as the main source of food. Nevertheless hunting, in the form of fishing provided more food for humans than ever before in the last century. Fishing also gives us a perspective on the domestication process. Humans have practiced aquaculture for a very long time; it was documented by the Ancient Romans and in China some four thousand years ago. Yet, people have continued fishing, simply because, in most cases, it has been the easiest way to get fish. With increasing energy prices and depleting fish stocks, aquaculture is gradually taking over from wild catch.

Before taking to farming people had not only developed a large number of tools for hunting and fishing, but also tools to harvest plants, such as digging sticks and sickles. We cannot compare the methods of agriculture of the first human beings with those of the farming societies that emerged after thousands of years of trial and error. That would be like comparing floating on a log with sailing in a boat. Farming wasn't a single ready-made technology waiting to be picked up or discovered; it was a complex of technologies, biology and human knowledge and, ultimately, a society. The philosopher Jean Jacques Rousseau[19] maintained that society as such must have emerged before farming because many functions and institutions need to be in place for farming to be possible. This is clearly a valid point. If we see the transformation as a gradual process we can avoid some of the pitfalls of trying to sort out what came first.

In the domestication process, we humans have, intentionally and unintentionally, changed our symbionts, the plants and animals we domesticated. Through selection we sought to increase the yield of those parts of the animals or crops that we found most interesting, which differed in different cultures. This has led us to develop dairy-sheep, wool-sheep, meat-sheep and skin-sheep, and even among these there are many varieties. But domestication also comes with a cost: most domesticated grain, for example, has a protein content that is only around half that of their wild ancestors. Domestication has also created an amazing diversity. Just look at dogs or cabbages to see what enormous diversity we have created in a rather short time. It is fascinating to consider how wild cabbage has resulted in crops as different as kale, cauliflower, pak choy, kohlrabi and white cabbage. Through selective breeding, the dog has developed into hundreds of varied breeds; with heights that range from 15 centimeters in the Chihuahua to about 76 cm in the Irish wolfhound.[20]

Some good foods have never been successfully domesticated. In many places gazelle meat is very popular. But the gazelle is too territorial and nervous to be successfully domesticated. The end result is that in many places the gazelle has become extinct as a result of overhunting, while the docile sheep and goats have increased in numbers and filled the earth. The same goes for many plants that we have liked but not been able to domesticate successfully. For those we have farmed, becoming domesticated has been an enormously success-ful survival strategy, and there are good reasons to ask who has 'conquered' whom and who has domesticated whom.

The Columbian exchange, the mix of the New and Old World species, resulting from the European conquest of the Americas and the opening of sea routes tying all the continents together, had an enor-mous effect on our farming and food systems. The most direct effect was a giant leap in the number of crops and animals available for farmers. The Americas got domesticated animals, and the small grains (to mention just the most important ones). The Old World got maize, potatoes and cassava, crops that were rapidly integrated in the farming systems to the extent that, despite their status as newcomers are seen as part of 'traditional' agriculture systems. Many Native North Ameri-can people saw the benefit of the horse and made it an integral part of their culture. Overall the exchange increased food production potential substantially. Potato production in Europe increased the possible yield of food per area unit considerably compared to grain growing and in

China maize and sweet potatoes increased food supply and nutritional quality.[21] It is remarkable how few new domestications that have taken place since the Columbian exchange. Salmon, sugar beet, ostrich and rubber come to mind as the rare exceptions over the last few hundred years. For the rest we are living on the advances of people living many thousand years ago. In essence, they determined what we eat today.

If they ever think about it, most people seem to initially imagine that cooking of most foods began after they were farmed, but that is to turn the co-evolution of food, cooking and farming on its head. In Abu Hureyra, Northern Syria, 11,000 years ago, people ate gazelle, wild cattle, sheep, goats, pigs, birds and fish. In addition around one hundred and fifty different species, including wheat and rye, have been identified from carbonized seeds. Yet, there are still no indications from this site that the people had started farming. Gordon Hillman of University College, London, studied contemporary Turkish ways of turning emmer wheat into bulgur. From harvest to getting the wheat ready to process there are fourteen steps – threshing, primary winnowing, coarse sieving, storage, parching, pounding, secondary winnowing, medium coarse sieving, fine sieving, washing to semi-clean, storage, second fine sieving and hand sorting. And from ready to process to bulgur there are another five steps – par-boiling, sun-drying, bran removal, winnowing, cracking, and sifting.[22] Only then is it time to boil it!

Clearly people must first have gone through the tedious process of preparing wheat into a digestible food, before they ventured into domesticating it. Therefore, we find traces of cooking wheat and other small grains that significantly predate the first domestication.[23] Some maintain that the desire for alcohol was the main incentive for growing grain. *Saccharomyces cervisiae*, a fungus that we normally refer to as yeast might even claim a position as one of the first domesticated species according to a paper by two geneticists from Washington University School of Medicine in St. Louis.[24] Alcoholic fermentation certainly suggests the emergence of a more sedentary life style. Both beer and its raw materials were difficult to move around, so once humans got a liking for beer (or wine) they had a good reason to stay in a place where they collected the raw materials needed for them. It is a topic of fierce debate among scholars if bread or beer came first.[25]

Before farming, humans had also developed an array of tools for transforming food such as querns, stone vessels, mortars and pestles. Food were cooked, roasted and smoked, and some storage took place.[26] Cooking food over fire made it more palatable. Some claim that we get 20-25% more energy from cooked food and that this also allowed our brains to grow. In other words, we were smart to discover fire, and that discovery led us on to become even smarter. It also makes foods safer by destroying poisons that plants developed in order not to be eaten. Frying or grilling creates a whole new pallet of flavors; browning onions or meat changes their taste remarkably. Humans benefitted from this ten thousand years before the French chemist Louis-Camille Maillard discovered the main reactions – which later was given his name – that bring out the best of everything, from coffee to bread.

Gradually, our ancestors found out about new food technologies. Similar to cooking, grinding is a method to improve palatability of food and thus increase the nutrient uptake. Eighteen thousand year old finds from Palestine and Egypt show that grinding must have been an important activity as skeletons, usually of women, show specific work related injuries from the position of the body laboring over the quern (mill). Also the teeth of people eating the stuff had breakages, perhaps from small pieces of rocks or hard grains. They had no tooth decay though.[27]

Fermentation has similar benefits as cooking, increasing flavor, improving digestibility, and preserving perishable foods. It can also decrease toxicity, or create new toxins that we like, alcohol being the foremost. Fermentation also interacts with the micro-cosmos of our guts – where we have an estimated 100 trillion bacteria, ten times the number of human cells – in a favorable way and has probably contributed to its development. Controlling the fermentation process for making a cheese or a wine is a delicate art; one could see it as a kind of herding, managing the bacterial herd to feed in the way we want.

Pottery was the next important innovation. It allowed for boiling food in water as well as for the storage of many things out of reach of insects, predators or vermin. Boiling in water opened up the possibility of preparing a whole new range of foods. Some peas, beans and lentils are not edible without cooking, some are even toxic. The use of clay pots to cook cereals gave us porridge and in general increased our ability to utilize cereals. Some claim that this increased women's fat reserves and their fertility. Infants could also be weaned earlier with the use of porridge, contributing to an increase in the population as women became fertile again more quickly.

The ability to store food is essential and the huge role that grain has played for human civilization and nutrition is certainly linked to the relative ease with which it can be stored. However, storing grain was a challenge before pottery and plaster developed, and it is no coincidence that pottery and agriculture are strongly linked. Storage technologies were an important prerequisite for the sedentary life and dependence on cultivated crops. The technologies themselves also enabled us to utilize resources which could not otherwise be utilized. What is known as Europe's LBK[a] culture (around 5,500 to 7,500 years ago) shows the first evidence of milk being a big part of the diet. These people possibly also made cheese and yoghurt. Later on, pottery became a basis for all sorts of fermenting technologies. In Iran a wine has been found which is 7,000 years old.[28]

As with so many later instances in the history of food, these improvements came at a price, there are indications that the mortality of children increased and the new food stuck to the teeth and tooth decay start to afflict humans.[29] Cooking in water destroys much of the vitamin C and frying meat creates carcinogenic substances. A piece of wisdom deducted from humanity's experiences with food and farming is that there is no perfect technology, no perfect diet or farming system. Damage control follows in the footstep of innovation.

The social and cultural role of food and eating is almost as important as the biological role. Raw, unprepared food is preferably eaten on the spot as there is extra work involved in carrying it, and there is the risk that some other animal would take it. It is therefore a fair assumption that before cooking, people would have mostly eaten where and when anything edible was found.[30] But already some *Homo erectus*, living half a million years ago in what is now China, carried carcasses back to the cave and cooked them. Most likely cooking also increased the sharing of food and as such strengthened the band. We bond and celebrate together with food and drink. On special religious or secular holidays (many of them having their origin in farming), certain foods should be eaten or sacrificed to gods. Food is also one of the stronger markers of ethnicity.

At the same time as food binds us together it also marks hierarchy and class. Status relationships within the family are sharply delineated by such rules as whether a woman eats with her husband or separately, when and whether a man eats with his children, if they all eat the same food etc. In pastoralist culture the ownership of cattle, the most important food resource, equals social standing; without cattle, a

---

[a] From the German *Linearbandkeramik*, named after the kind of pottery used.

man is condemned to low social status.[31] All through history the rich have had access to more and higher quality food than the commoners, a self-reinforcing process as they and their children thereby become stronger, healthier, smarter and more attractive. While there were many different kinds of food described in Mesopotamia, wine, honey and some meat was largely consumed by the elite,[32] while foot soldiers, construction workers and servants got about 2 liters of barley and salt and a little fish day after day.[33] In the poem *Moretum* by the Roman Virgil, the food of a simple farmer is described as consisting of bread and a stew of vegetables and some herbs, as well as cheese. The middle classes consumed meat, vegetables, egg and fruit while the upper class indulged in ham, honey, wine, oysters and fish.[34] Before, as today, poor people were more likely to suffer from malnutrition and this is particularly the case for lactating mothers and children.

Cooking has had a significant and diverse influence on the development of civilizations. When the Greeks founded a new colony, they didn't only carry seeds and livestock for breeding, they also carried a cauldron and a spark of fire from the mother city.[35] In some cultures, statesmanship was identified with cooking. In the Chinese classics, cooking is a frequent metaphor for government. Legend has it that Emperor Tang, founder of the Shang Dynasty appointed a cook as prime minister.[36]

At the same time as eating is a social act it is also a very personal and private act. With the exception of sex and a few medical procedures there are no other ways that we let the outer world consciously enter into our body. In this way food also links our bodies with nature. No wonder that we have a complex and often complicated relationship with food.

It is also no coincidence that the words culture and cultivate share the same stem (the Roman *cultus*). Agriculture and how we farm has had a very strong influence on culture and society. Irrigated flood plains were the basis for many strong civilizations, while swiddening farming could never support the population densities to allow for a strong central kingdom or empire. Pastoralists were mobile and often fierce warriors, but their nomadism didn't support the establishment of strong centralized societies. They could conquer sedentary civilizations for a while, but were mostly absorbed by the conquered culture in the end.

Even if farming incurred more toil and less leisure for individuals than foraging, it formed the basis for stronger societies as it provided storable energy reserves. By and large food production, as opposed to foraging, laid the foundation for what we today call civilization. Those

sedentary societies with more people, and better skills in communication and organization could – and perhaps had to – develop higher
degrees of specialization. By mechanisms not clearly understood, but
certainly linked to the division of labor, those societies also became less
equal, in many cases authoritarian. This led to the development of the
city and the state. Again, this new transformation was not advantageous for the individual. Neolithic villagers were less healthy than
hunters, foragers and herders and health deteriorated even more in
cities; city dwellers were shorter, lived briefer lives and suffered more
from disease and bad teeth.[37] Despite this, the human city, emerging
some seven thousand year ago was the most powerful organism ever
seen on planet earth, and this was only the start.

4

From sickle to combine harvester

For centuries, the technological development of agriculture, much like in human society at large, was slow. It was only really with the Industrial Revolution that farming experienced very rapid technological developments. Mechanization and the use of external energy resources, in particular fossil fuels, resulted in a dramatic increase in productivity per person. But this doesn't mean that agriculture didn't develop at all before then. Improved tools increased productivity in soil preparation, weeding and harvesting – the three most labor-demanding elements in most agricultural systems. Crop rotations, polycultures, the use of manure and limestone and many more 'soft' technologies were developed and had at least as much impact on agriculture development as the harness and the plow. Farming in ancient Egypt was well developed and it was probably here that oxen were fist harnessed for animal traction, a very important step in farm technology. Egyptians also practiced advanced crop rotations with wheat, barley and legumes.[38]

Europe underwent a population boom in the period 1750-1900, and the land was under serious pressure to produce more. In the nineteenth century, there was a great increase in agricultural production and productivity. This began in Flanders, parts of Germany and later in England. Even if it is often called a revolution it was a rather slow process of agriculture intensification and modernization. Agrarian historian Bernard Slicher van Bath concludes that new methods spread by 50-70 kilometers every 30 years in France. In earlier European systems, land was left fallow (unused), every second year or more; in some places, the land was fallow for two years out of three. Fallowing allows the land to regenerate and yield decently in the coming years. In many parts of Europe, hay was grown on permanent meadows and cattle only grazed on permanent pastures. Manure was collected and brought to the infields. In this way there was a movement of nutrients from the meadows to the farmed land. The saying "the meadow is the mother of the field" expresses this relationship. Another very land-demanding system was the northern European *plaggen* system that was based on grass sod that was cut and applied to the land as fertilizer. This allowed continuous grain production without crop rotation. The system required an outfield area of at least five times the size of the cultivated fields.[39] The result of this vastly extractive practice was a heath landscape, one that is as loved as the permanent meadows that were also the result of environmental exploitation.

In the new system, the strict division between infields and meadows was abolished. More grassland was brought under cultivation, more fodder was grown in the fields and more manure was recirculated to the crops. Instead of letting the land rest fallow, it was used to produce fodder. Through the introduction of crop rotations of leguminous plants, plants that bind nitrogen from the atmosphere, a lot of fodder could be produced. At the same time, productivity in grain production went up. Intensive row-cropping of potatoes, sugar beets and other root crops and cabbages also produced more food – and fodder – per hectare than grain production. In France on the eve of this first agriculture revolution, around the year 1700, fallow lands occupied 10 million out of 24 million hectares of arable land. At the end of the eighteenth century, 75% of these fallow lands were being cultivated.[40] And at the same time, the rearing of animals also increased considerably.

Even if it sounds like a revolution, there was not a lot that was really new in this. Most of the practices were already known a long time before. The Roman farmer and writer Columella, living in the first century AD, explained that the integration of livestock and cultivation of fodder increases productivity. The Romans had well-developed crop rotations and also a high level of specialization, and commercialization, which didn't come back in Europe until the 19th century.[41] And it was the level of commercialization which, more than anything else, defined which technologies which would be used, rather than the existence or knowledge of certain technologies. I will return later to discuss the main drivers for this development.

The new methods required more labor and this increased employment; "the average number of hours worked per year by a family of agricultural laborers and small peasants must have increased tremendously in the period from the agricultural revolution to the time when agricultural machinery became widespread," concluded Danish agronomist Ester Boserup, in her famous analysis *The Conditions of Agricultural Growth*.[42] All in all the intensification led to a doubling or more yields. Grain acreage in France remained stable but yields increased 2.1 times in the period 1800-1900. Fodder crops were increasingly grown, and meat production increased by a factor of 3 and milk production more than doubled. The population increased from 27 million to 39 million and food intake rose from some 2000 to 3000 calories per day. All in all, production and consumption doubled and this was all before chemical fertilizers and tractors, which came with the second agriculture revolution.[43]

China and parts of Japan and India underwent a similar kind of intensification much earlier than Europe. This was also the reason why those countries were much richer than Europe before the Europeans took to aggressively colonizing most of the rest of the world. The Chinese agriculture system was very labor intensive and was focused on soil conservation and fertility management. Farmers recirculated any waste, including human waste, meticulously and they used river mud, lime and other off-farm resources. They didn't fallow land but had intensive crop rotations. By and large they used labor to create or restore fertility, where Europe relied on the slow process of natural regeneration through fallowing. This was also underscored by the tax system, which was mostly based on the area of land owned and not on a share of the harvest. The tax per hectare of farmland during the Qing dynasty was 15 times higher than in Prussia at the same time.[44] The Chinese peasants simply had to produce as much as possible from the area in order to survive.

Parallel to the European agriculture revolution in the 1800s there was also a vast expansion of agriculture land. The primary target for the expansion were grasslands, savannahs, prairies and steppes used by nomadic or semi-nomadic people in all continents (in Europe, most of this transition had taken place earlier). People were driven off their customary lands, mostly through violence or the threat of violence. Vast tracts of fertile land were brought under the plow by European colonizers, other lands were used for large scale livestock ranching. This massive exploitation of natural capital was probably as important as the silver from the South American mines in providing a one off injection into the nascent global economy, largely controlled by a few European states and the emerging power-house, the United States.

The second agriculture revolution came with specialization, mechanization and the use of chemical fertilizers and pesticides. In *Naturalis Historica* Gaius Plinius (23-79 AD) describes a reaping machine: a box on a chassis pushed by donkeys. On the front of the box there were iron teeth which broke off the ears of wheat; the ears accumulated in the box. So the idea of using machines in farming is old, but with the exception of irrigation equipment, didn't spread much. There were several reasons for this. Farmers often didn't pick up certain technologies because there was plenty of cheap labor; the technologies were immature and, in particular, tool making was poorly developed; iron was very expensive; there was a lack of appropriate power sources. Most farmers had no strong incentive to produce more as there were no markets to sell to and no competitive pressures forcing them to constantly improve. As economic historian George Grantham puts it when discussing the period preceding the introduction of fossil fuels in the economy: "It is the history of markets rather than the history of technology which explains the growth of agricultural labor productivity".[45] Another, often overlooked, condition is that agriculture practices influence each other, and the introduction of one new technology will interact with a multitude of other factors, on farm, in the household or even in the market place.[46]

A number of more or less, often less, practical farming machines were invented in the 19th century, but it was not until the end of the century that mechanization started to play any major role in farming. The exception was wheat reapers, which spread early in the Unites States, so that by 1870 four-fifths of the cereal area was cut by reaper. Combine harvesters, which also thresh, were developed in the 1880s but their spread was severely limited as they were so heavy that they needed between 25 and 50 horses to pull them and to get power to the different processes within them.[47] Mechanization was an American specialty, driven by two coinciding factors, large fields with few physical barriers and small gradients and a shortage of labor. American colonizers made great efforts to ensure the supply of labor, not only through slavery. In the early nineteenth century, the typical North American woman had between seven and eight live births in her lifetime[48] – this is higher than the birth rates of any country today. While immigration also contributed to the increase in population there was still a constant labor shortage.

The tractor was the main symbol and the epicenter of mechanization, as it allowed for a multitude of machines to be pulled (the word comes from Latin *trahere* which means to pull). It was only in the 1930s that the combined power of tractors overtook the power of the horses in the United States.[49] In most countries tractors have still not yet taken over from humans and draft animals as the main source of power. The first tractors were heavy and very expensive. They were like a metal draught animal pulling basically the same machines that a set of two, four or eight horses could pull. The combination of increased labor costs, cheap oil, the innovation of the hydraulic system and the power transmission from the tractors to the implements (e.g. a harvester) paved the way for the breakthrough of tractors. In Europe mechanization was initially limited to large estates. There were only 270,000 tractors in Europe at onset of the Second World War, compared to 10 million 50 years later. The Soviet Union mechanized farming early, driven by a combination of large land resources and a desire to industrialize farming.[50] There was also a lack of farm labor as a result of the combination of the enormous losses of life in World War II, famine and Stalin's reign of terror which resulted in mass deportation of whole villages. Today there are around 1.6 tractors per farm worker in the United States and Canada, 0.9 in Europe but less than one per hundred farm workers in Asia. The introduction of tractors meant that the land previously used for grazing and growing food for horses and oxen for animal traction became available for the production of food and fiber for human consumption.[51] In the United States it is estimated that by 1960 the tractor had replaced 23 million draft animals, and 79 million acres of land used to grow feed for them could be reallocated to other uses.[52] In this way, mechanization freed up more land for crop production. In addition, mechanization allowed for quicker soil preparation and harvesting, which sometimes increased yields or reduced losses. For example when potatoes are picked with a machine at an optimal time there will be fewer losses to frost or disease than if the hand harvest drags on for a month.

Rural electrification also played important part in the mechanization of farming as electricity is used for fans, water pumps, milking machines, conveyors, refrigeration, etc. The development of machines to process agriculture produce was also important. Early such innovations were the sugar mill and the cotton gin (the machine which separates the fibers from the seed in the cotton 'ball'). Without the cotton gin it would have been virtually impossible for the English cotton mills to expand as fast as they did. Another remarkable industrial innovation that was readily picked up was barbed wire. It was patented 1874 and by 1907 the yearly production in the United States was 200,000 tons.[53] Barbed wire also had profound social and economic consequences in the cattle ranching areas of United States and globally it is a powerful symbol of the expansion of private property at the expense of communal land stewardship.

Agriculture was a driver of growth and at the same time the foundation for a successful early industrialization. Despite increased productivity, at a certain time agriculture and forest could no longer keep pace with the demands for resources and fossil fuels began to replace biomass as the primary energy source. And, with fossil fuels many industrial products and machinery became sufficiently afford-able to be profitably used in farming. The importance of iron in farming can hardly be exaggerated; with iron mountings on ploughs, spades and hoes, the efficiency of these tools increased manifold. Before the industrial revolution iron was too scarce and expensive to be used in such an extent. Once iron became cheap it was widely applied in farming for everything from plows to barbed wire, and thus increased productivity.[54] Through mechanization the time spent in the production of a given quantity of wheat shrunk by around 40 times in United States between 1800 and 1960.[55] The mechanization of farming released agricultural labor for work in the growing manufacturing and other sectors.

Farmers are eternally obsessed with controlling pests. Anyone with a garden has experienced frustration, desperation and anger after seeing their crops destroyed by myriads of larvae or eaten by rabbits. Ancient literature describes the use of various concoctions, ashes or minerals against different pests; that they didn't use dangerous chemi-cals was not because of environmental awareness but because they were not available. Sulfur has been used in grapes for a long time as well as Bordeaux mixture, a mix of lime and copper sulfate. In the 1930s America, the chemicals farmers used were based on the ancient poison arsenic fortified with various toxic compounds that gave them different colors that inspired trade names such as Paris Green or London Purple.[56] Many outside the farm sector believe that pesticides, used against insects, are the most widely-used toxic chemicals in farming but herbicides, used to kill unwanted weeds in the field, are much more widely-used. 2-4D was commercially released in 1946 and became the first 'successful' selective herbicide. This was also one of the active ingredients sprayed by the United States during the Vietnam War, with the purpose of killing the crops in rebel lands and to defoli-ate areas where their enemies might be hiding out. United States learned this technique from the British who employed herbicides to destroy the crops of communist insurgents in Malaya, today's Malay-sia. DDT was used as an agent for mosquito control during World War II and is still used to control swarming locust and mosquitoes today. In 1944, Du Pont started mass production for civilian use. A few years earlier, scientists in Germany looking for new nerve gas agents during World War II synthesized parathion, an organophosphate insecticide, which remains widely used today.[57] The use of these pesticides co-evolved with the use of chemical fertilizers.

Nitrogen is the main building block of proteins, amino acids, and nucleic acids such as RNA and DNA. It is the most common element in air, which consists of some 78% nitrogen. But almost all this nitrogen is biologically inactive, inert. It can be converted into active forms, such as nitrate and ammonia, through thunderstorms, fire and biological processes such as symbiotic nitrogen fixation by Rhizobium bacteria (which live in the roots of leguminous plants and supply the plant with nitrogen in exchange for energy) or fixation by blue-green algae. Justus von Liebig (more about this giant later) is credited as the first person to understand the critical role of nitrogen for plant growth even though he made some erroneous assumptions on how nitrogen is used in the cycle of life. Phosphorous and potassium are also essential elements the lack of which often limits growth. Nitrogen, phosphorus and potassium are known as macronutrients and are blended into artificial NPK fertilizers, each letter being the chemical symbol of one of these elements.

The active forms of nitrogen are dynamite for plant growth but they are also essential for making gunpowder. The link between fertilizers and war is old. In Sweden, France and Germany from the 16th to 18th century farmers were forced to deliver saltpeter, a nitrate compound, to the governments to make gunpowder. That nitrate was extracted from the urine and manure of livestock. This meant that large quantities of nutrients were taken from farming, depleting soils and literally exploded into thin air. The antithesis of converting swords into plowshares. The opposite happened after World War II. When the war started, the United States government constructed ten new plants to produce ammonia for munitions. All were located in the interior of the country. Several of them were built alongside natural gas pipelines so they could use the gas as raw material for their production. By the end of the war, the country had the capacity to produce 1.6 million tons per year. When the nitrogen was no longer needed for bombs, what were they going to do with all this capacity? The answer was, to use the nitrogen-rich ammonia to fertilize the nation's fields.[58]

Before chemical fertilizers were available much use was made of guano, sedimented bird droppings. Massive deposits of these were mined from the coasts of Chile and Peru in the 19th century. In the early 1850s a British officer observed guano being loaded, from a single island off the coast of Peru, counting forty-four ships from the United States, forty English ones, five French, two Dutch, one Italian, one Belgian, one Norwegian, one Swedish, one Russian, one Armenian and three Peruvian. Then, in 1853 a process was discovered for mining the nitrate fields in the arid parts of Peru and Bolivia. By the 1860s these nitrate fields had become even more important than guano, the supply of which was almost depleted. Nitrates were in high demand not only

for fertilizers, but also for the recently invented TNT and other explo-
sives, crucial for the war machineries.[59] Chile, Peru and Bolivia fought
a five year war, *Guerra del Guano*, over the control of these resources.
Bolivia lost access to the sea, something it still contests today. Chile,
with British backing, took over most of the resources. This period of
Chilean history is referred to as the Saltpeter Republic.

There was no way of economically producing a chemical nitrogen
fertilizer until Fritz Haber and Carl Bosch developed a process, carrying their names, to convert the unlimited supply of molecular nitrogen
in the atmosphere into ammonia. Haber and Bosch had a factory ready
in 1913. Because Germany was cut off from supplies of nitrate by the
British naval blockade the factory was converted to produce bombs
instead of fertilizers, giving Germany an almost limitless supply of
ammunition.

During the first agriculture revolution labor input was still high.
Sweden and Finland have reliable occupational records stretching back
to before industrialization, which show that around eighty percent of
the work force was engaged in farming until the mid 1800s.[60] Contrary
to common belief, the agriculture population and work force continued
to grow in parallel with urbanization and industrialization (as is still
the case in many developing countries). Few farmers were forced off
their farms or lured away to the industries even though many of their
sons and daughters were.[61] Only Belgium, the United Kingdom, and
Switzerland experienced a reduction in number of agriculture workers
before 1910,[62] and in the United Kingdom, at least, this was largely
made possible by importing a lot of food. During the second agriculture revolution, increase in productivity per worker in agriculture was
very rapid, outpacing that of industry. The overall productivity
(measured as 'total factor productivity', i.e. the combined productivity
of land, labor and machinery and other invested capital) of agriculture
in United States and the United Kingdom grew slightly slower than
the rest of the economy 1870 to 1913, at the same rate between 1913
and 1950 and dramatically outperformed it after 1950.[63]

Knowledge and the ways in which it is generated and disseminated
have also been transformed profoundly. Earlier, farming was developed by the farmers' own experiments, trials and errors. Knowledge
was developed as part of the farming process and was transferred, 'on
the job', to the next generation. It was also shared freely within, and
between, communities. Science and formal education were of no
significance to farmers. When science started its exploration of agriculture, most early efforts were devoted to understand what was really

going on in the field. When you hear people talking about precision farming or something else that sounds very scientific, don't believe them: we still today don't know enough about what goes on in incredibly complex and microcosmic ecological systems of the soil. The influence of science on farming started with Justus von Liebig's discovery of nitrogen as an essential plant nutrient, and his formulation of the 'Law of the Minimum'. This described how plant growth is determined by a critical limiting factor, for example, if there is a shortage of water, there is no point in using more fertilizers as the plant primarily needs water to grow.[a] I believe this point is (and was) well understood by farmers who have never heard of Justus von Liebig or the Law of the Minimum: farmers in drought prone areas of Africa do not apply the recommended quantities of fertilizers as they know that if there is no rain it will all be in vain.

Justus von Liebig (1803-1873) was also a pioneer in nutrition and food processing and, as he will pop up in many places in this book, he deserves a brief introduction. When he was twelve years old, the largest known volcanic eruption occurred at Mount Tambora, in Indonesia. The explosion was heard more than 2,000 km away and the dust and ashes caused a volcanic winter in the Northern hemisphere. This led to major crop failures and a famine after 'the year without summer' 1816. This is said to have shaped von Liebig's later work, even if there is no indication that the young baron himself suffered. In 1824 at the age of 21, he became a professor at the University of Giessen, where he established the world's first major school of chemistry. He had a profound influence on agriculture and nutritional science. He was also a very enterprising person transforming some of his ideas into commercial undertakings.

Breeding is a very knowledge intensive part of farming. The initial domestication of plants and livestock was followed by plant and livestock breeding which provided impressive results long before the laws of heredity and genetics were known. Progress was achieved through better selection and various chemical or radiation treatments to increase the frequency of mutations in crops. The work continued the process of redistributing plant growth to the parts of the plant we desire. Plant breeders managed to increase the share of the biomass in wheat that went to the grain from around 35% in the 1920s to 50% in

---

[a] This is often depicted as a wooden barrel with several staves with the shortest one being the limiting factor.

the 1990s.[64] With more scientific knowledge plant breeders also went for hybrids. Hybrids are, simply put, first generation plants (called F1s) bred from two separate inbred parent lines. They are very homogenous in growth and are often more vigorous. The fact that the plants are all the same has a number of advantages for their management as the proper timing for sowing, weeding, fertilizer application and harvest is easier to determine. If you have, as I have, grown cabbage hybrids then you know that you can harvest your entire field in one go as all the plants are ready at the same time. If you are less successful you have to make a second cut.

This also highlights that a farm technology is rarely neutral. One technology assumes, or leads to a certain ecological, economic and social system and cannot be seen or discussed in isolation from this. If you grow old varieties, your harvesting is spread out over a longer period, excellent for your household or for supplying a local market, but very impractical and costly when you pay for labor by the hour and supply distant buyers or a food processing factory. Of course, the very homogenous field also provides a wonderful table for pests, which can spread very rapidly across countries and even continents, which is another result of those modern seeds. So the hybrids usually need more protection from pests.

Hybrid maize spread in the United States in the 1930s and allegedly increased the return for farmers by up to 300%.[65] Hybrids have a trait that is interesting for commercial seed companies – but not so good for the farmer – they are not stable in the coming generations. If you sow the off-spring of a hybrid you get all sorts of plants. This forces the farmer to buy new seeds every year. Lately, genetic engineering has played an increasing, and controversial, role in the development of new varieties. Genetically modified plants (often called GMOs, GM crops or biotech crops) were grown by 17 million farmers on around 170 million hectares of land in 2012. The United States has more than 40% of the total GMO acreage, followed by Brazil, Argentina, India and China. Cotton, maize and soybeans are the main GMO crops.[66] GMOs share several traits in common with hybrids, they are patented and farmers cannot, or are not allowed, to multiply them, forcing them to buy new seeds every year. I will discuss GMO use more in a later chapter.

The history of artificial insemination has a dark streak; the first reported case, in 1884, was not on livestock but on a woman who didn't know it happened. In 1884 a Philadelphia professor of medicine, William Pancoast, deposited with a rubber syringe semen from the 'best-looking member of the class' in the uterus of an anesthetized woman. The six young men of the senior class who witnessed the operation were pledged to absolute secrecy. The woman was not informed, unlike her infertile husband; his 'honor' and self-esteem were apparently more important than her consent to the procedure. The case was reported 25 years later in a medical journal.[67] In the 1930s artificial insemination was first used on a larger scale in livestock breeding, initially in the Soviet Union. Today, animal breeders use many modern technologies such as embryo transfers and hormonal treatments to influence the sex of offspring. The sheep Dolly was the first cloned animal in 1996, but there has so far been little practical use of cloning for livestock, and the trials have not been too successful.

Apart from GMOs, there have been few groundbreaking new farming technologies introduced recent decades, but productivity has continued to increase considerably. To some extent this is due to a result of ever tighter control of the processes. This is linked to an increased use of information technology; farmers were early adopters of computers and even more so mobile phones, allowing the farmer to sell his crop or order spares while driving the tractor, or to get instant weather forecasts. They can now carefully monitor both milk yield and the exact quantity of feed for each individual animal. When harvesting the computer will record the variation in yield in different parts of the field and the application of fertilizer can be adjusted. Pesticide applications can be adjusted to the density of weed stands etc. With the spike in energy-prices in mid 1970s (the first oil crisis) it also became apparent that continued productivity increase could not be based on processes that waste energy. In recent times mechanical inputs and the use of fertilizers have stabilized and farmers have become more selective in the use of the later. When energy price go up, the use of fertilizers goes down, unless food prices increase even more than oil prices.[a] No-till farming has spread, partly because it is good for the soil, but probably more because it saves diesel.

Marketing itself has also become a lot more streamlined. The number of production and marketing contracts that govern the sale of products has increased. Contracts covered almost one third of the crop production in United States in 2011, compared with less than a quarter in the mid-1990s. Larger operations are more likely to use contracts, which can reduce the price and marketing risks faced by farmers.[68]

---

[a] There is a diminishing return on the use of fertilizers and, at a certain level, the fertilizer costs more than the net return of the increase in yield.

Equally important in this managerial revolution is the management of capital. Denmark is a very successful agricultural exporting nation but its 40,000 farmers have a total debt of 350 billion Danish kroner. This corresponds to US$1.6 million per farm,[a] or U$25,000 per hectare of land.[69] In United States the total farm assets in 2014 amounts to US$3 trillion,[70] corresponding to US$1.2 million per full time job.

This increased use of capital assets in agricultural production makes the management of input supplies and credits as important factors of success as land preparation.[b] Financial management, futures contracts and hedging, tax planning and tighter integration between suppliers and customers all shape the success (or otherwise) of the modern farm entrepreneur, who is normally a well-educated, savvy, person far from the archetypical traditional farmer. Farming as a lifestyle is often seen as an abomination, shunned by government, agri-business and big farm organizations alike. All over the world farm advisors, farming unions and governments alike promote the concept of farming as a business as opposed to farming as good husbandry and stewardship.

The second agriculture revolution completed the transformation of agriculture to a market-driven, linear, production system. A small labor force and huge energy and capital inputs transform purchased inputs into commodities to be sold in an increasingly global market place. At the end of the 19th century, the cost of purchased inputs was still in the range of 10% of the value of the gross output from farms; it was 12% in France, 8% in the United States, Germany and Sweden and 24% in the much more commercialized United Kingdom and the Netherlands. One hundred years later the cost of purchased inputs was between 40 and 75% of the value of the farm sales. The global use of artificial fertilizers, for instance, increased ten-fold in the fifty years from 1950 to 2000. Over the 120 years from 1870 to 1990 labor went from being two-thirds of the costs of a farm in high-income countries to less than one fifth, despite huge increases in the wages for farm

---

a Of course of those 40,000 farms there is also a number of mostly small farms which have no, or very little, debt, so the debt load of the commercial farms is much higher.

b This is also a reason for why farming is no longer a way to prosperity for poor people in developing countries, something I will discuss more later on. It is also a major reason for why it is hard to recruit young people to the farm sector.

labor.[71] Mechanization has also fundamentally reshaped the agrarian landscape, with 'obstacles', such as trees, removed at a rapid pace and open ditches being replaced by subsurface drainage systems. As each machine needs to run as much as possible, mechanization has gone hand in hand with specialization. Crop production has become separated from livestock keeping. When fewer fodder crops were needed for horses and specialization increased, crop rotations changed to grains in monoculture, which increased disease and weed pressure. Fertilizers and pesticides were introduced to compensate for a lack of crop rotations which in turn drove even more specialization. Employees needed more skills and salaries increased, which in turn necessitated more mechanization. In one or two generations, in high-income countries, there has been a total system shift in farming to a system that is characterized by a high dependency on the use of specialized machinery, chemical fertilizers and pesticides, market orientation, specialization and indebtedness. And the effects of this on nature, society and our food have been profound.

5

People

Besides commercialization and the use of energy (expressed in mechanization and the use of chemical fertilizers), growing populations and what they consume constitutes the third megatrend that influences farming and what we eat. The world population has increased from 1 billion at the beginning of the nineteenth century to 7 billion at the end of 2011. Such growth certainly justifies the expression 'population bomb' the title of a best-selling book by Paul R. Ehrlich published in 1968. Many believe that size of the population is the biggest threat to a sustainable future of human beings on the planet.

Human population was probably less than 10 million 12,000 years ago. Population growth was very low for a long time, perhaps just 0.001% per year (compared with 1.8% in 1990). With the transition to agriculture, many more could be fed from a fixed area. A period of rapid growth ensued; in 10,000 years, the population grew 100 fold. At the time of the Industrial Revolution, the population in many parts of the world had reached new ecological limits. Less intensely exploited areas were rapidly filling up with settlers from an 'overpopulated' Europe. Through the deployment of huge amounts of fossil fuel, first coal followed by oil, it was possible to, once again, take a giant leap to new levels of population.[72]

Improvements in technology could, in each kind of society, generate some possibilities for expansion; for example, spears and digging tools could allow hunters and gatherers to harvest a larger share of the surplus of their habitat; the introduction of crop rotations and other improved agriculture methods could perhaps double or triple the yields. Technology expanded our ability to feed more and more people on the planet during the industrial phase, but limitations are now arising from all sides. It is hard to see what similar radical change of conditions would allow humankind to make another giant leap in population. Some say synthetic foods, while others look to interplanetary colonization, but none of these ideas are really feasible, at least not in not in the lifetime of my newly-born grandchildren.

The size of the human population is a challenge, but there are many examples of how high population density forces a more sustainable use of the landscape. For example, in Germany and Japan it was first the exhaustion (or the threat thereof) of forest resources that compelled people to manage the forests with a long term view and it was increasing population that made farmers abandon the extractive practice of sod cutting to fertilize their soil.[73] Similarly, regardless of how much environmentalists and foresters condemn swiddening agriculture, it will continue to be the norm until population density reaches a certain level, simply because it is the most comfortable, secure and sustainable way of getting a good return on labor inputs.[74]

The Egyptians, who operated a fertile but limited land resource, knew several thousand years ago, that it was beneficial to alternate cereals and fodder crops such as clover or alfalfa,[75] but it was only under the pressure of population that crop-rotations integrating fodder production and grains became widespread in Europe. Similarly, the high population density led the Chinese to utilize human excreta efficiently for millennia, whereas in sparsely populated Africa such practices are rare and often even taboo. Edith Boserup made the observation that soil fertility may be a result of the use of intensive methods of cultivation rather than the other way round.[76] Clearly, regions where land is in short supply generally have considerably higher yields than those places where land is abundant.[77] And when land is abundant it is often badly managed. George Washington commented the farming practices of his country fellows: "here it is more profitable to cultivate a lot of land poorly than a little land well",[78] which, to judge from the dustbowl years that followed, is what many of them did.

In the tenth century with 10 million inhabitants, France was afflicted with famine, three centuries later it fed 20 million people thanks to new systems based on animal drawn plows. In the end of the eighteenth century France again appeared overpopulated. One hundred years later it fed nearly 40 million thanks to the first agriculture revolution. Similarly, 500 people per square kilometer was long considered the limit for the rice growing deltas of Asia, today they feed more than 1,000 people per square kilometer.[79]

There are a number of signs that the world's population is stabilizing. The number of children born annually reached a peak around 1990 and the growth in the world population today is mainly a result of people living longer. The global growth rate of population has been decreasing since its peak of 2% in 1965-1970. In 2010, forty-three countries, including Japan, Russia, Germany and Italy, have populations that are stagnant or decreasing. A larger group of countries, including China and the United States, has reached the stage where new families will be smaller. When the next generation in these countries reaches fertility, their population will stabilize. The third group, which includes many of the African countries, such as Ethiopia, Congo and Uganda, will have doubled its population by 2050. The United Nations predicts three alternative scenarios for population size for 2050: 10.8 billion, 9.2 billion or just below 8 billion.[80] Most seem to bet on the middle alternative.

The horror scenario described in the enormously influential 1798 *Essay on the Principle of Population* by the economist Thomas Robert Malthus, has maintained its appeal over 200 years, and is quoted in almost any publication that deals with population or resource use. His observations coincided with the start of the demographic transition of England, following an unprecedented population explosion. This pattern has been repeated in country after country, and just as Ireland was the frightening example 150 years ago, Nigeria, Uganda or Ethiopia are now.

Large numbers of people is a reality that we have to live with and adapt to. Yet, the problem is not so much the numbers but how much environmental 'space' each person takes. It is not only the size of the population that matters, it is also how and where they live. The term 'ecological footprint' – a measure of how much resources one uses – captures this well. For a citizen in the United States the ecological footprint is around seven global hectares, while for a person in India it is a tenth of this. This means that an American uses ten times more of nature's resources than an Indian, so it is quite apparent that the world can 'afford' one more Indian much better than one more American. Similarly, the challenge is not, yet, to provide more food to feed the billions, but how and where we produce the food, what kind of food people eat and how much they throw away.

It is important to consider how and where people live. History has been written in cities and power has resided there, so this might give us a skewed view of the importance of cities. In 1800, a mere three percent of the world's population lived in cities. By 1900, this had increased to just ten percent.[81] In 2008, the world's urban population exceeded its rural population for the first time in human history.[82] It is not only the number of people living in cities that have changed, the cities themselves have changed. In 1800, there were two cities in the world with one million or more inhabitants – London and Beijing. In the year 2000 there were almost four hundred. And the average size of the 100 largest cities increased from 2 million inhabitants in 1950 to 6.3 million inhabitants in the year 2000. This has been made possible with modern transport technology and globalized markets, without these, it is simply not possible to solve the logistics of megacities. And as a consequence, the ecological link between the city and the surrounding land has all but disappeared – at least for food and farming. [83]

Cities emerged in Mesopotamia some 6000-8000 years ago. With them came a marked differentiation and specialization in the population, payment of taxes to a deity or king and a state religion; those not producing their own food were supported by the king and there was trade and import of raw materials. Landlords didn't farm themselves but did so with a farm-bailiff, through tenants, or with slaves or serfs. All this was possible with the surpluses generated by farming through irrigation and plowing. Most of the early city-states were more or less self-contained ecological units. When many people, especially those with power, were no longer directly involved in farming there was the risk that the city developed in ways which the surrounding land could not support. For instance the cities might overexploit the surrounding lands to get more produce which could be traded for luxuries from other countries. Often this led to environmental degradation, with the cities shrinking or totally disappearing into oblivion.[84]

But there were ways for the cities to – seemingly at least – free themselves from this dependency. Sea transport, canals, railroads and the commercialization of farming all help break the chains that link the city to its hinterland. This allows farm produce from one place to be shipped to different markets and traders and retailers in the city to source from many different farm areas. Ultimately the relationship between land and city was translated into market transactions and money. Cities are of course as dependent on rural areas as before, in the same way that our whole civilization is as dependent on nature as our hunting ancestors. The difference is in the form of the dependency. The urban people are no longer dependent on any particular agriculture area, but on more than one billion people involved in farming, anywhere on the globe.

The city's dependency on rural areas is something that most will probably understand intuitively. That rural areas were equally affected by the city is perhaps less well understood. In the 1826 treatise *The Isolated State*, German geographer Johann Heinrich von Thünen showed that production in rural areas would be organized according to the land rent, yield per unit of land, production costs, market price and transport costs to the city market. Market gardens and dairies would be closest to the cities. With increasing distance there would be firewood growing followed by grain production and finally livestock, which could be transported by the hoof to the city. At a certain distance farms would be too far from the city and there would be no commercial production with farms orienting themselves to self-sufficiency, perhaps exporting its people as migrant workers to get whatever cash was needed. Apparently this was a simplified model which didn't consider mountain ranges, deserts or different soil qualities. For a city on a river or with railroad connections, these circles would become ellipses instead. But, by and large, the model had very good explanatory powers. If the city had access to the sea, it would often import foods through the harbor, which also had huge implications for the rural areas. Land-locked Madrid forced its surrounding farmland to grow grain whilst, five hundred years ago, Amsterdam could ship in grain from the Baltic sea, thus opening the opportunity for its farmers to specialize in other, more lucrative, crops.[85] And ancient Rome was encircled by a sprawling suburbia. Most Roman villas were farm production units which apart from feeding those who lived there were also engaged in producing high-value crops which could generate high profits. There was no clear limit between city and farmland "giving the beholder the impression of a city stretching out indefinitely" as recorded by a Greek visitor.[86]

Von Thünen's model has still some value today, even if food production itself is no longer subject to the city-hinterland relationship. Today the inner ring is filled with supermarkets and ring roads, followed by golf courses, stables and recreational areas, all directly used by city-dwellers. Water catchment, sewage emissions and landfills for waste are still geographically attached to the cities to a large extent. But effective transport operations and global supply chains have chopped off most ties between the city and its rural hinterland. The rural areas are largely no longer producing for a nearby city but for an anonymous global market. Once the truck is loaded and leaves the farm the goods become enmeshed in a process of global circulation, bereft of identity and place, much like electrons that run through electrical cables.

London was nicknamed 'The Great Wen' by William Cobbett, a radical pamphleteer who saw the rapidly growing city as a pathological swelling on the face of the nation. Many cities in history have been 'consumption cities', i.e. they have taken a lot more from their hinterland than they gave back. Rome, the political capitals of medieval China and early modern Europe are such examples. Of course, not all citizens of the city were just consumers, some were craftsmen, builders and blacksmiths, but by and large very few goods or services were shipped out from those cities, while there was a constant flow of goods and people into them. Over thirty percent of the workers in 18th century Madrid were servants to the upper classes and even in London very few were engaged in manufacturing.[87] Because of the deplorable living conditions among the poor in many of the cities, they couldn't even maintain their population, but were dependent on a constant supply of migrants taking the place of those who succumbed to disease.[88]

There is no evidence that the city of Rome, with its one million inhabitants, sold anything of special value to the rural population or that it provided any other useful service than that of protection.[89] The city engaged in all sorts of activities to display and assert its powers: building castles, temples, arenas and through the arts. The huge quantities of food and other products needed for such cities also implies a need for a lot of infrastructure, canals, roads, stores and a whole supply chain that fed merchants, drovers, ship crews etc. In this way the division of labor between city and land created new jobs and opportunities. British historian Neville Morley thinks that even if one sees Rome as a hungry belly swallowing up all the surplus from the rural areas, this does not mean that its effects were solely negative: "the belly's hunger is what forces the rest of the body to rouse itself and exercise its strength and ingenuity. Freed from the burden of supporting a capital city, the country would happily slumber until doomsday."[90] This is exactly what happened when Rome did collapse. To my ears this sounds quite plausible but it also sounds like similar arguments throughout history voiced in support of exploitation.[a] After all, what is wrong with people happily slumbering?

Many cities of today are not political capitals but economic powerhouses, either because of trade or industrial production. Regardless of the nature of the city, urbanization affects food production in many ways. Urbanites eat more processed and pre-prepared foods, partly in response to long working hours and more competing things to do and partly due to a lack of appropriate space for cooking and storage. Urban diets are also markedly more globalized than rural diets, and imported food has a higher share of the market. The emergence of supermarkets and larger scale retailers also changes the trading structure, putting smaller traders out of business and then rippling back down the supply chain to disadvantage smaller producers. There has been a major a shift in employment within the food industry, with

---

[a] Compare with the 'white man's burden' as a defence for exploitation of colonies.

fewer people working in agriculture and more working in transport, wholesaling, retailing, food processing, catering and marketing. All this has profound effects also on rural areas.

For the Balinese, the cultivation of land is a creative art and a communal effort. The people of Jatiluwih have created a true masterpiece – an intricate pattern of finely curved rice terraces in brilliant shades of green, blue or yellow depending on season and stages of growth of the rice. The village has deservedly been named a UNESCO world heritage site. At the time of my visit in 2007, the women were harvesting rice, with the young girls assisting. Young boys were swimming in a nearby stream, while the grown up men were idling in the shadow of a huge tree – assumingly pondering over important matters... They grow organic red rice with traditional methods. Yields are good, some five tons per hectare, and as they take two crops per year, it is a lot. The certified organic rice fetches a price well above the normal. The village is not only beautiful; the system is also ecologically and economically sustainable. But I am told by the women that it is not socially sustainable because the young prefer to work in the Balinese tourist industry. A more glamorous and better paid job, where you can be clean, indoors and comfortable.

Around 1980, the economically active population employed in industry and services exceeded that employed in the primary sector (agriculture, forestry, mining and fishing).[91] The global agricultural population – defined as individuals dependent on agriculture, hunting, fishing, and forestry for their livelihood – still accounted for over thirty-seven percent of the world's total population in 2011, the most recent year for which data are available. Although the agricultural population shrunk as a share of total population between 1980 and 2011, it grew numerically from 2.2 billion to 2.6 billion people during this period.[92] In all countries, the share of farmers in the population is decreasing and farmers and farm workers have lower incomes than people employed in industry. In the richest countries, farmers and farm workers are less than two percent of the workforce. In the poorest countries, farmers and farm workers exceed two-thirds of the population.

Paradoxically perhaps, even relatively poor countries are starting to experience labor shortages in farming, prompting journalist Fred Pearce to ask "never mind the land and water, will there be enough people to work on the farms?"[93] The exodus of people from rural areas and the reduction of people involved in farming have far-reaching consequences. Most agricultural ecosystems are dependent on human beings, and with continued urbanization, despite population growth, more and more areas are becoming depopulated. What these depopulated landscapes will look like in the future and how they work have not been planned, and so societies end up paying farmers or entrepreneurs to 'maintain' the landscapes or preserve the 'cultural heritage'. This problem is not confined to high-income countries. Some areas with traditional terraced rice paddies, such as Jatiluwih, experience labor shortages to maintain the infrastructure.

Driving through Mato Grosso in Brazil or the Great Plains in the USA it is ironic to see that the most successful farm areas are largely dead. Farms have modernized and mechanized and there are fewer people needed. Food processing and distribution has also been rationalized so there are very few job in those trades in rural areas. The end result is that there are very few people left in those highly productive agricultural landscapes. Even food itself is scarce; twenty percent of rural counties in the United States are considered 'food deserts', where people have to drive more than 10 miles to get their food,[94] which is often expensive and of low quality.

So where are the people, the consumers and the households in this story? Some scholars emphasize the importance of individuals' and households' aspirations to increase their consumption, and to indulge in new luxuries, as a major driving force for the development of all aspects of the new industrial society, including food. Jan de Vries, professor in history and economics has popularized the term[a] the 'industrious revolution', to describe how households work longer hours and spend a greater proportion of their working time (in the broader sense that includes household labor) engaged in the market economy. This in turn made possible the consumption of more market goods, consumer goods such as lamp oil, rum, tobacco, sugar, linen, as well as kitchen ware and furniture etc.

By the end of the 18th century the Dutch East India Company and their rivals had shipped more than 70 million pieces of porcelain from China to Europe. Cotton textile consumption in the North Atlantic market grew between 3.2 and 5.1% per annum between 1700 and 1850. Tea imports to Europe went from a trickle to 14.5 million kg annually, corresponding to 7 billion cups of tea,[95] which meant drinking tea had spread far beyond the upper classes. This was particularly the case in

---

[a] Initially coined by the Japanese historian Akira Hayami.

Britain where per capita consumption had reached 0.7 kg by 1780 – corresponding to a cup per person per day. Such changes are of great import, not only in economic terms, but also in signaling a whole new type of human society. "Tobacco, sugar and tea were the first objects within capitalism that conveyed with their use the complex idea that one become different by consuming differently" concludes anthropologist Sydney Mintz in *Sweetness and Power*.[96]

Increased consumption in the upper classes also necessitated more labor as servants. This opened up many new income generating opportunities, not the least for females. Despite all the fuss about the Industrial Revolution, only 10% of adult employment in England was in manufacturing in 1831. In England there was one retail shop per 52 inhabitants in 1759 and similar ratios are reported from the Nether-lands.[97] In addition to small retail shops many urban immigrants tried to earn their living as street hawkers. A London journalist, Henry Mayhew, made impressive research of these trades and counted more than 16,000 such hawkers in 1851. Many of them sold fish and vege-tables, but surprising numbers sold items such as ginger beer (900) and even ice cream (20). He described the smell of the numerous pig-sties close to the center of London, the sight of tens of thousands of cattle driven to market through the streets and the cries of costermongers and milkmaids.[98] This gives some perspective on the tendency for every other person to be selling something to their neighbors in the poor countries of today. It also gives credit to the statement that England was a nation of shop-keepers expressed by Adam Smith and Napoleon I alike.[99]

Americans also showed an early taste for consumption. At least ten percent of the annual income of North Americans was spent on imports from Britain. Newspaper advertisements show that many different products were imported in the second half of 18th century. We can read adverts for fine Genoese Vermicelli, Florence Wine in flasks, Turkish Figs in chests, Gloucester Cheese and "just landed from the North of England, a fresh Parcel of pickled mushrooms and Ketchup in Quart Bottles". The newspapers themselves are an example of an emerging consumer society as advertisements made up the bulk of the newspapers in North America in the 18th century.[100] The commercial foundations for the further expansion of global trade and branded food were there.

According to de Vries, households shifted from market contact, where the market supplemented household production, to market orientation, and finally to full integration in the market economy. This shift took place earlier and more profoundly for urban and rich households than for rural peasants. Urban households needed food and the market became the main mechanism for distributing and allocating food, a new role. This created a demand and an opportunity for rural households to also enter the market economy. They did so by producing more surpluses for the market and by engaging in more household based income generating work, such as weaving for a merchant. Others took to seasonal work in construction or in distant cities. But it took a very long time before the market economy fully took over the agriculture process itself, peasant life and village organization.[101]

Households, both urban and rural households, not only redistributed their work towards markets, they also worked more and harder. A combination of the elimination of saints' days, longer working days and new and cheaper light sources led to a considerable increase of the time worked in England, the Netherlands and northern France, perhaps by as much as twenty-five percent more than in the years preceding the industrial revolution.[102] In this perspective the industrial revolution is a continuation of an increase of work that had already started before the steam engine.

The increased human energy spent on remunerative work and consumption led to a reduction in the time spent on traditional household work, driving people to adopt the forerunners of convenience foods. Sweet tea, wine, beer or coffee with bread replaced porridges and pancakes as meals, considerably reduced the time spent on cooking. The bread itself changed in character, from heavy rye loaves to white wheat bread and meats was increasingly transformed into bacon, hams and sausages which can be quickly fried or cooked. This was compounded by the cast iron stoves and later by gas stoves which were not only more fuel efficient (and less polluting) but were also better adapted to quick cooking than an open hearth.

This process didn't stop with the industrial revolution. Today we are witnessing a transformation of ever more aspects of life into the market economy, even of things that before were parts of people's private lives or civil society. Instead of contributing time for voluntary work, people pay a sum per month, to the poor in other countries, the WWF, or the local sports club. Instead of nursing a sick family member, medicines are bought and professional services, such as nursing homes, are used. The industrialization of home cooking by more home appliances, by ready-made foods or the hybrid of eating out and at home – take away food – is just another expression of this development. Adding to this is the increasing proportion of single-person households or households with few people, as compared to the 'old days' when households were much bigger (including more children but also, often, the elderly). The effort of cooking is disproportionate to the number of people eating and it is relatively much more work for singles to cook their own meals than it is to feed extended families. This also greatly influences the social aspects of eating, facilitating the transformation of eating from sharing a meal to munching fast food.

People in pre-industrial societies spent some 80% of their disposable income[a] on food, and another 12-14% of clothing, mostly made from on agriculture raw materials.[103] Around the year 2000, consumers in high-income countries spent an average of 13% of their total household expenditures on food, whereas consumers in low-income countries spent an average of 43%. These shares ranged from a high of 55% of total household expenditures in Indonesia to a low of 7% in the United States.[104] This is the result of both a drastic increase in peoples' incomes and sharp fall in the prices of farm produce. At the end of World War I, a sample basket of staple food items cost what an average American would earn in 10 hours of work. By 1995, that cost had dropped to less than two hours.[105] To earn enough to buy a kg of wheat a laborer in Sweden had to work thirty times longer in 1930 than in the year 2000.[106]

The share of income spent on food has certainly shrunk, but in absolute numbers, people spend a lot more money on food today than they did before. Although the raw materials that agriculture produces have become much cheaper, they are less often consumed in an unprocessed form. As the share of processed and ready-made food increases, the cost of food increases. And when people earn more money, they spend more on food. Which, of course suits the food industry very well. Plunkett Research estimates the total United States retail food and beverage industry revenues for 2013 to be in the range of US$1.8 trillion. Of this, the catering industry represents a third and employs more than 9% of the people in employment at 980,000 locations.[107] Eighty percent of the cost of food eaten at home in United States is spent on non-farm related expenses. Labor in the supermarket and the factory has replaced labor in the home.[108] We have not been able or willing to swap our ever-increasing productivity into more leisure but are rather constantly engaged in consuming more things.

------

[a] Admittedly, the concept of "disposable income" is not easily applied to pre-industrial societies, as they are mostly non-market societies.

6

The making of food into commodities

The construction of the Eire Canal reduced the cost of shipping grain from the Great Lakes to the east coast of the United States from US$120 a ton to US$6 a ton. And most grain didn't stop there, much was exported on to Europe. The end station of the canal, New York, increased its share of national exports from less than 10% in 1800 to 60% fifty years later and its population went from 10,000 people to over half a million in the same period.[109] The effects on European farming were equally profound. And this was just a start. When Atlantic steamers took over from wind powered vessels, the costs were reduced again. A bushel of wheat cost 60 cents in Chicago in 1870 and twice the amount in London. By the end of the century, transport costs, and thereby the price difference, had shrunk to 10 cents[110] which meant that prices for American grain dropped below the cost of production in many parts of Europe. Wheat exports from the United States to Europe went from 5 million bushels to close to 200 million bushels in the same time.[111] While transport became cheaper, new, or more efficient, methods of preservation, such as freezing and heat preservation opened up further new commercial opportunities. Institutions and physical structures to store, mill, slaughter, finance and distribute the increasing volumes of agriculture outputs also emerged shortly thereafter for the growing range and volume of agriculture inputs. This was the infancy of agribusiness and food marketing which today play a key role in the food chain.

The transport revolution, driven by steamships and railroads was the start of an intensive process of globalization. Certainly, there was global trade long before this. Notwithstanding how impressive early trading empires were, and despite all the might and splendor of Venice, Seville and Amsterdam, the economic activity of most people was grounded, until well into the nineteenth century, on local and regional self-sufficiency. Before the age of the train and the steamship it was difficult to transport bulk commodities over long distances. Even without tariffs there were few competitive pressures, and trade in basic foods was driven by pressing necessity rather than profit.

We may not always think about it, but the origin of trade is found in ecology and not in economy. The merchant was an ecological plumber moving supplies from an area of surplus to one of shortage, greasing the cogs of ecology as well as human society. Trade made it possible for human beings to establish themselves even where some basic resource was absent. One tribe had access to a resource that the other was missing. In some places flint or obsidian was abundant, and in other places hunters had no access to those stones for making spears and arrows. In other areas there was no salt, which was important for preserving meat and curing skins. In some rare cases this situation might have led to war, but more often it led to peaceful exchange. The role of trade in ecological adaptation has, in some cases, meant that communities have been able to specialize in forms of production that are very well adapted to their ecological context. Through trade with the plains, the peasants of the Alps could shift entirely to pasturing livestock thus avoiding the need to plow fragile mountain slopes while their Mediterranean colleagues occupied themselves with viticulture and olives. In this way, trade in agricultural produce, even staple food such as grain, promoted sustainability, long before the term was coined.[112] Today, however, trade is no longer driven by ecological adaptations or human needs. It is driven by unlimited competition and profit-seeking. How did we end up here?

In order to understand this we need to trace the developments of markets and the processes by which more and more parts of human society have become subject to commercialization. This commercialization has had a profound influence on all aspects of human society, from how many children we have to what we eat. In early human society markets played a minor role; most exchanges were not organized as a 'trade' or through the 'market' but more often as gifts. The reciprocal exchange of gifts is a socially important act and an essential part of creating relations. Gifts were also the foundation of status. Instead of extracting wealth from others, traditional leaders were often supposed to share with their peers or to organize big parties. A gift creates mutual dependency. Food sharing was, and still is, a form of wealth distribution, and plays a very big role in aiding social cohesion. In Papua New Guinea, people exchange piglets with each other to maintain relationships. In some cases the sharing is extreme, for example, among the Arapesh a man does not eat food which he himself has grown. In India, sharing with kin and jāti (community) members has been compulsory, while social sharing with friends has been casual and alms-giving optional.[113] Sharing and giving food have thus been a norm in most human societies.

While food sharing has been the norm, not all people shared food, "non-sharing is the characteristic of societies in which there are no stable social groupings above the family and where the accumulation of individual wealth and power is paramount".[114] Yehudi A. Cohen, an anthropologist, identifies many examples of societies characterized by the non-sharing of food, including the Alorese, the Marquesans, highland peasants in Jamaica, the Yakut of Siberia, and the Yurok Indians.[115] He could have included modern capitalist society.

Armies on the march were drivers of markets. In order not to alienate future subjects, armies often had to tread carefully and often exchanged or 'bought', food and other supplies with coins from the royal mint. Just consider the impossibility of supplying the army of Alexander the Great with food from home when it marched to India. In 11 years, from 335 B.C. to 324 B.C., the army battled its way across 35,000 kilometers (22,000 miles). Clearly, food had to be bought, stolen or received as a tribute. One can assume that the exchange was not very equal. It is interesting to consider what went through the mind of a farmer in Punjab, an economy not yet built around money, when told to part with his or her oxen in exchange for some pieces of metal with a picture on them. And once that was done, what could those coins be used for? What was there to buy in a non-monetary economy? Mostly the rulers got their money back in the form of taxes. The state paid its soldiers with coins, the soldiers use coins for buying food or drink and the farmers paid the coins back to the state as tax. In this way the state never needed to deliver anything, just take. But in doing so, the state also created a market.

Social differentiation is another driver of trade. Quite early on there was trade in luxuries, shells, pearls, incense, exotic foods for the elite, including high-value products that justified the costs of long-distance transportation. They clearly had no ecological role and no immediate economic role. The growth in early trade coincided with the rise of hierarchy and social stratification because those seizing power needed to differentiate themselves with powerful and magic objects.[116] The philosopher Seneca criticized that the Roman elite who brought "from all regions everything, known or unknown, to tempt their fastidious palate".[117] In addition to this luxury trade, strategic products were imported for the military,

The fact that there was trade should not be taken as an indication that 'the market' played an important role in ancient societies. Merchants were important in Sumerian society but their activities were carefully managed by the rulers, to the extent that they could be seen as "quasi-ambassadors".[118] The emerging great kingdoms and empires were strictly planned bureaucracies; societies were more or less 'socialist' in the sense that everything was produced for society and individual rights were almost non-existent. Production was recorded – which required and demanded the emergence of the use of letters and numbers – and what wasn't needed locally was kept in central storage facilities.[119] In Egypt, the pharaoh imposed taxes in the form of goods delivered to the state. Huge granaries, often located in the temples, kept stocks of grain which were more precious than the reserves of central banks today. Egyptian laborers were paid in bread or beer.[120] The temple for Ramses II had storehouses big enough to feed 20,000 people for a year.[121] So, a lot of goods were moved, but they were not moved through any markets in a modern sense.

Rome, whose population reached a million inhabitants, was much concerned with its food supplies. One public storehouse in Rome held an astonishing 225,000 square feet of granary space, almost eight times the size of the Colosseum.[122] Free adult males, more than 200,000[123] received a monthly ration of grain, sometimes subsidized and some-times for free, which kept them calm. This free ration, *annona*, was later expanded to oil, wine and pork.[124] The government also had to feed the army. This meant that much of the food was kept out of market circulation and was distributed by the government. Grain from Egypt and Sicily didn't flow into Rome as a result of the entrepreneurial activities of traders. There were private grain shipping companies and they were paid for their work by the government. The provinces shipped their grain to Rome because they were forced to. They had to pay taxes to the central government and could do so either in currency or in kind.[125] Even when there were markets they were mostly under strict government control. One tomb relief from Rome shows govern-ment inspectors monitoring and issuing receipts at every step in the making of bread.[126] Other types of societies developed other types of stewardship, distribution and division, but markets didn't play a major role in any of them when it came to distributing daily necessities.[127] [128]

In general, rulers were greatly concerned with food, to keep the population alive and working and avoiding them becoming restless. A secure food supply was also critical to withstand aggression or natural disasters. Food was also central in emerging modern societies, although the market was seldom trusted, particularly in times of hardship. Attempts at stabilizing grain supply became part of the job of the emerging nation-states of Europe. The most ambitious central-ized systems of food provisioning developed in France and in Prussia under Frederick the Great.[129] Paris reached some 650,000 people in

1750 and the task of feeding the city was formidable, even more so as Paris was far from the sea. The government organized the supplies of Paris from the surrounding land, according to distance: in bad years, grain would be drawn in from as far away as the Mediterranean coastal areas. There was a grain police with a network of informants. Merchants were all licensed, hoarding was a crime and there were strict rules preventing millers, merchant and bakers going into each others' businesses. Like so many times before, food regulations were hard to enforce and a black market thrived.[130] The historian Steven Kaplan calls the French king 'the baker of last resort',[131] and the king's failure to feed the people was at least in part a cause for the French Revolution. In Paris the price of bread and the number of bakers were regulated up to 1863.[132]

Before the industrial revolution Europe did have local markets where food and goods from the countryside and city were exchanged, and they were sometimes important. In 1208/09 the Winchester manors in England sold 50 tons of grain, 146 cattle, 1,277 sheep and lamb, 4,135 cheeses and 118 hens on the market.[133] But we shouldn't believe that most food was distributed in that way; on the contrary, most (surplus) food was given to landlords as rent, to the church as tithe, to the crown or was used for big events. In the Swedish town of Gothenburg records from the middle of the 17th century show that ten times more oxen and steers were slaughtered 'for family needs' than 'for sale'.[134]

For most of us it is probably hard to visualize what life looked like in pre-industrial European farming communities. In many parts of Europe, even if land was held 'privately' by tenants or farmers, the agricultural calendar was governed by a village commune or the court of a manorial lord who owned the soil. There it was decided when to sow and harvest and when land would be open for grazing. Beyond the fields were pastures and woodlands which mostly were commons, used for collective grazing and fuel collection. Animals were often kept in a joint village herd, overseen by a communal herdsman. The number of animals kept was restricted and crops, wood or even manure could not be removed from the village without a permit. All in all, it was a very different society and the influence of markets was weak.[135]

The markets were also not particularly free; there were many regulations on prices and over who could trade and where. In medieval England there were laws regulating the price for many foods; an 1378 ordinance of the City of London regulated the prices of hen pies, roast snipe, larks, herons and pigs, to mention just a few. In 1529 there were new laws with maximum prices for meat.[136] Authorities regarded bread as fundamental for the subsistence of the population and did not leave its production or distribution to the market. The Assize of Bread from the reign of Henry III in the 13th century regulated the price and weight of bread in great detail. These rules were in force, with some changes, until the beginning of the 19th century. Similar rules existed for beer.[137] A Swedish ordinance from 1622 required that a permit to be issued for each animal to be slaughtered and defined the cost of slaughter, quality classifications and the price of the meat, if sold. Meat prices were even seasonally differentiated. The number of meat mongers was regulated and there was a tax on both the slaughtering and the sale of meat.[138] In 1771, during what is commonly called the Age of Freedom (!) in Sweden it was prohibited to import up to 871 different products.[139]

At this time there was not one European market. There were not even national markets, but many separate local and regional markets. There were very weak connections between national and international markets and traders who engaged in international trade were largely shut out from local markets.[140] In France there were regional barriers to trade that meant that grain markets were not national, with the exception of Paris which drew on the whole country as catchment area.[141] In German speaking parts of Europe domestic trade was severely restricted up to the establishment of 'free trade' in the first half of the 19th century. Before that, small shopkeepers (*krämer* in German) belonged to local guilds, which prescribed what commodities could be offered and at what price, and also influenced the place and size of the shop or stall in the weekly markets. They could only sell goods not produced in their town. Only the few great merchant families who were engaged in long-distance trade were exempt from such regulations. The grain markets were largely local and strictly regulated. In times of shortage prices were fixed, sales out of the town were prohibited and houses searched for hoarded grain. The government distributed grain to the poor for free or at subsidized prices.[142]

While markets and trade were highly regulated up to the 19th century in most European countries, changes were underway. They didn't come abruptly and the emergence of a 'free market' (there has hardly ever been any really free market in the meaning of an unregulated market) was not a linear process. It emerged slowly. By the end of the 13th and the beginning of the 14th centuries, a trade network from China to England and from Scandinavia to Africa had been established. In Europe, the main beneficiaries of this were the Italian city-states, in particular Florence, Milan, Genoa and Venice. These states were mercantile states, where traders and manufacturers had a lot of influence. It is in Florence and later Genoa that the toolbox of managing money and transactions developed. Meanwhile, to the north, Dutch traders had taken control over the lucrative trade of grains from the Baltic Sea. Their profits far exceeded what could be reinvested in the trade. Some of the money went into farming and was one of the reasons for the modernization and increased productivity of Dutch farming. Even food self-sufficiency was abandoned as a goal when Dutch farming commercialized. Holland imported grains while Dutch farmers grew flax, madder (the dye plant *Rubia tinctorum*), made cheese and had other commercial production.[143] [144] The farming system was greatly intensified with increasing yields per area unit as well as increased labor input per area unit. Manures, crop rotations and nitrogen fixing plants were developed and yields of grain reached levels that were not improved upon until the late 19th century.[145] It is difficult to distinguish between causes and effects but clearly agriculture intensification and development were key elements of the Dutch Golden Age.

Colonization was also a strong driver for the development of international trade as seen in the case of sugar, mainly from Brazil and the Caribbean (more about it in chaper twelve). An equally important factor was that colonization gave the emerging industries in the colonizing countries a market for their sales. The British crushed the Indian textile industry and through that established world dominance in cotton fabrics. In North America most trade was with England and there was little trade between the North American colonies.[146]

Many early cities were supplied by others means than trade, such as government collection of taxes in kind, landlords living in the cities getting supplies from their estates etc. In the 11th century, eighty percent of the public rice demand for the one million inhabitant city of Kaifeng in China was met by taxes in kind.[147] But for an industrial town with salaried workers, a market would often be the way of organizing the supply of foods and other goods.[a] Such arrangements clearly require a transport system so that farmers – or specialized traders – can bring their wares to the cities. The growing cities of Europe constituted a market for food and there were large scale sales of oxen, driven over huge distances to major centers such as London,

---

[a] This was, surprisingly for some perhaps, also the model chosen in the Soviet Union and most communist countries.

Holland, Northern Italy and Augsburg. Some oxen were also transported by ship; several Swedish ports have records of live oxen exports
going back to the 17th century. In the middle of the 17th century an
estimated 15,000 Scottish black cattle were driven to England and by
the middle of the 18th century this had increased to 40,000 cattle per
year.[148] Ireland became increasingly important as a supplier and in
1812 almost 80,000 oxen were imported to England from Ireland, this
equaled an estimated twelve percent of all beef consumed in England.
In 1870 over 600,000 cattle were sent from Ireland to England.[149]

England became a large net importer of food. Up until 1842 all its
meat was from the British Isles (including Ireland), but by the end of
the century 40% of all the United Kingdom's meat was imported. As a
result of the inflow of cheap grain from United States and wool from
Australia and New Zealand, production of wheat, barley and wool
dropped to more than half and more than 5 million hectares of plowed
land became pastures, heath or forest.[150] From being almost self-
sufficient in food production in the early 19th century, by the onset of
WWI Britain imported almost two thirds of its food and around four
fifths of its bread grain.[151] [152]

It is important to recognize both the extent and importance of this
early global food trade, but also that this was without parallel at that
time. After the abolition of the Corn Laws 1846[a] England took a free
trade stance, while most other countries protected their agriculture
sector. The effect on agricultural production of regulating trade could
easily be seen and can be seen still today. Neither France nor Germany
protected wool production, which led to a halving of the sheep herd in
France and a reduction to just twenty percent in Germany between
1870 and 1914. Yet these two countries protected the domestic production of meat and cereals and their production continued to increase.[153]

In Western Europe, urbanization and the transport revolution,
with canals, steamships and railroads, meant that markets rapidly
became the main driver of agriculture development. Farmers could
and had to specialize. As cheap grain flowed into Europe from North
America and Russia grain production was no longer profitable.
Farmers in countries such as the Netherlands and Denmark opted to
specialize in pork and dairy, while buying imported feed. Today, one
can still clearly see a relationship between livestock concentrations and

---

[a] The Corn Laws were designed to protect cereal producers against
competition from less expensive foreign imports between 1815 and 1846.

access to high capacity harbors or sea ways for shipping in all the feed needed. This specialization and commercialization broke the link between the city and the rural areas, and this was reflected in a further 'liberalization' of trade.

Despite the rapid shift in market conditions, the commercialization of agriculture was a slow process. As noted before, as late as 1900 only ten percent of the world's population lived in cities, and cities were where markets thrived. Grain, the most important commodity, didn't become a fully tradable commodity until the end of the nineteenth century in Asia.[154] In China in the 1840s only 10% of the rice harvest was traded and still in 1936 it was only 29%. The French historian Fernand Braudel estimated that as recent as the sixteenths century only one percent of the total grain produced around the Mediterranean was internationally traded.[155] At the beginning of the 1900s, the United States, Canada and some of the more advanced European economies had a commercialization rate of more than 75% (which means that three quarters of production was sold in the market and one quarter was consumed on the farm or distributed by other means). But in most countries much less than half of the production was sold.

The process goes from market contact, to market orientation and finally ends in market integration. In the market contact phase farms sell a limited surplus to get income to buy some consumer goods and pay taxes. With market orientation they adjust their production to supply markets, changing the mix of crops and actively seeking market opportunities. They seek to increase production of tradable goods, but still strive to base the production on local resources. With market integration the whole farming process is guided by the market and the farm is integra-ted in markets for inputs, credit, land and labor. Increasingly farms are sub-contracted suppliers to agri-business corporations, such as the case of chicken producers (more about that later). Market orientation can have many advantages but it also requires more resources, and ultimately those with fewer resources will not be able to capture the new opportunities. This is the case in developing countries today and it was the case in Europe in the process of agricultural transformation.

The process of market integration doesn't only affect how farmers distribute their surplus but also the productive factors farmers need in order to have anything to sell. For three major factors needed for agriculture production, seeds and breeds, land and labor, there were no markets in most societies. Land formed the basis for military, judiciary, administrative, religious and political systems, and was also the economic unit of most importance in an agricultural society. There were few places were land could be bought and sold in anything resembling a market before the emergence of the capitalist society. In many cases sale of land was simply not allowed or not possible as it was not individually owned. Often it was communally owned or owned by the state, feudal lords or other powerful institutions, such as monasteries. Converting land from public or communal stewardship to private ownership was therefore an essential part of the commercialization process.

The origin of private land mostly lies with the state. The king would allocate land to a single proprietor in exchange for real or promised services. This was also the strategy of most colonization, for instance in Brazil. Between 1534 and 1536 King John III divided the huge land mass of Brazil into 15 "captaincies", which were given to Portuguese noblemen who wanted and had the means to administer and exploit them. The heritage of this can still be seen in the extremely tilted distribution of land in Brazil. In North America the British king assigned the lands of Maryland to Lord Baltimore and of Pennsylvania to William Penn. To try to gain settlers, Maryland used what was known as the 'headright system' where settlers were given 50 acres[a] of land for each person they brought into the colony, whether as settler, indentured servant or slave.[156] This private ownership[b] was in stark contrast to the tradition of the Native Americans. Massasoit, a Wampanaog leader who helped the Pilgrims to survive their first years had another perspective: "the land is our mother, nourishing all her children, beasts, birds, fish, and all men....How can one man say it belongs only to him?"[157]

But privatization of land was not only restricted to colonies. Where land was under communal control the state often took it by force or forced its transformation into private property. For instance in the United Kingdom, from 1800 to 1860, some 2 million hectares were 'enclosed' in this way, and huge tracts had already been transferred to private landlords earlier.[158] An increased demand for wool meant that it was more interesting to get income from large-scale sheep farming

---

[a] In this book I use hectares as the main measure for area unit, for ease of comparison, but in this and similar cases I use acres and other measurements as they appear. One acre is approximately 0.4047 hectare, and is approximately the size of a soccer pitch.

[b] The first settlers actually had a vision of communal ownership of land, inspired by early Christian community.

than from extracting rent from the land; so tenants and others were driven off the land and were replaced by sheep, something that still can be seen in the landscape of the British Isles. A survey of land ownership published in 1873 showed that a quarter of the United Kingdom's land surface was controlled by just 353 landowners.[159] In imperial Russia at the beginning of the twentieth century common land ownership was still the rule. In an effort to curb revolutionary tendencies the Russian authorities wanted to transform the communal ownership of land to private family farms. But the peasants were not very interested and only some ten percent of the communal land was redistributed during the ten years leading up to the 1917 Revolution.[160]

After the American Revolution, the states owned huge tracts of land. Some of this was transferred to the federal government, which with conquest and purchase expanded the territory rapidly. Originally, land was auctioned to settlers with 1 or 2 dollars as a minimum price and with a minimum size of 640 acres – pricing out the typical pioneer. Instead large parts of the land were bought by speculators, making use of generous credits from the government.[161] The Homestead Act of 1862 allowed setters to claim 160 acres for free in designated areas. But only parts of this land was sold or given to settlers. Between 1775 and 1855, the federal government gave away some 70 million acres as bounties to men and officers from the Army and Navy, mirroring a practice established long before. Already Socrates says "you need but use your eyes to see how many private persons, not to say crowned heads, owe the increase of their estates to war."[162]

Of the 500 million hectares of land disposed of by American authorities between 1860 and 1900 only about 80 million went to homesteaders. During the same period 108 million acres were sold mostly to speculators and the remainder, some 300 million hectares were given to states and railroad companies, which in turn sold most of it to speculators or farmers.[163] Depending on whose estimates one believe railroads got between 91 million and 183 million acres.[164] Overall most land passed through the hands of speculators and many farmers turned speculators as well. "In general they were all land speculators – whether they owned 80 acres or 8,000,000 acres" writes Willard W. Cochrane in *The Development of American Agriculture*. That all this land has been taken from the Native American at an earlier date is of no relevance for the farmer of today. Private ownership is for some reason sacrosanct, even when it is founded on theft.

It is important to recall this history of land, which is one of the reasons for why farms and farmers all over the world often are indebted in one or the other way. There are few places on earth where farming communities transformed nature into productive acres and kept control over that land throughout millennia. There are even fewer where an individual broke his or her new land and continued to manage it, a by and large idealized view of pioneer farmers which has little grounding in reality. The transition of land to a market was one of the driving forces and preconditions behind the integration of agriculture into the market economy. Farmers needed cash income for rents and land leases, which forced them to produce for the market, and once that was established there was no going back. Today, the privatization of communal land is still promoted as a key modernization strategy in areas where communal ownership prevails.

Farmers have always saved seeds from their own crops and have also exchanged seeds with each other in various ways. Still today, in many parts of the world, informal markets or exchanges are important ways to renew seed stocks. This is especially the case where the seed is also the desired product, such is the case for grains. Even in the highly commercialized United States as recently as 1973 wheat growers in Kansas only bought commercial seeds to plant 5% of the acreage.[165] Farm-saved seeds and seeds from informal sources are responsible for providing more than 90% of the seed produced in most countries.[166]

Commercial seed breeding emerged late. In Europe there was some commercial production of vegetable seeds in the 17th century,[167] although the most important seeds were outside of commercial circulation. The first commercial seed crop in the United Sates was not produced until 1866 – cabbage seeds produced on Long Island. Early seed trade entrepreneurs felt the growth of their business was stymied by the government programs of free seed distribution as well as the self-replicating nature of seeds. In 1883, the American Seed Trade Association was formed and called for ending the government programs. But the program was very popular with constituents, and the United States Department of Agriculture's (USDA) seed budget was kept intact – at one point it accounted for a full 10% of the agency's overall annual expenditure. It took 40 years of lobbying to convince Congress to cut the USDA's seed distribution programs.[168]

Historically, the agricultural 'labor market' mostly involved slaves or serfs, with few examples of workers freely offering their services.[169] Most farm labor has been supplied by the farm households themselves. In parts of the world there has been rather well developed 'market' for tenants, small farmers renting land from landlords. This could be a long lasting arrangement that endured for decades or just apply to a single crop; as such the conditions varied greatly. One description of the many forms of such contracts from Italy in the 1880s runs to 813 pages. Payments were made in kind or in cash, or often as share-cropping arrangements, where the tenant and the landowners share the proceeds of the crop sales. The tenants' share ranged from just 20% in Tamil Nadu in India to up to 80% in Argentina in the 1890s. The later was a result of labor shortages and land abundance.[170]

Farmers also wanted and needed income for a multitude of reasons. The very existence of interesting things to buy is perhaps an undervalued driver of commercialization. In many poor rural areas there were simply very few things available to buy which might motivate people to sell. Equally there were very few buyers of the goods you might want to sell as most people produced the same things. But once there is liquor in the store, cotton cloth, watches or antibiotics for your sick child your motivation to earn money increases. Mobile phones seem to play an important role in increasing market orientation in many developing countries today. The purchase and use of them require cash and the phone itself is used for selling and getting market information.

Some claim that smallholders will never voluntarily move into the market economy but must be coerced into it through many different pathways. Sometimes the means are brutal, such as the British enclosures; trading monopolies or outright colonization. But more often they are more subtle: credit programs that create dependency; compulsory schooling that mean farmers need to pay for school fees, uniforms, books, loose family labor and see their children acquire other values; land titling, i.e. the transformation of land from communities to individuals etc. Another way to force people into commercial farming is to introduce taxes that have to be paid in cash, a system that forces subsistence farmers into commercial farmers – or laborers. As the Kenyan environmentalist and winner of the Nobel Peace Prize Wangari Maathai describes:

> When the British decided to collect revenue and finance local development, they did not want to be paid in goats. They wanted cash. They also wanted to create a labor force, but they did not want to force people to work. So they introduced an income tax for men in most parts of the country that could be paid only in the form of money. This created a cash-based rather than a livestock-based economy.[171]

Today, farms are integrated in global markets not only for what they sell but also for what they need, the inputs, which range from seeds to jerry cans to diesel and fertilizers. Even the most basic farm tool, the hoe, is often imported; for example, in East Africa the hoes often come from India or China. The use of external inputs, in particular chemical fertilizers and pesticides, has increased enormously. Credit allows farmers to increase investments and risk-taking in their production. But it also forces them to get a cash income to pay the interest. Credit also drives farms into private ownership as communal land or land with unclear tenure cannot be used as collateral for a loan.

The period between 1850 and 1914 was a real break-through for commercialization and globalization. This was also helped by the wages of urban people rising faster than the prices of most food, spurring further demand. For a long period, there was even an inter-national currency, the gold standard. Goods, capital and people started to flow at an ever increasing rate. From 1826 to 1913 almost one million kilometers of railroad tracks were built.[172] This had a profound effect on agriculture. Prices were generally lower, but they were also more stable as the transportation network and relative free trade allowed for shipping from surplus areas to deficit areas. Previously grain prices were extremely volatile, and could differ by a factor of up to 7 from the cheapest to the most expensive; now prices rarely reached double that of the cheapest.[173]

Between the World War I and the 1950s, global trade expansion took a pause. But world trade accelerated dramatically during the early 1970s, growing seven fold in real terms from 0.45 trillion dollars in the early 1960s to 3.4 trillion dollars in 1990. From 1850 up to around 1950 agriculture products constituted around half of all international trade, after that trade in other products skyrocketed, so while agricultural trade continued to increase, its share of global trade was down to ten percent by the end of the 1990s.[174] In the period before the Second World War, annual trade in grain rarely exceeded 30 million tons,[175] while today trade in cereals exceeds 300 million tons. Population growth and growth in agriculture production is increasingly geographically de-coupled, which means that global trade in food is likely to grow – if the global food system can continue to function. A very important caveat.

In economic theory, poor countries should compete in trades that require a high labor input and have low capital requirements. Histori-cally, agriculture has been such a sector. But today's agriculture, in the rich countries at least, is characterized by a low labor input and very high capital input. Mechanization has crushed the comparative advantage of poor countries and poor producers. Poor farmers can only be competitive in crops which have not yet been successfully mechanized, such as coffee, tea, flowers, avocadoes and green beans. At the beginning of the 1960s developing countries had a trade surplus in agricultural produce of around US$7 billion, but by the beginning of the new millennium that balance had shifted to a deficit of around US$20 billion and, if we exclude Brazil this figure is much higher, at US$27 billion.[176] [177] It is not only the money flow that has drastically changed direction, but also the flows of calories. In the late 1960s developed and developing countries were more or less producing their own calorific needs, but in 2009, many more developing countries had become net importers of food. Sub-Saharan Africa went from a four-teen percent surplus of calories to a thirteen percent deficit.[178]

It is not only importing countries that are stuck in dependency, to some extent the dependency is even more extreme for exporting countries, or at least for farmers in exporting countries. In an average year in the 1980s the output from about thirty percent of the agricul-tural areas in the United States was exported, in 1988 it even reached a high of nearly two-fifths. Cotton is the most export-dependent crop: 86% of the United States crop was exported in 2011. Meanwhile, more than one quarter of the textiles imported to the United States are actually made from cotton exported from the United States. To compli-cate the picture even more some of those textiles are then exported again.[179] Food exports is of course a marketing opportunity and it also gives the United States an almost unique role as a world supplier of food, with Brazil as a runner-up. But it also means that the agriculture sector in the United States is completely dependent on a world economy, which it cannot control. A mixed blessing.

Japan's food self-sufficiency rate in calorific terms stood at seventy-three percent in 1965 but has since plummeted to around forty percent since the mid-1990s, the lowest for any major developed country.[180] Norway, Belgium, Haiti, Dominica, Somalia, Saint Kitts and Nevis, Gambia, Zimbabwe, Dominican Republic, Armenia, the Netherlands and Panama all had a net calorific self-sufficiency of less than fifty-five percent in 2009. The Netherlands, a small country and one of the world's most urbanized, despite its low self-sufficiency, is the fifth biggest exporter of foods in the world, and has a huge agriculture trade surplus in monetary terms. Belize, Hungary, Guyana, Bulgaria, Canada, New Zealand, Ukraine, Australia, Uruguay, Paraguay, Argentina all produce more than 150% of their calorific needs, and the food giants Brazil and United States have surpluses of 41% and 24% respectively.[181] China went from calorific self-sufficiency in 1967 to a deficit in 2009, mainly driven by large-scale imports of soybeans and palm oil.[182] Chinese imports of soybeans to feed its 500 million pigs is the largest trade flow in today's food system, sixty percent of all internationally traded soybeans are bought by China.[183]

In 2013 Maersk's *Mc-Kinney Møller* made its maiden voyage from the Daewoo shipyard in South Korea. For a while it will be the biggest ship in the world. It carries 18,000 containers, each of them 20ft long, 8ft wide and 8ft high. That's enough space for 36,000 cars, 111 million pairs of trainers or almost a billion cans of Coca-Cola. Over the next two years, Maersk is overseeing the construction of another 19 similar "Triple-E" vessels, to be deployed on the Asia-Europe route. This ship is a powerful, albeit often neglected, symbol of globalization. In fifty years containers have transformed shipping from an old-fashioned business into an industrial enterprise.

Malcolm McLean, a trucking entrepreneur from North Carolina wanted to integrate trucking on land and shipping, which so far had been separate businesses. He converted a World War II tanker into the *Ideal-X*, with a reinforced deck to sustain the load of 58 modified lorry trailers. This signaled the birth of the shipping container. The world's first purpose-built container crane started to operate in 1959 and loaded one 40,000-pound[a] box every three minutes. The productivity gains from using this container crane were staggering, as it could handle more than 40 times the average of a longshore gang. There are now more than 17 million container units in the world, with every container having its own unique number that is linked to information about who owns the container and who is using it to ship goods.[184] Individual satellite tracking is well on its way.

Prior to highly mechanized container transfers, crews of longshore-men would pack individual cargoes into the hold of a ship. Loading took a lot of time, there was high risk of damage to the goods by bad weather or theft. A common joke at the New York piers was that the docker's wages were 'twenty dollars a day and all the Scotch you could carry home.' Most food traded could either be easily transported in bulk or was expensive food for which transport costs were a small part of the price. Today most of the food traded is processed food, including simple items such as crackers, muesli and ketchup. Even beer and water are shipped across the seven seas to be sold in distant markets. The trade in processed foods is increasing more rapidly than other agriculture trade.[185] Containerization has greatly reduced the expense of international trade and increased its speed, which has had an impact on trade in consumer goods. The use of containers has elimi-nated up to twelve handlings from factory to end consumer. Three

---

[a] 1 pound is 0.4536 kg.

researchers at the University of Lund, Daniel M. Bernhofen, Zouheir El-Sahli and Richard Kneller, concluded that the effect of containeriza-tion on North-North trade are much larger than the effects of free trade agreements.[186]

In 2012, I visited two very different farmers; Bob Stewart in Illinois and Susan Mkandawire in Zambia. Bob farms in the Corn Belt, south of Chicago and Susan farms not far from the international airport in Zambia. They are both maize growers, and as farmers they shared worries over the weather, prices, access to labor and many other things. They were also very different, or at least they operate under very different conditions. Bob's yields of maize are regularly more than 10,000 kg per hectare while Susan, in a good year, gets around 2,000 kg per hectare, i.e. Bob harvests more than five times as much per area unit. That is remarkable. But what is much more remarkable is how much land they farm; Bob's farm is 3,200 hectares while Susan manages less than half a hectare.

Bob works the farm with a brother and three full time employees, their father and Bob's wife are also involved in the operation. In peak season they have four more helpers; each person thus manages more than 400 hectares, i.e. they spend less than five hours of work to manage the total land area that Susan farms with her husband, Fred. Because they are very poor, Fred takes on other jobs outside the farm when he finds them; at the time of my visit he was occasionally working as a watchman. Apart from the maize they also grow vege-tables which are sold in the market in Zambia's capital Lusaka. But let's focus on the maize. Together they spend some 266 hours per year tending their 0.4 hectares of maize. They hire a team of oxen to do the land preparation; which saves them 120 hours on land preparation by hand, still the dominant method in Sub-Saharan Africa.

Through the ease of transportation and storage (mainly driven by the fossil fuel economy), there is more or less a global market for grains, pulses and oil crops, with similar prices all over the world, tariffs or other government interventions being the only other factor of importance. These prices are determined by the producers who can combine large areas with mechanization, i.e. those than can use a lot of resources and a lot of external energy. The dramatic increase in *labor productivity* we have seen in the farm sector is linked to the increased use of external energy sources, be it for pumping water, driving tractors and combine harvesters or making chemical fertilizers. It is almost self-evident that Susan in Zambia has not a chance in hell of competing with Bob in Illinois. This example begs the question of whether global food markets really work to our advantage. Poor people and poor countries are supposed to get a comparative advantage from low labor costs. But this mechanism is totally broken when the cost for labor is depressed far below sustenance levels, not to speak about reproduction, that is raising a family. Because of productivity gains in developed countries, agriculture prices dropped by some 60% in the period 1960-2000. As the productivity of the poorest farmers remained much the same, it is obvious that they have lost out. Their value of production, regardless if they eat it themselves or sell it, has gone down considerably, making them poorer both in relative and absolute terms.

Early trade was about ecological adaptation, transporting essential food or other essential goods to a places where they were lacking. Very little in present international trade is based on that. Instead, trade in itself creates shortages. Today, Sweden only produces half the beef it consumes. This is not because there is no land or resources available in Sweden. On the contrary, the country has let a million hectares of meadows revert to forest and a lot of arable land is idle – or grazed by horses that people keep for a hobby. International trade can be a safety valve for food shocks by moving food from one part of the world to the other. Yet it has dramatically reduced each region's self-sufficiency and made all of us dependent on global supply chains for our daily food. Some of the trade is really difficult to understand or justify. More or less identical products are exported and imported by the same countries. As the ecological economist Herman Daly points out: "Americans import Danish sugar cookies and Danes imports American sugar cookies. Exchanging recipes would surely be more efficient".[187]

It is a mistake to conclude that there is a linear process driving farmers into increased levels of commercialization. In times of collapsing markets, natural disasters, unrest or war, self-sufficiency and non-market exchange is bound to play a bigger role. The Roman peri-urban sprawl with agricultural estates, villas, engaged in intensive commercial production went the same way as the Empire. At the fall of Rome the area fell into neglect and finally reverted to extensive pastoralism.[188] The pastoral beauty of this Roman Campagna inspired the painters who flocked into Rome in the 18th and 19th centuries, when it was the most painted landscape in Europe.[189]

We can also see the same patterns today. In banana-producing Jamaica food prices soared in the mid 1970s as a result of the first oil price shock. But banana prices were not keeping pace with the cost of food. This resulted in many smallholders reverting to subsistence farming, growing for themselves, or growing food crops for the local market. Interestingly, this coincided with improvements in their children's nutritional status.[190] When the Soviet Union collapsed, farming in many parts of the fallen empire reverted to self-sufficiency. During Soviet times Armenian producers had supplied the Union with brandy, grapes and fruits, but when the Union crumbled and war broke with Azerbaijan, people ripped out the vines to grow wheat.[191] Commercialization in reverse can also be observed recently in Argentina during the economic crisis 2001 and presently in Euro debt ridden Greece, Spain or Portugal or in Detroit where urban farms are being established on the ruins of the automotive industrial culture.

The commercialization of agriculture and food has had profound implications for how we view food and what we eat. As historian B.W. Higman notes in *How Food made History*: "Only in recent time have consumers in some countries come to think of food as a packaged good, to be obtained almost exclusively by purchase, and come to regard anything taken directly from the well as potentially dangerous".

7

The food chain

While there are many theories about the importance of irrigation, the plow or chemical fertilizers for society there are few that expand on the importance of cooking, making bread or brewing wine. This might be a result of a gender bias, since food processing[a] along with cooking, in most cultures (but not all) has been a predominantly female activity, and even a low-ranked female activity undertaken by the oldest daughter or the daughter in law. Be that as it may, the effect of cooking, food storage technologies and food processing on society has been profound.

Food processing is closely related to storage and transport. Many of the main food processing technologies have their origin as storage technologies, often accidents or mistakes in storage. The contents of long-forgotten pot tasted nicer than expected, and the grain that got wet and germinated and then was dried again fermented into a nice brew when soaked again in water. Sushi, which we today associate with perfectly fresh fish, was originally fish that was stored in rice where it fermented, allowing it to be transported inland or used as a travel ration. For a long time salting and curing were the main methods of preservation, and these were known in ancient times. The Romans cured ham with processes similar to those still used for prosciutto in northern Italy. Sausage making was also developed in ancient times, and apparently derided equally early: the Greek poet Hipponax identified the sausage with the penis and stories about what really goes into sausages have been told ever since.[192]

Salted fish was delivered to Athens from as far away as from Spain, and there were many definitions of its qualities, with terms

---

[a] I asked food historian Rachel Laudan if she could suggest another word for food processing as to my ears it sounds bad. She responded "food processing is a dreary word: that's why I called my book *Cooking in World History* not *Food Processing in World History*".

describing origin, shape and saltiness, indicating a well-developed trade.[193] The marriage of fish and salt was completed in the making of salt fish sauce, which was made in Ancient Greece and brought to heights and world fame by the Romans. The Romans used fish sauce extensively and it was affordable for most of the population. There is a close similarity between the Roman *garum* and the *nuoc-mam* of present day Vietnam and *nam-pla* of Thailand.

The making of fish sauce and many other food processing technologies developed into commercial professions in Rome. Professional bakers emerged with new baking technologies and the donkey-driven mill. In many cases, these new technologies represented a substantial investment and were only possible if the machinery was used in a commercial way, not just for the household. Secondary trades also developed with some areas producing millstones and others amphora for storage and transportation.[194] And trade in foods and the inputs needed for food preparation became a full time occupation. Salt and spices were very important traded goods and formed the basis of the riches of the Italian city states in the 14th and 15th centuries. Medieval trade in Britain was in the hands of salters.[195]

Freeze-drying of vegetables and meat took place in many cold climates; the Inca freeze dried the staple potato, still today known as *chuño*, or *papas secas*. Trade in ice was reported already in antiquity and, in India, ice was brought from distant mountains to Akbar's court in Lahore in the 16th century.[196] But it was used only for luxuries, cool drinks and for making ice creams, culinary interesting but irrelevant for the food system at large. This was also the case when ice houses first appeared in England in the 17th century.[197] But this was to change.

The first shipment of American ice to England in 1844 puzzled customs officers who had no idea how to classify it: it got stuck there for so long that all the 300 tons melted. Bur this didn't deter Frederic Tudor, the 'Ice King' of Boston, who harvested ice from Lake Wenham and shipped it all over the world. He had ice-houses in Cuba, Jamaica, New Orleans, Calcutta, Madras, Bombay, Sri Lanka and Singapore, as well as a shop on the Strand in London which would put a fresh block of ice in the window with a newspaper behind it so that passers-by could marvel at how clear the ice was. The shop window was regularly crowded with people staring at the ice. America exported 146,000 tons of ice in 1856; amazingly, this was financially viable even though up to three quarters of the cargo melted on the way. During the 1850s the Norwegian lakes, which were much closer, became Britain's major source of ice; by 1900, Norway was exporting a million tons a year, and half of that went to Britain.[198]

Artificial ice making was discovered in the middle of the 18th century, but wasn't commercially viable until hundred years later.[199] The first attempt to ship frozen meat was on the S.S. Norfolk which sailed from Australia to England in 1873, but on arrival the 20 tons of beef and mutton were spoilt. But in 1877 *Le Frigorifique* managed to ship frozen beef from Argentina to France and at least part of the cargo was edible. Things started to move quickly; by 1880 trade in frozen meat was a normal business and 30,000 carcasses of frozen mutton was shipped from the Falkland Islands (Malvinas) to England in 1886. Three years later 143 ships with a capacity for 6.5 million mutton carcasses were competing for trade.[200] Freezing was developed to enable long-distance trade, but gradually developed as supermarkets stocked frozen foods and refrigeration technology moved all the way into households. As recently as 1939 only two percent of British households had a refrigerator.[201] As a transitional arrangement some shops had freezer lockers where clients rented a space, something I vaguely remember from my own childhood. Thus, it took almost two hundred year from the discovery of the principles of artificial refrigeration to it becoming an everyday technology. Today, New Zealand can supply global markets with chilled meat transported at minus 1 centigrade in controlled atmosphere which can be kept for 90 days and still be called 'fresh'.[202]

In the novel *East of Eden*, by John Steinbeck, Adam Trask fails in shipping iceberg lettuce to distant markets and is ruined. Perhaps he was just a bit too early, because the shipping of iceberg lettuce by rail later became a real success-story. After First World War iceberg lettuce emerged as the first year-round vegetable which could be shipped by rail from California to the East Coast. The lettuce was originally called crisp head, but was commonly referred to as iceberg lettuce, because of the huge quantities of ice needed for the shipping. It was one of the first designer crops, a compact lettuce which could stand the near freezing temperature needed to keep it fresh for the long journey. This enabled huge scale production in monoculture fields. It didn't only enabled this but it required it, as the cooling facilities were costly and the need to fill whole wagons with lettuce and supply the markets with a steady stream of lettuce was all important. In this way it had most of the characteristics that still drive ever increasing size in farms[203]; a food technology that requires a constant supply of large volumes of a uniform quality shipped to anonymous mass markets.

Before refrigeration, beef was difficult to preserve; cattle were killed year round and the meat sold and consumed while still fresh. The same applied for lamb. There was potted meat, where cooked meat was pressed in a pot which was sealed by melted butter or fat,[204] but it was not a significant commercial product. Hogs, on the contrary, were only killed in cold weather and their fat was rendered into lard and their flesh carved into hams, shoulders, and sides, which were covered with salt and packed in wooden barrels, which is the origin of the expression meat packer.[205] A bacon industry emerged in the end of the 1700s in Wiltshire, England. As in many other cases it was the demands of the military and shipping that drove this development. The ration for ordinary seamen in 1808 was 6 pounds of salt meat per week. During the latter half of the 19th century, bacon industries in Denmark and Ireland were established to supply the British market.[206] Exports from Ireland continued even during the Great Famine of Ireland during which a million people died.[207] Due to poor hygiene and inadequate storage facilities saltpeter and salt were not always enough to guarantee good storage, and even heavier preservatives were in use. Boric acid or borax or a mix of them were used in England until 1927 when they were banned. The multi-talented Justus von Liebig also stands as the first large scale maker of meat extracts, *Extractum carnis Liebig*, a kind of concentrated meat stock which later was named *Oxo*, a trademark that still exists. At the time, people were persuaded that it was an effective substitute for meat, and that it was particularly suitable for building up the strength of invalids. He also took up the production of corned beef in South America, a product that received a huge boost by the Boer and First World Wars.[208]

> [The wheel] began slowly to revolve, and then the men on each side sprang to work. They had chains which they fastened about the leg of the nearest hog, and the other end of the chain they hooked into one on the rings upon the wheel. So, as the wheel turned, a hog was suddenly jerked off his feet and borne aloft. At the same instant the ear was assailed by the most terrifying shriek; the visitors started in alarm, the women turned pale and shrank back. The shriek was followed by another, louder and yet more agonizing – for once started upon that journey, the hog never came back; at the top of the wheel he was shunted off upon a trolley, and went sailing down the room. And meantime another was swung up, and then another, and another, until there was a double line of them, each dangling by a foot and kicking in frenzy-and squealing.

This is how Upton Sinclair in *the Jungle*, describe the slaughtering of hogs in Chicago at the turn of the century.[209] In United States, Cincinnati, 'Porkopolis' was the first real meat center, but it was in Chicago that the first industrial meat processing was developed, starting with the inauguration of the Union Stock Yard in 1865. There was substantial machinery used in a conveyor belt style processing line–one could call it a disassembly line–with high division of labor and mechanization that included steam powered meat cutters and sausage stuffers.[210] The meat packers also developed what is nowadays called vertical integration; the same company owning or controlling most stages of the production process by taking over farming and transport as well as the processing of animal by-products, such as offal. In 1883 more than 5 million pigs, 2 million cattle and 0.75 million sheep were slaughtered in the Chicago Union Stockyards.[211] This can be compared with the city's population at the time of 750,000. The effluent from the stockyards caused much pollution. In 1885, typhoid, cholera, and dysentery epidemics killed more than a tenth of Chicago's population. When the city reversed the flow of the Chicago River in 1900, it was largely to prevent the stockyards' massive waste from flowing into Lake Michigan.[212]

But the handling of meat didn't only threaten the environment it also harmed people. Around 1900 the science around meat hygiene developed rapidly and the links between poor hygiene and public health became clear. Upton Sinclair's novel described the scandalous methods used for slaughter and the suffering of the animals. But even more he described the unscrupulous exploitation of labor, the hardships of the people living there and the collusion between the state, the judiciary and the meatpackers. More as a side line Sinclair tells about the adulteration of products and the filth involved in the production.[213] The latter caught most of the attention, causing a public uproar, contributing to the passage of the 1906 Pure Food and Drug Act and the Meat Inspection Act, the first laws in the United States to protect consumers from corner-cutting by the food industry.[214]

The sailors who opened the can containing three month old sardines on the French ship assigned to first test Nicolas Appert's canning technology in 1806 were probably nervous. But they needn't have been, and the taste was to their satisfaction. This event marks the starting point for canning in general and for canned sardines in particular. The innovation of tin cans instead of more expensive, heavy and easy-to-brake glass jars was a corner stone for the expansion of the sardine canning industry of France.[215] A friend of Appert's, Joseph Colin in Nantes, set up production of sardines in oil based on the traditional recipe in 1822 and others followed so that, in 1847, there were twelve canning factories. In 1900 French production of canned sardines reached its peak with 23,000 fishermen landing 50,000 tons of sardines. Some fisheries remain but today France imports sardines from Morocco, Spain and Portugal.[216] For the communities involved in this fishery the sardine has been part of their identity for ten generations. There is a church named Notre Dame de la Sardine and there are sardine festivals and masses. In Saint-Gilles-Crois-de-Vie fishermen kiss the first sardines out of the sea in spring.[217]

Sardines were the first mass scale canned foods, and were soon followed by many others.[218] As with many other food preservation methods, canning became part of cooking itself, making new products, with new tastes that didn't exist before. Fresh peas, boiled peas, frozen peas and canned *petit pois* are clearly distinctively different products, and one might very well like one of them and detest another. Initially, most of the food processing took place on farms or in households. But with the commercialization of the food sector, food processing developed into separate industries – a process that took less than a century in Western Europe and USA. Food processing plants were initially small, but mechanization, competition and improved transport drove up the sizes. At the end of the 19th century the modern mills in Berlin had fifty times the capacity of those fifty years earlier, and modern bakeries had kneading machines which replaced fifty workers. Increasingly the companies were stock corporations and even before 1900, many were multinational corporations. At this time the industry itself became a driver of change. Steam energy, electricity and improved infrastructure all paved the way towards increased market orientation and increased competition which became powerful influences over the emerging, dairy factories, creameries, slaughter houses, margarine producers or biscuit bakers.[219]

Other parts of the food industry changed as well, having an impact on both consumption pattern and the working conditions of farmers. In the Netherlands the shift from manual power to steam took place in the beginning of the 20th century and it increased the size of the creameries. Steam power didn't only increase the speed of production but also the efficiency.[220] The agrarian historian Jan Bieleman at Wageningen University concludes that factory dairying meant much more than simply producing butter on a larger scale. Factory dairying was a companion, or even the engine, of a true revolution in farming and an important factor in the emancipation of the peasantry. It allowed a small farmer to earn an income from just a few cows, to get skimmed milk in return, which they could convert into pork.[221] The work of the women in the household, earlier oriented to butter-making was released for eggs and other small business. In this particular case, the industrialization was a boon for small producers, but by and large the effect of industrialization of food processing had the opposite effect, it drove farmers into bigger production to satisfy the demand of the factories. Today, most dairies in developed countries don't even want the milk from small farms as the marginal cost for picking it up is too high, and small producers, once again, make exotic cheeses for sale in farmers' markets.

The slaughterhouse is a direct result of urbanization and the commercialization of farming. It also carries a lot of symbolism as it separates the barbarous killing from the art of secondary butchery, sausage making and *charcuterie*; it covers up the process by which living creatures are transformed into commodities. Before the advent of the slaughterhouse, the whole process was mostly done by the same people in the same place. In the early 1800s central slaughter-houses were established in major urban centers such as Berlin, Paris and New York. This was partly driven by the logistical and hygienic night-mare of having hundreds of small butchers killing animals in all parts of the cities. In Berlin, which had had 420,000 inhabitants by 1850, there were 780 private slaughter-houses. One can hardly imagine how it could look when all the animals would be driven to these and slaughtered under very primitive conditions. And the smell was nauseating, "the pestilence stench that spreads through the houses every night" according to an article in the *Tageblat*.[222] In 1810, Paris established five public slaughterhouses. The process there never went as far as in Chicago, as the Parisian butchers remained artisans, working in teams rather than destitute industrial workers in a (dis)assembly-line.[223] The pricing of meat in Paris was also based on subjective estimates – of weight and quality – by traders and butchers and very far from the commodity approach in United States and many other places.[224]

Until 1880 groceries were sold from more than 9,000 market stalls in 20 farmers' markets in Berlin. The hygiene of these left a lot to desire and waste management hardly existed. The authorities redirected this trade to specialist and grocery stores as well as to a central market supplied by the railroad. The state also invested in a road network to facilitate transport into the city and from 1838 onwards railroads were built.[225] The architecture of these central markets says something of their huge importance and symbolic meaning. The market of Paris, Les Halles, rebuilt in cast iron and glass during the Second Empire was a landmark of modernity in the city, the wholesale and retail center of a thriving food industry.

Gradually industrial food processing moved into multi-ingredient products, preserves etc. In Britain, one third of the output value of the food processing industry were convenience foods, broadly defined, already in 1935 and growth rates for breakfast cereals, confectionary and ice cream outstripped those of bread, sugar and margarine.[226] American companies played a big role in Europe, creating whole new market segments. In 1924 between 85% and 90% of all canned and bottled food in Britain was imported, most of it from the United States or from American owned companies in Canada or Argentina.[227] The Americans also brought with them a knack of advertising and promotion. "You can't just manufacture cereal. You have to get it halfway down the customer's throat through advertizing. Then they've got to swallow it", C.W. Post, founder of General Foods (now part of Kraft Foods) reportedly said.[228] Quaker hot oats were promoted in a spectacular way as early as the 1890s, where huge banners draped over the cliffs of Dover could be seen for miles out in the sea. Kellogg's launched a very aggressive campaign in Britain in the 1930s and within a few years, most families with children regularly had Kellogg's cornflakes for breakfast.

Sales and marketing became drivers of company development rather than production. Manufacturers discovered that marketing was an easier road to profit than investing in production. Competition took the form of more and more elaborate advertising and packaging.[229] Advertizing costs increased and food advertizing was directed to more processed, branded, foods while basic food stuff like potatoes and milk were rarely advertized, as there was little market differentiation.[230] One pioneer in branding was Nabisco which devised the brand name "Uneeda" for their crackers and, through heavy advertising, captured seventy percent of the American cracker market by the beginning of the 20th century. Others tried to compete with "Iwanta" and "Hava" crackers.[231]

A pioneer of branding in the broiler industry was Perdue Farms. In Perdue's marketing of its branded produce, Frank Perdue made fun of unbranded poultry parts by calling them 'unidentified frying objects'. Between 1968 and 1970 they spent 300,000 dollars in radio and TV commercials. Their strategy paid off. In 1968, Perdue had three percent of the New York chicken market, four years later one out of six chickens eaten in New York was a Perdue chicken. Today, Perdue spends approximately five cents per pound in advertising – increasing the sales price of their branded products by an estimated eight cents. Of course 300,000 dollars is next to nothing for food advertising today[232]; in 2011 food, beverage and candy companies spent US$8.4 billion on advertising and the four largest retailers spent another US$4.4 billion.[233] Add to this advertizing for cafés, restaurants and others selling food and the amounts are mind-boggling.

At the time of writing this book (2013/14) there is a retail war going on in India, where the retail industry is estimated to be worth around US$500 billion, corresponding to 14-15% of Indian gross domestic product. Almost 90% of the Indian retail business is made in tiny, family owned shops. But the 'organized retail segment' is expanding at 20% a year, driven by the emergence of shopping centers and malls and a growing middle class. Foreign companies had largely been locked out from the Indian market but in 2012, India opened up for foreign direct investments in the retail sector. As the governmental *India Brand Equity Foundation* told foreign investors "India offers immense scope of growth and opportunities in this arena. Thus, organized retailers have a lot of room for further penetration in this flourishing economy."[234] But allowing foreign retailers like Carrefour, Tesco and IKEA into India has been hugely controversial, with opponents saying it could ruin the livelihoods of the millions of small traders and family-run shops. To soften the blow, a new law requires foreign retailers to source 30% of the products they sell from small and medium-sized Indian businesses. This is not to the liking of the transnational companies. Scott Price, Walmart Asia CEO, said in October 2013 that the rule of sourcing from local small and medium businesses is the 'critical stumbling block' to its plans to open retail stores in India.[235] This is a clear sign of how the control of the supply chain or, as it is often called today, the 'value chain' is a key strategy in supermarket chain expansion.

The Great American Tea Company was founded 1859 and opened the first chain grocery stores.[236] In a similar development on the other side of the Atlantic, Thomas Lipton established a chain of stores in Great Britain in the 1870s and 1880s.[237] As the United States entered the great depression in the 1930s, collapsing demand led to changes in food retailing. Michael Cullen opened the first 'supermarket' in 1936 under the King Kullen label. To lower costs customers had to do more of the work themselves with self-service and cash-and-carry. After the depression, food processing developments, the mass use of automobiles, the rapid expansion of suburbs and newfound household affluence together contributed to the continued expansion of the supermarket. The sale of refrigerators in the United States grew dramatically, increasing the ability of households to store perishable food, and thereby lowering the number and frequency of shopping trips households had to make. In four years after the World War II Americans bought 21 million automobiles and 20 million 'ice-boxes'.[238]

The capacity for shopping is determined by the size of your wallet and of the space required to store it. But it is also limited by the physical ability to carry the stuff from shop to home. Sylvan Goldman, owner of a food store in Oklahoma City, noticed that customers usually quit shopping when the baskets became too heavy, an early and direct example of 'shopping fatigue'. In 1937, he invented the shopping cart which greatly increased customers' ability to hold and purchase more goods at the same time.[239] With automobiles, iceboxes and shopping carts all was set for the next steps in retailing. In Minnesota, the Southdale Shopping Centre, established in 1956, was the first enclosed shopping mall signaling the start of the 'mallification' of America, emptying city centers and further cementing the dominance of the automobile as the preferred mode of transport.

Supermarkets and the food industry became good bedfellows. Before supermarkets, many products were handled loose, which didn't allow for much branding. The food industry had packaged food with attractive branding and backed it up with commercials, increasingly on a national and later an international level. This put pressure on small shops to stock all these items. But bigger shops could store more items and a shop designed for self service by the consumer fitted much better in this world of pre-packaged food. Later on, as supermarket chains became bigger and more powerful, they also started to dictate conditions for the food industry, and their demands drove small food processors out of business in a similar way that the big food processors helped to drive small shops out of business.

All of these factors helped drive small farmers out of business. The strict quality requirements and strict business conditions for supply security, penalties for failure and slow payment instead of the earlier cash-on-delivery affect farmers and small food producers a lot. Those conditions favor those with more resources who can climb the ladder and invest in their production, in cooling facilities, in trucks, in toilets, bore holes for cleaner water and what not. Farmers who don't want to, or cannot (more often the case), follow this trajectory are marginalized. Small scale food processors are also harmed by the concentration in food retail as they are unable to meet the new buyers' quantity and pricing requirements. Governments have also assisted in the concentration of agri-food businesses by imposing regulations, which mostly favor the bigger actors, at the very least because it is they who have the capacity to keep up with the ever-increasing demands. Public outrage over food scandals is often directed against the big actors, but when regulations are put in place to placate the public they often hurt the small ones disproportionally.

Carrefour opened the first hypermarket, predecessor of the supercenter, in 1963, in Sainte-Geneviève-des-bois, France. With a floor area of 2,500 square meters, 12 checkouts and 400 parking spaces, the venture joined a nonfood retailer and a food wholesaler, completely encompassing the concept of total one-stop shopping. Today, such a shop is rather small. The average size of a hypermarket had increased to 16,000 square meters by 1989. But those are dwarfed by some recent shopping malls.[240] The Golden Resources Mall in Beijing, nicknamed the Great Mall of China measures 557,419 square meters, spread over six floors and is 1.5 times the size of the Mall of America. Golden Resources Mall was the world's largest shopping mall from 2004 to 2005, when it was overtaken by South China Mall in Dongguan (which never took off and has very limited occupancy).[241] Not only have shop areas become bigger, there has also been consolidation in the business so that fewer companies control all parts of the chain.

Multiple retailers have taken over the food market, not only in high-income countries but also in developing countries. This has direct and indirect effects on everybody, from farmers to food shoppers, and places small independent food shops under immense pressure. In Argentina, the number of food shops dropped from 209,000 to 145,000 in the 10 years between 1984 and 1993. In Latin America supermarkets now dominate retail sales and they grew in one decade (from the mid 1990s to mid 2000s) as much as they grew in five decades in the United States. Multiple retailers are also rapidly expanding in China, India and Africa.[242] [243]

It is not only in India where there has been resistance to these developments in retailing. Several European countries have tried to regulate size, location and shopping hours to limit the commercial pressures on small shops and to safeguard the interest of workers. In 1996 the French government introduced the Raffarin Law, stating that any store larger than 300 square meters had to gain full regional planning consent in order to be built and this process requires the agreement of representatives of local businesses. In Britain laws were considerably more relaxed. The French law seems to have had some effect; in 2011 there were more than 80,000 independent retailers in France, double the number of Britain, which has a similar size of population.[244]

Even if many might believe that supermarkets want to sell cheap foods, the reality is that they earn a lot more money from selling processed foods than from unprocessed foods. People who buy processed foods have a far larger food bill than those who buy unprocessed foods. In addition, there are few losses with processed foods as they are treated to have long shelf life. As for the food industry, it is in its own interest to change our consumption patterns towards eating its industrially processed food rather than unprocessed products.

Industrialization and commercialization have transformed the entire food chain. Firstly, the chain has become much longer. There are many actors and intermediaries between the primary producer and the consumer. Secondly, the chain has also become a lot more complex and differentiated. Each operation is specialized in only one stage of the chain, often something that we don't even see as a separate stage. This starts already at the farm, where farmers increasing buy in services, and continues all through the chain. The ancillary services needed for the actors in the chain have also greatly increased, as complexity requires a great deal of expertise. It is often too costly to develop this expertise in-house. As a consultant, I have myself spent considerable time, and other peoples' money, troubleshooting in the value chain. Third, there is also a narrowing of the chain in the sense that the links between the actors are stronger, there is close interaction between suppliers and producers to meet the specifications. This last point also implies a transfer of power, further and further away from farmers towards the end users or rather the last link before the end user, retailers or caterers.[245]

Farms mostly produce unprocessed foods which are not branded at the points of sale as branding is difficult. Few farmers can invest in the machinery needed for food processing, and even if they did, economies of scale and the supermarkets' requirements will keep them out of the larger sales channels. Branding requires more resources than farmers normally can muster so the few unprocessed products which often are branded, such as fruit (think bananas), are in the hands of agribusiness. As a result, farm produce only constitute a small and diminishing fraction of food prices. In the United Kingdom agriculture and fishing capture only seven percent of the total food chain revenue of £412 billion.[246] In Sweden, the price of raw materials for the food industry dropped by twelve percent between 1995 and 2005, but the price of processed products from the food industry increased by almost ten percent over the same period.[247] For products such as breakfast cereals, the farmers' share is just a few percent of the retail price. No wonder the food and retail industry want you to eat highly processed breakfast cereals instead of (a low processed) porridge.

The easiest way to understand this shift is to look at the distribution of the food dollar, food pound or food euro. In the United States in 2011, out of each dollar spent on food, the farm sector got 10.8¢, food processing 22¢, packaging 4¢, transport 3.5¢, retail 12.2¢, food services 31.2¢, energy 5.5¢, finance and insurance 6.1¢, advertising 2.4¢ and legal and accounting 2.1¢. The farmers share has gone down by more than thirty percent in just twenty years, and the share for the farmers and their employees work is now less than 2.7¢, more or less the same as the advertising costs of the food industry.[248] As much money is spent on convincing us to eat branded products as to remunerate the people who actually produce the food in the field.

- 8 -
The Emperor's new dish

If you have eaten in a Japanese restaurant, the chances are high that you devoured Yakuniku, grilled meat. You probably believe it was developed from a long tradition of street vendors selling barbecue. Nothing could be further from reality. At the age of twenty, Emperor Meiji staged a remarkable new year's party in Tokyo in January 1873. As part of his efforts to modernize Japan in the direction of the model of an enlightened nation state – Meiji means enlightened rule – guests were dressed in western clothes and French-style food was served. Most remarkably, there was beef and the Emperor himself ate beef in public. With this he broke a more than thousand year old taboo. The first decree against eating meat in Japan was issued 675 and was repeated several times before that extraordinary party.[249]

'Food is a weapon' proclaimed posters from the United States government during World War II. They could have said 'Food is power'. We cannot understand food and agriculture if we look away from those with power, and we cannot understand power if we look away from food and agriculture. I have already discussed the influences of ecology, commercialization, energy and technology on the food we eat. Other shifts in diet are the consequences of power politics. For example, by introducing coffee and sugar-cane to the Americas, Europeans not only altered local foodways, but also made the economies of America part of global markets.[250] The colonial powers guarded their plant materials in the same way as the multinationals guard their genetically modified seeds today. The first coffee plantation in Brazil was established in 1727 when Lt. Col. Francisco de Melo Palheta smuggled seeds from French Guyana. For most of the 19th and early 20th centuries, Brazil was the biggest producer of coffee and had a virtual monopoly in the trade.[251] Rubber went the opposite way. The rubber tree is indigenous to Brazil and South America remained the main source of the limited amounts of latex rubber used during much of the 19th century. In 1876, Henry Wickham gathered thousands of Para rubber tree seeds and these were sown in Kew Gardens, England. The seedlings were then sent to India, Ceylon, Indonesia, Singapore, and British Malaya (now Malaysia). Malaysia was later to become the world's biggest producer of rubber.[252]

   The Soviet Union went so far as to even change cooking and eating habits in its efforts to create the new human, the *homo sovieticus*. A domestic kitchen was branded reactionary and an obstacle to the new scientific approach to nutrition. The *stolyvya* (public canteen) was to be the forge by which Soviet society would be created. 'Down with kitchen slavery' was the war cry. Alexandra Kollontai, an anarchist-leaning Bolshevik, who later was safely stationed (exiled some would say) at the Soviet Embassies in Stockholm and Oslo, said that it was essential to separate marriage from the kitchen.[253] This was not such an outrageous idea at the time, it was shared by feminists and social reformers of the West as well (you will read about some of these in the next chapter). The Soviet Union also introduced something that could be described as democratic luxury, represented by champagne, cognac, chocolates and caviar sandwiches. These state-sanctioned mass-produced clones were sold across the Soviet Union for the same, very affordable price, allowing a Soviet worker stopping at a kiosk to enjoy a glass of champagne and a caviar sandwich. Considering the general low availability of consumer goods in the Soviet Union the availability of these luxuries must be seen as an effort to make people feel that life was quite good after all – one can almost hear the question, 'tell us how many workers in America can have champagne for breakfast?'[254] The meddling with food went so far that during Stalin's reign the official canon of Soviet cooking, the *Book of Tasty and Healthy Food*, 1952 edition, was purged of dishes that originated from ethnic groups which the great ruler disapproved of, including the Jews and the Kalmyks. Ironically, in the August 1953 edition, the quotes from the master chef himself all disappeared.[255]

When I grew up in Sweden all our bread was sweetened, and I thought that was normal. But recently I came to realize that this was a result of public policy forty years before I was born. During World War I, there was a shortage of grain in Sweden, but a surplus of sugar. Therefore, the authorities commanded bakeries to mix sugar with the flour to keep people sated and happy. Once eating the sweet bread we got used to it – it became something we chose. Under conditions of war or other hardship, old habits may be surrendered more easily and new ones established with less resistance than would be the case in peaceful circumstances.

   World War II reshaped the food preferences of American citizens, both those who were drafted into the armed forces and civilians at home. This transformation of diet was influenced by the food industry and government alike. The President of Coca Cola, Robert Woodruff, ordered that every man in uniform should be able to get a bottle of Coca-Cola for 5 cents, wherever he was, and whatever it cost the company. In 1943, General Dwight D. Eisenhower sent an urgent cablegram to Coca-Cola, requesting shipment of materials for 10 bottling plants. "During the war, many people enjoyed their first taste of the beverage, and when peace finally came, the foundations were laid for Coca-Cola to do business overseas." is how the Coca Cola Company describes the effect on its web site.[256]

In a similar way, the Camembert makers of Normandy were very successful in selling their cheese to the French military in World War I even though they faced fierce competition with Gruyere. Camembert won the battle, and became itself part of the stories of the Great War, it was later demanded by the million surviving conscripts,[257] and later still became a major French export product, its break-through as fare for soldiers in the trenches of Ypres now forgotten.

The needs of the military have long been a major driver of technology change in food. It is not only penicillin, aircrafts and the internet that are results of military demand but also canning. Napoleon, who is widely quoted, accurately or not, as saying, "An army marches on its stomach," offered an award of 12,000 francs to anyone who could devise a practical method for food preservation for armies on the march. The award went to Nicolas Appert who developed a method of sealing food in glass jars. For obvious reasons it was impractical for an army to transport food in glass jars, so the army went with canning in tins.[258] One major obstacle was that can openers were not invented for another thirty years – at first, soldiers had to cut the cans open with bayonets or smash them open with rocks.

Huge armies on the march or in trenches provided a development field for logistics, food processing and not the least mass catering, which also served the masses in the rapidly growing cities. Anthropologist Katarzyna J. Cwiertka studied the food in Japanese canteens and observed that the menus in modern day Tokyo are made up of dishes that are luxury versions of those served in the Imperial Japanese Army and Navy half a century earlier. She concludes that: "it was the process of nation building, largely sustained by imperialism, expansionism, and post-war economic affluence that shaped the outcomes that we know today as Japanese cuisine[259]". This observation provides a new perspective on the famous dinner of Emperor Meiji.

Rulers have always been preoccupied with food supply and prices. Even the worst dictators can hardly ignore a starving population. If a government cannot safeguard a food supply for its people (or at least its urban populations) it rapidly loses its credibility and license to rule.

As such, government policy has played a big role in shaping agriculture and what we eat. Some describe the efforts of feeding an imperial army in the same terms as the efforts to control oil supplies. The Roman expansion was to a large extent based on the control of grain, which was shipped from Sicily, North Africa and Egypt to Rome and further to the armies. The state prohibited the production of wine in these provinces to ensure they produced food, while on the Italian peninsula production was oriented to olives, wines and luxuries for Rome.[260] Such edicts have been repeated throughout history. Once the settlers in Maryland and Virginia learned how to produce tobacco, and the market in Europe grew they were so eager to earn money that they even neglected to grow food for themselves. This was so serious that the governor had to issue regulations directing the colonists to plant a minimum part of their land with food crops.[261]

Historically, most countries maintained strategic food reserves to cushion against possible bad harvests and be prepared for war. Earlier, I discussed the granaries of Egypt, Mesopotamia and Rome and how the Roman Empire worked to safeguard its food supply. China established a national grain reserve in 54 BC and all the provinces created stores of rice for an inevitable catastrophe.[262] After a terrible flood of the Yellow River in 119 BC the government supplied 725,000 people with food for several years.[263] Today, aware of the Chinese love of pork the government maintains a strategic pork reserve.[264] In the United States strategic food reserves were established in the 1930s. The stores were gradually depleted until 2008, when the USDA decided to convert all that was left into its dollar equivalent. "And so the grain that once stabilized prices for farmers, bakers and American consumers ended up as a number on a spreadsheet in the Department of Agriculture" writes food journalist Frederick Kaufman.[265]

Now the food system operates on a just-in-time rather than a just-in-case basis, meaning that every part of the system needs to run smoothly if the whole thing is not to break down and leave us hungry. In 2012, the global food reserve was estimated by the United Nations Food and Agriculture Organization (FAO) to be only seventy-four days.[266] This is made possible by the super-efficient transport machinery, by food being produced in different seasons in different parts of the world and a freely flowing trade system and global comptetition. But such a system is very sensitive to disturbances. In just five days in 2000, the truckers' fuel price protests in United Kingdom led to hoarding and panic buying and supermarkets warned that they were running out of food. There is currently enough food in the system to feed the United Kingdom for about ten days.[267]

Many people don't trust this system. And if people don't trust the government they will take things in their own hands. Web sites in the United States and United Kingdom offer food reserve solutions. For £12,000 one can buy the *Bespoke 12 months Deluxe Family Pack*, a food pack for four people a whole year from Emergency Food Storage UK. It is not just individuals who distrust the system. At the time of the food price hike in 2008, many governments imposed export bans to safeguard the needs of their own population and those with insufficient domestic production made bilateral food deals with food producing countries.

Food and agriculture often constitute the main obstacle to free trade deals, because they are very sensitive issues that are deeply embedded in society. But it is also because food is such a basic need, a need which states, in one way or the other, have to guarantee their citizens. And, as I discussed earlier in most periods of human society the food supply has not been mainly maintained through a free and open market.

The British Corn Laws imposed a duty on imports, inversely proportional to the domestic price. This protected British farmers and landowners. But it was not in the interest of the industrial capitalists who wanted cheap food for their workers and cheap raw materials for their industries and who lobbied heavily against those laws. When the laws were abolished 1846, state intervention in food trade in Europe was minimal. When the effects of the commercialization of food and farming and fierce competition from overseas became apparent, government intervention in markets increased again and import duties re-emerged in most developed economies. Britain continued to hold a free trade stance though, with devastating effects on British food production, but arguably very beneficial effects for the economy at large and the capitalists.

At the onset of World War I, Britain imported 60% of its food and roughly 80% of its grain for bread (basically wheat), as a result of its laissez-faire trade policies and the enclosures. Initially, the government thought the market could ensure food supplies, but quite soon it had to step in, even more so when Germany's submarine fleet started taking a toll on merchant shipping from January 1917 onwards. The British government increasingly regulated both the price and the supply of bread, "whatever else was in short supply, the supply of breadstuffs had to be maintained".[268] It took control over imports and shortly thereafter, in April 1917, took control over the mills from the private sector. In 1918 all staple foods were regulated in price and many were rationed. People were encouraged to produce their own food and herds of cattle and sheep were reduced. The policies worked so well that it is estimated that during the war the average provision of food was 3,500 calories, compared to 3,400 calories in the years preceding the war (although the quality of food didn't necessarily improve, for instance fruit and vegetable consumption plummeted). Even more interesting is that the difference between the diets of the rich and the poor decreased in war time.[269] This was a result of the government intervening in food distribution and access, since the market simply cannot achieve equitable distribution. It is inherent, almost a definition, that distribution in an unregulated market is inequitable, as it is based on economic purchasing power, not on needs. To say this is not to say that the market 'doesn't work'. It works as a market should, but that doesn't necessarily give the results that society wants. The invisible hand doesn't always do the right thing.

Public support to the farm sector reached new highs in the postwar period. Despite the free trade rhetoric of the United States it has intervened heavily in its agriculture sector using price supports, production controls, import and export quotas and export subsidies in order to support farm incomes and control overproduction. The first comprehensive policy was put in place in 1933 with the Agriculture Adjustment Act.[270] New regulations have been introduced and others taken away, and as global markets have shifted so have policies, for instance price support has been taken away. In 1985, the first environmental program, the Conservation Reserve Program, was created[271] with the objective of removing 45 million acres of erosion-prone, and relatively unproductive lands from farming.[272] Lately policies have subsidized the production of maize for bio-fuels.

The United States also covers its food stamps program (now called the *Supplemental Nutrition Assistance Program*) from its agriculture budget. This is because the program's origins were more about offsetting agriculture surpluses than helping the poor. In most other countries, such a program would fall under social or health departments. The European Union did the same but on a smaller scale when it introduced a school milk program from the agriculture budget. In the 2010/2011 school year, around 300,000 tons of milk and milk products were distributed to more than 17 million pupils in schools in 26 Member States.[273]

In the European Union, agriculture policy interventions have been even bigger, and slower to change than in the United States, largely an effect of the decision making procedures of the Union. In 1973 the Common Agriculture Policy was well-established based on price support, intervention buying, public stocks (the infamous butter mountains and wine lakes), and export subsidies. Subsidies to farmers have since been decoupled from production and are now largely based on acreage while export subsidies have been removed. The policy has since been complemented by a rural development component and various kinds of environmental support measures, e.g. support for organic farming. Nonetheless, support of farm income remains the key goal[274] and with twenty-seven member states, all with very different farming sectors and economic conditions, it is difficult to reformulate European agricultural policy, which continues to be the Union's largest single area of expenditure

For the past twenty years public support to the farm sector has oscillated between 30% and 40% of total farm income in OECD countries.[a] The value of public support to the agriculture and food sector was US$407 billion in 2010, roughly one percent of GDP. The trend is a (slow) reduction in support and a shift from production-driveing support mechanisms (e.g. price support) to support for ecosystem services, rural development and farmers' incomes. Agriculture policies in high-income countries have not been very efficient in delivering their objectives and have been directly harmful to farmers in other countries, as surplus production has been dumped in global markets, thus pressing down already low global prices. This in turn induces more subsidies from these governments.

In the past, most high-income countries stimulated higher production and 'structural rationalization' (making farms bigger). Today, in most high-income countries farm policies are made up of a jumble of measures and programs, often with contradictory objectives. The same country might simultaneously support the promotion of genetically modified organisms and organic farming; or might pay farmers to leave farms to allow for structural rationalization while also promoting farmers' markets to give small farmers a market outlet, or have start-up grants for young new farmers. Both the United States and the European Union have subsidized tobacco production, despite other public policies aimed at curbing smoking. In the Unites States total tobacco subsidies 1995-2012 amounted to US$1.5 billion.[275] The European Union phased out tobacco subsidies in 2010, but at the time of writing (early 2014) there is a massive lobby to re-introduce them.

---

[a] The Organization of Economic Cooperation and Development (OECD) is an intergovernmental think-tank whose members include most of the world's rich countries.

Very few countries have a truly 'liberalized' (which in international policy speak means de-regulated with little support or other government regulation) farm sector. Of the OECD countries, New Zealand is the most liberalized. By and large those where there is little support are major exporters with competitive agriculture sectors and those with higher levels of support at net food importers, such as Japan, Korea, Switzerland and Norway.

In 1996 the Swiss constitution was amended by a referendum (with a firm majority) to explicitly include reference to the multifunctional nature of agriculture – agriculture's role in contributing to food security, resource conservation, landscape and rural settlements.[276] Today various support and remuneration from the government provide more than half of Swiss farmers' incomes. This level of support comes at a price. It involves spending much tax payers' money and setting high tariffs to protect Swiss farm produce. Meat imports faced an average tariff of 126% and milk of 102% in 2012, and this is reflected in very high consumer prices – and Switzerland being almost self-sufficient in these produce. The self-sufficiency rate for animal products was 95% in 2009 while it was just 48% for the plant products which are less protected. Almost one third of Switzerland's substantial agriculture budget is spent on ensuring domestic food supplies. Switzerland, in contrast to most other countries, still maintains emergency food reserves for a variety of food stuffs that can last for several months. One possible negative effect of Switzerland's high support levels is that it can trigger surplus production which has to be dumped in global markets, thereby suppressing the world market prices. While Swiss agriculture support does have such effects these are small and shrinking. Despite the high level of protection, there are also forces of competition at work within the country and these still exert pressure for farms to get larger. Almost forty percent of Swiss farmers in 1990 have since quit farming. Yet, many small farms persist. Many see this as a positive thing, others share the view, expressed in a 2013 report from the OECD, that "Switzerland's heavy support sustains inefficient farming structures".[277]

Governments in many developing countries invest few resources in the farm sector, certainly in comparison to the sector's importance within their economies. What money is spent often goes into inefficient and harmful subsidies, especially subsidies for chemical fertilizers. In India, subsidies reached new record heights in 2009. The Food Corporation of India spent US$10 billion for food subsidies and the Ministry of Fertilizers spent US$20 billion dollars for subsidies of chemical fertilizers. To this one can add federal support for food security and crop insurance as well as state programs for energy, seeds, seedlings, livestock, tractors, pumps, irrigation, etc. Despite all these support measures, Indian farmers are under huge financial stress and debts are incurred by buying inputs such as seeds, fertilizers and pesticides. Just in 2007, 16,600 suicides were reported among Indian farmers.[278] Ironically, they often use pesticides, bought with credit, to finish their lives.[279] In the 1980s, the World Bank investigated agriculture policies in eighteen developing countries and found that in most of them, Brazil being a notable exception, governments extracted more resources from their agricultural sector than they invested, a striking difference to OECD countries.[280] Of course, one could argue that it is not possible for poor countries with a large agricultural sector to support their farmers, as the burden on nascent industries and services would be too heavy.

The key objective of most farming policies has been to transform farmers into market actors who buy and sell produce, need financial capital or credits, services, etc. Governments intervene by subsidizing credits, tax exempting or even subsidizing inputs such as fertilizers, investment supports and limits on the level of farm rents.[281] Ironically, once farmers go here, encouraged or compelled by the state, social interventions are geared to mitigating the negative effects of a commercial farm sector. One reason for this is that farming doesn't easily lend itself to the same logic as industrial production.

There is a long history of regulations to prevent the adulteration of food. Already in ancient Egypt and Rome priests or officials inspected meat.[282] The German *Reinheitsgebot*, dating back to 1487, stipulated that the only ingredients that could be used to produce beer were water, barley and hops. In 1912, almost ten percent of the 24,964 examinations of food samples in London were found to be adulterated. In November 1905, the Civil Service Cooperative Society was prosecuted for selling tins of spinach containing copper sulphate, used to retain the green color of the spinach. Milk and dairy products were often subject to adulteration; samples of 'Irish butter' taken from 14 shops in 1911 turned out to be largely margarine.[283]

National governments, municipalities and city councils were those normally entrusted with food quality and safety inspections. But when citizens don't trust the government, or the government doesn't live up to the expectations, people will find other ways to ensure that the food they eat is safe. In Germany in the 1870s citizens developed local 'associations against the adulteration of food'. Initiated by the writer Ernst Leistner in Leipzig in 1877, they informed the public about possible food adulterations, through lectures, newsletters, meetings and guidelines for shopping. Chemical tools and devices along with domestic user manuals were distributed and exhibitions organized where adulterated and pure food were shown in order to train people to see the difference. Their newsletters featured larger studies and tests in specific fields and advice for readers and discussed important new regulations. Members could bring in food for examination and the associations initiated controls of companies and markets. As a precursor to modern certification schemes individual companies voluntarily placed themselves under the scrutiny of the associations as a means of building trust with consumers. Germany passed a comprehensive food law in 1879, and interest in the associations subsequently dwindled.[284]

New food safety standards and procedures have mostly been introduced in response to public outrage or scandals. In the nineteenth century, despite many warnings, the British authorities had no inspection mechanism for live animals brought into the country or transported on the extensive railway network. When three million animals died of cattle plague in 1865 they were forced to introduce stringent controls.[285] The pattern was repeated more than hundred years later with the BSE-crisis, better known as the Mad Cow Disease which killed 144 people in the United Kingdom and led to the culling of 4.4 million cattle.[286] This was repeated again in 2001 when a major outbreak of Foot and Mouth Disease caused a crisis in British agriculture and tourism. Over 10 million sheep and cattle were killed in an eventually successful attempt to halt the disease.

With the emergence of food industries and longer supply chains the need for regulations increased and the safety risks became of national importance, today even of global importance – and the subject of trade disputes. It is not necessarily the case that large companies are more likely to cheat or have a lower hygiene standards than smaller ones, probably the opposite. However, the bigger the company and the longer the supply lines, the more people are affected by fraud or unsafe food. The more forward-looking representatives of the food industry understood the benefit of certain minimum standards that guaranteed that competition didn't undermine product safety. After all, a food scare for one product often damages consumption of the whole product segment, regardless of supplier.

The food industry has been quite successful in implanting the idea that human hands equal filth and stainless steel and plastic equate to hygiene. This is now spreading to developing countries. A supermarket manager in Madras, India proudly states that "everything in the store is prepackaged – nothing should appear to be touched by the fingers".[287] And to a large extent the food industry has had support from the government in this image building.

Both society and supermarkets have increased the demands and the number of standards a food producer has to fulfill. Apart from, hopefully but doubtfully, providing consumers with safer food, this has also led to many small-scale producers quitting as they cannot invest in upgrading their technology to meet the ever-increasing demands. In the same vein, traditional food processing methods are indirectly becoming illegal or in other ways impossible in the market-place. For example, in response to an oil contamination scandal in 1998, the Indian government imposed rules that every oil mill must have its own laboratory and chemist, which led to a million small mills closing down.[288] At this moment a battle over raw, unpasteurized, milk is raging in many countries, with governments trying to ban it. While some of these regulations may be well founded, they follow an industrial logic with the idea that less natural and more processed produce is better. When this is combined with a global food business and trade, there is an increased risk of large scale food poisoning of consumers with pathogens they have never acquired any resistance to.

Because of the many scandals in agriculture and food, there are frequent calls for more rules for food safety, new certification or quality assurance schemes. Mostly, those rules favor the big over the small, the modern over the traditional, and the formal over the informal. As such they tend to favor a further corporate take over of the food sector. Lately, many countries have also adopted food policies where they advise their citizens what to eat. The driving force behind this is often a mix between concern about health of the citizens and a wish to promote certain types of products, mostly as a result of pressure from important lobby groups. This is the topic of the next chapter.

9

What is good for you!

Mexicans are becoming increasingly fat; seventy percent of Mexicans above fifteen years are now overweight, giving them the dubious distinction of having the highest proportion of fat people in the world (just ahead of the Americans). Mexicans consume more soda per capita than any other people in the world, and diabetes is the leading cause of death.[289] The National Congress recently struck a blow for public health in November 2013 when it passed a one-peso-per-liter tax on soda and an eight percent tax on 'junk food'. The question 'What should we eat for dinner today', seems to be more pressing than ever before in human history. Governments, the medical profession, dietary gurus and the food industry give different response to that question and each has their own agenda.

Apart from energy, a proper diet needs to supply us with proteins, vitamins, minerals and fats. Throughout history people have always eaten things that were not strictly necessary, because they liked them or they were seen to have other special values. Even the hungriest person may refuse a certain food because of a taboo or just fear of the unknown. There are many ideas, ideologies and fads regarding what is best to eat. But it seems incredibly difficult to ascertain this; we appear to be able to live a rather healthy life utilizing a wide range of foods, and we seem to be able to develop a liking for a very wide range of foods. Quite clearly most of the likes and dislikes are not there by nature, but acquired, although our preferences for sweetness and fat seem to be hard-wired in us.

The kind of food we prefer is to a large extent determined by our culture – but our food culture has to a large extent been determined by our farming systems or, if we were fisherfolk or hunters, by those systems. And whatever system(s) people depended upon, most of their foods were simply foods that were available in sufficient quantity and could be acquired with reasonable efforts. The Mediterranean diet, often lauded for its alleged health benefits, was not developed by people seeking a healthy diet; rather it was a direct result of the ecological conditions in the area, where olive oil, a range of nuts and wine grew well and could be complemented by fish, and cheese from goats and sheep. In the more temperate north and north-west of Europe, a dairy based farming system led to high consumption of milk, cheese and butter. Towards the east, where it was drier, grains and grazed cattle were the basis.

Did the dawn of farming and our modern food supply systems improve our diets? This is a thorny question. There are some objective things that can be measured to infer the effects of a given diet, these include; stature, weight, life expectancy, dental status and susceptibility to a number of diseases. However, none of these alone is an indicator of superior nutrition. Stature comes out as one of the most useful measures as it can be studied in skeletons. While people today are generally taller than before, historical data shows, not a linear process of improvement, but rather movements back and forth.[290]

In ancient Egypt, five thousand years ago, men reached 170 cm and women 160 cm. In following periods body height shrank and there was also a more marked difference between people of different classes with poor women being shortest, an indication of a more hierarchical system. During the Roman Empire average height diminished at the same pace as the empire declined and the downward trend continued throughout the Middle Ages. In the Americas, stature increased among hunters and gatherers until five thousand years ago. In general when people picked up farming their height decreased.[291] Lately however, stature, life expectancy and weight have all increased.[292] The main reason is probably increased supply of food.

With the second agricultural revolution the food supply increased considerably, which is visible in statistics for body height and life expectancy; in 1750, life expectancy was 37 years in England, only 26 years in France and 51 years in the United States. One hundred years later it had reached 69, 67 and 68 years respectively.[293] One reason[a] for the very short life spans before was an undersupply of food and diets with very little variety, rather than dramatic famine. This in turn led to weakness and illness. This was a vicious cycle, as those who are sickly and weak simply cannot work as hard as those who are well fed. This is clearly seen in modern day India and Africa. The body first needs energy for maintenance and after its basic functions are satisfied the rest supplies the energy for the actual work that needs doing. A person

---

[a] Clearly improvements in hygiene and better medical services also played a role here.

with an intake of 3200 kcal per day is able to do far more than twice the work than someone on 1600 kcal per day. The first 1,600 kcal is used just to stay alive and dream about the food one would like to eat and the things one wants to do. In recent times it is not only the quantity of food available to most people that has increased a lot but also its quality and nutritional composition. The share of cereals in the food ration has decreased and the consumption of meat, dairy products fruits, vegetables and oils has increased.[a] Sometimes a change in diet led to very rapid changes. In Japan the height of 12 year olds increased by 5 cm per decade between 1950 and 1970.[294]

Improved access to food played no little role in the industrialization of Britain. In 1800, Britain imported about 13% of its dietary needs while those in farming produced more than twice the quantity of food they needed for themselves, with the surplus available to feed the growing numbers of industrial and service workers. This increased access to food improved the efficiency of people's bodies and they could use a much higher proportion of food energy for work output as opposed to simple body maintenance. The Nobel Laureate economist Robert William Fogel calculated that the efficiency of the 'human engine' in Britain increased by 53% between 1790 and 1980. This increased efficiency would account for half of the economic growth in Britain since 1790.[295] Even if this calculation has been contested, it is an interesting perspective. From my observations of the energy levels and health of the very poor farmers I have met, I think it is significant. The increased consumption of food was certainly a result of the improvements in farming and the increased incomes of many people. This also had profound effects on health and contributed to the "transition from infectious disease and premature death to chronic disease and long lives" as expressed by food scientist Fabrice Etilé from the French National Agronomic Research Institute.

In the 1950s and 1960s there was a rapid transition to much more processed food, a transition that is still in full swing, moving from its origin in the United States across the world. After the Second World War, Finland underwent a transformation from a largely peasant society into an urban industrial society, and the change in diet followed suit. Most people had lived in rural areas and the main foods

---

[a] Obviously there are limits to the benefits of increased consumption of some of these products, and one can also see a decline in meat consumption in some countries today, for a multitude of reasons.

were regional products; dairy products, rye, oats, barley and potatoes supplemented by meat and fish. Fruit and vegetables were hardly ever eaten except for wild harvested mushrooms and berries. During the 1960s, the commercial food system took a firm grip of Finland as the population moved to the cities (or migrated to Sweden for jobs). The proportion of local foods diminished, traditional staple foods lost importance and the consumption of fresh and frozen fruits and vegetables increased. In the period from 1950 to 1973 the annual consumption of rye decreased from 48 kg per capita to 24 kg, while sugar went the other way from 28 kg to 45 kg. Even more spectacularly the consumption of fruit and vegetables grew from 33 kg per year to 81 kg. Farm households ceased growing most of their own food, even products they had, such as milk and meat, were increasingly bought as processed and packaged industrial products. Not only was there a big change in diet, even more astonishing was the 'delocalization' of the Finnish food system on several levels, national, regional level and even the household level.[296] Finland is but one example of a development that has been, or is, repeated in country after country and shows how closely the economy and people's diets are linked.

At the same time as diets have become more varied and individualized they have also become less localized; there is a convergence in global diets. One of the more striking examples of this is that, for some time, Indonesia hosted the biggest wheat mill in the world, despite the fact that they don't produce any wheat at all. The wheat was imported for the production of instant noodles, a very popular fast food in Indonesia,[297] the fourth most populous country in the world. The country consumed a staggering 14 billion packages of instant noodles in 2012.[298] The history of wheat in Indonesia began in 1969 when the United States extended food aid in the form of wheat flour and wheat to Indonesia. Indonesia now imports some 7 million tons of wheat and wheat flour, almost 30 kg per person, the cost of which far outweighs the total agriculture development budget in this 250 million people nation.[299]

With the westernization of diets, various degenerative diseases have followed, putting totally new demands on the health sectors. The average diet has become lower in fiber and higher in saturated fats, sugar and salt and, in general, people continue to increase their intake while working less hard physically.[300] While there seems to be no great medical disadvantage to being tall, possibly with the exception of an increase in head injuries, increased waistlines are more problematic. For a long while obesity was a sign of wealth and well-being and fat women were seen as beautiful. Today there are still a few cultures that maintain this ideal, but by and large obesity is today seen as a major problem. Overweight and obesity are major risk factors for a number of diseases, including diabetes, cardiovascular diseases and cancer.

Globally, obesity has nearly doubled since 1980. According to the World Health Organization, in 2008, more than 1.4 billion adults were overweight. [a] Of these over 200 million men and nearly 300 million women were obese.[301] Once only considered a problem in high income countries, overweight and obesity are now dramatically on the rise in low- and middle-income countries, particularly in urban settings. The spread of obesity comes in the footsteps of modern processed food made from refined (white) wheat flour, maize, sugar, sweeteners, fats, including sodas and beer. Those products are cheap, easy to eat, and appeal to universal triggers of satisfaction.

More than one third of Americans are obese and US$147 billion is spent every year on health problems related to obesity in United States.[302] The overall food consumption, in calories, of the average American has actually changed less than we might think. The average consumer put away 3,550 calories per day 1910, which decreased to 3,160 calories in 1951 and then increased to 3,600 calories in 1988.[303] Unfortunately there are no statistics for the actual use of calories for activity in the same period, but it is a fair guess that the physical need for food energy must have decreased considerably in the same period.

While some maintain that calories are calories and the only thing that matters is how many you eat, there are reasons to believe that things are more complicated than this. The emergence of platforms for marketing fast food is commonly considered a leading force in the increased incidence of obesity and diabetes in children (17% of American children aged 2 to 19 are obese). An 2004 American study analyzed the food consumption patterns of 6,212 children, and reported that fast-food consumers ate more total fat, more saturated fat, more total carbohydrates, more added sugars, more sugar sweetened beverages, less fluid milk, and fewer fruits and non-starchy vegetables than others. The researchers suggest that children who consumed fast-food were nearly twice as likely to become obese than those who did not.[304]

The simplest explanation for obesity is that food rich in calories is cheap and easily available. After all, it is one of the fundamental 'laws'

---

[a] Overweight is normally defined as a Body Mass Index of 25 or more and obesity as a Body Mass Index of 30 or more.

of the market that a low price will increase consumption. Some say that the poor cannot afford good food, or that they lack knowledge, and that is why they eat junk food, and that is also why the poor (in high income countries) are more often overweight. Others maintain that nutritious foods don't have to be expensive and that many poor people buy processed food instead of healthy raw materials. As I have explained earlier, the poor often lack proper facilities for cooking, or they have to work so hard, or spend time on other activities that they don't have the energy to cook. But it important to realize that from a calories-per-dollar perspective the choice of junk food may be rational.

Two researchers in the United States concluded that you get 1,200 calories in a dollar's worth of potato chips but only 250 calories if you use the dollar to buy carrots. The research, presented in the American Journal of Clinical Nutrition, shows that obesity is promoted by foods "that offer the most dietary energy at the lowest cost". Incidentally, children show the same preferences; they prefer chocolate cookies and potato chips to vegetables and fruits.[305] It is perhaps a bit simplistic, but the calories per dollar equation is certainly a useful piece in the obesity puzzle.

We rarely eat fat, sugar, salt or wheat flour alone but together they can be formed into an amazing number of food products, and seasoned to suit all tastes. What they have in common is that they are cheap, are possible to make in industrial process, are easy to eat (which mostly means that they are not healthy and that we easily eat too much of them) and they are quick to prepare.

A group of Harvard economists thinks that obesity in the United States is caused by the reduced time spent in cooking and getting food, and that the food industry makes cheap food available in an easy way. Simply put, the effort – the time cost – to get the stuff into your mouth is lower. They illustrate their point with the humble potato. As most of us know it takes a lot of time to peel potatoes. Despite this, potatoes have been widely prepared in people's homes for hundreds of years. Yet they were rarely transformed into French fries because this requires a number of additional steps. This also limited the serving of French fries in restaurants. In the postwar period, a number of innovations allowed the centralization of the production of French fries. They were then frozen and shipped to the point of consumption, where they were quickly reheated either in a deep fryer (in a fast food restaurant), in an oven or even a microwave (at home). Today, the French fry is the most popular way to eat potato in the United States; from 1977 to 1995, total potato consumption increased by about 30%, almost exclusively due to increased consumption of potato chips and French fries.[306] I would add the availability of cheap cooking oils as an additional reason for the French Fry expansion. The story is very similar in other countries, but with some local variation so that in Switzerland the consumption of *rösti* has increased.[307]

The same research showed that the increase in caloric intake is because people eat more often, not that they eat more at any one sitting. The number of snacks in the typical day increased dramatically over this period. Whereas only about 28% of people in 1977-1978 said they had two or more snacks per day, 45% reported two or more snacks in 1994-1996.[308] Other research shows that one fifth of all food consumed by Americans aged between 18 and 50 took place in the car. Finally, research on the role of supermarkets in changing diets concludes that the most universal effect of the ascent of supermarkets is that supermarkets encourage us to consume *more*, whatever the food.[309]

Faced with increasing costs for health care as well as public opinion, governments have slowly started to tackle an obesity problem which they have played a role in creating. In the Health Care Act passed in 2010, the United States government required that all restaurant chains with twenty or more restaurants post calorie counts for menus. Even local governments are issuing regulations aimed at the food industry. The city of New York required in 2007 that chain restaurants prominently post the nutritional values of menu items. New York also tried to ban the sale of large sodas, on the grounds that the high quantities of sugar in those drinks are a health hazard. However, the courts later struck down this ruling.[310]

One cannot have this discussion without remembering that while so many people eat too much, an almost equal number don't get enough food to eat. According to the FAO's most recent estimates 12.5 percent of the world's population (868 million people) is undernourished in terms of energy intake.[311] While the obesity epidemic is raging, another epidemic is killing even more people. An estimated 26 percent of the world's children are stunted, 2 billion people suffer from one or more micronutrient deficiencies. The costs of undernutrition and micronutrient deficiencies are estimated at 2-3 percent of global GDP and the cost of all diseases, for which overweight and obesity are leading risk factors, were estimated to be about 2 percent of global GDP in 2010.[312] While hunger is mainly a problem in poor countries, a surprisingly large number of people in rich countries experience a food shortage. In the United Kingdom some 4 million people cannot afford a healthy diet and one in five parents and one in ten children regularly go hungry because they do not have enough money for food.[313]

The current interest in diets is not new. I read with some amusement about the iconic *lardo di Colonnata* (a lard product) that, just a generation ago, was ascribed healing properties, curing all things from an upset stomach to a bad back.[314] All through history, there have been ideas about which foods are good for you and which are not, and there have been many cultural and religious rules. Ancient Chinese physicians identified four categories (grains, fruits, vegetables and domesticated animals), each one with five foods in each group being considered to be especially nourishing and useful for treating disease. The 3,500 year old ayurvedic script Caraka-Samhita mentions twelve such food groups.[315] The Roman Cato the Elder wrote in *De Agricultura* "When all the veins are blown up with food, they cannot breathe through the body, and that gives rise to illness. When from overeating the bowels will not move, if you take (as I advise) an appropriate amount of cabbage, you will develop no illness from overeating."

Linked to the wholesale introduction of white flour and an increase in degenerative diseases many 'reformed diets' emerged at the end of the 19th century. Margaret Barnett studied some of the fads of the period and her description could equally hold true today:

> Even those who could not or would not take the fads seriously, however, must have found them hard to ignore. Their fame was spread by hundreds of books and articles, cartoons, jokes and jingles, catchy advertisements and even plays and novels. For the general public, there were lectures, food reform societies and sports fixtures where cultists vied with 'normal' eaters to demonstrate the physical rewards of a particular regimen. Sanatoria and spas, meanwhile, overflowed with wealthy hypochondriacs availing themselves of fashionable new dietary cures.[316]

It is only the last hundred years that we can talk about a scientific approach to food. This originated in the desire of rulers to control the food supply and know what was essential or not, and to deal with diseases that harmed the human engine. Scurvy was common among sailors and by soldiers deprived of fresh food for extended periods. Scurvy can lead to open wounds, loss of teeth, jaundice, fever, neuropathy and can be fatal. It was documented as a disease by Hippocrates and Egyptians recorded its symptoms as early as 1550 BC.[317] Since the 16th century it was well known that scurvy could be prevented by special foods, e.g. lemons – a typically 'unscientific' grandmothers' cure. However, it was not until 1747 that, in the first ever clinical trial, James Lind formally proved that scurvy could be treated and prevented by citrus fruits such as limes or lemons. Today, we now know it is caused by vitamin C deficiency, but vitamin C as such was not clearly identified until 1928.

All throughout the 19th century leading scientists, such as von Liebig, thought that protein was the essential energy for the muscles since they were largely composed of proteins. The development of nutritional science in the 19th century was largely driven by an economic perspective, the question of how to feed workers or soldiers in the most affordable way. For the army it was essential to know that they got best value for money in their selection of foods. And in Europe, the revolutions of 1848 triggered an interest in how to feed the masses.[318] One of von Liebig's students was Carl Voit who, together with Max Rubner and Wilbur O. Atwater, developed modern nutritional science.[319] From the late 1870s to the mid-1940s, the German debate over nutrition and the social question was framed around the concept of *Volksernährung*, feeding the people. One important question was how much and what kind of protein the human body required. Voit stated that an average working adult needed 118 grams of meat per day following Liebig's 'meat makes meat' thesis which implied that animal protein in the diet was a necessary condition for human health. Rubner emphasized that rational nutrition also had a political payoff saying that "A well nourished population is easily governed". He urged the state to create a central food office for systematic nutritional studies; establish workers' restaurants in the cities to provide low-cost nutritious meals; redesign apartments to contain small kitchens so that families could eat cheap and nutritious meals at home, rather than squandering money on unwholesome food purchased on the street; educate school-age children, especially girls, about the basic principles of hygiene and nutrition and set up school lunch programs to deal with the problem of childhood undernutrition.[320]

A crucial moment for food science occurred 23 March 1886 when the student A.W. Smith entered a calorimeter, a device used to measure the combustive energy of engines. In the small room he studied academic treatises and lifted weights and ate measured quantities of bread, baked beans, potatoes and steak. Meanwhile, thermometers, hygrometers, condensers, fans and pumps measured what occurred.[321] Wilbur O. Atwater, a professor of chemistry at Wesleyan University with the help of fellow scientists Edward B. Rosa and Francis G. Benedict developed this 'respiration calorimeter' to measure precisely the energy provided by food and used by the human body for various activities. Based on this, Atwater created the system to measure that energy in units, known as calories. Finally, there was a common standard against which all foods could be measured.[322]

Many today try to avoid calories, by ingesting low or no calorie food. In Atwater's time the view on calories was different – they provided a scientific benchmark for feeding the masses. The calorie, Atwater declared, would determine "the food supply for the future". With this physiological economy the minimum nutritional and energy needs could be determined for different social groups, taking into account their energy use and economic resources. The American government welcomed this new way of quantifying foods which made it possible to compare milk with meat or bread and thus substitute between them while still being able to satisfy basic nutritional demand. If workers could be fed scientifically the wages could be kept lower as there would be no wasteful consumption. The calorie became an important ally in the global expansion of American wheat, its primary export at this time. This went so far that the governor of Michigan, Chase Osborn, in 1920 proposed a system of international trade using the calorie as the currency.[323] In 1925 the League of Nations established a global dietary standard of 2,500 calories for a laboring adult.

The scientific approach to food met with some resistance. Gourmets took exception to this new way of viewing food, which inserted a wedge between taste, pleasure and need. The American Medical Association warned in 1917 about focusing too much on calories. Atwater's science led him into a conflict with his church and his own belief in temperance when he concluded that a bottle of wine supplied the body with energy in the same way as fat and carbohydrates.[324] Nevertheless, since Atwater's time thoughts about 'calories' have kept many people awake at night, and fed a mushrooming industry dedicated to calculating and, either, increasing or reducing their intake.

The transformation of the rations of the Japanese Army, discussed earlier in this book, was to a large extent a result of the realization that Japan's soldiers, and indeed most Japanese, were underfed. This led to a wholesale reform of army cooking based on the concept of 'value for money', i.e. as many calories as possible for minimal cost.[325] This message was brought to the general population through recipe books and exhibitions and was part of a larger package of controlling the size of the population and Japan's aggressive expansion into Manchuria with the purpose to establish 'imperial self-sufficiency'.

So the humble calorie played a key role in global politics. Gandhi recognized the political implications of the calorie and refused to let modern science become the basis for setting universal food norms, which implicitly meant domination by the British Empire. He urged his followers and the people of India to tune their diets to their culture and the subjective needs of the body, unique for each living person, instead of referring to objective calories. He also resented the scientific separation of food from growing and cooking, which he saw as extensions of the same thing. For Gandhi, food was also a discussion about urine, frying oils and manure application.[326] And all of it was politics. A perspective that is still true today.

"The nutritional needs of the body can already be reduced to chemically known substances that can be synthesized or extracted from natural products", wrote Nevin S. Scrimshaw,[327] a leading food scientist from the Massachusetts Institute of Technology, who was awarded the prestigious World Food Prize 1991. An important effect of the role that science and politics played in nutrition was that common people could no longer be entrusted to decide for themselves what they should eat. False needs expressed ignorance and should be cured by proper instructions from scientists.[328] We have since been raised not to rely on taste or pleasure to determine what to eat, but to defer our selection of food to experts. I believe this view is mistaken. Deliberations over nutrition only play a relatively small role in our decisions about which foods to choose and there is no natural link between what we like and what is good for us. A prime example is sugar and sweetness. Most people have a liking for sweet things. This liking might have been useful historically as there was little risk of anyone getting too much of the most rapidly available energy resource that there is. But with the industrialization of sugar production there are no limits to how much sugar we can consume.

Author and journalist Michael Pollan, in his *In Defense of Food: An Eater's Manifesto* refers to the obsession with the single elements of our food as "nutritionism". He says this has three components: seeing nutrients as more important than food; needing scientists to guide our food choices; and the view that the sole purpose of eating is to gain (or maintain) physical health. The scientific approach leads a form of reductionism which focuses on single nutrients because "one can't make research on broccoli". But even then we don't eat broccoli as a whole meal but compose different dishes with it and we don't eat the same things throughout the day, the week or the year. So how can I understand the effect of my annual diet? Our food has so many components and the way we mix them is important, as is the interaction between what we eat and what we do, how we live and how much physical exercise we take. This makes it virtually impossible to draw any conclusions from fragmented 'nutritionist' research, which is why we receive such a flood of, often contradictory, health messages.[329]

We cannot detach nutrition from the food system at large, including not only how we cook, but also how food is stored, processed, distributed and farmed. In its annual flagship report, The State of Food and Agriculture, 2013, the FAO writes that, "Food system transformation and the nutrition transition go hand in hand. To address the nutritional challenges in a given context it is first necessary to understand the nature of the food system and identify key entry points throughout the system."[330] It is critical that we don't reduce matters of nutrition to a discussion about the food choices of the individual, when the reality is that most nutritional choices are made on the farm, in the food industry, by supermarkets and through government policies.

Nutritionism has suited the food industry well. After all, the strength of the food industry is to mix standard components and create a constant flow of new products. 'Now with omega-3' or 'more iron/antioxidants', or whatever is temporarily in fashion are good marketing pitches. Vitamins, fiber, minerals and lately special proteins for body builders are all ingredients that can be mixed in never-ending combinations and marketed with nutritional arguments – and be marked up a notch compared to the same product without these extras. Dieting and nutritionism create their own industry, so the same companies that first earned money from making people fat, can earn even more from making them slim again. Americans spend between US$40 billion and US$100 billion on dieting.[331] 'Meal replacement' shakes and protein bars are sold to those who have ingested too much Coke and too many French fries. In 2008 alone, Nestlé made changes to more than 6,000 products to cater for nutritional issues, real or perceived.[332] Sometimes the attempts to address one problem can lead to a new one. For instance, in the 1980s the food industry and fast food restaurants were encouraged to shift from frying in highly saturated fats, such as beef tallow and palm oil, because of the effect of these fats on cholesterol levels. But the fats they chose to use instead, known as transfats, were later shown to be even worse.[333]

Governments' interest in what their citizens eat continues, but the agendas are changing. The first set of public guidelines – Recommended Dietary Allowances (RDAs) – was accepted in 1941 in the United States. In January 1977, after having held hearings on the national diet, a set of nutritional guidelines for Americans that sought to combat leading killer conditions such as heart disease, certain cancers, stroke, high blood pressure, obesity, diabetes, and arteriosclerosis, were developed. The *Dietary Goals for the United States*, also known as the *McGovern Report,* recommend that Americans eat less fat, less cholesterol, less refined and processed sugars, and more complex carbohydrates and fiber. The committee's 'eat less' recommendations triggered strong negative reactions from the cattle, dairy, egg, and sugar industries. Under heavy pressure, the committee held further hearings, and issued a revised set of guidelines in late 1977 which adjusted some of the advice regarding salt and cholesterol and watered down the wording regarding meat consumption.[334] In the 1989 edition the authors, at a certain point, recognize that people eat food and meals and not nutrients and add, "However, RDAs should be provided from a selection of foods that are acceptable and palatable to ensure consumption".[335] The motivation for this acknowledgement is just to be sure that people will eat the right things.

In contrast, it was not until 2005 that the French government issued any recommendations, and even then the issue of nutrition was subordinate to that of national culinary excellence. France stands out as a country where the quality and culture of food plays a much more prominent role than in most other Western countries. Cookbooks in France are more literary, intellectual and focused on culinary values than say in, Britain, where the focus has been on household management and 'home economics'.[336] French children are 'taught' taste; each autumn during *La Semaine du Goût* (the week of taste) some 3500 chefs visit French schools to initiate children into the secrets of cooking. Meanwhile, restaurants offer reduced price menus for students and some serve special children's menus.[337]

Today, enormous energy is invested in promoting diets of all sorts. Some of them are based on human history, in the sense that the diet that we have had for a long time is seen as natural and therefore we are likely to be well adapted to it, e.g. the paleo diet. In this book, I will keep to other elaborations. After all, even though many people seem to believe that we can eat what we want, the reality is that our food choices are quite limited. They are limited by the choices made by our ancestors and by ecological and economic conditions. The farming system in Sweden, by necessity, produces quite different things than the farming systems of Uganda, Greece or Japan. What we eat is, and should be, a reflection of what we can produce. That of course can change, but the change is usually gradual and slow and many of the factors are determined by local conditions.

The 'best' diet might not be possible for economic or ecological reasons. A diet of nuts and raw food probably cannot feed 7 billion people, and a vegan diet would have tremendous repercussions on the landscape and the economy. To date there has never been a truly vegan agriculture system on any large scale, even if there are some individual farms that operate without animals or without using animal manure. Parts of the Japanese farming system probably come closest, but these are not entirely vegan. Japan's meat taboo led to the country being among the world's primary extractors of fish, seafood and whales. It is no coincidence that Japanese trawlers are found in most of the seven seas. Even India, where large parts of the country are vegetarian has a farming system based on dairy cows and buffaloes in many parts, and India is competing with Brazil to be the largest exporter of bovine meat in the world.

Those who recommend a substantial reduction of carbohydrates, or that we should not eat grains need to suggest what other sources we can use for the energy we need. Grains have been the bulk of human food in most cultures. This is not primarily a dietary choice, but a 'choice' based on what has been available in sufficient quantities to sustain large populations. Fat is globally a scarce product and two thirds of all vegetable fat today come from very large-scale palm oil and soya plantations. Those who say we should eat more olive oil and less palm oil, need to figure out how to considerably expand olive oil production. Olive oil is today a minor part of the global fat supply, with less than ½ liter per person, compared to around 7 liters of palm oil that are produced per person. Given that olives can only grow in a very narrow climatic range it is simply not possible to make olive oil the main vegetable fat for the human population. This is not to underplay the vast devastation that oil palm plantations have wrecked in the rainforests of Borneo and Sumatra, but just a factual statement that illuminates the many difficulties in translating dietary ideas into a viable production system.

There is a link between the health of the soil and the health of our bodies, or at least I am convinced there is. This is no new thought, but scientists are now finding some evidence of this. A soil that has a rich diversity of life is more likely to produce nutrient rich food and there is an interplay between bacteria in the soil and in our gut.[338] And everything in the food system between the soil and our gut influences our health. There is an interplay between the soil, the farming methods and the crop varieties, food processing and our health. When we change one thing, we change many more. The development of white wheat flour and the effects on milling and wheat varieties used is a clear example of this.

In the 1960s, researchers in Sweden were scouting for old seeds to send to the newly established gene bank on Svalbard, which has now developed into what is called the Doomsday Seed Vault. They were hugely surprised when visiting the Kaupang farm on the island of Gotland in the Baltic Sea. The farmer, Ragnar Pettersson, had kept in cultivation a number of old, almost ancient wheat varieties, including summer wheat, white, red, blue and black emmer, and borstvete, a variety of wheat that appears to be unique to Gotland. Petterson grew them together because that gave his wife Maria the best flour for bread-making. Today, those varieties, and other old varieties found later, in total 30, have been multiplied in commercial production and are marketed by an association, *Gutekorn*. One of the biggest selling points of Gutekorn's products is their nutritional value. The ancient grains differ in the amount of gluten they hold and they are rich in minerals, making them rich in flavor. Einkorn, for instance, has relatively little fiber, is fattier than wheat, and is rich in beta-carotene and low in gluten. Emmer wheat is a good source of antioxidants and has higher protein content than bread wheat. A top baker in Stockholm promotes the flours from Gutekorn.

Another example of this is the transformation of cattle, from being fed on grass, fresh or dried, to increasingly being fed diets of grain and soybeans. This is not only 'unnatural' but it is bad for the cows since grass is still the best cattle feed. Not only is it better for them, but it is also better for the end consumer if the beef or the cheese is 'made of grass'. Grass-fed milk, meat or eggs contain better fats, with higher levels of omega 3 and conjugated linoleic acid (CLA). In one study from the United States, cows grazing pasture and receiving no supplemental feed had five times more conjugated linoleic acid in milk fat than cows fed typical maize diets.[339]

While yields have been constantly increasing over the last century, the nutritional level of agriculture products has not. There are many indications that the food harvested today is less rich in valuable nutrients, and contains more water and carbohydrates. According to American studies, there were statistically significant reductions for six nutrients between 1955 and 1999: a 6% drop in protein, 38% in riboflavin, 16% in calcium, 15% in iron and vitamin C and 9% in phosphorus.[340] The differences are mainly explained by changes in the varieties grown or bred, indicating that modern varieties have not been bred with sufficient attention to nutritional value. How we grow also plays a big role. Irrigation and the use of chemical fertilizer have a big impact, mostly negative. Studies that compare organic and non-organic (conventional) products show that, on average, organic food has a higher content of 'good' things, such as vitamin C, dry matter and omega-3 and a lower content of 'bad' things such as nitrates and (quite obviously pesticides).[341] Further, the nutritional content of goods for the market is often sacrificed for storage ability, shape or size (so they can be more readily boxed), ease of handling and transportation and physical appearance rather than for nutritional value.

The 20th century was marked by the 'scientification' of food and the development of many a new technologies. Still, people are suspicious of industrial foods and government controls. After all, food authorities all over the world tell us that it is perfectly safe to consume a low dose cocktail of pesticides and chemical food additives. But equally, what was considered safe twenty years ago is not considered safe today. The dietary recommendations from authorities and scientists were so far off the mark that most grandmothers' advice would have done better. And the constant tinkering with the ingredients and additives by the food industry is frightening. Even more so when they go all the way into changing the genetic makeup of crops and animals. It is ironic that historically we needed to civilize food through preparation, processing, in order to make it fit for consumption, to make it safe and clean, while today people seek natural, organic or even raw food to avoid the dangers of processed foods. Michael Pollan says that we should 'touch the hand that feeds us'; that we need to have a relationship with the farmer and the food processor who produce our food. It is through relations – and not through more rules, liabilities and declaration of content – that we will get both safe and nutritious food.[342]

The obsession with nutrition neglects the link between food and culture and society, not to mention farming, and this contributes to further distancing these elements rather than better integrating them. In the end it undermines local food cultures. The industrial model sees farming as being about providing NPK and water to plants that are driven by photosynthesis. The soil is seen as just a medium for the roots to grow in. This view is reinforced when we reduce food to proteins, vitamins and hygiene. In this view the role of the food system is basically to transform the NPK into nutrients for people in the most efficient, which means cheapest, way. But this perspective neglects the immense life in our soils, the millions of organisms living there and all their interactions. It also neglects the many interactions between the human body and the environment and totally fails to recognize that the whole food system is a socio-ecological system with millions of interactions and relationships. No wonder people eat junk food and get sick. No wonder our soils are unhealthy.

Part II: Primi

MAKING LUWOMBO
I am making Luwombo[a].
Carefully choosing and apportioning contents,
Ensuring only the best of ingredients,
To lovingly wrap in my well smoked banana leaf
Mpombo.
For I am making Luwombo.

I am making Luwombo,
Vigilantly placing my banana leaf stalks,
To keep my delicacy delicately propped,
Steaming it gently till the juices pop
Penetrating, stewing, brewing,
Slowly…slowly…slowly
As for you my city urbanite friends,
You may toast your pop tarts for the pop charts.
And in this place I may seem like the last,
The Kisembo,
But, I know, that I am making Luwombo

I am building a skyscraper,
While you toss up your buveera,[b] plastic-thatched shacks overnight,
I dig… and dig… and dig deep the foundations
For my monumental legacy
And maybe tonight I'll sleep under a tree,
But when I am done I will live in the penthouse suite,
For I am building a skyscraper.

I am making Luwombo,
And as I slave over my hot, smoking sigiri,
You may spin your soft, easy cotton-candy
But when my food is ready,
I can go to bed happy,
As you hold your stomachs–hungry
And then, where will be your mocking lugambo?
You see, THAT is why I am making luwombo.
Susanne Anique

---

[a] Luwombo is a Ugandan dish of meats steamed in banana leafs.
[b] Buveera is what plastic bags are commonly called in Uganda.

10

Filling and nourishing

In Modena, Italy, I hosted a dinner for a number of friends. It was a rather typical dinner for that area, antipasti, pasta, main courses etc. It wasn't the best food I had eaten but it certainly was good. Towards the end of the dinner I asked if people wanted desserts. Most agreed. My four African friends politely declined and said that they would go and look for 'food'. First I was a bit offended by this, but then I realized that for them the Italian fare was not really 'food' as it lacked the fundamental ingredient in a proper meal, which is built around a staple, such as maize, bananas or cassava and cooked into a heavy porridge. It goes under names such as Nshima, Ugali, Posho and Matoke depending on the language and raw materials. They are adamant about the need for this staple and insist on an accompanying relish, which preferably has meat and at least some oil and vegetables. This relish has the dual role of providing taste and also makes it easier to swallow the sticky lumps of porridge. Of course, it also provides the much needed vitamins, fat and protein. This basic recipe is not unique to Africa. Most cultures have been dominated by a single staple which has been accompanied by a number of other foods. In many places it was porridges like Nshima, in others it was bread or tortillas. Mostly the staples were grains.

The history of farming, and the history of human civilization, is to a large extent the history of grains. It is no coincidence that *sperma* in Greek and *säd* in Swedish refer to both the seed of man and to grain.[343] In a few, mainly tropical, climatic zones root crops (such as potatoes, sweet potatoes, yams and cassava), breadfruit or bananas have been the foundation of food, and in fishing, nomadic and pastoral cultures fish, seafood, milk or meat have been very important. But by and large grain has ruled – and still does. The global increase in meat consumption doesn't take away the importance of grain, rather the opposite, since grain is now also the main feed for livestock, in contrast to earlier times when animals ate everything but the precious grain, which was reserved for humans and the gods.

Roots and grains have many advantages as foodstuffs. They are rich in calories and nutrients. Roots can often be harvested year-round or left in the ground without rotting, and grains can be stored in granaries to provide food in the difficult seasons of cold, drought, or heavy rain, depending on the region. Most societies came to depend on one, two or three favorite roots or grains to provide most of their calories, that is, as their staple foods. Other foodstuffs, such as meat, fruits, and vegetables provided flavor, variety, and nutritional balance. It is remarkable that the few staples humans selected already many thousand years ago still dominate our food.

Between grains and roots, grains were generally preferred for their ease of transportation and storage and also because they offer more variety in cooking than root crops and can be used to produce everything from liquor to bread. Half a kilo of wheat, rice or maize provides us with three quarters of our daily calorific needs, while we need four to five times more of a root crop. All high civilizations, based on cities, had grains of some kind as their base. The exception is the quinoa and amaranth of the Inca, which technically are not grains but the seeds of a herb. The agriculture system of the Inca Empire was considerably more diverse than most other systems as it spanned several totally different agro-ecological zones, each one suitable for a range of different crops, or pastoralism.[344]

Cereal grains are edible seeds from the grass family (Poaceae or Graminae). They include wheat, rice, maize, barley, oats, sorghum, and millet. 100 g of whole grain provides about 350 kcal, 8 to 12 g of protein and useful amounts of calcium, iron (though phytic acid may hinder absorption) and the B vitamins. They lack vitamin C and, with the exception of yellow maize, they also lack carotene. For a healthy diet, they should be consumed with other foods rich in vitamins A and C and in minerals. The protein of most cereals is deficient in the essential amino acids lysine and tryptophan and, as such, cereals need to be supplemented with other sources of protein such as pulses (beans, peas, etc.) or animal products. Examples of such combinations are lentils (*dal*) with rice in India or with wheat in Pakistan and North India, beans with maize tortillas in Mexico, tofu with rice Japan and bread with cheese in Northern Europe. [345]

Over the course of history most people have satisfied three quarters of their calorific needs with grains. Still, feeding cities or armies with grains was not easy. A packhorse could carry up to two hundred and fifty pounds of grain, enough for ten people for ten days. Water transport was much more efficient. A merchant ship in the ancient Mediterranean could carry as much as four hundred tons. Land transport cost seven times more than river transport and twenty-five to forty times more than going by sea, which confined larger cities to navigable rivers and places with a good harbor.[346] [347] Still today most cities are on the coast or on navigable rivers.

Grains, their production, storage, preparation, and consumption have shaped our world in more ways than most of us think. They have shaped states, culture and language. The primacy of rice as a staple food is echoed in the Japanese language. '*Gohan*' is both the word for 'cooked rice' as well as 'meal.' The use of *gohan* in Japanese is extended with prefixes to give *asagohan* (breakfast), *hirugohan* (lunch), and *bangohan* (dinner). Some also explain the traditions of harmony, consensus-seeking, and the feelings of dependency with the conditions needed to produce rice. Historically, wet rice cultivation was a labor-intensive task, where families pooled their labor and shared their irrigation facilities. This necessitated an emphasis on group interests, group decision-making and the avoidance of conflict between families, who would continue to be neighbors and workmates for generations. At various times in history rice even functioned as a hard currency. In this context the Japanese 'obsession' with protecting their rice farmers is more understandable.[348] The importance of maize in some American cultures and wheat or barley in the Mediterranean and Middle Eastern cultures show similar characteristics. "Give us this day our daily bread" in the Lord's prayer is one such indication. In ancient Greek religion and myth, Demeter is the goddess of the harvest, who presided over grains and the fertility of the earth. She also gave humans law and order, an indication of close link between civilized society, grains and agriculture.

Today, cereals still play a huge role in feeding the world. Between 1960 and 2000 the global population doubled while global grain production increased by 127percent.[349] The total production of cereals in 2012 was in the range of 2,300 million tons: one third of this is used for feed for animals, half is directly consumed by people and the rest is used for biofuels and industrial production. Even if people eat less porridge today, they eat a lot of ready-made foods which, if we disregard all the colorants, sweeteners, preservatives and aromas, are largely based on grains. In North Africa, India, Turkey, Myanmar and Vietnam people consume more than 200 kg of cereals per year, representing almost 2,000 kcal per day. The average American gets 554 calories per day from maize, 768 calories from wheat and 91 calories from rice.[350] These three grains are by far the most important in terms of global consumption.

For most of history, the rice-growing cultures of South and East Asia were more populous and powerful than any other cultures. This can to a large extent can be explained by the high productivity, per area unit, as well as per labor unit, of irrigated rice. It was only with the industrial and capitalist revolution, that the European wheat eaters got the upper hand and wheat eaters came to outnumber rice eaters. But since 1999 rice once again feeds more people than wheat. Centuries of trade and exportation have spread rice cultivation and consumption to every continent and it has become a very important food in Latin America. However, most of the world's rice is grown and consumed in Asia – where sixty percent of the earths' people live. It is planted on about eleven percent of the world's cultivated land. The traditional method for rice farming is to flood the fields while, or after, setting the young seedlings. More than 75% of all rice is produced on irrigated land. Rice can be grown even on a steep hill or a mountainous area by making use of water-controlling terrace systems. It is also perfectly possible to grow rice without flooding, but irrigation inhibits the growth of weeds and deters vermin.

The origin of Asian rice (*Oryza sativa*) is still disputed, with some believing that the impulse for domestication occurred simultaneously in the Ganges Valley and East Asia. Recent molecular studies show that Asian rice was domesticated in the Yangtze Basin some 8,200 to 13,000 years ago, and spread from there.[351] There is also African rice which is thought to have been domesticated some 2,000 to 3,000 years ago in the inland delta of the Upper Niger River.[352]

In addition to being a rich source of dietary energy, rice is a good source of thiamine, riboflavin and niacin. Unmilled rice contains a significant amount of dietary fiber. Lysine is the limiting amino acid and rice is generally low in protein (mostly between 6% and 8%). Many traditional dishes throughout the world combine rice with animal products, fish or beans, groundnuts or lentils which all complement the nutrients in rice. As with wheat, unpolished rice has a higher nutritional value than polished rice. Unfortunately – again as for wheat – people mostly prefer white rice. In many cultures, rice forms an integral part of the culinary tradition. For example: dry flaky rice is eaten in South Asia and the Middle East; moist sticky rice in Japan, Taiwan, Korea, Egypt and northern China; and red rice in parts of southern India. Many countries have signature rice recipes, such as sushi, fried rice, curry, paella, risotto, pancit, or beans with rice.[353]

The population of rice consuming countries continues to grow and the world will have to produce 40% more rice by 2030. This increased demand will have to be met from less land, with less water, less labor and fewer chemicals. To meet the challenge of producing more rice from suitable lands we need rice varieties with a higher yield potential and a more stable yield. There are over 100,000 traditional rice varieties collected from a range of climates. These seeds serve as a large pool of untapped germplasm for modern seed-breeding.[354] But in the field the varieties of rice is rapidly disappearing.

Olga Linares at the Smithsonian Tropical Research Institute in Panama followed the development of agriculture among the *Jola* people of Senegal over a long period. In 1965, farmers in just one village used nineteen different varieties of rice, six of which were traditional African rice varieties. For them it is important to grow a mixture of fast and slow maturing types so as to stagger the harvest as insurance against extreme weather conditions, such as drought. Different varieties are selected according to the soil, even within the same field. There was a constant exchange between the women, who were in charge of the seeds. A woman would trade a variety that is best suited to rain-fed fields for one that grows well in mangrove fields. Another woman would trade a fast-growing variety for a slower-maturing one depending on her needs.[355] *Jola* women also applied criteria about taste, ease of pounding, and how varieties cooked. A *Jola* could usually tell the general region from which a particular variety came and how long and how it had been stored by its taste. The preferences for rice varieties reflected a wide range of criteria, from ecological or environmental to cultural and even religious. However, with modernization these traditions were gradually eroded. Thirty-five years after her first visit, Linares again made an inventory of the rice varieties grown in the same village and now there were only nine grown, and only one traditional variety.[356]

Rice farming is undergoing rapid changes. And the change is not only a result of farmers' choices, but is also driven by external pressures from agri-business and governments. In the state of Kerala in India, the government promotes what they see as the three essential parts of modernization of rice production: mechanization, increased use of chemical fertilizers and pesticides and the use of modern varieties. It pays up to 70% of the cost of mechanical rice transplanters, allegedly because of a shortage of labor. Over centuries farmers have developed many rice varieties suited to the soils, climate and rainfall and that also provide better nutrition and taste. But the government wants them to change, and promotes high yielding and hybrid varieties of rice as their productivity is high and there is more demand for them in the market".[357] However, these new varieties need more chemical fertilizer and pesticides to thrive.

The process through which maize was domesticated is not totally ascertained. Most scientists hold that it was domesticated from the annual plant *teosinte*, Zea mays ssp. parviglumis, native to the Balsas River valley in south-eastern Mexico. Stone milling tools with maize residue have been found in a 8,700-year old layer of deposits, and this points to maize having been developed from teosinte in that area some 9,000 years ago. Considering that teosinte has skinny ears with a dozen kernels wrapped in a stone-hard casing, the transformation into cobs carrying 500 naked kernels is indeed a remarkable accomplishment. Even more so as it was done by people who had no knowledge of the science of hereditary seed breeding.

Maize is still a very important food in Mexico. More than sixty native varieties are grown on medium to marginal land as specialized ingredients for more than 600 preparations as food and beverages, including some 300 types of *tamales* (a traditional dish made of maize dough which is steamed or boiled in a leaf wrapper).[358] The average Mexican gets more than 1,000 kcal per day from maize. Irrigated farms are mostly industrial operations using commercial hybrids and achieving yields of about 10 ton/ha, comparable to their counterparts in United States. Those on medium-to-poor quality land tend to farm smaller plots, often rely on native seed varieties, and produce yields of 2-3 ton/ha; some produce a significant surplus for the market. Meanwhile, those farming marginal lands tend to be subsistence or sub-subsistence, with yields of 1 ton/ha. Mexican smallholders use one hundred times as much labor in their maize fields than farmers north of the border. As a result, maize is increasingly imported, making Mexico the second maize importer of the world (after Japan where it is used for feed). In the 1960s, imports were mostly negligible, while in the last decade imports account for around one third of maize consumed in Mexico.[359]

In the last decade the global maize trade has normally been more than 100 million tons. The quantity is still less than for wheat (145 million tons in 2011), but the growth in the maize trade has been bigger, linked to the increase in livestock production.[360] And in no other country does maize play such a role in modern agri-business as in the United States, the country which now supplies Mexico with most of its imports. Maize covers more than one quarter of crop land in the United States making the country far and away the largest maize producer and exporter in the world. In the record year, 2007, it produced 331 million tons, more than 40% of the world's production or more than a ton per American.[361] The United States is also the biggest consumer of maize, using 290 million tons (11.5 billion bushels) per year.[362] According to the movie *King Corn* fifty percent of the biomass of many Americans can be traced to maize consumption.[363] Throughout the day Americans eat maize in all its forms: breakfast cereal, marmalade (maize sweetener), margarine (maize oil), all the animal products (all fed on maize), snacks, candy, beer and bourbon are all made of maize.[364]

Between 1910 and 1950 four important events changed production practices in the fertile American Corn Belt[a]: the substitution of horse power by the tractor, the introduction of new high-yielding hybrid seeds and of chemical fertilizers and the development of viable mechanical picker-huskers for harvesting maize.[365] Between 1870 and 1940 yields were more or less stagnant, but from 1940 they increased rapidly. In 2000 the average farmer got 8.5 tons per hectare, compared to 1.7 tons per hectare in the pre-war period.[366] The area under maize remained quite stable. Until after WWII less than 7% of the American maize harvest was exported. By 1980 exports had reached 35%, although in most years the figure was in the range of 20%.[367]

Maize is a highly productive plant but has a disadvantage compared to rice and wheat, there are more deficiencies in its nutritional content and so it requires more supplemental foods. The expansion of maize, together with that of soybeans, enabled the industrialization of animal production. Both are high yielding plants lending themselves to large scale production, trade and processing. Maize is also easier to grow in monoculture than many other plants. As a result, maize is today often grown in big fields on farms which produce little else. But this comes at a high price for the soil and the massive use of fertilizers and pesticides affects biodiversity negatively. The intensively farmed maize fields are probably less nature-friendly than highways, which all have refuge areas where wildlife can thrive. Maize is not only one of the foundations of industrial livestock production. There are more than 4,200 different uses for maize products, and more are being found each day. Apart from the many food products it is a raw material in diapers, shampoo, gasoline, plastics, paper and antibiotics.[368] These are all offshoots from the maize milling industry.

Maize milling was originally done by pounding the grain with a, usually wooden, pestle in a mortar, often referred to as querns. These were slowly replaced by gristmills which mill the dry maize. Today most maize is processed by wet milling. One hundred kilograms of

---

[a] An intensively farmed part of the Midwest of the United States

maize can produce 57 kg of starch, 60 kg of sweetener, 42 liter of fuel ethanol or 40 kg polylactic acid plastic (PLA), plus by-products such as distillers' grains and maize oil. Of the sweeteners the most prolific is the high-fructose corn syrup followed by glucose and dextrose. Maize contains 3% to 5% oil and, despite this low oil content, is the second most consumed oil in the United States. It is mainly derived from the germ which has a high oil content. The oil can be extracted by expellers or more commonly through extraction with hexane (a constituent of gasoline). Maize oil goes through a number of processing steps, refining, bleaching, winterizing (to reduce the melting point so it remains liquid at lower temperature) and deodorization (taking away the bad smell).[369] There is a rapid growth in the maize milling industry in United States, most of it in Illinois and Iowa. "Recent estimates say that the wet corn milling industry exports US$3.3 billion worth of goods in a year – that is a lot of dough" wrote market analysts EMSI, slightly tongue-in-cheek, on their web site.[370] A lot of the dough today is made from maize liquor in the form of ethanol fuel, which I will discuss further in chapter twenty-two. It is worth noting that maize is a main beneficiary of agricultural support in the United States and maize subsidies totaled US$84 billion in 1995-2012.[371]

Mayan creation myths tell of three stages of creation. First, the creator, *Heart of Sky*, made men out of mud, but they spoke nonsense and crumbled. The second attempt was with wood, but the doll people had no blood, did not sweat and had nothing in their minds. The third attempt was successful, when the gods made maize dough and mixed it with their own blood to produce present day humans, literally 'maize people'.[372] Perhaps the fast-food fed North Americans are just modern incarnations of maize?

The earliest cultivated forms of wheat were einkorn and emmer wheats, first cultivated some 10,000 years ago in the south-eastern part of Turkey. Bread wheat developed some one thousand years later. Two very important properties of the wheat plant had to be manipulated to adapt it to farming. First it was necessary to stop the shattering of the ear (also called head or spike) at maturity, which resulted in seed loss at harvesting. Second there was a need to change from hulled forms to forms where the chaff (casing) didn't stick to the grain in order to allow the processing of the wheat into porridge or bread. Wheat spread via Iran into central Asia, reaching China by about 5,000 years ago and to Africa, initially via Egypt. And it reached most parts of Europe some 5,000 years ago. It was introduced by the Spaniards to Mexico in 1529 and by the British to Australia in 1788. Most wheat grown worldwide is bread wheat, and most of the remaining 5% is durum wheat, which is better adapted to the dry Mediterranean climate than bread wheat and is often called pasta wheat to reflect its major end-use (it is also used for regional foods such as *couscous* and *bulgur*). In the 10,000 years it has existed, more than 25,000 types and varieties of wheat have adapted the crop to a wide range of environments. If there is sufficient water and mineral nutrients available and pests and pathogens are controlled, yields can exceed 10 tons per ha. But the global average yield stands at less than 3 tons per ha.[373]

Wheat can be stored for many years without losing much of its nutritional value,[374] even if the often repeated story of 3,000 old wheat seeds from a Pharaonic grave germinating is a just a smart marketing myth. Another blessing of wheat, compared to other grains, is that doughs formed from wheat flour allow us to make a wide range of breads and other baked products (including cakes and biscuits), pasta and noodles, and other processed foods. A ship biscuit from 1852, purportedly the oldest existing in the world, is displayed prominently at the maritime museum in Kronborg Castle, Elsinore, Denmark,[375] and still looks edible. Hard tack, pilot bread, ship's biscuit are all versions of a simple type of cracker or biscuit, made from wheat flour, water, and sometimes salt. Inexpensive and long-lasting, these were used for sustenance in the absence of perishable foods, commonly during long sea voyages and military campaigns. They were also one of the first industrialized food products after sugar. Already by the 18th century they were produced in assembly lines in dockyards and by 1833, the British Royal Navy introduced steam-powered machinery to roll the dough and later a Jonathan Dickson of Carlisle invented a mechanical biscuit stamp, an early example of branding.[376]

Until the 19th century, bakers obtained their yeast from beer brewers, continuing the symbiosis between beer and bread established more than five thousand years earlier. However, beer brewers slowly switched from top-fermenting to bottom-fermenting yeast and this created a shortage of yeast for making bread.[377] This process got a real boost by invention of artificial refrigeration which made it easier to make *lager* (lager means storage in German) beer. In response, the Association of Viennese Bakers offered a prize in 1845 for the production of a good yeast strain that was not dependent on brewers. Ironically, it was a brewer, Adolf Ignaz Mautner, who won the prize for the production of press-yeast in 1850. Meanwhile there was a rapid development in milling technology. The marvelous mills of Budapest had steel rollers with a capacity to mill 1 billion pounds of wheat per year. Roller mills allowed the production of white wheat flour, which wasn't really possible with stone mills. The yeast and the new mills changed the baking-industry throughout the Austrian empire, and at the Paris Exposition in 1867 the Viennese bakery was recognized as the best in the world. The development was so sensational that the United States government printed the *Report on Vienna Bread* by Eben Norton Horsford in 1875 in which he stated that the purity, whiteness, yield and keeping qualities of the wheat flour of Austria were unequaled in any other country. But this was to change, as everyone followed in the footsteps of Austria.

This industrial development had many effects, reaching far outside the factory gates. White wheat bread in all forms is easy and quick to eat, has not too much taste in itself and can be complemented with various forms of spreads or covers. With industrial yeast it was also quick to produce. It is more voluminous, more porous, and easier to chew. In this sense the bread became something of a pioneer fast food. Another, possibly bigger, effect was that with earlier stone-milling technology the oils of the wheat germ was set free in the flour and caused it to go rancid and have a foul smell if stored for a longer term. Wheat flour was thus a fresh product, milled daily and households bought small quantities from local mills to have fresh flour. The white wheat flour didn't contain the germ and could be stored for a long time, which meant that traders could buy and store bigger quantities and transport it from where it was cheap to where it was dear. This was the start of a rapid consolidation of mills, aided by the railroads and canal networks, which enabled big mills to both source grain and sell flour over a dramatically bigger area than before. In a few decades small mills closed down and in a later stage the same forces led to the concentration of baking into huge factories. Industrial bread was born.

The industrialization of milling created new opportunities, but also its own set of problems. Whole wheat flour is more nutritious than refined white flour and contains more fiber, protein, calcium, iron, selenium, folic acid, vitamins and omega-3 fatty acids.[378] Quite soon after the large-scale introduction of white flour a number of diseases emerged. These were often referred to as "western diseases" as they seemed to follow in the footsteps of the spread of a diet of white bread and sugar. This explains why the British working classes, for whom bread was the main source of sustenance, were more malnourished in 1900 than at any time since Tudor times (the period between 1485 and 1603) according to an article in the British Medical Bulletin.[379] There was an early counter-reaction with strong arguments being made in favor of whole grain bread and the emergence of breakfast cereals and muesli. In 1880, May Yates founded the Bread Reform League in

London to promote a return to wholemeal bread, particularly to improve the nutrition of the children of the poor.[380] It was evident that some of the problems were a result of the victory of white flour, and industry and government responded with a counter-measure in line with the new industrial process, thinking and profits: fortification.[381]

Flour treatment agents or additives, euphemistically called 'flour improvers' alter the appearance and properties of flours in order 'to better suit their intended purpose'. For example, inspired by a fashion that arose in the 19th century for whiter-than-white bread, bleaching agents such as chlorine are used to whiten flour (unbleached flour has a pale cream color). Oxidizing agents, such as phosphates and ascorbic acid, are used to develop gluten in flour, making it better for baking bread. Potassium bromate, is widely used in United States as an oxidizing agent but has been found to be carcinogenic and is banned in Europe.[382] The German company Mühlenchemie lists no more than sixty-two flour 'improvers' on their web site. Many of the additives are composed of several active ingredients, so the total number is even much higher.[383]

As with many other shifts in technology, the new milling method had repercussions not only on the processing and the final product but also on the raw material. This is often the forgotten part of the story of our food industry. The new milling technology needed harder wheat that could more easily be worked by the new high-speed machinery. Soft wheats, good for stone milling, were replaced by hard wheats. The hard Turkey Red wheat brought to America by Russian immigrants became a major export commodity, largely as a result of the new milling technology, and wheat production in United States tripled in fifty years.[384] Similarly, the new industrial baking processes needed wheat with certain qualities in order to work well. Only much later did anybody question if these improved technical properties were detrimental to the nutritional quality of wheat.

White flour is not the only reason for our bread having a lower mineral content, cultivation methods and seed breeding that values higher yields ahead of nutritional value have also contributed. Wheat protein is well suited for human nutrition except for a low lysine content. The lysine content is comparatively lower in white than in whole grain flour and lower in heavily fertilized wheat. One variety of wild emmer wheat in Israel has a protein content that reaches forty percent,[385] more than three times higher than in normal wheats. The long-term experiments at the English research station Rothamstead – which required vision and commitment to establish and maintain – show that the introduction in 1968 of the new 'Green Revolution' varieties of wheat was accompanied by a considerably lower content of zinc, iron, copper and magnesium in the flour.[386]

There is also a close interdependence between the new varieties and the new cultivation methods. Semi dwarf varieties of wheat were introduced because they had shorter straw and less roots, which meant that more of the biological production went into the seed (the kernel). But this only worked if the plant got more 'support' from the farmer, in the form of artificial fertilizers, pest and weed control. Higher yields also often have a dilution effect, with the protein and mineral content going down and the carbohydrate content going up. The highest wheat yields are recorded in West and North West Europe where farmers use a lot of chemical fertilizers to keep the protein level high enough for industrial bread-making. For example, United Kingdom farmers currently apply 250-300 kg N per ha in order to achieve the 13% protein content required for the bread-making process that is most common in the United Kingdom. The quantity of fertilizers used is well above what the plants actually take up. The rest is washed away into the waterways as nitrates or goes up into the atmosphere, some of it as the potent climate gas, nitrous oxide (laughing gas).[387]

In this way, white wheat flour embodies most of the characteristics of the industrialization of food: stripping it to its basic components, giving a longer shelf life, making further preparation easier, enabling large-scale processing, storage and handling, requiring food additives but giving a lower nutritional value. All this is also combined with an increase in environmental damage. This industrialized food system industry drives, and is driven by, changes in marketing and distribution that together determine what and how we eat and how we interact with each other. The genes of the wheat, the yeast and all the processes involved in making our daily bread are all shaped by industrial and marketing imperatives.

11

Green and white

A researcher followed a group of Baluchi, Iranian pastoralists living in Pakistan, and was astonished when a man could recognize some faint prints in the gravel as being those of *his* cow and set off looking for it. Several hours later the man appeared with the cow at the camp without anyone raising an eyebrow. The Baluchi nomads can even identify lineal descendants from a good foot print of a camel. They never mark their animals in any way and do not count them for fear of the Evil Eye.[388] They are an example of a form of farming which, in terms of the world's land surface is the most important of them all, the conversion of grass into food.

Apart from the special grasses called grains, the seeds of which we eat, we also grow grass on a fourth of the planet's surface as pasture for animals. Many of these grasslands existed previously but many were also managed by human hunters before the domestication of animals. Other grasslands, e.g. most of the grassland in temperate climate Europe are converted forests, wetlands or drained lakes or created in other ways by humans for livestock grazing. Livestock has played a very big role in human civilization. As can be seen from the etymology presented at the start of this book there are also very strong links between the word 'food' and 'livestock'. Cattle have been a major indicator of wealth and in many places still are. The word capital originally comes from the Latin word *caput*, meaning 'head', i.e. how many 'head' of cattle a person had. Even *cattle* itself also derives from this same origin. The cow is the most important representative of the ruminants and will be the star of this chapter, but most of what is said about the cow applies equally to sheep or goats (referred to as 'decimal cows' by a lecturer in goat keeping I once listened to).

And cattle and grassland are intrinsically linked, since grass has been the main food for cattle and other ruminants, such as cows, sheep, goats, camels, llamas, yaks, giraffes and many others. The most important difference between ruminants and non-ruminants such as humans, horses, dogs, and pigs is that ruminants have a stomach with four parts where more than 200 different bacteria and 20 types of protozoa help the animal to break down fibrous food like grass. The cow's rumen, the first and biggest part, is like a large fermentation vat, with a volume almost the size of an oil barrel. As important for the digestion is the large quantities of saliva, up to some 150 liters(!) per day which the animal mixes in with the feed. After a short period of mastication, when the saliva is added, the feed is swallowed in the shape of a ball. When the cow ruminates, the feed returns back to the mouth and is masticated again.[389] There are many advantages in letting animals eat grass and convert it to other products. One clear advantage is that we don't have to harvest, as that is done by the animals which concentrate it. Another advantage is that there are many lands in the world where it is not practical or possible to till in any way. They may be too steep, too rocky, too cold, too hot, too dry or too wet, all conditions that make arable farming very difficult. Historically, almost no land that was good for arable farming has been left for permanent grazing, for the simple reason that when conditions are good for arable farming that is usually a more productive way to produce food.

The bottom line, which is of tremendous importance for us, and for the cow, is that ruminants can feed on grasses and other cellulose materials, stuff that we cannot eat. The grass is converted into meat, leather, wool, fat, a number of medicinal products and, not least, milk. Domesticated cattle come from two or three major lineages that are derived from independent domestications of aurochs (*Bos primigenius*). *Bos taurus* and *Bos indicus*, were domesticated in Near East and the Indian subcontinent respectively,[390] cattle might possibly also have been domesticated in Africa. It is not clear however when these animals were first milked, although humans have consumed milk for many thousands of years. There are finds of traces of milk in pottery from the Near East which are nine thousand years old and from Eastern Europe eight thousand years ago.[391] This supply of milk, meager as it might have been, had some distinctive advantages. It provided sustenance in times of food and water scarcity in Africa and the Middle East; provided additional nutrients (especially calcium and lysine) to a cereal-based diet and was an alternative to sunlight as a source of vitamin D.

Pastoralism may look sloppy and disorganized and pastoralists are often accused of being primitive, not maintaining the environment, or even being cruel to their animals. Mostly, these allegations come out of ignorance. Pastoralists live very close to their animals and their environment. That their grasslands are dry and barren is mostly not because of the pastoralists, but rather the opposite. They are the only ones (apart from miners and oil companies) who can turn this landscape into something of value for humans. Nomadic pastoralists move around, not because they are bad managers of the environment where they live, but because the conditions where they live change seasonally and often erratically. Their management systems have mostly been based on common ownership of land, and their culture was often oral, not written. This made it easy for dominant sedentary cultures to take over the fertile spots of their lands and push them onto marginal lands – where indeed they sometimes cause environmental degradation.

There are many different forms of pastoralism. Some are integrated with the farming system, such as seasonal pastoralism in parts of Europe, where sheep, goats and cattle are taken to the mountains for grazing in the summer and are kept in the villages in the winter. In other cases, for example in parts of India, farmers and pastoralists live side by side and exchange goods, mostly meat for grain. The pastoralists graze fields after the harvest and the fields get manured by the cattle. Finally there are fully nomadic pastoralist societies where it is not just the herders, but the whole people, who move with the herds, sometimes across national borders. The cattle ranches established in the Americas, Southern Africa, Australia and New Zealand are a form of fenced-in-pastoralism, enabled by barbed wire.

Most pastoralists depend heavily on their livestock's milk products for nutrition; both directly by consumption and through sales of dairy products to adjacent farmers to acquire grains or other foods. Live animals can also yield blood and this has been historically exploited in Eastern Africa. The Maasai bleed cattle with a special hollow arrow and mix the blood with milk. Some Turkana, Maasai and Tuareg people get more than two thirds of their calories from milk and meat.[392] A survey of Mongolian herders shows that they eat an astounding 184 kg meat per person, half of which is horse meat, and 786 kg of milk products, mainly milk and butter. In their diet, animal products supply three quarters of the protein and almost all the fat.[393] Globally, extensive pastoralism produces some 10% of the meat consumed by humans and supports around 20 million pastoral households. Pastoralism supplies about 80% of the agricultural output of Sudan, Senegal and Niger.[394]

The flexibility so characteristic of pastoral nomadism and the ability to transport goods and people have meant that pastoralism has long been associated with two other major livelihood strategies, trade and warfare. The Mongolian empire was for a while the largest in the world, and for a period of three thousand years China tried to protect itself from the nomads of central Asia.[395] The Chinese aversion to milk consumption may have its origin in a desire of creating a cultural divide against the nomads, in addition to the physical barrier of the Great Wall. For sure, most Chinese are lactose intolerant, but lactose intolerance is the 'natural' stage for humans and not a sign of any deficiency. Once a population take up milk drinking this intolerance gradually wanes.

Many countries have policies designed to settle pastoral people. Compelling pastoral nomads to settle, however, has rarely been successful, socially, economically or ecologically.[396] A comparison between Mongolian herders and herders and livestock keepers in Inner Mongolia (which is part of China) show that when the nomadic people were settled and given individual tenure of land, which was the case in Inner Mongolia, their management of the land deteriorated. Interestingly, when asked what main function grassland serves, 44% of those still roaming around said natural beauty and only 22% stated fodder provision while among the settled people, 86% answered fodder provision and only 3% responded natural beauty.[397] In many places the livelihoods of pastoralist are under enormous pressure, from encroachments into their natural environment and climate change, but even more from the industrialization of livestock. As a result of what is known as the livestock revolution, built on cheap maize and soybeans, the relative price of meat has plummeted tremendously. But the pastoralists' cost of production has not decreased at all, on the contrary. In essence they have become poorer.[398] Some try to counter this by 'rationalizing' pastoralism, using modern technologies, helicopters or snowmobiles. But the environments in which pastoralists live and work aren't so easy to manage in an industrial way as crop lands or sheds of animals shot full of medicines.

The pastoralist doesn't aim at maximizing production at any point of time, but to maintain and increase stocks. In a monetary economy, that could be expressed as not looking for profit but rather to increase the size of the bank account. Considering the origin of the word capital, it is not surprising that livestock acts as a store of wealth. In good years the stock grows and lean years it shrinks again.[399] Consistent with the origin of the word, even today in Nigeria most of the benefit of goat keeping is in providing a 'banking service', because livestock can almost always be converted into cash.[400]

When discussing the role of animals in the agriculture systems and on our plates, the focus is often upon meat (which I discuss more in chapter twenty-two) and tends to omit milk. But that is a mistake. The production of milk is a more efficient way of transforming grass into protein than meat production. Milk from cows is now on par with rice as the world's economically single most important farm product; about eight percent of all farm income comes from cow milk.[401] Dairy products represent almost half of the calorific intake from animal products in developed countries and around 14% of the total calorific intake. On average, 215 kg of milk is consumed per person in developed countries (this includes not only liquid milk drunk but also milk used for cheese, butter, dried milk, yoghurt or ice cream). In developing countries, milk consumption is much lower and dairy products represent only 4% of the calories.

Pastoralists are prime examples of cultures totally built around livestock, but in some other systems animals have also played a large role. India has had a well-developed dairy culture for a very long time, after all this is where the cow is sacred. In 1987, the average Indian consumed ten times more milk than the average Chinese. Today the average Indian consumes 69kg per year and India is the biggest milk producer in the world producing almost one sixth of the world's milk, half of which is buffalo milk (it is less complicated to raise buffaloes as the buffaloes are not subject to the same religious rules as cows). India has sixty percent of the world's buffalo milk production.[402] The Indian cow has developed along very different lines than the European cow and she has played much the same role as the pig in China or Europe, a converter of waste of all kinds. Indian cows hardly ever compete with humans for food. A survey conducted in 1997 showed that Indian cows were mainly fed with grasses, grazing and crop residues. Cultivated forage crops represented a mere 5-8% of their diet and concentrates (normally bought in oil cakes and maize) even less.[403] The cattle and the buffaloes also provide animal traction which allowed people to grow more food for themselves (or labor less) and to get them and their produce to market. Cow dung has been a very important fuel, once more an effect of ruminants' ability to concentrate resources for our use. The same argument that is used today against eating meat can also of course be made against using dung for fuel – it is a waste of resources as there is more energy in the grass than in the manure. It is, but it is much more work to collect the grass, and the dung can be made up into very concentrated briquettes for burning, which burn slowly and for a very long time, allowing the cook to work while cooking. The sacred place of the cow in Indian society makes a lot more sense when you look at the system as a whole, rather than assume that the cow in India has the same role as a cow in Oregon, the Netherlands or New Zealand.

The mixed farming systems of Europe are yet another version of feeding animals on grass. In these systems grass or herbs are grown in rotations with grains and other field crops. These mixed farming systems have been very productive and were resilient over centuries. They were also extremely important for the income of farming families. As late as 1948 milk represented 40% of the income of Swedish farms, meat 22% and eggs and poultry 6%.[404] In the Balkans, the Alps, Scandinavia and other mountainous areas of Europe there has been (and in many places still is) seasonal migration, transhumance, where cattle, sheep and goats are taken up to mountain pastures for grazing, often a considerable distance away from the permanent settlement. Normally, cheese and butter is produced in those summer grazing locations, providing a store of protein for the winter months or to be sold.

Commercialization and industrialization have significantly changed the rearing of cattle. This change has had effects far beyond their consumption of feed. It has had profound effects on whole agriculture systems as well as on the food we eat. In the past cows in Europe grazed and ate hay from clover-grass leys (cultivated grass-lands) which were part of a crop rotation. Today they feed on bought in concentrates (grains, soya or oil cakes) and, most often, silage from heavily fertilized grasslands that are detached from their ecological function in the farm. An English farmer Simon Fairlie puts it like this; "the low yielding cows are nitrogen providers whereas the high yielding cows are nitrogen takers". [405] Because each cow now gives so much milk, the calves and the old cows produced by the dairy system are not sufficient for the provision of meat and this has given rise to specialized cattle breeding for beef. This development has also changed the animals themselves. In the past most cattle were 'multi-functional', being used for animal traction, meat and milk, to mention just the most important uses. With specialization, cows have increas-ingly been bred for one specific purpose, and a dairy cow breed (e.g. a Holstein) is very different from a beef cow (e.g. a Hereford or an Angus). And, in turn, very different 'value chains' have been built up around beef and dairy production. These are shaped by the different conditions of producing milk and beef, but even more by the huge difference in marketing and logistics for milk, a fresh product that is delivered by the cow, usually twice a day, and meat, in the form of calves that grow into steers in a year or two.

While milk has been very important in the Northern and Western European farming system, the consumption of fresh milk was not very widespread, apart from by children in the countryside. Milk was generally transformed into cheese, yoghurt, butter and other products which could be stored and transported, and also sold for cash. The commercialization of fresh milk was hampered by the speed with which milk goes sour. Getting pure milk into the dirty conditions of the heart of Victorian London was hard work. In 1850, most of London's fresh milk was produced within the city itself, but by 1910, eighty percent was brought in by railroad, from as far away as from Devon.[406] Londoners were not particularly enthusiastic for the local milk produced in thousands of crowded inner-city cow-sheds. There was no refrigeration and fresh milk could not be stored for more than a few hours. Even keeping the churns and measures clean was difficult when the water supply was polluted.[407] Because of low standards of hygiene and frequent adulteration of the milk there was considerable demand for milk drawn from the cow while the customer was watching. This could be satisfied at the cowshed, but also doorstep milking of cows and goats, which were driven around the streets, was popular.[408] All these factors led Londoners to embrace 'railroad milk' wholeheartedly. Merchants Mary Ann and John Sainsbury (who founded the retail chain carrying their name) made this novel milk available around the clock by having a pump, 'the mechanical cow', outside their shop.[409] The transport costs fell constantly and by the 1890s so much milk was carried to London from the West Country that the Great Western Railway was known as 'The Milky Way'.[410]

Even if conditions for the cows and the hygiene in the stable probably was a lot better outside London, the quality of the milk was not safeguarded by shipping by railroad and this milk was often 24 hours old before it was delivered. All dairymen claimed to serve fresh or 'new' milk as it was called, and some even added hot water to convince the customer that the milk was still warm from the cow. Because Londoners expected the milk to have a rich yellow color there was also widespread use of annatto dye. Chemicals were also added to prevent the milk from going sour. "A conspiracy of silence on the part of the trade and of apathy on the part of the public was instrumental in maintaining these practices as an essential element in retail profitability" concludes Peter Atkins, Professor of geography in Durham.[411]

Not only the milk underwent changes, also the marketing of milk changed a lot as a result of the change in milk supply. During the 1860s and 1870s a few milk joint stock companies emerged, including the Express County Milk Co. (1864), the Aylesbury Dairy Co. (1866), and the Dairy Reform Co. (1871). Their success in raising capital and attracting customers led to a wave of new enterprises. At the turn of the century the ten largest companies controlled over 40 percent of all London's dairy outlets. This consolidation was also driven by technical development in the dairy industry itself, and as has been repeated many times since, government regulations paved the way for the larger companies at the cost of the smaller outfits. One important driver of change was the installation of pasteurization and bottling plants in the early twentieth century; an investment that was well above the capacity of smaller players. United Dairies was formed in 1915. By the end of the war it controlled about two-thirds of London's wholesale milk supply and one-third of the retail milk trade.[412]

Milk consumption rose at this time, partly as a result of increased incomes and partly because women increasingly worked away from home and could not breast-feed.[413] Another version of milk emerged, sweetened condensed skimmed milk. Butter was already a quite standardized dairy product which was possible to store, trade and export, leading to an emerging butter trade. As a by-product of butter making, fresh machine-skimmed milk was widely utilized in the Netherlands for animal feeding, in particular for pigs. However, in 1896 the Dutch margarine producer van den Bergh (later Unilever) also established a milk condensing factory. Condensed milk had advantages in that it was free from bacteria and, when sweetened, could be stored at room temperature, even in opened tins. At a time when nobody had a refrigerator this was important. Working class families became the main consumers. But the working women didn't know that the cheap and convenient condensed skimmed milk was not an adequate replacement for milk or breast-feeding. In 1917, C.E. Bloch studied cases of serious eye diseases among Danish infants in an orphanage. Their diet consisted mainly of skimmed milk, and Bloch concluded that the absence of fat was the main cause of the disease. Soon the existence of vitamin A and D and their presence in milk was ascertained and from 1923 a British regulations required condensed skimmed milk to be labeled as being 'unfit for babies'.[414]

Even with today's efficient logistics and globalized trade, fresh milk is mostly consumed in the country of production, with the global trade mainly being based on milk powder, a product which is easy to standardize and store, a prerequisite for a tradable commodity. The price of milk powder essentially determines the world market price for most dairy produce as all major milk buyers turn any milk they cannot sell fresh, or profitably turn into other dairy products, into milk powder. So even if consumers don't shift from cheese to milk powder, the price of industrial cheese is very closely linked to the price of milk powder. And there is a big chance that the milk powder comes from one of the most isolated places on the planet.

The global giant in the milk trade is not India but New Zealand.[415] Every third minute a container of dairy products – mostly milk powder – is shipped from New Zealand.[416] Nearly all of the milk produced in New Zealand is exported. As a result New Zealand, which only accounts for a little over two percent of total world milk production has about one-third of the global cross-border trade in dairy products.[417] With annual exports in excess of NZ$13.7 billion (around US$11.6 billion), the dairy industry is New Zealand's biggest export earner, accounting for more than 29% of the country's exports of merchandise.[418] This industry is totally dominated by one player, Fonterra, a farmers' cooperative which collects around nine tenths of New Zealand's milk production. Their website explicitly recognizes the level of market power that they have: "Because Fonterra purchases such a large proportion of New Zealand's total milk, there isn't a 'market price' for milk that is independent of the price paid by Fonterra".[419] This domination means that the 'world market price' is determined at the fortnightly auctions of one single actor. It is a remarkable achievement – or a scary expression of globalization – that dairy farmers all over the world will have a sleepless night awaiting the results of Fonterra's auctions. That the booming New Zealand dairy industry also has a dark side doesn't get much attention. "What no one wants to talk about is that the current 'white gold rush' is leading New Zealand to a freshwater quality disaster," says Kevin Hackwell, advocacy manager with Forest & Bird, a local NGO.[420]

"Fifty-five square feet of rainforest is destroyed for every quarter pound hamburger that comes from a cleared rainforest cattle farm." This and similar statements, with unclear scientific backing, have made many aware of 'the hamburger connection', the link between meat eaters in Europe and United States and deforestation. The origin of notion of the threat that the hamburger poses to the rainforest was a rapid expansion of cattle grazing in Latin America, often established on formerly forested land and mainly destined for export to Europe. In Honduras, between 1952 and 1974, forests shrank by 33,000 hectares and crop land also decreased as a result of more cattle grazing.[421] The production of food for the local market also shrank as a result of this. And those who earned money from the cattle were not those who went short of food. This process was repeated, on a much larger scale, in Mato Grosso and adjacent states in Brazil, so there is a certain truth in the hamburger connection. But, by and large, the recent expansion of livestock numbers has been driven more by the expansion of soybeans and maize than by the direct grazing of cattle. Cattle rearing in Latin America is rapidly transforming from being based on 'natural' grazing to industrial feeding.

The pampas, the vast grasslands of Argentina, has long been cattle country, and beef exports made Argentina into one of the world's ten richest countries at the end of the 19th century. But today, the image of cows grazing idly is becoming more and more a thing of the past. Grain-fed, feedlot cattle are becoming the norm. Around a third of all Argentinean beef now comes from cattle reared in grain-fed feed-lots. In 2005, Argentina's ranchers and farmers produced more than 3.1 million tons of beef, exporting some 745,000 tons onto the world market. Argentina was the third largest beef-exporting country (behind Brazil and Australia) in the world, still allowing its own population to have the second highest level of beef consumption in the world. In March 2006, Argentina's government – in an effort to lower the rising price of beef to its people – banned beef exports for 180 days. This was followed by a 15% export tax on fresh beef. The government assumed that ranchers and farmers would continue to raise cheap beef. But instead, they cut their herds and converted their pastures to soybean production. Getting two crops of soybeans per year instead of taking three years to raise cattle to be sold on a domestic market with artificially depressed prices, is a no-brainer for Argentinean land-owners, who now mostly rent out their land to huge agribusiness operations. As a consequence, the acreage of soybeans in Argentina increased from 37.6 million acres in 2005 to more than 48 million acres in 2012. "Land that has been converted to soybean production is not going to go back to pasture," says Carlos Becco, head of Soybean for Syngenta in Argentina. "That land is worth too much now to be put back into permanent pasture".[422] [423]

"It is like being a comedian, it is all about timing". Jack Erisman explains how he manages the weeds in his organic fields in Pana, Illinois. He is swimming against the tide in a sea of maize grown by his neighbors. The Corn Belt has, as the name suggests, been conquered by corn (maize). A century ago, farms in the Corn Belt were a lot more diverse. They all had their own cows and hogs, chicken and horses; there was pasture, and there were many people employed on the land. The land was good for maize and farms produced it very cheaply. When chemical fertilizers became readily and cheaply available after WWII these farmers expanded their maize production. The maize was bought by large specialized livestock operations; which produced meat at a lower price than the diverse farms. As a result over time these farms quit livestock production altogether and shifted into monoculture maize, sometimes in rotation with soybeans.

Meanwhile, livestock cattle breeding was divided in two stages. In the rolling hills of Montana you see cattle grazing everywhere. But if you look closer you will see that the only adult animals are the mother cows and the odd bull. Geneticists have still not succeeded in totally alienating cows and calves from the environment which is their natural habitat. This may be on their hit list for the future, but for now it is not viable to lock up cows in pens and feed the calves from birth in feed-lots, factory farms, or concentrated animal feeding operations (CAFOs) as they are called in the United States. But, when old enough, the calves are sold as 'feeder cattle' to these concentration camps, where they spend the rest of their lives in confinement, fed on maize (for energy) and soybean cake (for protein). In this way American beef is produced in three different sites, the Corn Belt, permanent pastures such as Montana's and finally in feed lots. Some feedlots in the United States now have more than 100,000 cattle.[424] This model is now being successfully exported to Brazil and Argentina. The system is similar in Europe, but population density, zoning, environmental and animal welfare regulations place limits on the size of factory farms in Europe.

Jack Erisman's fields contain maize, for sure. There are many varie-ties, blue, red, yellow, white and popcorn maize, all organically grown. He also grows soybeans, ray, wheat, clover, vetch and many more things in a seven year crop rotation. But his two hundred head of Murray gray cattle, mixed with Angus are 'grass-fed' and rarely eat any maize or soy. He sells these grass-fed cattle meat for a premium price to a special market, saying a lot about how modern farming has developed. What is – what should be – normal has become an exclu-sive niche. Grass is still the best feed for cattle. Not only is it better for them, but it is also better for the eater when the beef, milk or cheese is 'made of grass'. In recent years some consumers have come to recog-nize this and show their appreciation by paying a better price for grass fed beef. Yet at the same time a combination of market forces and governmental protectionism are driving Argentinean farmers into plowing up the Pampas and confining their cattle within feedlots.

12

Sweet

The English first arrived in Barbados in 1624 in the *Olive Blossom* and took possession of the island in the name of King James I. In 1627 the first permanent settlers arrived from England and they, or rather their indebted workers,[a] planted tobacco, cotton, ginger and indigo. Little did those first settlers know that in a short period their whole island would be covered by sugar cane, and that the wealth produced by Barbados and Jamaica would, literally, fuel the British Empire for a century and more. Sugar production and trade were important drivers for colonization and slavery and the cause of wars between sugar trade-controlling nations in the 19th century. And sugar rose to become one of the world's the most important food stuffs. The average person consumes about 24 kilograms of sugar each year, equivalent to over 260 food calories per person, per day.[425] In the United States sugar and sweeteners (including corn syrup, etc.) constitute 17% of the calorific diet,[426] making the United States the world's largest consumer of sugar and sweeteners.[427]

There should be no doubt about that humans have a predisposition for the sweet tastes. Even breast milk, our first food, is very sweet, containing around seven percent lactose. We don't only use sweetness as a positive way of describing food, we also call our loved one 'honey' or 'sweetie' and we 'sweeten' our offers or make 'sweet-talk'. The extraction of juice from the sugar cane plant and the domestication of the plant probably occurred in New Guinea many thousands of years ago. From there it spread over Asia. Some two thousand years ago people in India found out that one could refine the juice into crystals. The early use appears to have been medicinal rather than culinary. In most of Asia sugar remained little used until people came more firmly under European colonialism and imperialism. Sweetened tea or the

---

[a] A large proportion of white emigrants to the Americas were indentured workers, i.e. under contracts where they were bound to work for board and lodging for many years to pay for their trip overseas.

claim, and then claim within 187 days of that draw date. Claims over £50,000 must be made in person. **If you believe you have won over £50,000 telephone the National Lottery Line.** For all claims over £500 (over £5,000 if claiming by post) you will be required to complete a claim form and show proof of identity. For a claim form telephone the National Lottery Line.

To claim by post, please send your ticket (and completed claim form for prizes over £5,000), at your own risk to The National Lottery, PO Box 287, Watford WD18 9TT.

SIGN YOUR TICKET. MAKE IT YOURS.

Name	
Address	
	Post Code
Signature	

Safe custody of your ticket is your responsibility. If your ticket is lost, stolen, damaged or destroyed, you can make a written claim to Camelot no later than 30 days after the winning draw date, but it will be at Camelot's discretion whether or not to investigate and to pay the claim.

THE OPERATOR OF THE NATIONAL LOTTERY
The National Lottery is operated by Camelot UK Lotteries Limited under licence granted by the Gambling Commission. The principal office of Camelot is Tolpits Lane, Watford WD18 9RN.

GAMES RULES AND PROCEDURES
National Lottery games are subject to the relevant Rules and Procedures which set out the contractual rights and obligations of the player and Camelot. Games Rules and Procedures are available to view at retailers or on the website, and copies can be obtained from the National Lottery Line. Camelot is entitled to treat a ticket as invalid if the data on it does not correspond with the entries on Camelot's central computer. Players must be 18 or over. Play responsibly.
If you are concerned about playing too much, call GamCare on 0808 8020 133 (freephone).
www.gamcare.org.uk

TR14

THE NATIONAL LOTTERY®
For information visit the website at www.national-lottery.co.uk or call the National Lottery Line on 0333 234 50 50. Calls cost no more than calls to 01 or 02 numbers. If your phone tariff offers inclusive calls to landlines, calls to 03 numbers will be included on the same basis. A separate MINICOM line for the hard of hearing is also available. A proportion of National Lottery sales goes to the Good Causes. For further information please refer to the Players' Guide.

GUIDANCE ON HOW TO PLAY
For how to play and prize structures see the Players' Guide (available from retailers), see the website, or call the National Lottery Line. Results can be found through recognised media channels, retailers, the National Lottery Line or the website. Tickets issued in error, illegible or incomplete can be cancelled if returned to the issuing terminal within 120 minutes of purchase and before close of ticket sales from that terminal on that day.

GUIDANCE ON HOW TO CLAIM A PRIZE
For details about how and where to claim prizes see the Players' Guide or visit www.national-lottery.co.uk/prize. If you hold a winning ticket you must claim your prize by post, or in person at a retailer, or Regional Centre as appropriate, within 180 days of the applicable draw date, or within this period notify the National Lottery Line of your intention to claim, and then claim within 187 days of that draw date. Claims over £50,000 must be made in person. **If you believe you have won over £50,000 telephone the National Lottery Line.** For all claims over £500 (over £5,000 if claiming by post) you will be required to complete a claim form and show proof of identity. For a claim form telephone the National Lottery Line.

To claim by post, please send your ticket (and completed claim form for prizes over £5,000), at your own risk to The National Lottery, PO Box 287, Watford WD18 9TT.

SIGN YOUR TICKET. MAKE IT YOURS.

Name	
Address	
	Post Code
Signature	

Safe custody of your ticket is your responsibility. If your ticket is lost, stolen, damaged or destroyed, you can make a written claim to Camelot no later than 30 days after the winning draw date, but it will be at Camelot's discretion whether or not to investigate and to pay the claim.

THE OPERATOR OF THE NATIONAL LOTTERY
The National Lottery is operated by Camelot UK Lotteries Limited under licence granted by the Gambling Commission. The principal office of Camelot is Tolpits Lane, Watford WD18 9RN.

GAMES RULES AND PROCEDURES

Good luck for your
1 x Fri draw
on Fri 17 Nov 23
1 play x £2.50 for 1 draw
£2.50

EURO
MILLIONS®

1644 033782035 200379 016293

Your numbers

Lucky Stars

07 08 10 27 37 -- 03 11

Your UK Millionaire Maker Code

Guaranteed UK Millionaires every week

MJXT85171

AMAZING THINGS HAPPEN WHEN A
LOT OF PEOPLE PLAY A LITTLE
SEARCH 'DREAM BIG PLAY SMALL'

CHECK IF YOU'RE A WINNER

▼ SCAN WITH THE NATIONAL LOTTERY APP ▼

1644 033782035-200379 016293 Term. 43560701

[   ] Fill the box to void the ticket

sweet food often served in Chinese restaurants in Europe or the United States have no roots in China. Until the 20th century sugar production in China was on a small scale and it was mainly used to supply people with a quick sweet treat, chewing a piece of cane. The making of sugar was known but sugar didn't enter Chinese cuisine on any large scale until recently.

Sugar cultivation and the manufacture of sugar spread from Asia through the medieval Islamic world. It was first known and consumed in Europe after the eighth century.[428] The Crusaders started specialized production in the Levant (roughly the Middle East), which spread to North Africa, Andalusia, Cyprus, Crete and Sicily. The industry was small-scale, labor-intensive and did not produce any large quantity of sugar, so it remained a luxury product. Unfortunately, the Europeans didn't only take up the crop from the Arabs; they also kept the use of slave labor, and scaled it up to levels the Arabs never dreamed of. And the importance of slavery in satisfying the cravings for sweetness was to remain for many hundred years.

Sugar production was moved further West as part of colonization. The expansion of sugar to the Canaries, Madeira, Cape Verde and Sao Tomé allowed Portugal bases that affirmed its control over the mid Atlantic. Sugar cane was first carried to the New World by Columbus on his second voyage in 1493. Beginning around 1516 commercial cane production took root in Santo Domingo (Hispaniola), but it was in Brazil that sugar really rooted itself and the 16th century was the Brazilian century for sugar. In 1625 Brazil was still supplying almost all of Europe's sugar. Tropical America had a climate that was favorable for sugarcane cultivation, and an abundance of land to grow it on, water for the processing, and the forests needed to provide fuel for the factories. The main limiting factor was labor. The Portuguese tried to satisfy this by employing the indigenous population. But as that population declined in the face of Old World diseases and violence, they turned increasingly to Africa.

Not long after, the entire American sugar industry depended on slave labor, and more than 10 million people were captured and forced into the hulls of ships crossing the Atlantic.[429] Abysmal living conditions for the slaves resulted in very short life spans and low natural reproduction, meaning that new slaves were needed all the time. For example, Barbados had 40,000 slaves in 1700 and the slave population in 1800 was 66,000 despite an astounding 263,000 slaves having been forced to Barbados in those hundred years. Some of them would have been re-sold, but the figures still present a grim picture of the living conditions.[430] In some cases the plantations owners supplied them with food, in other cases they got rum, which they could use as currency for buying food, obviously the rum often ended up being drunk instead.

The successful slave revolt in the French colony of St. Domingue (now Haiti) during the 1790s signaled the beginning of the end of slavery, even if it took almost a century until the slaves of Cuba and Brazil finally gained their freedom. Many of the former slaves continued to work on sugar plantations, but the planters also sought other sources of labor. Between 1838 and 1917, the British recruited indentured workers from their Indian empire. These were bound by contract for many years to work for board and a very small salary. Laborers also came from Madeira, China, Japan, and the Pacific islands to work in the cane fields.[431] In the light of the enormous fortunes made from the sugar plantations it is even more appalling that the conditions for workers and slaves were so miserable.

The cane plantations didn't only violate the people, they also took brutal possession of the landscape and all living. All the land within a certain distance of a factory was put into the service of the plantation, primarily for growing cane, and mostly in pure monoculture, year after year. To facilitate transport, supervision and planning, land was often divided into identical squares with roads around them. Roads were cut along the slopes, streams were filled up or diverted and the forest was cut down, all leading to severe erosion. Plantations also needed food for the workers and a substantial quantity of firewood as well as pasture for the all the draught animals used for transport, mills and plowing. Even if the sugar plantations tried to organize their own supply of the heavy firewood, most of them imported a lot of food and the livestock needed for traction and powering the mills.

The colonial nature of sugar was underlined by the fact that the refining of sugar didn't take place at the point of production but in Europe. England imposed high import taxes on refined sugar in 1685, which ensured that refining would take place there and not in the colonies, or elsewhere. But the British would also not sit still and look while Portugal earned fortunes from sugar production. From humble beginnings in the 1640s sugar production expanded from Barbados to Jamaica, and in a few decades the English Empire was self-sufficient in sugar, the popularity of which spread rapidly. Initially it was still an indulgence for the elite. The plantations supplied the English upper classes with sugar, and the rich plantation owners imported all sorts of luxury from the Motherland. The plantation owners also played a big role in politics, many of them were Members of Parliament. It was on their initiative that the navy started to include rum (made of sugar) in the rations, starting with a half pint per day in 1731 which rapidly was increased to a full pint per day.[432] While some for sure lost fortunes in sugar plantations, it was by and large a very profitable endeavor. In late 17th century Barbados, the income from a 200-acre (81-hectare) cane plantation was enough to support the lifestyle of a duke in England. A hundred years later, the trade from Jamaica alone, sugar, slaves and rum, was worth more than all the trade with North America.[433] Throughout the 18th century sugar was the most important imported good in England, France and Portugal, exceeding the combined value of all other colonial imports. The economic power of the sugar economy also found expression in very dense populations. Barbados would become the most densely populated and productive place in the English-speaking world, and by the late 1600s, eighty percent of the island was already planted with cane.[434]

As production increased, prices dropped and new markets developed. Sugar became perhaps the first globally traded mass-market product. And it went from a rarity and luxury to become a necessity. By 1750 sugar has become so widespread in England that 'the poorest English farm laborer's wife took sugar in her tea.' Per capita consumption is estimated to have been around four pounds (just under two kilos) in 1700 and reaching eighteen pounds a hundred years later. And it didn't stop there, the consumption kept increasing to the extent that by 1900, sugar supplied almost one-sixth of the calories of the English diet.[435] The consumption of sugar was, to a large extent, tied to the consumption of three other colonial crops, tea, coffee and cacao, all bitter products. The bitterness itself should have been no reason for the sweetening though. All three were normally consumed without sugar in their place of origin.

In England, sugar was mainly used by the poor to sweeten tea. So cheap was the combination of tea and sugar that it largely replaced beer as a drink. Beer would probably have been more nutritious, but the hot tea with sugar when combined with some bread was not only a drink but a substitute for a proper meal. It is much quicker to prepare a cup of tea and bread than a proper meal, and sweet tea with bread was an early fast-food: very fitted for the living conditions of the emerging English working class, where both man and wife worked hard for long hours. Time for cooking was scarce and fuel for cooking was expensive in the cities. Over time sugar increasingly became a poor man's food, or perhaps, even more, a poor woman's food. Observations from Britain in the late 19th century state that "We see that many a laborer who has a wife and three or four children is healthy and a good worker. What we don't see is that in order to give him enough food, mother and children habitually go short, for the mother knows that all depends on the wages of her husband". Treacle (syrup) and pudding often constituted a meal for the mother and children.[436]

Sugar production was not only an agricultural activity; it also included a number of processing steps. Even if the final refining was done in Europe, the cane first needed to be squeezed and then the juice had to be crystallized into raw sugar. In the seventeenth century the inefficient Mediterranean-style mills were replaced by a mill made of three vertically mounted rollers that could be turned by animal, water, or wind power. These mills did not require the stems to be chopped into pieces before milling. More efficient milling demanded, in turn, more efficient production of sugar. And more efficient manufacturing demanded that the factory had a stable flow of raw cane coming through its doors, i.e. bigger plantations. There were also notable improvements in the design of furnaces, allowing a production-line organization for transforming cane juice into crystal sugar.[437] One could claim that the industrialization of the sugar mill was a precursor to the development of industries in England in the coming centuries.

Later, there was also an influence in the other direction. With the industrialization of Europe and the development of steel, steam engines, railroads and coal, the sugar industry got new tools and machines. These could greatly increase the capacity of the sugar factory, allowed the use of internal rail transport in plantations and also the transportation of cane from inland areas. This drove up the scale again; in 1750 a plantation of 2,000 acres was big but hundred fifty years later 10,000 acres was needed to qualify as big.[438] A growing demand for purity and a stable quality led companies to employ more and more specialist staff, such as chemists. This in turn led to large central factories gradually replacing traditional mills.[439] In 1917 a smaller scale plant could crush 1.25 tons of cane per hour and a modern factory 200 times more. In addition the modern plant, through better technology, could get much more sugar out of the same quantity of cane.[440] Constantly falling prices accelerated this transformation as it was impossible to work profitably with the old technology and capacity when prices dropped.

The development into larger units of production has continued and sugar production has been taken over by multinational companies. Raízen, one of Brazil's top five companies in terms of revenue, has almost a million hectares of sugar cane from which they produce 66 million tons of sugar cane. It has twenty four plants to convert this cane into an astounding 1.9 billion liters of ethanol, 4.2 million tons of sugar and annual electricity sales (the leftovers from sugar production are used to fire steam boilers for electricity generation) of approximately 1.8 million MWh, sufficient to power a city of five million.[441]

It was long known that the beetroot contained sugar, but it was only in 1747 that a German professor found out how to extract the sugar. For Germany, which did not have any colonies at that time, supporting a sugar beet industry was part of a European power-struggle, and was an important strategy in reducing its dependency on England and France. A factory was built with governmental support in the early 1800s. A number of factors helped the beet industry in the early years. The abolition of slavery in the English and French colonies interrupted supply and countries had placed import taxes on cane sugar but not on beet sugar. Several countries even paid substantial subsidies to beet sugar exports.[442] During the Napoleonic Wars the British Navy blockaded French ports preventing sugar cane from being imported so sugar beet farming started by necessity in France. By 1880, beet was the main source of sugar in Europe.

Equally importantly farmers realized that beet could be a valuable way to diversify the farming system. European farming was in crisis, mainly as a result of imports of cheap grain from Russia and the Americas.[443] Beet improves the crop rotation and the leaves make good fodder, the intensive row cultivation during the season cleans the fields from weeds. Even today, European farmers cling to their beet contracts. From very humble beginnings the international trade in sugar beet grew spectacularly and was on par with cane sugar at the time of the First World War. During the First World War beet production plummeted. Imports of sugar from cane increased, and by 1920 sugar cane again had 70% of the world's production. Beet sugar never took back its market share. These days cane sugar again accounts for about 80% of global sugar production.[444]

The five largest producers of sugar in 2011 were Brazil, India, the European Union, China and Thailand. Of these only the European Union produces primarily beet. India, the European Union, China, United States and Brazil are the leading consumers.[445] The global market for sugar and sweeteners in 2011 was worth nearly US$99.1 billion.[446] By weight sugar is the most important agriculture product, a staggering 1,774 million tons of sugar cane were produced 2012, that is 250 kg of cane per person[447] which equals the combined quantity of maize and wheat. Yet, because of high productivity only around two percent of the global crop area is used for sugar production. Sugar from cane is increasingly also used for ethanol production and forms the basis for other industrial products.

The Unites States is no exception when it comes to government intervention in its sugar production and trade. The sugar industry has enjoyed trade protection since 1789 when Congress enacted the first tariff against foreign-produced sugar. Tariffs and quotas keep the sugar price high, which was one reason for the rapid development of maize-based sweeteners. Few other countries have taken to high-fructose corn syrup (HFCS) like the United States, but as Credit Suisse says in a report "the principal requirement for HFCS to flourish is government support".[448] The replacement of partly imported sugar with HFCS made from government subsidized maize lowered the price of the sweetener in sodas by a few cents. This reduction in costs was not passed on to the consumers in the form of lower price but was instead transformed into bigger sodas for the same price.[449] A staggering 43% of the sugar is consumed in sweetened beverages. Between 1955 and 2000, the consumption of soft drinks increased from about ten gallons/person to 54 gallons/person. It has since dropped from this peak by around 20%.[450] Today, people consume a lot more sugar in processed foods and beverage than they pour in their tea. For instance in Canada only twelve percent of the sugar is sold in retail packages and used directly by households (and possibly smaller coffee shops), the rest is used by the food industry and catering sectors.[451]

The real price of sugar has fallen tremendously since its medieval origins. Based on wages an English worker of today would have to earn £2,600 to buy herself a kg of sugar in 1270 prices.[452] Sugar is now affordable for all but the poorest in the world. It is one of the cheaper ways for someone to fill their energy needs. The impact of the increase in sugar consumption on our health is still debated. The United States health system spends nearly U$3 trillion annually on healthcare costs. Obesity alone accounts for 20% (or US$190 billion) of United States national health expenditures and diabetes and metabolic syndrome account for a similar figure, so 30-40% of health-care expenditure in the USA goes to help address illnesses that are tied to the excess consumption of sugar. Forty million people will be diabetic by 2020 according to projections by Credit Suisse.[453]

By and large, sugar played a globally pioneering role in the transformation of agriculture into large-scale monoculture plantations, a system that has been devastating for nature. It has also had profound effects on global diets, most of which have been negative. Sugar was also played an important role in the development of the modern capitalist market-society. The consumption of sugar facilitated the transformation of British rural poor into a labor proletariat, which could work the mines and the factories, or be servants to the upper classes. Sugar generated profits all the way; in the production of cane, the refining, the trade, the further processing and marketing of sweet products, the sale of sweet tea and rum to workers and exports of consumer goods, food, processing technology and slave labor to the plantations. In these respects sugar represented one of the most important foundations for exploitation and capital accumulation at that time. Sydney Mintz reports from his field work in Puerto Rico in 1948 of how aware the local people were of the power of the market: "though half of them were illiterate, they had an understandably lively interest in world sugar prices" and those that remembered the global slump in sugar prices 1919-1920 were especially aware of "the extent to which their fates lay in the hands of powerful, foreign others".[454] The impact of sugar has also led to extensive government interventions in sugar production and markets. Sugar markets are often said to be the second most politicized global market, after oil.[455] Tariffs, quotas, monopolies are all part of the sweet talk.

13

Fat

It may come as a surprise, but globally fat is the scarcest of the big three elements of our diet, protein, carbohydrates and fats. In France, Belgium, Austria, the United States of America, Luxembourg, Italy, Switzerland and Spain people consume more than 150g of dietary fat[a] per day, while in Bangladesh, Eritrea, Ethiopia, Rwanda and Burundi the average person consume less than 30g.[456] Because of the scarcity of fat and the limitations on producing enough fat in many parts of the world the global trade in vegetable oils accounts for almost forty percent of total production, a higher trade share than for any other major food commodity. All the four most important agriculture export streams (by value) are for two oil crops, soybeans and oil palm, which says something about their enormous importance in our food system. In 2011 exports of soybeans from United States and Brazil and palm oil from Malaysia and Indonesia were worth some US$68 billion, almost equally split. Consumption of vegetable oils is growing faster than that of any other major food category and they now contribute ten percent of all food calories globally compared to five percent forty-five years ago.[457] In absolute terms the production of vegetable oils has increased eight fold in fifty years. Most of this growth is attributable to palm and soy bean oil. Previously, fat and oils were a rich man's food in the same way that sugar was until the large-scale sugar plantations were established. Now, with extremely large scale soybean and palm oil plantations, the price of vegetable oil has gone down considerably and calories from vegetable oil are almost as affordable as calories from grains[b] and other traditional staples.[458]

It is no wonder that trade in fat is important. Fat has many important functions as a nutrient. It is a concentrated source of energy and

---

[a] Dietary fat includes all fat consumed, not only pure oils and fats. Dietary fat includes the fat in milk, avocado or meat.

[b] One hundred grams of palm oil contains 880 calories compared to 370 calories in the same mass of wheat. The price of palm oil has been between two and four times higher than that of wheat over recent decades.

provides essential building blocks for the cells in the body. Fat is a carrier for fat-soluble vitamins A, D, E and K and it contains essential fatty acids. Linoleic acid and α-Linolenic acid are called essential because our body needs them, but cannot synthesize them. They are indispensable for growth and renewal of cell membranes. The brain, retina and other neural tissues are particularly rich in essential fats. Fats are also needed by the body to support growth and development, and for the development of the brain and visual systems. International dietary guidelines (such as those of the World Health Organization) recommend that, in a healthy balanced diet, 55% of our daily energy should come from carbohydrates, 15% from proteins and up to 30% from fats.[459] The taste of many foods are enhanced by fats, and as with sugar, the supply from nature is quite limited, so a natural craving for fat has been normal and fitting for human survival.

Before the fossil fuel revolution natural fat and oils had many roles in the economy. They were, as they still are, used for frying and baking. But they were also used for lubricating machinery, softening leather, waterproofing clothes, soap-making and many other uses. Humans probably first used fats taken directly from animals for smearing on leather or their own skins (the natives of Tierra del Fuego supposedly used fat as an extra layer of clothing to ward off rain) and also for medicine. Evidence of olive oil processing has been discovered from the Golan Heights, dating some 6,000 years back.[460] The Romans used olive oil as frying medium, as an ingredient, for medicine, for perfumes, as a lubricant and as a fuel. The use of oil palm may date as far back as 5,000 years in Upper Egypt. In India, ghee, clarified butter, has been a symbol of purity and an offering to the gods for at least 5,000 years.[461]

Lanterns powered by natural vegetable oils and in particular whale oil began to spread from Amsterdam in 1663 to Paris, London and further to other cities.[462] Whaling was to a large extent driven by the need for lantern oil. There was some use for the bones while (in Europe) the meat was discarded. European whalers killed more than thousand whales per year after 1670 when oil lanterns had become widespread. Later on the Americans vigorously picked up whaling. At its peak, in 1846, the American whaling industry had 736 vessels and employed more than 70,000 people.[463] The main American whaling port, New Bedford, Massachusetts, was thus known as "The city that lit the world."[464] Globally, more than 2 million whales, 20,000 per year, were killed in the twentieth century.[465] Over time urban coal gas, kerosene and electricity reduced the demand for whale oil and fat for lightning, coinciding with decline in the number of whales.

Oil from the palm *Elaeis guineensis* has long been used for cooking in West and Central Africa; the oldest finds are five thousand years old. It became a highly sought-after commodity by British traders for use as an industrial lubricant for machinery, for soap and candles. Palm oil is extracted from the flesh (pulp) of the fruit which contain 45-55% reddish oil, whereas palm kernel oil is derived from the kernel (seed) of the palm. Palm kernel oil is often used in commercial cooking because it remains stable at high temperatures. It can also be stored longer than most other vegetable oils. Trade in palm oil from Nigeria to England started in earnest in the 19th century and reached 1000 tons 1810. But it was its use in margarine and baking that would bring the oil palm to global prominence as one of the most important crops in the world. Margarine production from palm and palm kernel oil and from copra (the dried meat of coconuts) started in the 1870s and in 1905 exports of palm kernel oil from British territories reached 157,000 tons. Demand increased rapidly and so did prices.

West Africa had insufficient capacity to increase production so people started to look for new places where palm would thrive. Recently, the last remaining of four remarkable trees in Bogor (Java) died.[466] It was the last of two palms from Reunion and two from Amsterdam (originating from West Africa) which were planted in the Bogor Botanical Gardens in 1848. Descendants of these four palms were planted in Deli in Sumatra and were called the Deli Palms. For a long time they were used only for ornamental purposes. But then Adrien Hallet, a Belgian, established a 2,600 hectare plantation between 1911 and 1914 in Sumatra using seeds from the Deli palms. In twenty years the volume of exports of palm oil from the Far East far exceeded exports from Africa.[467] In this way, just four palm trees gave rise to the whole palm oil industry of the Far East. An agricultural and economic success story – and like most agriculture success stories, an environmental disaster.

Worldwide the production of palm oil has increased from 15.2 million tons in 1995 to 46.7 million tons in 2010, produced mainly in Indonesia and Malaysia. As of early 2011, oil palm plantations covered 7.8 million ha in Indonesia. Most plantations, as well as refineries are located in Sumatra and Kalimantan (the Indonesian part of Borneo). Between 1997 and 2006, four hundred thousand hectares of oil palm plantations were established every year.[468] Palm oil is now the fourth most important food crop in international trade, after wheat, maize and soya.[469] The palm oil industry provides direct and indirect employment to about 2 million people in Malaysia and close to 5 million people in Indonesia.[470]

Palm oil is the world's most utilized vegetable oil for the food and non-food industries. Most of the oil is used for food applications such as cooking, margarines, spreads, confectionery fats, ice cream and emulsifiers. According to Rainforest Action Network, palm oil can be found in almost half of the products in grocery stores in United States.[471] The proportion is presumably even higher in Europe which imports a much higher volume of palm oil. Palm oil recently got a boost because of health concerns over transfats, since it is a cheap replacement for hydrogenated oils. But most palm oil is used for cooking in developing countries; India and China are the two largest importers of palm oil. Ironically, Africa, where the oil palm originated, is also now a large importer. The only reason why not more palm oil is produced in Africa is that African producers simply cannot compete with the plantation industries of Malaysia and Indonesia. With the recent hike in petroleum prices and attempts to find renewable energy substitutes, there is now also an emerging demand for palm oil for making bio-diesel.

From an agriculture perspective, palm oil has many good properties as it is a perennial tree crop that gives very high yields, the world average annual yield is 3-5 tons oil per hectar. This is far more than any other oil crop, which means that less land is needed per unit produced. As a perennial tree crop it causes very little erosion as the soils are not plowed. Nevertheless, the rapid expansion has been accompanied by extensive environmental and social damage. This includes the loss of tropical rainforests due to land clearance and conversion to plantations, the destruction of wetland ecosystems following drainage, the pollution of waterways by improper disposal of mill wastes, apart from the 'normal' problems associated with the use of chemical fertilizers and pesticides (which I discuss in more detail later). The expansion has reduced wildlife habitats and threatens orangutans as well as the Sumatran tiger with extinction. Not only are trees cut down to clear land for oil palms, but many plantations are established on peat lands, which are mostly made up of organic matter. When drained the organic matter breaks down and emits very high quantities of CO_2.[472] This makes Indonesia the third largest emitter of greenhouse gases in the world – eighty percent of these emissions are from deforestation and land use changes.[473]

The other major oil crop is also implicated in deforestation. Unlike the seeds of most other legumes (except the peanut) the soybean is relatively rich in oil. It contains about 18% oil and 35% protein, both of which are in strong demand. The separation of those two major components has given rise to the soybean crushing industry. The great majority of the world's soybeans are processed into soy oil and soybean meal (or cake). The oil is degummed to remove the lecithin – an ubiquitous food additive – and usually refined, bleached, partially hydrogenated and deodorized before being used for an big array of popular products, including salad and cooking oils, shortenings, and margarine. Soybean oil is also used in 'environmental friendly' inks, paints, varnishes, soaps and for bio-diesel. Soybeans can produce at least twice as much protein per area unit than any other major vegetable or grain crop.[474]

Soybeans were first domesticated in the eastern part of North China a little more than three thousand years ago. It was one of the five main plant foods of China along with rice, wheat, barley and millet. It was used whole or fermented for tofu, soya sauce and similar foods. The idea of crushing soybeans to separate them into oil and meal is a relatively recent development in the long history of the human use of soybeans. Even in China, rape seed oil has been more important than soybean oil. Originally, one of the limiting factors for expanding soybean oil production was the limited use of the remaining product, the cake. When the Chinese started large scale cultivation of soybeans, the oil cake was exported as a fertilizer to Japan.[475] In an article from 1933, it was recognized that "the demand for the soybean cake is the limiting factor for the soybean industry".[476]

Henry Ford took a keen interest in the soybean and in the "marriage between farming and industry". In 1934, Ford cars were finished with a soybean lacquer and soy bean plastic was used for horn buttons, gear shift lever balls, light switch handles. The Ford Company built a US$5 million plant in Detroit to make soybean products. Ford was so enthusiastic about soybeans that he even composed whole dinners made of soybeans, such as the menu (below) from August 1934 where thirty wary reporters were treated by Ford at the Chicago Century of Progress Fair.

Soybean extravaganza
Tomato juice seasoned with soybean sauce.
Salted soybeans.
Celery stuffed with soybean cheese.
Purée of soybean.
Soybean crackers.
Soybean croquettes with tomato sauce.
Buttered green soybeans.
Pineapple ring with soybean cheese [tofu] and soybean dressing.
Soybean bread with soybean butter.
Apple pie (soybean crust).

Cocoa with soybean milk.
Soybean coffee.
Assorted soybean cookies.
Soybean cakes.
Assorted soybean candy.[477]

Before World War II, the United States imported more than 40% of its edible fats and oils. Disruption of trade routes during the war resulted in a rapid expansion of soybean acreage as the country looked for alternatives to these imports.[478] During the 1940s and 1950s major advances were made in soy oil refining, improving its use for cooking and salad oils, margarine, and shortening, and for the first time in history, the majority of the world's soybeans were crushed to yield oil and meal. The expansion of the specialized livestock production increased demand for soybean meal, which increased faster than demand for soy oil, keeping soy oil prices low.[479] After the mid-1950s, United States became the world's top supplier of soy oil and meal.[480] Lately, soybean production has expanded very rapidly in Latin America. Argentina went from producing just 1,000 tons of soybeans 1961 to 51 million tons in 2012, while in Brazil it went from some 300,000 tons per year in the 1960s to the bumper crop of almost 75 million tons in 2011. Soybeans are of such a fundamental importance in Brazil that in Mato Grosso land prices are quoted in bags of soybeans, which fluctuate with world market prices. The United States, Brazil and Argentina together produce almost four fifths of the world's soybeans, and soybean is the third most valuable crop in the world, after rice and wheat. But its role in international trade is even more important. A staggering 165 million tons (that is 24 kg for each human being) of soybeans, soy oil and soybean cake were internationally traded 2011, worth US$91billion, making soybeans the most important globally traded crop, with a value that equals that of wheat and maize combined. Half of the world's pigs – 500 million – now live in China and they are very largely fed soybean meal imported from Argentina and Brazil.[481] China imported some US$30 billion worth of soybeans in 2011. Very little of the soybean crop is directly used as human food.

In 1966, soy oil surpassed butter to become the world's leading edible oil or fat. In 1982 palm oil was in second place worldwide, sunflower seed oil in third, butter (fat content) in fourth, and rapeseed (canola) oil in fifth, all far behind soy oil.[482] Now palm oil has taken over; of the total vegetable oil production of 161 million tons 2012/13 palm oil and palm kernel oil (both from the same oil palm) contributed almost 40% and soybeans 27%. Two thirds of all vegetable oil now comes from those two crops. As we can see from table 1 (below) rapeseed and sunflower oil also play an promintent role in the global vegetable oil supply.[483]

Table 1. Major Oil Crops 2012/13

Oil crop	Share of production
Palm & palm kernel	40%
Soybean	27%
Rapeseed	15%
Sunflower seed	9%
Cottonseed	3%
Peanut	3%
Coconut	2%
Olive	2%

Source: USDA FAS, Major Vegetable Oils: World Supply and Distribution

In comparison total world production of butter was some 9 million tons,[484] which is more than the total production of coconut oil and olive oil, but still relatively marginal. Today, an average of 1.3 kg butter and ghee per person is consumed in the world, intake ranging from almost nothing in China to 2.7 kg in India and an average of 2.8 kg in developed countries.[485] In addition, almost 6 million tons of lard and 7 million tons of tallow are produced. Animal fat plays a minor role in supplying us with pure fat, around twelve percent, but still provides us with more than one third of all dietary fat because, in comparison with most plants, many animal foods contain a high proportion of fat.

Rapeseed, sunflower and peanut are often integrated in crop rotations with other crops. Rapeseed is mainly produced by China, Canada and the European Union. Relatively small quantities are globally traded and exports are totally dominated by Canada. The main producers of sunflower seeds are Russia, Ukraine, Argentina and the European Union, with Ukraine having more than half of global exports.[486] China produces almost half of the peanuts in the world, followed by India, Nigeria and United States.[487] While there are some large coconut plantations, this remains primarily a smallholder crop. The major producing country, and exporter, is the Philippines. In the past copra was collected by traders going from port to port in the Pacific Ocean but South Pacific production is now much diminished, with the exception of Papua New Guinea, the Solomon Islands and Vanuatu. As a result of falling prices of vegetable oils, increasing oil prices and preferences for renewable energy and other resources, there is a renaissance in the industrial use of vegetable oils They are used as environmentally benign oils in machinery and chain saws, for paints and not the least for bio-diesel. I will discuss this transformation later.

I discussed earlier how canning and white flour came about through competitions for innovation. The same is true of margarine. Emperor Napoleon III of France offered a prize to anyone who could make a satisfactory alternative to butter, suitable for use by the navy and the lower classes. The pharmacist Hippolyte Mège-Mouriès invented a substance he called margarine because of the pearl like white sheen (*margaron* means pearl in Greek[488]). He patented the concept in 1869 but had little commercial success and in 1871 he sold the patent to the Dutch company Jurgens, which later became Unilever.[489] The Dutch entrepreneurs realized that if margarine were going to become a substitute for butter, it needed to look like butter, so they began dyeing margarine a buttery yellow. We are used to margarine being a vegetable fat but the principal raw material in the original formulation of margarine was beef fat, tallow. Shortages in beef fat supply combined with technical advances led to commercial margarine being produced from a combination of animal fats and hardened and unhardened vegetable oils between 1900 and 1920. By 1945, original margarine had almost completely disappeared from the market. Margarine production involves many processing steps and chemicals including nickel, hydrogen and hexane. Because of the complicated process, as well as the marketing needs margarine production quickly became something reserved for big business.[490]

The competition between butter and margarine has continued throughout the twentieth century. In the United States, dairy firms succeeded in getting legislation passed to prohibit the coloring of margarine. In response, the margarine companies distributed the margarine together with a packet of yellow dye! The product was placed in a bowl and the dye mixed in with a spoon. This took some time and effort and the result was often unappealing, with uneven striped colors. In 1950, the United States government repealed the heavy margarine tax, and the market continued to grow as individual states reversed their bans on colored margarine.[491] It is an ironic twist that today the production of margarine is based on vegetable oils that have by-products which are excellent as feed for animals, also for dairy cows – the producers of butter. In terms of production butter and margarine are therefore mutually supportive rather than being competitors. As a result, increased consumption of vegetable oils is likely to also promote more animal fat and meat production, unless the industry find ways to convert the secondary products (such as soybean cake) into human food.

Fat gives us a lot of energy and the highest yields of fat come from tropical crops as these crops prosper under energy abundant conditions, i.e. when there is a lot of sun. In colder climates the fat content of crops is very low, which is why people traditionally have relied on pigs, seals, fish or cows to concentrate other feed into fats for them. Butter from grass-fed cows and fat from pigs fed on a combination of waste and grain can reportedly produce as much fat per hectare as soybeans or rape seed under English conditions.[492] The animal sources of fat have always been very important in Europe. But today, the ecological footstep of Europeans has extended to the tropical rain-forests which now produce palm oil and soy beans for oil and fodder. The animals provide a smaller part of the dietary fat of Europeans at present. Clearly, this is a result of the global trade in agriculture commodities undertaken solely on profit basis and has nothing to do with health, biology or ecology.

14

Crunchy

'We've got chicken every Sunday and the preacher comes around', sings Dolly Parton in *Chicken every Sunday*, showing that hers is not a bad family. Historically livestock was fed on grass, silage and hay, all crops that cannot be eaten by humans. Small quantities of pigs and chicken, which largely eat the same foods as humans and don't grow well on grass, were raised on waste products or sought their own feed in the farmer's yard, the thicket or the manure heap – a very popular place for chickens. This meant that pork and chicken were rare and expensive in most cultures, to be eaten on the day of rest. Today chicken in nuggets, wings or strips are munched 24/7. Americans eat 45 kg of poultry each year, most of which is chicken; Brazilian consumption increased from 11 kg in the late 1980s to 39 kg today and in China it went from one kg to ten in the same period.[493] There is hardly any other food that has increased its market share at such a speed in such a short period. Especially not one that has been around us for ages. Many explain this increase in the consumption of chicken by consumer preference for white, as opposed to red, meat which is based on health reasons. There is scant evidence for this. The main reasons for chicken's success are much simpler. It is the price, its ease of preparation and even the ease of consumption. I don't know how many of my readers that have tried a real village chicken that has scratched its food from the ground, with strong, long legs and not much meat on the body. If you compare that with a typical industrial broiler (special breeds for meat) chicken you will notice many differences. One of the most striking is that the flesh of the broiler is very tender. Another is that it doesn't have much taste, making it a good carrier of whatever seasoning or sauce is in fashion. These are two important features of an industrial food.

The chicken is assumed to have evolved from the jungle fowl (*Gallus gallus*) and was domesticated in either India or Southwest Asia. The chicken was a sacred animal in some cultures; the ever-watchful hen was a symbol of nurturing and fertility and eggs hung in Egyptian temples to ensure a bountiful river flood. Roman armies brought chickens along as forecasters. Their behavior was carefully observed before a battle; if they showed a good appetite victory was likely. According to Cicero, when one contingent of birds refused to eat before a sea battle in 249 BC, an angry consul threw them overboard. That didn't help at all as they went on to lose the battle. The Romans also had a good appetite for chickens; they invented the omelet and stuffing birds for cooking. Roman farmers developed inventive methods to fatten the birds – some used wheat bread soaked in wine, others cumin seeds, barley and even lizard fat.[494]

The chicken has come a long way to become the centerpiece of the second largest fast food chain in the world – KFC – with 18,875 outlets in 118 countries and territories in December 2013.[495] As mentioned before when talking about maize and beef, the widespread availability of chemical fertilizers allowed farmers to specialize in grain production and the proportion of land planted to grain and the yields increased substantially. This in turn allowed for even more mechanization, so grain production needed very little labor. The result of this was that grains became very, very cheap from a historical perspective. And new uses needed to be found for this grain, as humans can only eat so much of it. Some farmers took up the opportunity to specialize in animal production. Chickens are well adapted to eating seeds (which is what grains are), like many other birds, and they are very efficient in transforming grains into animal protein; into chicken wings, drumsticks, nuggets or whatever other innovations the food industry comes up with. Cheap grain has been an essential component in the chicken success story, the others were breeding, feed composition, mechanization and logistics.

Prior to the 1920s, chickens were mainly produced by farms having layers for eggs. The male chicken could be slaughtered at birth, provided that you could see the difference between the male and the female chicks, which is very difficult. Otherwise they were mostly raised for meat. Today 300 million male chickens of egg-laying hens are killed in the European Union each year as soon as they hatch, because it is uneconomical to raise them for meat[496] since meat from chickens specialized for meat production is cheaper. Many of them, and their American siblings, go to 'Instantaneous Mechanical Destruction' which is a technical way of saying that they are ground up alive.[497] Hens that no longer lay eggs also pose a disposal problem. In February 2003, the Ward Egg Ranch in San Diego County, California tossed more than 30,000 'spent' laying hens alive into a wood-chipping machine to dispose of them. Despite outcry from a horrified public, the district attorney declined to prosecute the owners of the farm, as the owners were following professional advice.[498]

Celia Steele of Sussex County, Delaware, is often credited as the pioneer of the commercial broiler industry. In 1923, she raised a flock of 500 chicks intending to sell them for meat. The business was so profitable that, by 1926, she built a hen house with a capacity for 10,000 birds.[499] Chickens, just like humans, depend on sunlight to produce vitamin D and they got sick from being locked up. For this and other reasons these early specialist growers did not keep the chickens in the houses all the time, they were allowed to roam free in the yard during the day and were brought back into the chicken house at night. The chickens would feed on worms and other insects in the yard and would be fed maize when they went back into the chicken house. Once farmers realized they could simply add vitamin D and other vitamins and medications to the chicken feed, they no longer had to let the chickens outdoors.[500] Meanwhile, technology for automatic feeding had been invented.[501] Now, the industrialization of both broilers and laying hens could proceed apace. The breeding of special hybrids into broilers and mechanization of the whole slaughtering process helped to reduce prices and increase volumes.

By 1952, broilers surpassed farm chickens as the main source of chicken meat in the United States.[502] Chicken consumption in the United States surpassed pork consumption in 1985 and beef consumption in 1992.[503] Almost all farms had chickens in 1900, while hundred year later only one farm out of twenty had them. In just over 50 years, the number of chickens produced in United States increased fourteen fold, while the number of farms producing chickens dropped from 1.6 million to just 27,000, a 98% decline.[504] Half of all broilers now come from farms producing more than 700,000 chicks per year.[505] According to the Council for Agricultural Science and Technology a flock of broilers generally consists of about 20,000 birds in a 'grow-out' house that measures 400 feet by and 40 feet with a minimum space per bird of one-half square feet. Farmers (it is debatable if the word 'farmer' is appropriate for someone who runs a land-less operation that converts maize into chicken meat) would rather build several houses than bigger houses, as the economies of scale are already reached at that size, and bigger flocks increase the risk of a major disease outbreak.

Antibiotics and anticoccidials are routinely used to prevent and treat disease; as chickens most certainly will be sick from being raised in such an environment, medicines are mixed into the feed – just to be on the safe side. Many contend that this puts humans at risk as bacterial strains develop stronger and stronger resistances. Excess nutrients, nitrogen and phosphorous are a major problem for large scale chicken production, even more so at it is increasingly disjointed from the feed production. Some 40% of American broilers are grown on farms that have no crop acreage, and thus no good use for the manure.[506]

Poultry in the United States are fed ground maize to supply energy and soybean meal to provide protein. Vitamins and minerals are also added in their feed. The improvement in the conversion of feed to meat has been a key factor for the success of the poultry industry. In 1925 a chicken took 112 days to reach 1.1 kg live weight and it needed 4.70 kg of feed for each kg of weight. In 2006, a chicken reached 2.5 kg weight in just 48 days and the breeder would have used less than two kg of feed for each kg of chicken.[507] The shorter cycles are of major relevance, they allow much more to be produced with the same infrastructure, lowering capital costs per kg: the shorter cycles mean chicken producers can take a profit seven times a year instead of three. In a world of quarterly capitalism that is a major consideration.

The link between expansion of chickens and that of soybeans is very strong. To produce one kg of chicken meat, three quarter of a kg of soybeans is used in feed in Europe. Most European chicken production is fed soybeans from Brazil or Argentina, while only two percent of the European farm land is used for protein crops. More than 90% of all soybeans in the Americas are genetically modified, so the recent chicken expansion is totally built on genetically modified soybeans.[508] When you eat a broiler today in essence you are eating genetically modified maize and soybeans.

In 1950, most of the American broiler producers were independent, today a very limited number of 'integrators' control most of the production. The integrator provides a grower with the chicks, feed, medication and technical advisors to supervise farm production. The company retains ownership of the birds and expects producers to grow their flocks under very specific management programs, often requiring growers to make expensive investments in housing facilities and equipment. At the end of the growing period, the company picks up the flock and pays the farmer by the pound. A recent USDA survey estimated that, in 2006, there were more than twelve thousand poultry farms with an average debt of over US$204,000.[509] The relationship between the giant integrators and the farmers is not always harmonious. Farm Aid describes how the large integrator Tyson Foods passes all its costs onto the farmers:

> When Karen and Mitchell got married in 1987, they decided to build two chicken houses to grow broiler chickens. They thought raising chickens would be a way for Karen to work while raising their three children at home. In 1990, the Crutchfields added a third chicken house, and in 1999 and 2000 they added three more houses in order to raise poultry for Tyson Foods, Inc. In the 25 years that Karen and

Mitchell raised poultry for Tyson, their compensation rate remained steady at under 5 cents per pound, yet they were required to continually make improvements to and modernize their facilities, keeping them in a constant state of debt. Last year, Tyson required the couple to install new computerized blackout houses, an update that would have cost upwards of US$300,000. "They control what you do and we finally said no," Karen recalls. "At that point, the cost it would have taken to update would have been like buying the farm again."[510]

Killing and processing chickens is dangerous and unpleasant work. Workers in this trade in the United States make less money than in other industries and are injured at twice the rate. One out of six poultry workers is either injured or becomes ill from their work every year. One common injury is 'neighbor cuts' where workers unintentionally cut the person next to them due to overcrowding. If the life of the chicken producers and slaughterhouse workers in the hands of integrators is hard, the life of a broiler is certainly harder. During the summer season the processing plant can get so hot that chickens being hung can suffocate in less than one minute.[511] Intensively reared chickens are selected for their very fast growth rate. They spend much of their time lying down and many of them suffer from lameness. Representatives of the chicken industry say that modern broilers don't even want to browse and scratch outside. Selective breeding has made the broilers so docile that even if they are given access to outdoor space they prefer to stay close to the mechanized trough, awaiting the next delivery of feed. The rapid growth also puts a strain on their hearts and lungs. In the United Kingdom alone, millions of chickens die in their sheds from heart failure each year. Around 20 million chickens per year are already dead by the time they arrive at European Union slaughterhouses.[512]

There is still some small-scale chicken production in poor countries. In Bangladesh and Ethiopia, essentially all chickens are from small producers. In Southern Africa, 85% of all households keep one or a few chickens and these mostly belong to women, providing them with a much needed income. But in countries such as Brazil and Thailand, chicken production has industrialized along the lines of United States, and they have become major exporters. Brazil has taken the world lead in chicken exports, although the United States is still the largest producer.[513] At the beginning of this century three quarters of global chicken production was in the hands of agri-business companies. In the United States, Tyson process 41 million chickens per week, the PHW Group in Germany has a 40% market share, 70% of the market for chicken breeding and control 80% of the market vaccines for poultry production.[514] Seara in Brazil has thirty two plants which slaughter about 1.7 million chickens daily.[515]

As with other global 'commodities', chicken is subject to trade politics. In 2008, the United States' exports of chicken products to China rose by 12.3 percent to 584,300 tons, and in the first half of 2009, about 305,600 tons of United States chicken products landed in China, making up 89 percent of China's total chicken product imports. Investigations by the Chinese Ministry of Commerce concluded that the United States chicken industry had dumped broiler products and caused 'substantial damage' to China's domestic industry. In September 2010, China slapped anti-dumping duties on imports of United States chicken products for five years.[516]

The development of broiler production was paralleled by developments in the processing, marketing and consumer side. As the Smithsonian Magazine says: "chicken farming has been a vast national experiment in supply-side gastro-economics".[517] The birds themselves are torn into pieces and reconfigured in a multitude of products such as nuggets and strips. In 1930 the, then, 40-year-old Harland Sanders – who never was a real Colonel – was operating a service station in Corbin, Kentucky, and it was there that he began cooking for hungry travelers who stopped in for gas. He invented what's called 'home meal replacement' – selling complete meals to busy, time-strapped families. He called it, "Sunday Dinner, Seven Days a Week." In 1955, confident of the quality of his fried chicken, Sanders devoted himself to developing the chicken franchising business, Kentucky Fried Chicken. Less than 10 years later, Sanders had more than 600 KFC franchises in the United States and Canada. Today, KFC, together with Pizza Hut and Taco Bell, is part of Yum! Brands, Inc., the world's leading restaurant company with over 40,000 restaurants and 1.5 million people employed in more than 125 countries and territories.[518]

Lately chicken wings have gained popularity and in the United States 1.23 billion chicken wings were eaten during Super Bowl Weekend in 2013. The National Chicken Council laments "A chicken has two wings, and chicken companies are not able to produce wings without the rest of the chicken. Therefore, the supply of wings is limited by the total number of chickens produced." Surprisingly there are no genetically modified chicken on the market. A four winged chicken ready for Super Bowl should not be a tall order – or why not six wings? Chicken breeders have, so far, stayed away from genetic modification, mostly because of fear of a consumer backlash. With the publication of the full chicken genome in 2004, all the breeders started investing heavily in genomics research. The breeding is extremely concentrated as a result of high research expenditure and the capital intensive nature of the chicken business. Did I say 'all the breeders?', there are not that many left; by the late 2000s only three sizable breeding groups remained for broilers: Cobb-Vantress, Aviagen, and Groupe Grimaud.[519] Cobb-Vantress has been owned by Tyson Food since 1994.[520] Two breeders control 94% of the supply of laying hens.[521]

All these developments have had profound impact on the main character, *Gallus gallus*. As the needs and industrial logic of producing eggs and chicken meat production are quite different, the chicken has been split in an even more dramatic way than cattle. In just half a century breeding has created two very different chickens, with totally different uses and efficiencies. A typical laying hen needs 1.99 kg of feed to produce 1 kg of eggs (and she will produce one egg per day), while a broiler hen will need 5.22 kg of feed for the same amount of egg. But the broiler is far superior in converting feed to meat. Broiler male chicks need 40 days to reach a weight of 2.2 kg while the males of the layers need 98 days to reach 1.8 kg. And, to produce one kg of live weight the broiler needs only 1.7 kg of feed, while the laying hen needs 3.8 kg.[522] Through selection and breeding, the breeders have thus created two different specialist chickens, each one incredibly efficient for its special purpose. Unfortunately both are less efficient than their common ancestor in being a chicken.

It is in light of this development we should see that chicken consumption increased five fold in a hundred years in the USA and ten fold from 1961 to 2009 globally,[523] while beef consumption has been more or less stable.[524] Globally diners still eat more pork than chicken 114m tons a year of pork compared to 106m tons for poultry, but chicken consumption is growing faster – by 2.5% a year. Chicken is also much more of a international traded commodity than beef or pork; some 13.3m tons per year are shipped internationally compared with 8.6m tons of beef and 7.2m tons of pork.[525]

The chicken industry provided a blueprint for the industrialization of livestock, in a similar way as sugar cane and iceberg lettuce set the blueprint for field crops and horticulture. More recently, the aquaculture industry has started developing along the lines pioneered by poultry producers. While shoppers can chose between salmon produced in Alaska, Scotland, Chile and Norway suggesting a link with locality, in reality there is hardly any difference between them. They are all raised using the same technologies and the same fish stock.

What all these models share in common is that they cut out small farmers and traders and substantially increase the use of bought-in inputs: feeds, medicines and breeding stock as well as knowledge. Production sites are normally located where feed, the major input is cheap, i.e. close to harbors. The production model bears a close resemblance with assembly industries, and there is little difference between production in one place and the other. The notion of place or culture in our foods has totally lost any meaning under these conditions: its sole purpose is to be consumed.

What is particularly disturbing with the commercialization of animal production is that it doesn't take into account that animals are living sentient beings. Through the commodification of animals, live or dead, their welfare and their ability and right to exercise their innate behaviors have become externalities, side factors of production, in the same way as the landscape is for plant production. It is this commodification that makes it possible to create those horrific 'production units' and the handling of animals as already dead goods in transport or slaughter. Of course, societies pass animal welfare regulations to get rid of the worst cases of abuses, and this is also in the interest of the industry itself as otherwise people might stop eating its products. But by and large, in industrial animal keeping, treating animals as living beings, as our evolutionary partners, is very much a secondary consideration and not a primary objective. The Roman agriculture expert Columella writes that after work the oxen should be groomed and their backs and legs massaged. He also recommends giving them wine, but not more than half a liter.[526] I am not sure this is representative of the relationship between man and beast in old times; I suspect that humans have caused many animals undue harm all through history. But the industrial way of raising animals is a system built on disrespect, covering up its cruelty under the veil of efficiency and science, making the abnormal normal.

Part III: Secondi

As I went walking, I saw a sign there,
And on the sign there, it said 'private property'
But on the other side it didn't say nothing,
That side was made for you and me
Woody Guthrie[a]

---

[a] One of many versions of a verse of the legendary song 'This land is your land'.

15

The global plate

Let's look at the ingredients of the global plate, what is actually produced and consumed globally.[a] The total agriculture area 2009 was 4.897 billion hectares. Of this 1.387 billion hectares were used for arable crops, 0.150 billion hectares for permanent crops (tree crops, berries and grasslands on arable land) and 3.360 billion hectares for pastures. If the land were divided equally between everyone on the planet, each one of us would have around 1,800 square meters of arable land, producing just over a ton of crops. This includes the production of animal feed and industrial crops, seeds etc., so you would not get to eat the whole lot. Half of that land would be used to grow wheat, maize, rice and soybeans. Of these crops, you would eat most of the rice, half of the wheat, a little maize and a few soybeans. The rest would go to feedstuff or industry. You would have tubers on 50 square meters and about the same area of cotton. A few oil palms would tower over your plot, together with two coconut trees and a cashew, a mango and an apple tree. Probably you would grow a few coffee trees and one or two cocoa trees under the shade of the bigger trees. Not to forget a rubber tree, for your tires, boots or condoms. Bananas, tobacco, onions and tomato will share another 50 square meters. The less productive oil crops, rape seed and sunflower would need quite a lot of space. In terms of the harvest, sugar cane is the heaviest load, one fourth of your output would be cane, which you can process to your sugar, or perhaps make ethanol for your car – but it will not drive you far. You would only get some 20 liters of ethanol even if you converted all this cane to ethanol, with nothing left over for your candy. From all that cotton, you would only get some three kg of cotton lint.

In addition to your plot of arable land, you would have some 4,800 square meters of mixed pasture for keeping cows or sheep (one cow for every five people and one sheep for seven are the global averages).

---

[a] The annex (Which I call 'the digestive') contains more detailed data, and some comments on the sources and methods I used for these calculations.

Some of it would be wet, but most would be arid. Together with your neighbor you would raise a pig (seven people share a pig) on crop residues and some of the maize. If you like chicken, you would use a large part of the maize and soybeans to raise three chickens; they would also scratch for food under the trees.[527] If you were a vegan, you could eat most of the soybeans and perhaps convert 100 kg of the maize to ethanol, giving you another 40 liters to drive.[528] In addition, food could be foraged from the forest and there is fish, algae and seafood from the sea. Enjoy your share.

Table 2 The global plot

Crop	M² in my plot	Production (kg)
Wheat	308	96
Maize	253	125
Rice	233	103
Barley, sorghum, millet, oats, rye and other cereals	225	39
Rapeseed, sunflower, oil palm, groundnuts and other oil crops	197	67
Soybeans	150	11
Beans, lentils, peas and other pulses	117	10
Cassava, potatoes, sweet potatoes and other tubers	78	113
Grapes, bananas, plantains, apples, mangoes, oranges and other fruits	64	69
Tomatoes, onions, watermelons, cabbages and other vegetables	56	111
Seed cotton	50	0
Sugar cane and sugar beet	45	300
Coffee, cocoa, tea and tobacco	40	4
Rubber, natural	14	0
The rest	117	2
Sum	**1,888**	**1,100**

Source: Own calculations based on FAOSTAT

A lot happens between global production in the field and global consumption in our homes (or wherever we consume our food). It is no easy task to trace food all the way along the chain. And data can look quite different depending on whether we discuss land use, calories, energy, protein or another indicator. As you can see from above maize, wheat, rice, soybeans and barley are the five most widely grown crops. Together they use 53% of the land (the annex contains a list of the top 60 crops). If we calculate the five top crops by weight we end up with sugar cane, maize, rice, wheat and potatoes. Together they represent 53% of the total harvest, sugar cane alone accounts for 22%.

We may not think much about how many kg of food we eat, but nowadays many think about calories. In 2012, the crop land produced some 14.5 quadrillion (that is 14,500,000,000,000,000) calories corresponding to 5,600 calories per person per day. This is considerably more than double the calorific needs of a population of 7 billion people. The top ten crops for calorie supply, in descending order, are maize, wheat, rice, soybeans, sugar cane, palm oil, barley, cassava, rapeseed[a] and groundnuts (peanuts). Maize contributes 22% of total calories, and the top five together two thirds. Of these crops, most of the maize and barley, and a considerable proportion of the wheat, are used as animal feed. A very small proportion of the soybeans produced are processed directly into food (such as tofu) or eaten as they are; instead they are processed into two parts, oil for human consumption and soy meal for animal feed. Rape seed and groundnuts (also oil crops) are used in a similar way, but a third of groundnuts are eaten as food. If we look at calories per hectare on a global scale, the two sugar crops, beet and cane produce the most calories (in the range of 40 million) per hectare (that is the annual calorific needs of more than 40 people), followed by palm oil, cassava, banana and maize.

Total global protein production is 418 million tons, this equals 162 gram per person per day, and is more than three times the nutritional needs of the world's population. Soybean is the most important protein crop; it produces 21% of all protein, followed by maize, wheat, rice, barley, rapeseed, seed cotton, potatoes, sunflower seed and groundnuts. The top four, soybeans, maize, wheat and rice contribute more than two thirds of all protein. Also here, a considerable part of the protein is used for animal feed, almost all the protein from soybeans, rapeseed, seed cotton and sunflower seed is fed to animals.

---

[a] Often called canola in North America.

Some crops are mainly industrial. The best example is cotton, a crop that takes up as much land as rape seed, approximately 3% of all arable land. The oil from cotton goes into the food supply and the seed cake is used as feed. The rest of cotton is not edible, we cannot digest the fiber. The same area – and cotton is often grown on fertile land – could be used for growing grain which could feed 500 million people.[a] There is also energy in various parts of the grains which we normally don't consume or cannot digest easily. These products are mostly fed to animals. There are also other industrial processes which convert maize and sugar cane into plastics, soybeans to printing ink and potatoes and cassava for starch. A considerable part of a few crops go to biofuels. Other crops produce no calories or nothing useful from a purely nutritional perspective, for example tea, tobacco and coffee.

Seed has to be taken aside from many crops, where the seed is the same as the produce, for example grains, beans and peas; the proportion needed ranges from 1 percent to up to 10 percent (and even more on land with low yields). Of the potato crop some 10 percent has to be saved for seed potatoes, while cassava is multiplied by stem cuttings and no seeds need to be kept aside. Then there is direct waste as well as losses in the processing. Grain yields are measured for the threshed product, but when the grain is milled, the bran and other parts are often not included in the final product but are mostly used as animal feed. A good rice mill can achieve a paddy-to-rice conversion rate of up to 72% but smaller, inefficient mills often struggle to achieve 60%. The waste at the food processing and retail industry levels are often reasonably documented as it is in the interest of those operating the mills and shops to quantify their wastes, and possibly reduce them. At the consumer level however, waste is poorly documented. I discuss waste more in chapter twenty-one.

A substantial part of the crops we produce are fed to animals. One third of the grain produced is fed to livestock, more than half of the oats, barley and maize. One quarter of tubers and most of the soybean crop, most of the cotton seed and, in general, the residual products from oil crops. All this is not lost but enters the food chain again (see more in chapter twenty-two) as meat, eggs or milk. In addition to these calculations, food is produced from permanent grasslands as well as from fisheries, hunting and wild collection. Let's try a summary.

---

[a] 35 million hectares could produce some 122 million ton of wheat, which could feed at least 488 million people (250 kg wheat per year equals 2,600 kcal per day).

Table 3 From farm to table

Item	Note	kcal/per capita/day
Gross crop production per capita		+5600
Used as seed	1	-130
Waste on farm & post-harvest	2	-560
Used as feed	3	-1543
From livestock products	4	+510
Biofuel	5	-480
Other industrial uses	6	-200
Waste in food processing	7	-400
Food from other sources		+50
Total food available		**2,847**

Sources:
1. Calculated from FAOSTAT data for the main 20 crops + 10% for the rest of the corps.
2. Based on FAO (2001), Global Food Losses and Food Waste, probably an overestimate.
3. Calculated from FAOSTAT data for the main 20 crops + 20% of the rest of the crops.
4. FAOSTAT. Some of this is from grazing and some comes from cultivated feed.
5. Calculated from United States Energy Information Administration (EIA) data on amounts of biofuel produced and the raw materials used. No calories are counted for the feed value of residual products as they come into the food system via livestock products.
6. Guesstimate, bio-plastics, starch, medicines, cosmetics and fiber.
7. Based on FAO (2011), Global Food Losses and Food Waste.
8. Wild fish, game and other wild collection. Own estimate and FAOSTAT

This coincides more or less with FAO data on food availability 2009. The figure is an average for all individuals on the planet, including children and the elderly. Small children don't eat much and old people also eat considerably less. By and large, even with a wastage rate of ten percent, there is more than enough food to feed the global population, *if* it was evenly distributed. Which it is not. But if food were evenly distributed, what would the global menu look like? The table below gives an idea. People consume some 1.8 kg of food per day (675kg per year). Looking at calories in our food, 46% came from cereals (with rice and wheat contributing 19% each), 18% from animal products, 10% from vegetable oils, 8% from sugar, 5% from root crops, 3% respectively from vegetables, fruits and alcoholic beverages and 5% from other (fish & sea food, algae and pulses). In terms of protein and fat, animal products play a much bigger role, contributing 45% of all dietary fat and 39% of all protein.

Table 4 Global food supply per capita per day 2009

	grams	kcal	%kcal
Wheat	181	532	19%
Rice	146	536	19%
Maize	47	141	5%
Cereals, other	28	82	3%
Starchy roots (potatoes, cassava etc.)	167	136	5%
Sugar and sweeteners	64	224	8%
Beans and peas	18	62	2%
Soybeans and groundnuts	20	56	2%
Vegetable oils	32	277	10%
Vegetables	361	87	3%
Fruits	200	92	3%
Alcoholic beverages	98	67	2%
Meat	115	230	8%
Animal fats	9	60	2%
Milk	239	134	5%
Fish, seafood	51	33	1%
Other	82	100	3%
Total	**1,857**	**2,849**	**100%**

Source: FAOSTAT, see details in annex.:

To make this more vivid let's try to make a day's diet out of it. Perhaps it would look like this:

> For breakfast you drink tea or coffee with sugar, eat three slices of bread (or cereal based porridge) upon which you use a vegetable oil based margarine and a sweet fruit-based condiment.

For lunch you eat tortillas, and two potatoes (or yams, cassava or sweet potatoes), with tomatoes and onions fried in vegetable oil. Once a week you also have a fish.

For dinner you eat boiled rice with a stew of beans, cabbage and a small piece of meat. You round off with a banana, an apple, an orange or half a mango.

In the evening you drink a very small soda or a beer and snack on roasted groundnuts or soybeans.

But the average food supply varies greatly geographically. The food supply per Indian is 2,321 kcal while it is 3,688 for the average American. The average Indian gets almost two thirds of their calories from cereals, pulses and root crops while these crops only contribute a quarter of the calories of the American. Sugar and fats contribute almost 40% of the American's calories but just 21% of the Indian's. Animal products, including fish, make up 28% of the calorie supply of an American but only 9% for the average Indian. Clearly, the agriculture systems that produce those two diets are very different and the ecological footprints of the diets are also very different.

Since 1961 the average global calorific intake has increased by 29%, from 2,189 to 2,831.[529] [530] Based on the changes in diets a number of messages can be formulated which give quite different signals – and newspaper headlines. *Total* global meat consumption increased by 300% between 1961 and 2009. But the *quantity of meat per person* increased by 110% while *the proportion of meat in the diet* increased by 63% in the same period.

Consumption of vegetables increased a lot more than meat consumption, by 300% per person. Vegetables are still rather insignificant as a source of food energy representing only 2% of total calorie intake. And although fruits and vegetables do not contain much energy or proteins, they are important for nutrition because of their content of vitamins and other important substances.

The most remarkable dietary change is the increase in consumption of vegetable oil which increased eight fold over the same period, and doubled its proportion in the average global diet. These oils now supply more calories than meat. This is a strong trend that deserves much more attention. Not the least since almost all the increase comes from oil palm and soybeans.

Fish consumption per person has also doubled. Because of the decline in fisheries, aquaculture is rising rapidly and farmed fish has just overtaken captured fish in terms of its share in the global diet. There is still more fish pulled out of the ocean than from ponds, but some of the captured fishery is used for industry – and also as feed for cultivated fish. Most spectacular is the development of aquaculture in China. The Chinese not only eat more meat than before, they have also increased their fish consumption, especially of farmed fish. The average Chinese eats 24 kilograms of farmed fish and 6 kilograms of wild fish, compared to the average for the rest of the world of 3.5 kilograms of farmed fish and 10 kilograms of wild fish.[531]

Another important piece of information is *where* the food is produced. One of the most important developments of the last hundred years, and particularly since the 1950s, is the increased disconnection between where people live and where food is produced. In 2011, 14% of the global grain production was internationally traded. Almost 30% of the sugar crossed a national border, 10% of the meat (chicken is the most traded meat), 7% of the milk, and more than one third of the fish. Half of the vegetable oil that is produced is exported and almost two thirds of the oil cake.[532] This trade is both a result and a driver of the global division of labor and the continued industrialization of food which has lost its connections with the landscape and the culture of where it is produced and where it is consumed. With this basic information of global food production, let us turn to the choices we have and that we make.

16

Whose choice?

As long as ecology and economy meant more or less the same thing our eating habits were closely tied to local patterns of food production. The modern idea of food consumption as a choice that is independent of local production would have been seen as surreal by our ancestors who relied on what could be produced and stored locally for the overwhelming majority of their food supply. Locality and food availability also influenced cooking and food preparation. People in central America cook their maize with lime and serve it with beans; this way of preparing maize makes the niacin available and the combination with beans complements protein deficiencies in both maize and beans. Similarly, fermenting soybeans makes them an ideal complement to rice, which is the staple food of those cultures where soya has been fermented.[533] After a few generations these foods became traditional and something people 'liked'. Similarly, most religious prescriptions about food can be traced back to either ecological or social conditions. Once established food preferences and taboos are quite strong and are often maintained even when their original *raison d'être* is long gone.

It is a paradox that while our diet and agricultural production methods have both changed a lot, there have been very few changes in the crops and animals that we use. Certainly, those that have been domesticated have been developed by intentional breeding, sometimes out of all recognition and sometimes just by accident. And there have been some shake ups, such as at the Columbian exchange, but, by and large, the characteristics of the main plants and livestock have determined most subsequent developments. We have brought very few new crops or animals into production in the last few hundred years. This cannot be because of lack of choice, after all there are millions of plants to select from. It is a very strong example of what is called 'path dependency'. Path dependency describes how earlier developments and choices largely determine later choices. The cost of taking another development trajectory is very high. For instance, if I have built a house with a certain design, heating system and internal walls the chance – or risk – is that as my family grows I might make various extensions to the house, but keep the basic building, rather than tearing it down and building a new one. With each new extension and modification of the old house, it becomes less likely that I will build a new one, even if the house is no longer in a very good shape or becoming more and more difficult to manage.

When food writer Anya von Bremzen, realized that her mythic childhood Soviet *kotleta* was the result of a Soviet emissary's investigations in United States in the 1930s, she exclaimed, "That's what it was? An ersatz burger that mislaid its bun?" We often maintain a romantic view of food and many of the dishes or habits we consider as being genuine or local are creations, in the same way that the hot dog or the hamburger are. Most 'traditional' foods are late comers, as are most 'traditional' farming systems. In *A Plea for Culinary Modernism*, Rachel Laudan explains that a number of dishes may not be as local as we believe. In Hawaii people eat *lomilomi* salmon, a salted salmon rubbed with tomatoes and spring onions. There are no salmon off the coast of Hawaii and spring onions and tomatoes were brought there quite late. The *baguette* only spread in France after World War II. Fish and chips emerged in the late 19th century and *Tequila* is a product of the Mexican movie industry.[534]

Even modern processed foods can become 'traditional and national foods', Tim Horton's donuts in Canada and Marmite, a spread used in England, are such foods. It is all the better if 'other' people don't like them; 'Love it or hate it'? is an advertising slogan used by Marmite. Kalles Kaviar, a Swedish roe product is marketed using the same strap line in a current TV commercial in which they serve bread with Kalles on the streets of Tokyo to unsuspecting Japanese who almost choke when they try it. The final voice-over says "Kalles Kaviar, a very Swedish taste". What we think is 'our' food is a strong cultural marker and there is often a lot of implicit, and sometimes explicit, discrimination when discussing 'our' food preferences. Identity is also created by what 'we' don't eat; avoidance of dog meat unites many Westerners[a] in their disgust for Chinese and Vietnamese cuisine. Even stronger are the many religious food rules, which both define who 'we' are and those who are 'apart'.

---

[a] For the record, I have eaten dog as well as whale and grasshoppers and crayfish (a Swedish national dish) and I do eat mushrooms, but not Kalles Kaviar or *surströmming*.

In order to make food from other cultures acceptable we often need to 'domesticate' it. Americans can pour ketchup on an unfamiliar food to make it American, Swedes would add more salt and sugar and a flavorless cheese. Curry makes a dish Indian. Salvadorian refugees in camps in Honduras completely reinvented macaroni when they received food aid from the Italian government. Instead of making an Italian style dish with cheese and tomatoes (which they didn't have) they set out domesticating it. Deep fried macaroni made a nice snack; toasted and pulverized and mixed with cinnamon, sugar and water it made a nice drink and; by grinding macaroni into flour it could be baked into bread.[535]

The threat of competition from outside leads us to begin to appreciate the local or traditional (whatever that is). "If nobody was attracted by the foreign, the local would be in no danger and there would be no need to protect it. The only reason to make noise about the normal daily bread on the table is if it appears to be replaced by rice, noodles or corn flakes" concludes anthropologist Richard Wilk from Indiana University.[536] This can be seen not only today but also in history. The much heralded regional cuisines of France were largely developed as a reaction to the dominance of Paris.[537] Many of the national cuisines we think of today are social and cultural creations that were originally part of a nationalist project. In the 1920s, Greek intellectuals were concerned about the effects of cosmopolitanism on Greek culture; this threat from the outside was the impetus to write the first pan-Hellenic cookbook for the still young Greek republic.[538] And the first pan-Indian cookbooks emerged as late as the 1980s.

Politics enter food in many different ways. In a previous chapter I discussed governments' efforts to influence diets, for a multitude of reasons, but there are other ideological influences on food. People who object to American imperialism respond by not eating hamburgers and the Americans dumped British shipments of tea into the Boston harbor (because of the high taxes levied on it) and turned to coffee instead. Readers might remember the efforts in the United States to rebrand French fries into "freedom fries" as a protest of lack of French support for the second war in Iraq. This was reportedly inspired by similar actions against Germany in World War I, when sauerkraut was called "liberty cabbage", and frankfurters were renamed "hot dogs".[539] Hot dogs stuck – despite being a funny expression (or perhaps because of this) – while (luckily) freedom fries and liberty cabbage didn't.

We might envisage cooking, for a poor household in the past as a simple thing, generally based on a few staple foods, the same ones every day.[540] But perhaps this vision is overly colored by accounts in literature of poor peoples' diets in the big empires, almost all of them based on grain production. There are many examples of 'poor' people with a much richer diet. A recent survey of eleven indigenous peoples (the Awajun, Bhil, Dalit, Gwich'in, Igbo, Ingano, Inuit, Karen, Maasai, Nuxalk and Pohnpei) from five continents in modern times show that they consumed a wide range of traditional foods – ranging from a low of 35 species for the Maasai to 387 species for the Karen people. The Igbo's 220 different traditional sources of food supplied 96% of the calories they needed, but nowadays among most of these peoples, traditional foods supply less than half of their daily energy needs.[541] Nonetheless, these peoples' culinary heritages are an indication that people have known about and used many sources of foods. Also, we should not forget the oft-recurring festivities linked to marriages, funerals, other rites of passages and religious feasts. These often included an abundant supply of nourishing foods and foods of higher values. In a village of a few hundred people there will be many such events every year. So perhaps people didn't have to eat 'everyday foods' every day.

On the other hand, our visions of our great-grand parents' relationship with food may be equally distorted by tales of excesses at grand feasts and literature that romantically describes the upper or middle classes in times gone by. In urban households it was most likely only the wealthy that had a good kitchen with any capacity for extensive or expensive cooking. In most countries until quite recently poor people in cities had neither the time, fuel or sufficient space to make traditional cooking that might be romantically envisioned as being 'like grandma's'. It was only if grandma had a servant in the city that it is likely that she could cook 'like grandma'. In rural areas it is more likely that people had more time for cooking and there was available fuel and space. However, for poor people in rural areas it is likely that the variety of food wasn't that great. Despite rural areas being the producers of food, it is in cities that most culinary innovations – for the better and the worse – have taken place.

As with farming, our cooking and food processing methods have been largely shaped by local conditions. For example, the Chinese tradition of sautéing food in small pieces in a wok is founded on a shortage of fuel for cooking. In contrast, brown cheese made by condensing the whey – a very energy consuming process – is a common food in Norway and Sweden where firewood was in ample supply. The long-boiled curries of India are well adapted to the use of cow dung and many Indians will swear that food cooked over cow dung tastes far superior to food cooked using regular gas. That dried food mostly developed in dry climates requires no further explanation. Cheeses are mainly made in temperate climates also for climatic reasons. Roquefort cheese or Parma ham are products which have benefitted from the local climate and storage possibilities to become what they are.

Just as the upper classes and courts shaped fashion in clothes and arts they also were drivers of cooking and food processing. Palaces spent huge resources on food, cooking and food processing as one of the main roles of a ruler was to throw parties that demonstrated his (they usually were a 'he') wealth and largesse. Half of the personnel, more than 2,000 people, at the imperial palace of Ancient China were involved in the preparation of food.[542] With the cultural ascendancy of Islam, the Muslims took over leadership in cooking around the Mediterranean after the decline of the Roman Empire. The Ottomans brought the art to new heights. In the 16th century the kitchen at the Topkapi Palace in Istanbul catered for 5,000 people on week days and up to 10,000 on holidays. The head cook had fifty *sous*-chefs. But it didn't stop there, in the 17th century, the kitchen became more refined and more and more specialists were added. There were six different halva kitchens, each with a hundred workers and 100 carts of wood were needed every day for the cooking.[543] Muslim cooking influenced the aesthetics of the table in the West and introduced new exotic ingredients and a taste for sweet things. Western cookbooks in late medieval times often had a distinct Muslim influence.[544]

Fashions in food, what is chic to eat, change over the course of time. Chicken went from a luxury to a poor person's food in less than a century, as discussed earlier. Salmon is on the same track, while oysters and cod are going the opposite way, the first is increasingly rare and the second still not very successfully cultivated. When a food is cheap and widely available it loses its function as a 'class marker'. White bread baked with yeast was a luxury for centuries and reserved for the wealthy. Now, when this is the standard fare, the elite goes for sourdough bread made with coarse flours. Pasta has gone a similar way to white bread, mainly thanks to the development of the kneading machine and mechanical presses.[545]

The home kitchen has been transformed repeatedly to suit new cooking technologies and new eating habits. Even the kitchen itself has been largely standardized. It started with cast iron stoves and cupboards and eventually the idea of a 'kitchen design' developed, partly inspired by industrial ideals of efficiency and modern concerns with hygiene. Catherine Frederick, at the Massachusetts Institute of

Technology, published *Efficient housekeeping, or household engineering,* in 1925, influenced by the logic of industrial production lines. "There was no space for slackers in Frederick's engineered households" in the words of Carolyn Steel, British architect and author of *Hungry City.*[546] Her ideas moved across the Atlantic and inspired the 'Frankfurt kitchen', the first mass-produced kitchen, of which more than 10,000 units were installed in Frankfurt alone in the 1920s.[547] The industrialization of cooking has become even more pronounced through the development of ready-made foods and food eaten out of the home. The scientific approach to cooking merged with feminism as Charlotte Perkins Gilman stated that it is impossible for "half of the world, acting as amateur cooks for the other half, (to) attain any high degree of scientific accuracy or technical skill".[548]

For a long time Chinese street vendors have sold food throughout the night. Poor city dwellers often do not cook their own food, for a multitude of reasons. The place they live might have no facilities for cooking and they often work very long hours. In addition, sharing a meal might be one of the few social interactions available. Already in Ancient Rome, the proportion of people eating out was high, and countries such as Thailand and Indonesia have an abundance of street food available in every city. The cost of eating out has only been marginally higher than buying food to bring home, and eating out gives people a wide variety of food, as they can benefit from hundreds of ingredients and suppliers. There is also very little waste when one buys small portions of street food, instead of trying to store food in inadequate storage facilities.

Most public eating places, taverns and inns have been simple, noisy, places often with poor hygiene standards. One ate what one was served. The wealthy have, in most times and places, eaten at home. Tea houses in China, by contrast, were sophisticated places for business meetings, performances and poetry and, in the West, coffee houses emerged as places of political intrigue and intellectual debate. The modern restaurant for sophisticated food is a Parisian innovation from the mid 18th century.[549] Restaurants were opened to serve foreign travelers and patrons who found the food, service, and atmosphere offered by inns, taverns, and eating houses intolerable. The restaurants offered their clientele a nouvelle cuisine, consisting of items such as orange-flavored ice creams, fresh eggs, fruits in season, as well as healthful and tasty bouillons known as *restaurants,* which lent their name to the establishments. These restaurants had menus, which allowed patrons to select and pay only for what they ate and they offered food at all hours.

Food consumption away from home represents a large and growing component of food expenditure in the United States. Families spent nearly 42% of their food dollars on food eaten away from home in 2008, up by 25% from 1970.[550] One hundred years earlier only 5% of the money spent on food in the United States was on eating out.[551] Full service restaurants represent 41% of the market (in value), fast food joints 37%, the remainder being schools, hotels, bars, stores and the like. The number of full service restaurants doubled between 1972 and 2007 and the number of fast food restaurants tripled in the same period, bringing the total number of restaurants to almost half a million; one restaurant for every 616 people. In almost the same period, the proportion of calories that American children got from eating out of home, increased from less than a quarter to more than one third.[552] Eating out as opposed to at home is on the increase almost everywhere; 22% of the food budget in Brazil and Indonesia is spent on food services, the British spend around one thrird of their food budget out of home,[553] while in Japan the share of food eaten out of home went from 7% in 1963 to 17% in forty years later.[554]

As in most other parts of the food system, there is consolidation in the restaurant segment where the largest 100 chains now account for more than half of total sales.[555] This is totally overshadowed by the market situation for coffee shops, which continue to be dominated by Starbucks. Naturally the food processing companies want a share of this burgeoning market: "While you're likely familiar with General Mills' business from the products that you see on grocery store shelves, you may be less familiar with our food-away-from-home Bakeries and Foodservice business – which has been an important source of our profit growth over the past several years" writes Maerenn Jepsen, external communications manager for General Mills in a blog post.[556]

Schools don't only train us in the subjects of the curriculum and as social beings, they also influence our food preferences. The provision of meals for school children was a European invention of the late 19th century, following universal education. Once established it spread. In the United States the National School Lunch Program was established 1946, perhaps as much an outlet for surplus agriculture products as for welfare reasons.[557] Institutional foods, in particular in schools and in the military greatly influence our food habits, and as the institutions themselves are built on mass-production, their influence is towards the industrial. Through institutional cooking, especially school meals, as they reach all children for a long time at an age when eating habits are being formed, governments have a substantial leverage on food habits.

The food system is shaped as an hour glass. There are millions of farmers and billions of consumers at each end and in between there are a few companies that manage the whole system. There are, very roughly, 25 million coffee farmers in the world, while 40% of the trade and 70% of the roasting is controlled by the five biggest companies.[558] The effect is that while coffee consumption doubled during the 1990s the price share going to the coffee-producing countries decreased from one-third to just ten percent.[559] This pattern is not unique for produce from developing countries; it is basically repeated all over the planet.

In the United States, four companies control 80% of the meat market, three companies control 80% of maize exports and 65% of soy exports and four companies control 60% of the domestic grain market. Just three giant enterprises, US-based grain traders/processors, Cargill, ADM and Bunge, handle the majority of grain that moves between nations. Most of the transnational companies in the food sector are from the United States or Western Europe,[560] but times are changing. Brazil-based JBS SA has acquired a number of meat producing companies in United States, Europe and Asia and is now bigger than household name companies, such as Unilever, Cargill and Danone. JBS SA's worldwide slaughtering capacity is 85,000 heads of cattle, 70,000 pigs and 12 million birds. Each day. In September 2013, Chinese Shunaghui International Holdings Ltd. bought US-based Smithfields, the world's biggest pork producer.[561]

A handful of companies control most of the food on the shelves. In the United States three-quarters of the sales of thirty-two food categories (types of products) came from just four companies in 2012. The top ten food and beverage firms (the three largest are Nestlé, Pepsico and Kraft) control an estimated 28% of the global market. The top five breweries have around 50% of the market while the top ten wine marketers have around 16% of the market.[562] And the same company often owns several, seemingly competing brands, to offer consumers a bigger choice – and keep competition out. The top four firms selling breakfast cereals in United States have almost hundred different 'brands'.[563] And if you cannot beat your competition, you can just buy them out. Increasingly, huge multinationals have bought up pioneer organic companies or other premium brands. Many companies integrate 'upstream' production (i.e. farmers and other suppliers) and 'downstream' sales (outlets, agents), which allows them to extend their control of the chain.

The most spectacular development in the food chain recent decades is not the might of Coca-Cola or Nestlé, but rather the increased influence of actors in other parts of the food chain, in particular the retailers. In 2008, Walmart recorded sales of US$436 billion from 7,657 stores (this correspond to the GDP of Sweden), Carrefour US$161 billion from 13,791 stores, Metro Group US$116 billion and Tesco US$109 billion. In 1992, the top five supermarket chains in the United States had a market share of less than 20%; by 1999, that share had increased to one third and in 2012 the four largest retailers sold more than half of the groceries.[564] In Australia, the two giants, Coles and Woolworths, now control about 80% of grocery sales[565] and in Sweden, ICA has half the retail market.[566] The dominance of the major retailers is almost total in Britain. The number of independent shops shrank from 120,000 in 1950s to 18,000 in the late 2000s, and only 8% of the greengrocers remain.[567] The parliamentary report *High Street Britain 2015* stated that "many small shops will have ceased trading by 2015 with few independent businesses taking their place".[568] The concentration in the retail sector is even bigger than we might think. Just as food processors run many brands, retailers run a range of 'concepts', each with its own target segment of consumers. In 2012 the Kroger Company, the second largest retailer in the United States had stores operating under many names, including Kroger, Ralphs, Food 4 Less, FoodCo, Jay C, Owen's, Pay Less Super markets, Scott's Ruler Foods and ten others.[569]

The power of the supermarkets is also strengthened by the spread of retailer-owned brands and private labels. The retail share of private labels among food products has reached almost 60% in Switzerland and between 20% and 40% in most other Western European countries.[570] In the United Kingdom 85% of all milk sold is under private brands.[571] The retailers try to uphold the idea that we have choices by introducing many different private brands. The biggest retailer in Britain, Tesco, has many own brands; Value, Standard, Finest, Discount, Light Choices, Organic, Free From, Whole Foods and finally Disney Kids, which was introduced in 2007 "to help parents by providing a range of nutritionally balanced food that children will engage with and enjoy". This range includes a Mickey Mouse shaped pizza.[572]

The production and supply of inputs to farms is also highly concentrated – the top five countries control 50-80% of the world's production capacity for the most used nitrogen, phosphate and potash (NPK) mix.[573] Despite a generally-declining United States economy over the last decade, fertilizer companies generated massive profits. The average fertilizer company outperformed the Standard & Poor500 stock market index by over 750% over a 10 year period, showing similar growth rates to celebrated tech stocks, such as Google and Apple.[574] In the early 1990s agricultural processing and input firms received 20% returns on their investments making them second only to pharmaceutical companies in profitability.[575]

The global commercial seed market in 2009 was worth US$27 billion, with the top ten companies having three quarters of the market. Three of them controlled more than half of the market and one, Monsanto, now controls more than one-quarter of the commercial seed market.[576] Five seed companies control around three quarters of the EU market for maize varieties. For sugar beet, just four companies control around 86% of the market, while 95% of the EU vegetable seed market is in the hands of just five companies. The consolidation of the seed giants is largely driven by investments in the hybridization of certain crops, or in biotech products, protected by patents. Varieties designed for industrial-scale production, such as F1 hybrids, need on average between seven and fifteen years to be developed – a very large investment of time and money. This creates a barrier to newcomers, and small companies – which cannot afford those investments – are bought up by the seed giants. The French Limagrain group has taken over fourteen sizeable seed breeding companies since the 1990s[577] and in the United States at least two hundred independent seed companies were lost between 1996 and 2009.[578]

The concentration in the agro-chemical market is even higher, with the top ten having 90% of the global market.[579] The commercial seed sector has also merged with the agrochemical market. Five of the top 6 agrochemical companies are also on the list of the world's biggest seed companies. Monsanto is the world's largest seed company and fourth largest pesticide company. Monsanto's seeds that are genetically modified to work together with their flagship herbicide, Roundup, constitute a clear example of a successful strategy. The breeders grip of the market is enhanced by the increasing importance of intellectual property rights in the global economy which allow companies to patent life in its various forms. This topic in itself would merit a book (and indeed many have been written), but the short story is that through patent laws and the World Trade Organization (WTO) Agreement on Trade Related Aspects of Intellectual Property Rights (TRIPS) seeds, genes, plants, animals and combinations thereof are all patentable. Patent laws in the United States even restrict the right of independent researchers to carry out research, e.g. on the safety and performance of a GMO crop, without the consent of the patent holder[580] – *de facto* allowing companies such as Monsanto to determine who can investigate the safety of their products. The Roundup Ready trait (the making of a plant resistant to the herbicide glyphosate) in soybeans added US$6.50 per bag in 2000 and US$17.50 in 2009, sometimes amounting to nearly half the price of the seed.[581] Seed costs now account for around 10 percent of total crop production revenues.[582] I hope someone will one day get around calculating the size of the stream of money from farmers to huge agri-business corporations through the patenting of seeds, veterinary medicines and pesticides.

A new group of actors has also come to play a critical role in the food supply chain. When food prices sky-rocketed in 2008 five main explanations circulated. First, that it was simply a result of dwindling food stocks (to some extent true); second, that food crops were being diverted to biofuel production (also true); third, that meat production was taking food away from the market (more about that later). The fourth explanation was that increasing oil prices increased the costs of food production, e.g. by making fertilizers more expensive (certainly true). Finally, speculators were named and shamed.

There are many ways you can speculate in foods. You can buy up real stocks and hoard, which has been a popular strategy during wars. But nowadays, most speculation is in future contracts (simply called 'futures') and derivatives thereof (options etc.). As with money, the link between the digits in the spreadsheet and the underlying asset is becoming increasingly opaque. Until recently the futures market in food was largely a tool for buyers and sellers to 'hedge' the price. A farmer could sell her harvest in advance for an agreed price, and the mill could buy for an agreed price. As it is a lot of work for the two parties to find each other and agree on the exact terms of delivery and there is always a risk that one of the parties doesn't fulfill its obligation, intermediaries organized this through standardized contracts. And inevitably some started to speculate in this: buying or selling without being a farmer, a mill or a trader in the food chain. Through such activities, the nature of commodity markets has changed profoundly and most contracts are now never translated into actual trade but are 'rolled over' into new contracts or liquidated before delivery of the actual goods. Only about two percent of futures contracts lead to an actual delivery.[583]

It is as noisy as a livestock auction. Papers are tossed on the ground and big guys are gesticulating in the special sign language of 'the pit'. It is a big advantage to be tall and loud here, which is why there are so few women to be seen on the floor of the Chicago Board of Trade, where I went in May 2012 to understand how these markets actually operate. David Lehman, Managing Director, of Commodity Research and Product Development Research and Product Research, told me that the volume of trading has increased five-fold in ten years. Ninety percent of all trade in futures of maize takes place at the

Chicago Exchange, and more than half of the wheat trade. More than one million contracts in agriculture commodities are sold each and every working day. Each contract is for a determined quantity (5,000 bushels, 12.7 tons) of a specified quality to be delivered at a certain time. The only variable is the price, which makes the contracts ideal commodities. The trade in maize contracts is about ten times the size of the world's actual production. One reason for the increase in trade is simply that it is possible, according to Mr. Lehman. With electronic trading a lot more people can participate without joining in with the screaming on the floor.[584]

Another reason is that the trade in futures has gradually been de-regulated, opened up for speculators and Wall Street to make 'investment products'. This started when Goldman Sachs created the first food commodity index product in 1991, which was only made possible by the gradual market de-regulation that took place in the previous years. Between 1922 and 1936, in spite of pressure from the corporate and financial sector, the United States government strength-ened the legislation regulating food futures markets, setting limits on the maximum number of contracts a single actor could trade.[585] "One of the key lessons that we learned after the Great Depression is that those futures markets must be regulated," says journalist Frederick Kaufman. "But we had a mania – not only a global but a national mania – for deregulation and 'liberalization' of trade policies in the 1990s. And all of a sudden, these markets turned from fairly stable moribund affairs into crazy, volatile, spiking, dipping, moving-all-over-the-place type markets. This is bad for everybody."[586]

Everybody except speculators, that is. Sometimes speculators are blamed for high prices, but they can also speculate on low prices. David Lehman doesn't agree that speculators cause high prices, but he admits that they can increase short term volatility, "speculators don't cause high prices, but there may be some short-term over-shooting. This is because of a herd mentality among traders.[587]" This is echoed in a report from the United Nations Conference on Trade and Develop-ment in 2011.

> Market participants also make trading decisions based on factors that are totally unrelated to the respective commodity, such as portfolio considerations, or they may be following a trend.... In such a situation, it is rational to follow other participants' trading decisions. A wide range of motivations leads traders to engage in this so-called 'inten-tional herding' on a perfectly rational basis, the most important one being imitation in situations where traders believe that they can glean market information by observing the behavior of other agents.[588]

Coming home from Chicago, I wanted to try this for myself. I registered on a commodity trading platform and purchased 3,000 contracts of a mix of wheat, sugar and maize, enough food to keep a smaller town alive for a year. After three days I made a profit of US$2,500 and two days later, I lost US$2,000 – and I was quite happy that I was using the demonstration version of the trading platform. More interestingly, I could also sell maize contracts, without first having had to buy them. I didn't understand at all how that could be possible. I mean, I had no maize whatsoever yet I could still sell it? Reflecting on what I learnt at the Chicago Board of Trade, I realized it really didn't matter, as I will never deliver on the contract anyway. Very few contracts are linked to any physical trade. In most cases, the same contract is bought and sold many times before it is due, and when it is due, the owner will have to pay up or cash in the difference with the actual market price.

In the supermarkets we find a large supply of fully prepared meals, including ready meals of all types and take away food for consumption at home. There are also partly prepared meals consisting of several meal components. In any week, 45% of Europeans and Americans prepare such meals.[589] The British seem to be world leaders in convenience food. Between 1994 and 2004 the sector grew by 70% and in 2006, sales in the United Kingdom were almost as big those in the whole of the rest of Europe.[590] As younger customers buy more ready-made meals than older ones, the trend is likely to continue.[591] It is also spreading rapidly to emerging economies where the consumption of convenience foods is increasing, partly due to increasing urbanization: retail sales of ready meals in India and China grew by 26.9% and 11.8% respectively from 2003 to 2008.[592]

We have seen how food processing and retail follow an industrial logic. The same is true of the production of convenience foods. The Greencore Group plc is a leading international manufacturer of convenience foods, with twenty-two convenience food manufacturing sites in the United Kingdom and the United States, employing 11,000 people. In a market worth over £2.1 billion Greencore Prepared Meals supply 150 million meals a year to a wide range of United Kingdom customers across the multiple, convenience and foodservice distribution channels. From the factory in Bristol they supply over 40% of the United Kingdom's chilled sauces and many other food products.[593] The web of suppliers to these operations is so complex that it proved very difficult to pin down the point at which horsemeat became beef in the European horsemeat scandal early 2013. The factory that supplied Tesco with its 'horseburgers' was using "multiple ingredients from some 40 suppliers in production batches, and the mixture could vary every half hour", according to the Irish department of Agriculture.[594]

Many see a link between female emancipation and the rise of convenience foods. The Head of Marks & Spencer's food division 1975-1987, Clinton Silver, claims: "feminism owes an enormous amount to Marks & Spencer and vice versa".[595] In the United States KFC ran billboards with a family size bucket of fried chicken under the slogan "Women's liberation".[596] I have my doubts about the link between convenience foods and female emancipation and to make cooking the centerpiece of a discussion about feminism reduces it to a question of the division of tasks. Aggressive marketing of ready-made food and more processed foods predates any important shift in female entry into the labor market, or other signs of gender equality. The rate of fast food and convenience food in the households also show little correlation to the proportion of women in the labor force. For example, Sweden has a very high rate of women who work (71% in 2012) yet a far lower rate of eating out of home and convenience foods than the United States (where 62% of women work) or the United Kingdom (where 66% of women work). As a matter of fact, the concept of a 'housewife', a middle class ideal, was strongest in Sweden in the 1950s, the same time that industrial food processing really expanded.[597] It may be that the industry and retailers deliberately depicted cooking as drudgery and took advantage of social tendencies in order to create a market for their goods, rather than the other way round.

The increased industrialization of food, and our tendency to let corporations do a lot more of the job for us, cannot really be explained by us not having enough time. The average person now spend much more time in front of the television, the computer, the game console or in the gym, all habits that have expanded enormously in parallel with the commercialization of eating. Many people clearly chose not to cook. Anya von Bremzen tells us how her grandmother – a career woman in the Soviet Union – used to say "Why should I bake, when I can be reading a book?" preferring to have a dinner made from frozen dumplings.[598] Interestingly, while less time is spent on cooking real meals, people nowadays spend more time eating, albeit mostly while multitasking; eating while driving, eating while watching TV, talking on the phone or walking to or from work or between meetings. A study shows that Americans spend almost eighty minutes per day on 'secondary eating'.[599] Social eating in restaurants has also increased in many countries.[600]

Food preparation, whether in palaces, restaurants or at homes has undergone great changes. The fast-food trend, eating out of home, ready-made meals for home consumption and the industrialization of home cooking are strongly related and mutually supportive even if they are competing for our preferences. Interestingly, the difference in food from these various sources is often very small. Instead of benefitting from the increased opportunities offered by eating out or buying ready-made food or cooking some semi-processed components, many seem to prefer the same food whatever the circumstances. Some go for pizza, others a salad. The trend is more easily understood if seen also in the context of changing living and workplace conditions and not only as a result of the aggressive expansion of capitalist companies. Urbanization, overcrowding in cities and the growing number of single person households contribute in no small way to this trend of 'eating out'.

Fast food and convenience food are, as expressed by sociologist Georg Ritzer in his book *The McDonaldization of Society*, efficient in the sense that they are the fastest way to get from being hungry to being full. The food is also highly predictable, standardized and controlled, built around the same logic as other industries.[601] Yet paradoxically, food away from home, fast food and the snacks at home have enabled a much higher degree of individualism in what we eat. An increase of food allergies and intolerance, real, perceived or just a result of more choice, give the notion of 'sharing a meal' a new meaning, or a lack of meaning, as meals as such are rarely shared.

As the notion of a meal loses its meaning, we see a continual spread of 'constant grazing' and the seemingly perpetual availability of food almost everywhere. In this context, the microwave oven represents one of the most groundbreaking inventions in food preparation since we learnt how to boil food in water. It has greatly facilitated and driven the spread of ready-made convenience foods, and it has made the individualization of 'cooking' possible. In this way it is also eliminating the essentially social aspect of eating; the bonds created by more than a hundred thousand of years of time spent around the campfire. "It reverses the cooking revolution, which made eating sociable, and returns us, in this respect to a pre-social phase of evolution" in the words of historian Felipe Fernández-Armesto.[602]

This trend is not only technologically driven though. Economic factors are equally important. And today it is perfectly normal for economists to not only refer to food as a commodity, but also eating. "In this study I have examined the determinants of the household production function characterizing eating, *a commodity* [my italics] whose production involves using purchased food and some capital goods in conjunction with time spent preparing the food, eating it and cleaning up afterwards", writes Daniel S. Hamermesh, economist from University of Texas in an otherwise interesting paper that shows, in 'economist-speak' that if restaurant workers are better paid, rich people will eat less food out of home.[603]

Modern food chains have undoubtedly greatly increased the supply of fresh fruits and vegetables, benefiting the diets of millions. The downside is that fresh fruit and vegetables are often produced with a lot of agro-chemicals, air freighted to us and are still quite expensive forms of food, so it is mainly the wealthy, or at least the comfortably-off, who benefit.

In 2009, food manufacturers introduced nearly 20,000 new products onto retail shelves in the United States. Most were candy, gum, snacks, beverages and other highly processed foods. The new releases must compete against the 320,000 items already on sale. The fierce competition for shelf space is one reason why food manufacturers invest heavily in marketing their products.[604] Another reason is simply to reap higher profits from a re-formulated or re-branded product. There is an irony that while we seem to have such an enormous range of choices, our real choices have shrunk. The stuff on the supermarket shelves are formulations and reformulations of the same major ingredients, raw materials derived from five main industrialized crops: maize, soybeans, wheat, palm oil and sugar. Add flavors and some suitable 'texturizer' and you can make great wonders. Modern food processing technologies has not affected all foods equally. Generally, there is little to be earned from foods that are consumed in more or less the same form that they leave the farm. The food industry and retailers are more interested in foods that involve significant preparation as it is possible to brand these and the margins are much higher. For typical breakfast cereals, the costs for the raw materials from the farms constitute just a small percentage of the sales price. It should come as no surprise that breakfast cereal makers spend much more in advertizing than oatmeal producers. Because of this, the whole food system is rigged against the non-processed, single ingredient products, as well as against home cooking.

When what you buy loses its meaning, the act of buying, shopping, becomes the meaning in itself. People spend endless hours in supermarkets selecting between very similar products. Shopping is reportedly the second largest pastime in North America. 'Therapeutic shopping' is being taken up with gusto also in many emerging economies. An ACNielsen global online survey conducted among 22,000 Internet users in 42 markets in 2006 revealed that 74% of the respondents admit to shopping as 'a form of entertainment'; when they do not actually need anything: "Shopping has become a national pastime in many Asian countries and is so entrenched in the lifestyles of Thais, Hong Kongers and Singaporeans, that governments have wisely turned this national characteristic into a major tourism attraction."[605] People's love of shopping is probably an underestimated cause both of obesity and of food waste.

All in all, the consumption pattern follows, not surprisingly, the same market logic as the production pattern; they are, after all, just a reflection of each other. The increase in eating out or buying ready-made food can be seen as an urban household's mirror reflection of the commercialization of farms. More and more time is allocated to paid work, time is seen as scarce – even though data would say the opposite – and reproducing resources in the household, or reducing expenses are not seen as priorities. At first it might be hard to understand how this can coincide with a record in cook book sales and a plethora of kitchen appliances. I recently read in a newspaper that it is increasingly common for people in Sweden to hire chefs to help them to cook (by some perverse politics this is even tax-deductable) and I hear that in the United States there is a service that offers to shape your hamburgers so 'you can lean back and enjoy' your own perfect home-made burgers.[606] This mirrors the fate of hunting, fishing and gardening. They have moved from being necessities for survival to expensive hobbies where the food harvested is no longer the most important thing. The gadgets, the experience, the nerdy knowledge of details are all expressions of this. Some may see this development as liberty and freedom from drudgery, other see more the loss of a feeling of belonging, the loss of one of the main rituals for bonding, social cohesion and a driver of unhealthy food and eating habits.

Modern consumer demand is to a very large extent created, not only (or even mainly) by advertising, but also by industrial and commercial processes that shape our whole world, of which advertising is just a small component. As I have discussed earlier, governments, the food industry, the fertilizer and seed industry giants and the supermarkets and even speculators, influence the food chain and the choices within it. When it is our turn to choose, most choices have already been made, by governments, by the various actors in the supply chain from the farmers to the supermarkets and by our predecessors. And with the enormous concentration of power in the food chain in the hands of very few actors those making these decisions have enormous powers over our daily food. But the lack of real choice is masked by the enormous supply of very similar products. The conditions under which we chose our food are a lot more important than the choices we have. In *Reconnecting Consumers Producers and Food*, six British researchers who studied alternative food schemes found that people whose food schemes offered the least choice (e.g. subscription schemes with fixed in-season contents) often ate the widest variety of food, more fresh food and cooked more meals from scratch. Through a lack of choice they were encouraged (and forced) to learn new recipes and acquire new cooking skills, and they were "in closer contact with the natural environment through their ability to appreciate the changing seasons and by seeing food as it comes out of the ground – misshapen or with mud on."[607]

The individualization and commodification of food has been a bonanza for, and perhaps the result of, the food industry. Commercial actors can now earn money from activities that were previously out of reach of the market (as they were done within the household), including cooking, food preparation and processing, feeding infants and brewing. Socialist utopians, such as Edward Bellamy,[608] and the Soviet Union and the Israeli kibbutzim had a vision that we would not cook at home. We would either get ready-made foods from factories or eat in collective kitchens. In some Israeli kibbutzes people were not even allowed their own kettles to make tea.[609] This vision, or part of it, has ironically enough now been materialized through the capitalist food industry taking over our food supply.

17

The great experiment in geoengineering

In farming, the availability of nutrients, particularly of nitrogen, potash and phosphorus – mostly referred to by their chemical symbols N, P and K – is a major limiting factor. All traditional farming systems have had some strategy for replacing nutrients in the soil. One is to rest the soil and allow a natural re-charge and release of nutrients from the soil and through atmospheric decomposition. (I discussed various ways of doing this, such as slash and burn, fallowing and swiddening in a previous chapter). Crop rotations with leguminous crops can fix nitrogen from the air and the nutritional demands of the various crops can complement each other. Phosphorous, from deeper layers or bound in the soil, can be 'mined' by some crops making it available to others. Nutrients can also come from irrigation water (especially sediments in flood waters), animal manure, night soil (human waste), plants, grass and other residues, a plethora of natural organic fertilizers. Farmers have used oil-cakes, feathers, leathers, bone, sea weed and fish as fertilizers. There are even reports that human remains from battlefields and ossuaries have been used as fertilizers. Yet all these methods have some limitations, and in most cases they require a lot of work or other efforts.

It is therefore no wonder that the farmers of the world took to artificial fertilizers with great gusto. They are easier to transport than bulky organic materials such as manure, easier to apply and give somewhat predictable results. Global annual use of nitrogen fertilizers increased from 11 million tons in 1960 to 85 million tons in 2003. Contrary to common belief most of the fertilizers are not used to replace what is removed by the crop from the field. The quantities applied mostly surpass this many times. Most nitrogen is simply wasted through denitrification, leaking, erosion and volatilization of ammonia.[610] According to David Montgomery, an American soil scientist, half of the fertilizer used in the United States is used to compensate the nutrient losses caused by erosion. In Rwanda the loss of nitrogen from erosion largely surpasses the amount added through fertilizers. At the end of the 1990s, countries with very intensive farming systems, such as South Korea and the Netherlands used more than 250 kg of nitrogen per hectare, much more than they took out in the form of produce, and these figures do not even include all nitrogen sources.[611] Globally, the nitrogen efficiency in grain production has deteriorated drastically and rapidly (probably mostly a result of decreasing marginal return). Around 1960, each ton of chemical fertilizer resulted in an increase in grain yield of 75 tons, whereas at the end of 1990 this resulted in just 25 tons.[612] And in China cereal grain yields increased by just 10% from 1996 to 2005, despite the use of chemical fertilizers increasing by 51%.[613]

Over and above the use of chemical fertilizers, there is also a substantial nitrogen supply through (natural) biological nitrogen fixation. Even though the nitrogen in chemical fertilizers and from biological nitrogen fixation comes from the same source (the air), one cannot treat these sources as equal, especially not with regard to their effects on the soil. In theory, there could be substantial nitrogen leakage from biological nitrogen fixation; in practice, this is difficult to substantiate. One reason is that the process, as most natural processes, is to a large extent self-regulating; if there is a lot of free nitrogen in the soil, nitrogen fixation from the air ceases, as it is easier (it 'costs' less) for the legume to take nitrogen directly from the soil than to swap it with a bacteria, which costs precious energy.[a]

The quantity of biologically active nitrogen[b] released annually into the biosphere has increased nine-fold in 100 years and nitrogenous fertilizers are the main source of this. In one of the most influential scientific articles of last decade, *Planetary boundaries: Exploring the safe operating space for humanity*, professor Johan Rockström and colleagues identify the nitrogen cycle as one of three areas – together with climate regulation and biological diversity – where modern civilization has surpassed a threshold for stable development.

Without knowing it, the average European bears costs of over €500 per year for farmers' use of Nitrogen fertilizers. The *European Nitrogen Assessment*[614] recognizes that synthetic nitrogen fertilizers have huge advantages but also notes that their use comes with a huge prize tag. The report states that the increased level of biologically active nitrogen

---

[a] Legumes supply bacteria with energy (from photosynthesis) in exchange for nitrogen.

[b] Most nitrogen in the atmosphere is in its molecular form.

in the biosphere might represent "the greatest single experiment in global geoengineering ever made". For a farmer it is profitable to use nitrogen fertilizer. The return of one Euro invested in nitrogen fertilizer is estimated at between two and five Euros. But someone else pays a bigger bill. "Environmental damage related to nitrogen effects from agriculture in the EU-27 was estimated at €20-€150 billion per year. This can be compared with a benefit of N-fertilizer for farmers of €10-€100 billion per year, with considerable uncertainty about long-term N-benefits for crop yield".[615]

The damage caused by fertilizers includes a wide range of direct and indirect effects. Through denitrification, nitrogen is lost as nitrogen gas which in essence is harmless, but some 5-7% is emitted as laughing gas, a potent greenhouse gas.[616] Nitrogen also plays a role in the formation of tropospheric ozone, which damages crops and plants.[617] Chemical fertilizers have enabled farmers to skip sound crop rotations and to monocrop, which leads to a reduction of carbon content in soils and, thereby, an increase in greenhouse gases (as the carbon is oxidized into carbon dioxide). Increased concentrations of nitrogen and phosphorus in the biosphere are two of the most important drivers of changes in ecosystems.

Globally, the discharge of nitrogen to the sea increased by 80% between 1860 and 1990. This run-off changes species composition and stimulates algal blooms and the associated dead zones.[618] In the United States, the Mississippi, the Columbia, and the Susquehanna rivers together discharge approximately 1 million tons of nitrogen (in the form of nitrates) per year to coastal waters – about 10% of all nitrogen applied in the country.[619] In the summer of 2013, the dead zone in the Gulf of Mexico covered around 5,840 square miles, an area about the size of Connecticut.[620] The extent of dead zones in the oceans has doubled every 10 years since the 1960s. Globally, about four hundred coastal areas are now periodically or constantly oxygen-depleted as a result of fertilizer run-off, sewage discharge and the combustion of fossil fuels.[621] The use of chemical fertilizers has also led to harmful levels of nitrates in some drinking water.[622] There are good, and frightening, reasons to closely follow the changes in the nitrogen cycle. We should not be surprised if the effects and costs of disturbing it turn out to be as dramatic as those for the carbon cycle.

Phosphorus is mined and is a limited resource. According to some researchers, the Earth's phosphorus reserves are expected to be seriously depleted within 50-100 years. 'Peak phosphorus', the point at which less phosphorus will be produced than previously because of limited supply and high costs is expected to be reached by approximately 2030.[623] Phosphorus is also very unevenly distributed on the planet. In 2009, two thirds of all phosphorus was mined in China, United States and Morocco,[a] with China alone mining more than one third. Since 2008, China has guarded its own long term supply by slapping on a 135% export tariff on phosphorus.[624] One complication with phosphorus fertilizers is that they often contain cadmium, a highly toxic heavy metal, of which the load in our food is already alarmingly high. Rich countries can choose the cleaner phosphates, or even purify contaminated ones, whereas low-income countries are left with the contaminated supplies.

It is often claimed that nitrogeneous fertilizers feed half of the world's population. There should be no doubt about the importance of chemical fertilizers, but this figure is based on erroneous assumptions. If you just cut away fertilizers from the existing systems yields would certainly plummet, perhaps even by half, but such a scenario is not realistic. In the same way as farmers have adjusted their production to the availability of cheap fertilizers, they would make adjustments to deal with a situation without (or with less) nitrogen fertilizers. That is exactly what organic farmers do and their yields are rarely that low.

Chemical fertilizers are not (yet) essential for feeding the world or for human survival, but they are essential for the global model of commercial agricultural production. Seen in isolation, all other things equal, chemical fertilizers increase yields considerably, but the extent to which they do so depends on the starting point. We cannot see them in isolation. They allow farmers – even whole regions or countries – to specialize in certain crops. They also allow farmers to skip crop rotations and focus on the commercially most interesting crops. Other areas develop industrial livestock operations, based on feed bought in from the specialized crop farm areas. Chemical fertilizers also enable cities to grow without giving any thought to recycling their waste. Buying fertilizers is also consistent with the ever increasing commercialization of farming. Because of the changes in production, monocropping and linear flows, pests and weeds become more prevalent, which makes farmers dependent on herbicides and biocides. In this way chemical fertilizers are one of the major building blocks of the modern food system.

Reflecting on his promotion of chemical fertilizers von Liebig exclaimed: "I have sinned against the wisdom of the Creator and, justly, I

---

[a] Most of the phosphorus is in the disputed territory of Western Sahara.

have been punished. I wanted to improve his work because, in my blindness, I believed that a link in the astonishing chain of laws that govern and constantly renew life on the surface of the Earth had been forgotten. It seemed to me that weak and insignificant man had to redress this oversight."[625]

Von Liebig discovered chemical fertilizers, but if he had invented pesticides he would have even bigger reason for coming to the conclusion he did. Farmers use chemical pesticides in an attempt to capture a larger share of the production of the photosynthesis per area unit, by killing all the weeds and competitors that might eat the crop. The volume of pesticides used internationally has risen fifty-fold since 1950. China is now the leading country in pesticide use and production.[626] Nearly 1,400 pesticides have been registered (i.e. approved) by the United States Environmental Protection Agency for agricultural and non-agricultural use.[627] But the price is high. "What we have to face is not an occasional dose of poison which has accidentally got into some article of food, but a persistent and continuous poisoning of the whole human environment," Rachel Carson wrote in Silent Spring 1962 already, and this remains just as true more than fifty years later.

In 1984, Bhopal in India experienced the world's worst ever industrial accident when around 20,000 people were killed when a pesticide factory blew up. The World Bank, which certainly is no anti-pesticide crusader, estimates that 350,000 people are killed by pesticides annually.[628] Most of the direct and visible harm from pesticides occurs in developing countries, where toxic substances, many of them banned in high-income countries, are used by untrained people without protective clothing. I have seen myself how farmers in Northern Uganda mixed pesticides in a bucket (which is also used for carrying water for people or animals) and then dipped, with bare hands, a bunch of grass into the liquid. Thereafter, the pesticide was shaken out over the crop, with a high proportion ended up on the skin of the person doing it. The farmers applying the pesticides could not read the labels and it was not at all clear that the substance being used had any effect on the pest he wanted to fight. And this is not an exceptional situation. A recent study by the NGO Pesticide Action Network assesses that of the total 1.3 billion farm workers worldwide about 41 million suffer pesticide poisoning each year. Pesticides are widely and easily available and are frequently used as a suicide method, especially among farmers who have seen their crops fail and risk losing their land and livelihood. The number of suicidal deaths in 2007 from pesticides was estimated as being as many as 370,000.[629]

The effect of pesticide residues in food on human health is difficult to ascertain, but according to a report of the United States President's Cancer Panel pesticides have been linked to brain, central nervous system, breast, colon, lung, ovarian, pancreatic, kidney, testicular, and stomach cancers, as well as Hodgkin and non-Hodgkin lymphoma, multiple myeloma, and soft tissue sarcoma.[630] The top-selling pesticide glyphosate, the active ingredient of the herbicide most commonly known as Roundup, was originally mainly used on weeds to clear land for planting, but is increasingly used to kill off the crop just before harvest, a process known as desiccation. When potatoes are sprayed with herbicides in the field immediately before harvest, this hardens their skins and reduces their susceptibility to late blight and germination, all of which improves the potatoes' shelf life. The active compounds of the herbicide directly enter the potato through the leaves; however, decomposition of the poison takes place in the body of the consumer. Researchers from the University of Leipzig found glyphosate in the urine of city workers, journalists and lawyers, who had no direct contact with glyphosate.[631] Other research shows that lettuce, carrots, and barley contained glyphosate residues up to one year after the soil was treated with glyphosate. Despite its ubiquitous use glyphosate is not included in compounds tested by the United States Food and Drug Administration's pesticide monitoring program, nor in the USDA's Pesticide Data Program.[632] It seems as if the authorities find it easier not to look for any problem.

In most countries there is no systematic follow up of pesticides in nature and no country monitors for all active substances; but what is found is still frightening enough. Eighty percent of all rivers in the United States contain pesticide residues and sixty percent of all wells have residues. The proportion of contaminated wells was almost as high in urbanized areas, due to use in home gardens, gravel or stone paths, golf courses etc. In France, pesticides are found in all rivers and half of all water sources had at least traces of them. Of the fifty substances that are monitored in the Netherlands, two thirds were found in ground water.[633] On the Great Plains in the USA researchers detected 2 insecticides and 27 herbicides in reservoir waters. Even after purification, treatment, drinking water contained 3-15 herbicides.[634]

Pesticides also damage biodiversity. An insecticide typically harms not only the target insect, the pest, but also several others, often also those that feed on the pest. The target insect might be valuable food for other organisms, which then are threatened. Herbicides reduce the amount of food for birds and other small animals living in the agriculture landscape. If a fungicide is used it normally affects various fungi, some of which compete with the fungal pest one tries to control. Bees are sensitive to pesticides and there are many examples of bee deaths caused by pesticides. Recently the neonicotinoid pesticides have been linked with the massive collapse of bee colonies on both sides of the Atlantic.[635] This is harmful not only for the beekeeper but also for society at large. Some estimate that the value of pollination of agriculture crops alone is worth around €150 billion, around 10% of total agricultural output.[636]

One study by the United Nations Environment Programme, UNEP, reveals that the costs of injury – lost work days, medical treatments, and patient hospitalization – from pesticide poisonings, in Sub-Saharan Africa alone, amounted to US$4.4 billion in 2005.[637] Another UNEP study suggests that the economic and environmental losses due to the use of pesticides in the United States amounted to US$1.5 billion in pesticides resistance and US$1.4 billion in crop losses, and US$2.2 billion in bird losses.[638]

Pesticides, antibiotics, veterinary medicines and anti-parasitic treatments have all increased tremendously in animal production. Here again the monitoring of the effects on health and the environment is highly inadequate. Every year 25,000 people in the European Union are hit by multi-resistant bacteria. The health-care costs alone for these cases are in the range of €1.5 billion. Some bacteria are already resistant to all known antibiotics.[639] The issue has now reached international politics and was one of the topics in a 2009 EU-US Summit, which established a joint task force on antimicrobial resistance issues.[640]

There are reasons to believe that the next major scandal for industrial livestock keeping will be related to antibiotic resistance. The guts of many animals are unable to adequately absorb these antibiotics, which consequently pass through them (via their manure and urine) and enter the environment. A study by the United States Geological Survey found antibiotic residues in half the waterways they surveyed. The carpet of antibiotics that we roll out into the environment by human medication and the medication of animals is almost certainly a reason for the increased resistance of some bacteria to antibiotics, a resistance that threatens to nullify the gains of one the most important medicines ever found. Around one half of all antibiotics in Europe are prescribed for animals, while in the United States livestock production accounts for eighty percent of all antibiotic use.[641] [642] In China national television exposed the 'instant chicken' production by Liuhe, a major supplier to KFC, which mixed 18 different antibiotics into the feed of broiler chickens, to speed up their growth.[643]

The World Health Organization says drug use in farm animals plays a 'significant role' in spreading antibiotic-resistant salmonella and campylobacter infections in humans while European Union food safety officials say it could also be a source of some antibiotic-resistant strains of methicillin-resistant Staphylococcus aureus and E. coli – both potentially life-threatening infections. A new, highly resistant type of E. coli, was recently found on a large number of dairy, pig and poultry farms in England and Wales. Dutch scientists estimate that between a third and one half of resistance in human infections in the Netherlands originated from farm animals.[644]

In 2008, Amy Sapkota of the University of the Maryland School of Public Health and her colleagues studied 10 conventional farms and 10 farms that had recently become organic. They tested for the presence of bacteria known as enterococci in poultry litter, feed and water and whether these organisms were resistant to 17 commonly used drugs. All the farms tested positive for the bacteria. But the organic farms, which didn't use antibiotics, had significantly lower levels of resistant bacteria. Forty-two percent of the bacteria from conventional farms were resistant to multiple drugs, compared to only 10% from the organic farms.[645] In Sweden the systemic preventative use of antibiotics in livestock is prohibited and livestock producers use less than a tenth of the quantities (per kg) used in Germany or Belgium.[646]

Another troubling development is the use of synthetic growth hormones in livestock production, including dairy farming. They include recombinant bovine growth hormone (rbGH) – to promote milk production; estrogen, testosterone, and progesterone – steroid hormones added to promote growth and production. Those hormones have no other role than to drive production. There are fears that hormones in our food are the cause of a number of disorders and disease, including breast and ovarian cancer. The hormones also spread in nature through manure and can be found in soils up to 195 days after being administered to the animals.[647] These hormones are prohibited in the European Union but are widely used in many other parts of the world, including the United States.

For individual farmers there are often good and justifiable reasons to use a pesticide, an antibiotic or a growth hormone, and if used at the 'right' time and place, this decision will mostly be economically viable and rational. But the end result of economically justifiable and rational decisions by half a billion farmers can still be – and certainly is in the case of pesticides – negative. The agricultural systems that are built around the use of fertilizers and pesticides create new needs for more pesticides. The system that is built on the routine use of antibiotics and industrial livestock systems breeds new diseases and resistant bacteria.

Scientists talk of the 'pesticide paradox' – by applying pesticides to a pest, one may actually increase its abundance or stimulate the emergence of a new pest.[648] The soil, the plants and the agriculture landscape are an intricate web and we have really no clue of the cumulative effect of the use of one single pesticide on this web, let alone the effect of hundreds of different ones in combination. The effect of the latter is often referred to as the 'cocktail effect'.

Many discuss chemical fertilizers and pesticides as solely technical or biological matters. But farmers' use of them can best be understood in the context of the system as a whole. The use of pesticides, chemical fertilizers, and antibiotics in livestock, are all part of the industrial agriculture system based on a mechanistic view of nature and life and geared towards profit. Humanity is playing a very dangerous game by using them indiscriminately.

18

Managing the planet

Humans are totally dependent on oxygen, plants and potable water, and all of these are provided by ecosystems. Ecosystems not only provide what we need, they also take care of what we don't need – waste; from the carbon dioxide we exhale to the sewage from the cities. The impact we have on ecosystems can lead to potentially irreversible processes with dramatic effects such as dead seas and climate change. The Millennium Ecosystem Assessment was initiated in 2000 by the (then) United Nations Secretary-General, Kofi Annan. It involved the work of more than 1,360 experts worldwide. Their findings, contained in five technical volumes and six synthesis reports, provide a state-of-the-art appraisal of the condition and trends in the world's ecosystems and the 'services' they provide. I am not entirely happy with the term 'ecosystem services' as it leads us to think about nature in a purely utilitarian way as well as in a market framework, both of which I believe is misguided.

Be that as it may, the experts concluded that two billion people are very vulnerable to loss of critical ecosystem services such as access to water and the threats posed by climate change and pollution by nutrients.[649] The composite value of these services is very high; but many of them are of such importance for human survival that their value simply cannot be calculated, such as the supply of oxygen. We cannot even imagine how we could organize the same services if the existing ecosystems were to collapse. Ecological economist Robert Constanza and others estimated in 1997 the value of global ecosystem services as being worth at least as much as the global GDP and possibly three times higher.[650]

Agriculture is the most prominent example of how, over millennia, we have increased the value of ecosystems – for us that is. But agriculture also highlights the dangers of focusing on just one ecosystem service, in this case the supply of food. The improvements in farming technologies have led to us controlling more and more of the farming ecosystem and taking an ever increasing share of the primary production, leaving less for the rest of the living world. It is this narrow perspective, augmented by the mechanisms of profit-seeking and market competition, which has led to degeneration of the agricultural landscape, to erosion and pollution.

Most ecologists classify the biomes (nature types or ecosystems) of the world largely as if they were not touched by human beings, but the reality is that human beings now influence most parts of the world. Erle C. Ellis and Navin Ramankutty identify 18 anthropogenic biomes and only 3 biomes that could be considered 'wildlands', most of them barren, permafrost or sparsely forested. The wildlands represent around 22% of all terrestrial land, but only 11% of the net primary production (through photosynthesis) because they are cold or dry, or both. All other nature types have been so heavily influenced by human beings that they should be considered man-made landscapes; 'human systems with natural ecosystems embedded within them'. And more than half the world's land is within farmed landscapes.[651] So even if farmland, in a narrow sense, might make up slightly more than one third of the land area of the planet, farming is the major determining factor for more than half of the biological production of the land. So farming doesn't only need ecosystem services and biodiversity, but today it is the most important determinant of most terrestrial ecosystems, for the better and the worse.

Many ecosystem services are linked to what is often referred to as biodiversity, which can be understood as the total network of species, varieties and their linkages; the abundance of life. Biodiversity provides the basis for food production, including genetic resources as well as productive, regulatory, supporting and cultural services. For food and agriculture it is important to maintain variety at all levels: diversity of genes, species and ecosystems. Many non-farm plants, insects and animals live in the farmed landscape. Many species also live in the border zones between the fields and 'nature'; which are often very rich in diversity. When agriculture practices and the farming system change, this affects all the species that interact with the farmed landscape. Some species can be directly harmed by very specific changes, such as the use of a pesticide or the destruction of their nesting areas. According to the International Union for Conservation of Nature, agriculture is responsible for 70% of all birds and 49% of all plants on the list of threatened species (the 'red list').[652] In the United Kingdom, 333 species in the agriculture landscape are in decline due to agriculture practices and the number of farmland birds fell by 44% between 1970 and 2012. Bee colonies have declined by more than 50% in twenty-five years.[653]

Agriculture can not only destroy biodiversity, it also creates a lot of biodiversity. From the first small steps towards farming, farmers all over the globe have created a fantastic diversity through selection and

cross-breeding. While the number of plant species that supply most of
the world's energy and protein is relatively small, the diversity within
such species is often immense. For example, the number of distinct
varieties of rice is estimated at more than 100,000. Farming communities in the Andes cultivate more than 175 local potato varieties.[654] It is
this diversity within species that allows for the cultivation of crops
across different regions and under many different climatic and soil
conditions. But the diversity has declined rapidly in the last century
and, according to the FAO, around three quarters of the agro-biodiver-
sity has been lost and another third of the existing germplasm could be
gone by 2050.[655] A survey of 75 crops in the United States shows that
97% of the varieties in the early public lists of seeds have disappeared.
Through the so-called Green Revolution the varieties of cultivated
paddy rice has become very limited. In Sri Lanka 75% of the rice
varieties come from one mother line, in Bangladesh 62% and in
Indonesia 74%.[656] Of 7,600 livestock breeds reported to FAO, more than
1,500 are at risk of extinction or are already extinct. In the beginning of
the 2000s almost one breed disappeared forever each month.[657]

Biodiversity is not only about individual species and varieties but
also how they belong together. In Turkey the whole traditional farmscape is disappearing. This landscape had both an impressive variety
of farmed crops and animals and a lot of wildlife that had found an
ecological niches in this relatively extensively managed landscape. As
a result of this, 6 wild plants, 14 of 20 cow breeds, 2 of 19 sheep breeds
and 2 of 5 goat breeds have been lost.[658] These landscapes are not only
full of biodiversity, they are also among the most scenic in the world. It
is for a reason the word pastoral has come to mean serene, of natural
beauty. Perhaps we all carry a sub-conscious memory of the African
Savannah where we developed as a species, making us like open
grasslands with scattered trees?

Diversity in plants and animals is particularly important for adapt-
ing to a range of farming conditions and environmental stresses, such
as temperature extremes, drought, soil salinity, pests and diseases, and
water quality. The availability of a broad pool of genetic resources also
contributes to breeding crop and animal varieties that are more
productive. It is essential to conserve genetic diversity within each
species. Modern agriculture has encouraged many farmers to adopt
uniform high-yielding types of plant or animal. But when food producers abandon diversity, valuable traditional varieties and breeds may
die out, along with their specialized traits. For the poorest farmers, the
diversity of life can be their best protection against starvation. According to the FAO "Losing these breeds is like losing a global insurance

policy against future threats to food security. It undermines capacity to adapt livestock populations to environmental changes, emerging diseases or changing consumer demands".[659] If all farmers grow the same variety there is a much bigger risk of a disease or pest rapidly wiping out the production over large tracts of land. An outbreak of wheat stem rust in the 1950s reduced wheat yields by 40% in the United States, resulting in a loss of income of US$3 billion and having a serious effect on the food supply.[660]

Farmers and breeders who want total crop uniformity – often a result of demands from the food industry and supermarkets – are literally throwing away most of the genetic possibilities accumulated through generations. It is essential that we preserve as large a share as possible of the gigantic common heritage of human beings, in the form of old varieties and races.[a]

The main cause of global warming is the burning of fossil fuel. But agriculture is directly responsible for some 14% of greenhouse gas emissions. Land-use changes (the conversion of forest, savannah or wetland to farmland), land-degradation and deforestation linked to agriculture represent another 18%.[661] Agriculture plays four important roles in climate change: 1) farming emits greenhouse gases, directly and indirectly; 2) changes in agricultural practices have a big potential to increase or decrease carbon stocks in soils; 3) changes in land use, caused by farming, have great impact (either negative or positive) on emissions; 4) agriculture can produce energy, which can replace fossil fuels. The last point I will discuss later. In addition to the effects of agriculture, the rest of the food system also contributes considerably to climate change, mostly through its considerable use of energy use from manufacturing agrochemicals to refrigeration and distribution.

Around thirteen million hectares of forest are cleared annually, mostly in developing countries. Logging for timber is one driver but the main driver is the expansion of agriculture. This expansion occurs both through large-scale expansion, with big corporations clearing forests for palm oil or cattle ranching, and on a small-scale by hun-

---

[a] Realistically, however, we can't hope to save *all* varieties and races that human beings have developed over millennia. In the same way that can't look after every single species in nature, neither we can take care of every variety of cabbage or breed of sheep. Some of these varieties are also functionally defective, for example, turkeys that can't reproduce or cows, like the Belgian blue, that can't give birth naturally. There are therefore clearly limits as to what we should conserve and protect.

dreds of thousands of smallholders seeking a better life. The soil's carbon stocks are many times bigger than all the carbon stored in green plants. The high drama, for the greenhouse effect, is not the cutting down of trees (although this can of course have devastating effects from other perspectives, such as biodiversity) but the loss of carbon from the soil which occurs when land is converted from forest, grasslands or wetlands to farmland. In this sense, plowing up grasslands might be worse than cutting down trees because the carbon content of grassland is often much higher. It is estimated that plowing the North American prairies and the famous black soils of the Pontic Caspian steppe of Eastern Europe have led to a loss of half of all their organic matter, and the process of destruction is still going on.[662] Even worse is the cultivation of organogenic soils (peat and marshlands made up of almost uniquely organic matter, i.e. carbon) in northern Europe and South East Asia. When these soils are cultivated this can lead to emissions as high as 20-40 tons carbon dioxide per hectare per year.[663]

When land is cleared for farming, after an initial rapid deterioration of soil organic matter the process continues and a new balance is reached after many decades. The level at which the soil organic matter content will stabilize depends on many factors, including climate, soil type, precipitation, choice of crops, livestock and the use of fertilizers. Approximately one-third of the increase in carbon dioxide in the atmosphere comes from the breakdown of organic matter, the humus, the life of the soils.[664] Carbon dioxide is also released from the direct and indirect use of fossil fuels in the agriculture sector, for instance, through the diesel used in the tractors and in producing chemical fertilizers.

Methane is emitted by ruminants, from paddy rice production and from manure. Knowledge about many aspects of the methane cycle is still scarce and incomplete.; for example, we do not know well enough how we can influence the break down of methane by metanotrophic bacteria in the soil or how fodder influences methane emissions from cows or how one can reduce methane emissions from paddy rice. We do know that rice production with no or little flooding releases less methane than normal practices. The methane emissions come from the rice plant itself (up to 90%) and there is a possibility of exploiting varietal differences to reduce these emissions.[665] There are indications that the methane emitted from grazing cows can largely be compensated for by an increase of carbon in permanent pastures. It is also doubtful that emissions of methane from domesticated ruminants should be seen as a contribution to climate change as they are part of a natural cycle. Domesticated livestock has to some extent just replaced their wild cousins, and if a big deer is replaced by a cow, the greenhouse gas emissions will remain the same. The American prairies contained at least 30 million bison two hundred years ago.[666] In addition, if land is not be used for pasture it will be converted into forest, left idle or converted into farmland. The last alternative would inevitably lead to more carbon emissions; according to a meta-analysis of 80 reports on the conversion of grassland to cropland, more than half of the soil carbon can be lost when grassland is plowed.[667] There are reasons to believe that as long as ruminants are grazing natural grass, their net emissions are rather small. It is a very different story when they are fed crops grown on agriculture land, such as maize and soy cake which generates 'double emissions', from the ruminants themselves and from the land farmed for their feed.

Agriculture is responsible for two-thirds of the emissions of laughing gas (nitrous oxide), the third most important greenhouse gas. These emissions are directly related to the nitrogen cycle. The increase in livestock numbers and the use of chemical fertilizers are the key drivers. The use of nitrogen fertilizers is extremely inefficient and a lot more nitrogen is added to the soil than is taken away with the harvest. The rest of this nitrogen 'gets lost'; some of it as nitrate runoff and some of it as emissions of nitrous gases. In addition, the production of nitrogen fertilizers also consumes a lot of energy. Reducing our use of nitrogen fertilizers can thus be a main strategy for reducing greenhouse gas emissions from agriculture.

Anyone looking into the management of ecosystems realizes that something has to be done to save them from further destruction and to restore many of them that have been degraded. The question is how? Clearly 'business as usual' isn't an option as there are no market mechanisms for food production that encourage ecosystem management. On the contrary, the continued specialization, mechanization and 'chemicalization' of farming pose major threats to ecosystems.

Increasingly, systems are being developed to make payments to land managers (usually farmers) to maintain or create new ecosystem services. As early as 1996, Costa Rica introduced a system which compensated landowners for carbon sequestration, biodiversity protection, water regulation and conserving landscapes. In 2001, the payments under this program had reached US$30 million and covered a total of 280,000 hectares (around 6% of the country's land mass).[668] Farmers in the European Union and the United States are paid for all kinds of environmental services: protecting landscapes and water sources, maintaining or restoring biodiversity. The United States pays

US$1.7 billion annually for 31 million acres in the Conservation Reserve Program.[669] Farmers in the Scoltel Té project in Chiapas in Mexico sell carbon sequestration, in the soil and in vegetation, for between US$300 and US$1800 per farm, big sums for households where the average income is about US$1000.[670]

Both the FAO and the World Bank are promoting carbon emission trading for carbon sequestration (carbon sinks) in soils; that is, paying farmers for increasing soil organic matter. The carbon sink capacity of the world's agricultural and degraded soils is said to be 50-66% of the historic carbon loss from soils or some 42-78 Gigatons of carbon.[671] Applying such measures in the farm sector is one of the cheapest ways of mitigating climate change and, in many cases, they also lead to other environmental improvements, such as reducing water pollution. Increased soil organic matter also leads to richer soils; that can retain water and are more resistant to erosion.

New York gets most of its water from an area stretching some 200 km north and west of the city. The authorities concluded that it was more efficient to manage the catchment area for good water quality than to invest in a purification plant. Such a plant would cost between US$6 and US$8 billion while the catchment management program cost US$1.5 billion. It includes measures such as purchasing some critical lands and providing education and support to farmers to reduce their use of chemical fertilizers and synthetic pesticides.[672] This is one of many examples of payments for ecosystem services.

There are potential problems with, and unintended side effects of, payments for ecosystem services, some of which are not initially seen. For example, in India, poor landless people have been harmed by community forest management plans because the plans limited their access to resources to which they previously had unrestricted access.[673] Other examples can be found when communal land is appropriated by private owners (part of the cause of the recent trend of 'land-grabbing') who suddenly see an economic benefit in selling these environmental services. A new scenario is emerging where farmers in developing countries can sell their services as carbon farmers to governments and companies in developed countries. This could become a business replacement for development aid, or a way to compensate farmers of developing countries for the distorting subsidies that their competitors in developed countries receive. But it also means that more of their activities are integrated in the global economy. These payments can also be seen as a new frontier of exploitation, where the rich countries use the land in developing countries as a 'dumping' ground for their waste, which is what these practices eventually amount to. The European Union has proposed a system where the sealing of soil (for buildings or road construction) is offset by "measures of equal value.... carried out somewhere else".[674] The logic of this is that Europeans will be paying for re-claiming land in Africa in order to continue building high-ways on their own agriculture lands. A strange world indeed.

The proponents of the market system believe that we can use the market to regulate 'negative externalities'; the damage to nature caused by farming. At present, we let someone else – nature, other people, future generations, tax payers – foot the bill for how we farm. For example, the external costs of farming in Great Britain were estimated to be some £1.5 billion, corresponding to £265 per hectare.[675] These calculations are conservative and only include proven costs; for example, they do not include any costs for the health effects of pesticides in food. And, as I noted earlier, farmers using nitrogen fertilizers create costs for society at large which are on par with (if not greater than) the economic benefits for them.

In theory, full internalization of costs (such as fees for natural resource use and waste) and compensation for ecosystem services (such as carbon credits or landscape payments) would allow, for instance, organic farmers to compete fairly with non-organic ones. If all the external costs – that is the costs for water purification, soil degradation and health effects, to mention just a few – were incorporated into the price of non-organic food those foods would be more expensive than they are today, some might be on par with organic food, some would perhaps remain cheaper and others more expensive.[676]

However, one can question the benefits of valuing ecosystem services in monetary terms, especially as the most valuable of these services have unlimited value and no known alternative. But there is also the question of how we perceive nature. It seems that we increasingly confuse 'value' and monetary values, and there is a case for us avoiding underwriting this confusion by assigning prices for natural and social capital.

In a complex system such as farming, the internalization of *all* social and environmental costs and compensation for ecosystem services would only be possible with very extensive and detailed regulations. Just look at the European Union's agri-environmental program which is but a small step in this direction. Such a system would probably still be neither fair, nor efficient, and would, in many ways, represent a control of farms more severe than under Soviet rule. Moreover, the payments to farmers for providing public goods will not reflect the value of the public good but the compensation the farmer needs to make the required effort – which may be considerably higher or lower than the value of the services themselves. So, if farmers are compensated for not spraying chemicals in a watershed, the level of payment will be to compensate the farmer from actual (or perceived) losses. In 2003 more than ten percent of England's agricultural land was enrolled in long-term contracts between the government and farmers to provide environmental services. There was a high uptake of the elements of the programs that didn't require fundamental changes to farming practices. But, in intensively farmed areas the uptake was low, as the incentives were not sufficient to persuade farmers to make more demanding changes.[677] In a sense the program was just 'greening the edges'.

There are no indications that the market for ecosystem services will be based on any of the scientific calculations that are now made to show the value of these services. The market value will be very different from the real value or the use value. This can be seen very well in the price for carbon credits, which has no relationship to the cost of climate change. The value of carbon markets worldwide dropped 38% in 2013 to US$52.9 billion. The EU Emissions Trading Scheme, which accounts for 94% of the world's carbon market value, has seen prices fall by almost US$18 per ton over the past two years.[678] The costs for paying in full for ecosystem services can also be very high. Mashahito Enomoto, Director of the Policy Division of the Japanese Ministry of Agriculture, Forestry and Fisheries told participants in a conference in 2012 that the estimated value of production from Japanese agriculture was 9.5 trillion Yen (some US$120 billion at 2012's rate) while the value of the ecosystem services were estimated to 8.2 trillion Yen, i.e. almost as much as the production value.[679]

"It is a fantasy to believe that we can devise a rigged market system in which 'corrected' prices would tell the whole truth about the opportunity costs of everything in the world, and automatically optimize the scale of the economy relative to the ecosystem, as well as the allocation of resources within the economy" wrote Herman Daly, the creator of the concept of a steady-state economy.[680] A recent governmental study on ecosystem services in Sweden concludes that economic valuation and compensation may, in many cases, not be the best way to maintain ecosystem services. It says that monetary valuation is not reliable or is completely unsuitable for complex situations that involve numerous ecosystem services, such as soil formation, water regulation and pollination. This, in a nutshell, is farming. It seems foolish to rely solely on market-based measures to tackle the biodiversity issues and ecosystem services associated with farming. Instead of fiddling with hundreds of different subsidies or fees that regulate what farmers should or should not do, we need to look at the whole system.

Farming is the most significant human management system of the planet; the future of humans on the planet largely rests upon how we manage our farmscapes. If we accept this then it has profound implications for agricultural policy for it means that 'managing the planet' is almost as an important task of the farming system as supplying food. But farmers are not very oriented to being land stewards through the market system. On the contrary, modern day farming has removed much of the land husbandry and stewardship which was previously an integral part of a regenerative farming system. It is not realistic that 'the market' will take care of managing the planet. It is also not desirable, as the Earth is our common home and responsibility and should be managed as such.

19

Fueling farming

In an earlier chapter I discussed two farmers: Bob in United States, with a big farm in the Corn Belt, and Susan in Zambia, a smallholder who relies on manual labor. Bob's labor productivity, measured in kilograms of maize per hour worked, is more than 500 times higher than Susan's. The single most important explanation for this is his use of energy to assist in the production. Susan has no access to external energy supplies, except for that pair of oxen she rents for land preparation before sowing, and indirectly through some chemical fertilizers that are subsidized by the government. Bob, on the other hand, uses very high quantities of energy, directly in the form of diesel and indirectly in the form of chemical fertilizers, embedded in machinery and used in the transport of goods in and out of the farm. On Bob's farm it takes energy the equivalent of more than one barrel of oil to produce maize on one acre (0.4 hectare).[681] Put another way, each worker on Bob's farm commands energy resources of a thousand barrels of oil. Considering that the energy content of one barrel of oil equals the manpower of some 14 people working a whole year, there is no wonder that labor productivity is very much higher in Illinois than in Zambia. But is it efficient? That depends totally on how we count, something I will return to later.

It is no coincidence that we use power as a measurement of the force extracted from energy *and* that the same word is used to describe social hierarchies. To have power is to command energy, in one form or the other. With the emergence of industrial capitalism, the power in society shifted from those who controlled solar collection on the ground (landlords) and human masses (the state and landlords together) to those who controlled the new energy sources (fossil fuels) and put them to work for trade or industrial production – the merchants and industrial capitalists.[682]

The poorest people have very limited access to energy; it is largely limited to firewood, manure or other combustible waste products collected by household members, often women and children. At the end of the 1990s I met farmers in China who were solely reliant on cotton straw as their only fuel for cooking. Any reader who is familiar with the cotton plant would understand that this is a source of last resort. Approximately 2.6 billion people rely on biomass as their main energy source.[683] Around 1.6 billion people have no access to electricity. By contrast, feeding a person in the developed world takes the equivalent of 1,500 liters of oil.[684] One can, of course, discuss cause and effect here: are the poor poor because they have no access to energy? Or is poverty the reason why they have no access to energy? Regardless of the chain of causality, it is clear that it is very hard for those without access to energy to compete in an international market with those who have very good access to energy.

The success of a species is mainly about its ability to capture energy. The enormous 'success' of humans can, to a large extent, be explained by our ever increasing command over energy resources. The arrowhead and the stone dagger made it possible for us to hunt large game and to use the energy of our arms better. Fire let us get energy out of wood, which made metallurgy and pottery possible, as well as settlements in colder areas. When we were hunters and gatherers, we captured the energy in game, fish, leaves and plants, we could only skim the surplus of nature. We had to capture as much food-energy as possible from the system to produce and reproduce. Reproduce not only children, but also the small society, the band, to which we belonged. This also included taking care of the elderly and sick, throwing the odd big party to keep spirits high, diverting energy to rock paintings, hair braiding, nose ringing and other forms of cultural expression. Farming meant taming photosynthesis (a form of solar energy) to meet human needs. Animals were domesticated not only for food but also for transport and power in agriculture. The use of wind for sailing dramatically extended our reach; new areas could be settled and trade allowed settlements in places that could not be settled in before. For each new form of energy, technological processes emerged that could control and direct the energy form more efficiently. We increased the heat of a fire with bellows; we developed harnesses, wagons, saddles, reigns, spurs and bridles for horses, each one of them essential to 'harness' the energy. Technology can, from this perspective, largely be seen as a process of 'directing' energy.[685]

The introduction of fire allowed humans to bring substantial energy sources under their command. The energy contained in the firewood was considerably higher than the energy of the food, meaning that, already with cooking, we developed an 'energy-deficient' food system. My visits to farmers practicing slash and burn in Latin America, Africa and Asia taught me that burning down trees is one of the easiest ways to prepare land for farming. However, the energy wastage is enormous. If we assume, as a rough calculation, that about hundred cubic meters of wood per hectare of land is burnt and that the land is used for farming for three years, this means that about 35 cubic meters of firewood is 'used' per hectare per year. This energy ratio is worse than today's industrial system.[686] Even today, firewood or charcoal made from firewood for cooking is a very substantial part of the energy source of the poor. Cooking represents more than a fifth of the total energy consumption in Africa and Asia and more than 90% of household energy consumption in some countries.[687]

The introduction of draught animals some 6000 years ago was another step in the conquest of external energy for human needs. Even today, almost 400 million draught animals are used to cultivate around half of all agricultural land. Of these, some 300 million are cattle, including buffaloes, and 80 million are horses, donkeys and mules.[688] Their daily energy output is somewhere between 1 and 6 kWh[689] compared with the 0.5-1 kWh output of human beings. Draught animals thus substantially extended (and continue to extend) the power (energy) that human beings use. They can increase the amount of land cultivated, especially in the countries with very seasonal farming: temperate or dry climates where speed in land preparation is critical. However, natural and biological conditions limit the use of these animals and their efficiency. In most agricultural situations, they can only be used for a rather short period of the year, but still have to be fed all year round.[690] Draught animals are also tremendously useful for transporting food and other products. Some of them, camels and donkeys come to mind, have mainly been used for this.

Before the large-scale extraction of fossil fuels, human society was largely locked into a biomass economy. Apart from the crops and resources from the sea, wood was the primary fuel. Most civilizations simply would not have existed without forests. This changed when profitable uses of fossil fuel, in particular mineral coal, were introduced. Fossil fuels represent some 80% of all energy supplies today. All indications point to us having reached what is known as 'peak oil'. The shale oil and gas boom in the United States is not a sign that peak oil isn't real. On the contrary, it is a proof that ordinary, easily accessible and cheap oil resources are running out and that we will have to make greater efforts to get precious energy in the future. This is bound to have huge consequences for our society, not the least for the farm sector. The costs of transporting soybeans from inland Brazil to China are already around one third of the total end price, with land transport costs being the biggest part, largely a reflection of fuel prices.[691]

Modern farming uses energy in many different forms: diesel for tractors and pumps; electricity for pumps, fans and indoor machinery, such as milking machines, etc. Fertilizers also represent a big energy use; 90% of the production costs of nitrogen fertilizers, 30% of phosphorus fertilizers and 15% of potassium fertilizers are for energy. In the United States, energy costs represent around one quarter of the production costs for wheat, maize and cotton and one seventh of the production costs for soybeans.[692] These figures do not include costs embedded in buildings, machinery, etc., so energy's actual share of the costs is substantially higher. The increase in energy use in agriculture was rapid in the period between the Second World War and the first oil price shock in 1973; while the agricultural labor force in England was halved between 1952 and 1972 energy use tripled. In the United States, energy use decreased between the mid 1970s and the mid 1980s as a response to increased oil prices; since then it has stabilized.

The Swedish Institute of Agricultural and Environmental Engineering studied the medium term (3-5 years) effects of three scenarios for a sudden decrease in the supply of fossil fuel energy. They chose this time period on the assumption that no technological development or other structural change would emerge that could significantly change current conditions. The three levels of fossil fuel supply studied were a decrease of 25%, 50% and 75% compared with current levels. With three quarters of the fossil fuel gone, a liter of diesel would cost almost US$25. With such a shortage of (and expensive) fuel it would not be possible to grow the same amount of grain, and the volumes grown would need to be used primarily for human consumption, rather than fed to pigs and chickens. Parts of the land left uncultivated would be used for grazing by ruminants. With a reduction of just a quarter it would be possible to feed the Swedish population adequately by increasing energy efficiency at all levels. But with 50% and 75% reductions, it would not be possible to keep the population above the breadline.[693] Over time, of course, farmers and society would adapt themselves to the new conditions. This has been the case before, for instance during the two world wars, when access to energy was much lower than it was before – see the example of how Britain converted from importing 60% of its food to self-sufficiency during World War One. Nevertheless, the study gives an interesting perspective on how dependent modern society is on energy.

In industrial countries, between 10 and 15 times more energy is used in the food system than is contained in the food we eat. The whole food chain consumes around 16% of the total energy use in the United States.[694] The USDA estimates that delivering the average American's 2,000 calorie diet requires nearly 32,000 calories of energy inputs.[695] Different kinds of agricultural production and different foods have different energy ratios. The energy efficiency of deep-sea fishing, meat production from feedlots and vegetables grown in heated greenhouses is very low. It is much higher for grains, grazing animals and root crops. Most agricultural systems have improved their energy ratios in recent decades, partly as a result of increasing energy prices and associated technical innovations.

In pre- and semi-industrial agriculture systems, most food was sold, eaten and prepared close to where it was produced, but modern food chains are highly centralized and globalized. Farm operations in the United States consume only 14% of the total energy used in the food chain, while handling, processing and retail on the one hand and preparation on the other, use more or less equal shares of the rest. This greatly influences the energy ratio of foods we eat, and comparisons of what we eat look very different than those made of produce at the farm gate. One third of all energy in the food system in the United States is used for snacks, convenience foods and beverages: their energy use is double the total for all meats. Food that requires cold chains and a lot of processing consumes a lot of energy post-harvest. Fruit and vegetables consume as much energy as dairy produce. At the farm level grains are most efficient (which is why they were traditional staple foods in the first place), but processing them demands a lot of energy.[696] If we look at the calorific contribution of different foods, compared to the energy used in the food chain, sugar, fats and grain come out well because they can be handled without refrigeration and are energy-dense. Fresh vegetables are some of the least energy efficient foods, even it is very healthy to eat them. This is also the reason why, historically, the consumption of vegetables has been modest. Today's sedentary, car driving office workers may have quite low energy requirements and be able to get by on a raw salad, but it is certainly not something that could keep a hard working farm laborer going for 12 hours.

When we add in what happens at the consumption level things get even more complicated. Here we need to add the energy use in households and food eaten 'out'. This includes the energy spent on frying and boiling, and storage in refrigerators and freezers etc. More than a quarter of the energy in the food chain in United States is used in households and one sixth in the food service sector, restaurants, cafés and catering.[697] Because most energy in the food system is spent after the farm gate, the design of the food system – how we process, distribute, store and consume food – plays a much bigger role than what we do at the farm level. This means any discussion of energy efficiency at the farm level, for instance if plants are more efficient than animals, only looks at a small part of the picture.

Our food system may have a poor energy ratio but this, in itself, is not an argument that it is fundamentally wrong. If that were so, all human civilizations would be fundamentally wrong, as they all have used firewood or other biomass for cooking. Even life would be wrong as plants are also highly inefficient – transforming less than one percent of sunlight into stored energy in biomass. But we should not have a food system where the energy efficiency is so low that it is completely reliant on access to unsustainable energy sources, such as fossil fuels.

Therefore, when seeking alternatives to today's food chains, taking net energy production as a prerequisite would lead us in the wrong direction. Even worse would be to say that we should not use any ancillary energy in the farming system. It is not always wrong to use additional energy. For example, a small quantity of water for irrigation, such as in a nursery or at a critical growth phase of the crop, can make an enormous difference in yield. Cooking remains an essential part of human life even if it is 'a waste of energy'. Also, the value of food cannot be measured in calories alone. If this were the case we would better off keeping to sugar (and sugar cane is also one of the most energy-efficient crops). Vegetables will always be inferior to grain when it comes to energy ratios, but they do contain a lot of minerals and vitamins. Meat is not primarily consumed for its energy content but for its protein content. And, some food is eaten simply because it tastes good or for religious or cultural reasons.[698] As for most discussions about farming and food, it is best to take a 'systems' perspective rather than argue that a particular crop or food should or should not be consumed because of its energy efficiency ratio.

Examining the energy ratios in agriculture give an interesting perspective but conclusions shouldn't be taken to the extreme. We are not (yet) in a situation where we have to balance energy from food against energy from oil, solar, wind, nuclear power or hydropower. But when we discuss the large-scale conversion of croplands to producing biofuels, it is clear that the link between food and fuel is real (I come back to this in chapter twenty-two). Our concerns about bad energy ratios should depend on assessments of the overall energy supply for humanity, and the prospects for renewable energy. I concur with Richard Heinberg of the Post Carbon Institute that it is a rather safe bet that, by 2100, global society will have less energy available for economic purposes, not more. That will lead us to make more direct choices about where and how to use that energy. But those who believe in the cornucopia of technological progress will have a very different perspective.

When energy prices rise, agriculture prices follow suit. This was seen when food prices rose following the oil price hike in 2007-2008.[699] Increased energy prices influence food prices through at least four mechanisms. Higher energy prices make production, at all stages, more expensive; it becomes more interesting to produce biofuels, thereby reducing food production leading to higher prices; it will increase transport costs that are directly reflected in food prices; and competition will be reduced in the food sector as increased transport costs reduce global competitive pressure.[700]

Rising energy costs will make those parts of our food supply which are most energy-inefficient, such as air-freighting food, and some cool chains, obsolete. The price of nitrogen fertilizers and pesticides will increase considerably and they will therefore be used less. Much of energy used in the food sector is quite difficult to convert to renewable energy. Electric tractors are possible to make, but they will certainly have less power than comparable fossil-fuel driven equipment. A group of researchers that have developed an electric tractor says that it will only work if the agriculture methods are changed to require less power in its operations.[701]

It is an open question if – in an energy deficient future – it will be cheaper to produce nitrogen fertilizers from solar energy than to bind nitrogen from crop rotations with biological nitrogen fixation. I would bank on the latter, as solar energy may turn out a lot more expensive when its production is no longer subsidized by coal and oil, which is currently is the case. An energy scarce future will also shift diets back to more grain and pulses and less processed and ready-made foods. Meat and milk from grazing animals would increase, while the recent growth of crop-fed beef, chicken and pork will be reversed.

Increasing energy prices will also realign the balance between the urban and the rural to some degree and will most certainly pose a big challenge to megacities of thirty million people in areas without food production. Their situation will be precarious. Higher energy prices will also result in a roll-back of markets. And in general, the rift between where food is produced and where it is consumed will have to narrow and long distance trade in food will be dramatically reduced. Sea transportation of quite large quantities is possible, even with sailing ships. As late as the beginning of the 20th century there were still thousands of great windjammers shipping grain between Australia and Europe.

20

The thin skin of the planet

Author Joseph Kinsey Howard describes a spring day in 1883 in North Dakota when a Scandinavian farmer was plowing. An old Sioux watched the prairie grass being turned under. The farmer stopped his team of horses, pushed back his black Stetson hat and rolled a cigarette. He watched as the Sioux knelt, thrust his fingers into the furrow, measured its depth, fingered the sod and the buried grass. Eventually this Native American straightened up and looked at the immigrant farmer. "Wrong side up," he said and walked away.[702]

Human existence is dependent on the thin skin of the planet; on 20-50 centimeters of topsoil. This topsoil is one of our most important resources and it is under constant threat. It takes between 60 and 1500 years to create a centimeter of productive soil.[703] Stones that are eroded by wind, water and plant roots contribute with minerals; dead organisms provide food for the special life forms in the topsoil, such as worms. They, in turn, help decomposition and free nutrients for new growth. Soil organic matter is what makes the difference between a fertile soil and weathered rock or sand. This soil organic matter is essentially made up of carbon; between 590 and 1180 million tons of carbon is fixed in the world's soils, and it plays many important roles. Land with high organic matter content is, almost without exception, more fertile. It has a better structure and is richer in nutrients. It is also more resistant to drought (as the organic matter acts as a sponge) and to water and wind erosion. When organic matter, essentially made up of carbon, is degraded it leads to substantial carbon dioxide emissions and vice versa; an increase in soil organic matter ties up ('sequesters') carbon dioxide and therefore increases the soil's role as a carbon sink. Soil formation can be a self-reinforcing process: a good soil will reproduce itself and actually improve over the years.

The same holds true for the reverse process, soil erosion, the loss of top soil. Erosion makes the soil vulnerable to more erosion until it can be completely washed away. Unfortunately, soil erosion can occur much faster than soil formation. What took a thousand years to build can be washed or blown away in just a few years, or in extreme cases, such as a land slide, in just an hour. Some erosion is unavoidable, it is a natural process, but farmers have increased the rate of erosion ten, hundred, even up to thousand times.[704] It was a concern for the rulers of ancient Greece as early as the sixth century BC. The lawmaker Solon proposed a ban on cultivating hillsides in order to prevent erosion. The ruler Peisistratus promoted planting of olive trees instead of cutting down forests and grazing livestock.

Some sources state that, globally, 5-10 million hectares of farmland become unsuitable for farming every year as a result of soil degradation.[705] Soils on steep terrains are particularly vulnerable. In Nepal, the loss of soil in mountain areas ranges from 20 to 200 tons per hectare per year.[706] Rwanda reports erosion rates of up to 557 tons per hectare per year.[707] This should be compared to the formation of new topsoil which ranges from 0.1 to 1.9 tons per hectare per year.[708] In the 1930s, as a result of extractive farming systems, the United States was affected by severe soil degradation resulting in the 'Dust Bowl' when sand storms clouded the sun for months at a time and led half a million people to become 'agricultural refugees' (an event whose after effects were dramatically recorded in John Steinbeck's *Grapes of Wrath*). Extensive conservation programs were initiated and have had some effect; but erosion is still rampant. The United States lost two billion tons of soil every year in the early 2000s, an incredible figure but still an improvement from the 1980s when erosion was estimated at three billion tons per year.[709]

Soil erosion is not only a problem of lost soil. In Rwanda, erosion causes the loss of almost one million tons of organic matter, some 40,000 tons of nitrogen, 280 tons of phosphorus and 3000 tons of potassium. According to the Rwandan Ministry of Agriculture[710] this is equivalent to more than the total quantity of chemical fertilizers used in the country. And, as noted in an earlier chapter, half of the nitrogen fertilizers used in United States just compensate for losses from erosion.[711] Thus soil erosion is very costly and creates huge environmental problems. But most critically, we lose something that is only reproduced very slowly.

In the United States[a] you can by top soil by the truckload for US$25-30 a ton. As 2 billion tons of topsoil is lost annually from the American farms, replacing it would cost more than US$50 billion. But, we should not forget that we cannot actually *produce* new soil at the speed or rate sufficient to compensate for these losses. And, we cannot

---

[a] Prices are rather similar in Europe.

produce soil for US$25 per ton, we can only strip it off from a place where nature created it and transport somewhere else. So the price of a truckload is no indication whatsoever of the real value of a living soil. The price of a truckload corresponds to the withdrawal fee of a bank account, rather than the withdrawal itself.

The dramatic collapse, or slow decay, of many civilizations can be traced back to soil erosion and harmful agricultural practices. In *Dirt: The erosion of civilizations,* David Montgomery discusses how most historic cultures have lasted between 500 and 1000 years. Civilizations start off with fertile soils created by natural processes. Abundant yields from those soils are the basis for a rapid development of the population and a civilization. But, sooner or later, a combination of soil erosion and population increase leads to the cultivation of marginal lands, the fertility of which rapidly plummets. Finally, the whole civilization collapses and the area is depopulated until nature replenishes the soils again.[712] It is a sobering insight that very few agricultural systems have proven to be really sustainable, and most of these have relied upon fortuitous external factors. The continued fertility of the Nile valley and other flood plains is mainly due to erosion upstream which brings new soil and new nutrients downstream every year. Egyptians have been aware of this for millennia and an early monument reads 'the Nile supplies all the people with nourishment and food'.[713]

As long as there is 'new' land available to farm, or there is forest that can be brought into periods of production and fallow, farmers' have a limited interest in caring for the land. The United States provides a good example of how an abundance of land led to bad management. Since independence, one-third of American topsoil has been lost. Up to three-quarters of the surface of New England was once farmed, but the land was depleted and large tracts were abandoned. In Georgia, the agriculture area shrank by 38% between 1930 and 1970 as land was depleted and farming moved westwards.[714] This movement was only arrested by a lack of virgin and fertile land that could be plowed and the arrival of cheap chemical fertilizers (detailed in an earlier chapter). The dust storms of the Great Plains in the 1930s shocked Americans; farmers, policy makers, and the public alike, into taking soil erosion seriously.[715]

One should not, however, believe that farming inevitably exhausts soils. This seems to be a common misconception, even among agronomists. On the contrary, a well-managed soil will normally increase its productivity over time, with the soil organic matter increasing rather than decreasing. This was noted by Columella, the most celebrated Roman writer on agriculture, in his work *De re rustica*. And, as I argued earlier, increased population pressure on the land can go hand in hand with increased productivity of the soils.

Since 1860, more than a billion hectares of farmland have been brought under the plow.[716] The availability of agriculture land per inhabitant is falling in sub-Saharan Africa and in South Asia. But hectares per person don't say too much. The 'natural' yield varies by a factor of almost 10, from the best to very worst producing land. The availability of agricultural land area is still increasing in developing countries but the increase has recently slowed down. Between 1960 and 2000 it grew by 5 million hectares per year, but today it is down to 3-4 million hectares per year.[717] We do not need to expand the amount of agricultural land in line with the human population as yield increases per unit area play a substantial role in meeting the needs of a growing population.

This said, the amount of new land bought into agriculture is actually higher than the figures given above suggest. Agricultural land is constantly being lost to human infrastructure (for example as cities expand) and as marginal lands are taken out of production. Some land is (re)converted to forests, some left idle and some has been eroded to the extent that it is barren. So the figures above are *gross* increases and do not include the land brought into agricultural use to compensate for these changes. Land use is more dynamic than most people realize, now as well as in the past.

Changes in land use run in several different directions: forests and wetlands are converted to agricultural land; erosion or competing demands on land use (for e.g. human infrastructure) lead to the loss of agricultural land; pasture land may be converted to forests or to other 'natural' lands or may be plowed for agriculture (often in combination with irrigation). In many developing countries forests are converted to farmland. In high-income and, increasingly, in middle-income countries the reverse is more likely to occur.[a] The agriculture lands of United States peaked in 1950 with 469 million hectares,[718] shrinking to 411 million in 2011.[719] Most Western European countries had their 'peak farm land' around the turn of the 19th/20th centuries; in France this occurred in 1850, in Germany, the Netherlands and Denmark

---

[a]   If this historical pattern holds, the expansion into the Brazilian Amazon will soon cease.

around 1910. Meanwhile, in Thailand agricultural land increased from 2 million hectares in 1910 to more than 20 million in the year 2000, and in the same period in Indonesia it increased from 12 million to 31 million hectares.[720]

Drained wetlands have always been an important source of agricultural land The Po valley and the deltas of the Mississippi and the Nile are all examples of drained wetlands. In Denmark, some 200,000 hectares of lakes and wetlands were converted to farmland when agriculture was expanding.[721] In the upper Mississippi watershed alone, 35 million acres of wetlands – that is an area the size of Illinois – have been drained and converted to other land uses, mainly farming.[722] In Italy, the draining of the marshlands in the coastal plains from the mid 1800s to the 1930s increased farmland by 2 million hectares (and substantial reduced mosquito populations.).[723]

In developing countries, there are some 300 million hectares of wetland that could be converted to farmland. However, there are many obstacles to achieving this. Draining can be logistically difficult and the drained land may have excessive concentrations of iron, aluminum or sulphuric acid, all of which are toxic to crops. These lands also have high environmental and economic values; for example, they might be breeding areas for fish, amphibians or birds. Wetlands also act as buffers for sudden water flows and therefore play a large role in flood mitigation. In China draining wetlands has led to a two-thirds reduction in the country's' buffering capacity against floods. This reduced capacity contributed to the disastrous floods of 1998, which caused damage valued at US$20 billion in addition to immense human suffering.[724] For all those reasons we should exercise caution in further draining wetlands. In high-income countries wetlands are no longer drained for agricultural expansion. On the contrary, many wetlands are being restored, for example the *Comprehensive Everglades Restoration Plan* in Miami (the United States) is supposedly the most expensive attempt at environmental restoration in history. It includes buying 187,000 acres of land from United States Sugar. After six years the company must cease farming the land, after which the state will convert the land back to its original natural marshland state.[725] The restoration of wetlands is motivated by care for biodiversity, reducing the leakage of nutrients to the sea, buffering floods and, more recently, for carbon sequestration.

On our way to Bob Stewart's farm in Yorkville, Illinois, we see many newly developed areas with 'McMansions' with generous compounds, built on very good agricultural land. Bob tells us that he sold some land to that development and used the money to buy more land in Farmer City, far from the urban sprawl. Ultimately, our land resources are limited, and when we pave fertile land, we need some other land for farming. Most big cities are located in rich farm areas which, unless they were trading towns, is why they grew in the first place – and it may take two or three hectares of average land to replace one hectare of good land. It is surprising how weak the statistical basis for assessing how much land human beings take for buildings, roads, and other infrastructure and there are no internationally agreed classifications. As such, the figures provided in the following paragraph are not directly comparable.

According to the most recent National Resources Inventory more than 23 million acres of America's agricultural land – an area the size of Indiana – have been lost to development between 1982 and 2007.[726] Not surprisingly, the eastern United States has a higher proportion of its total area (4-5%) given over to urban and suburban land-uses than the other regions.[727] The total sealed (covered by asphalt, concrete or buildings) soil surface of the European Union area in 2006 was estimated to be around 100,000 km² or 2.3% of the EU's territory (an average of 200 m² per citizen). Malta, the Netherlands, Belgium, Germany, and Luxembourg have all sealed more than 5% of their land. In Sweden there are 550,000 km of roads (some 60 m per person) covering 345,000 hectares of land.[728] In the more densely populated Denmark, human infrastructure is calculated to cover almost 20% of the land area,[729] though these figures also include parks, golf courses and water reservoirs.

Earlier, I discussed how land has increasingly been converted from common or public ownership into private hands. And, like most assets in today's world, it is subject to speculation. Because of a widely spread feeling that agriculture was 'something of the past', investors showed little interest in land for some decades. But they have short memories. There was a large move towards farm land in the United States in late 1970s, after a period of higher food prices that were linked to the oil price shock of 1973. But in the five years from 1982 land prices fell by 43%.[730] After the food price hike in 2007, there has been a resurgence of interest in land both nationally and globally.

I will not expand greatly on this topic here, the history of land grabbing is as old as writing I guess, but a few quick brush strokes are required. Most land, in anyone's ownership, today can be traced back to a land grab of sorts, whether it is located in developed or in developing countries. European colonization was built on land grabbing, for sugar cane, rubber, tea, coffee, beef or oil palm production.

The north of Sweden suffered multiple land grabs, initially from the indigenous *Sami* people by the Swedish government and commercial mining interests, and subsequent enormous land grabbing of forests by forest companies buying up settlers' land (earlier grabbed by the government and given to settlers) for peanuts.

The Land Matrix Database tracks recent trans-national land deals. By the end of 2013 it had recorded almost one thousand land deals covering a total of 34 million hectares. Most of the buyers are investors from the United Arab Emirates, Malaysia and the United States and the land bought is often in poor conflict-ridden countries such as South Sudan, the Democratic Republic of Congo and Mozambique. Food production is not the only purpose with the land deals. They include a number of projects for afforestation and carbon sequestration, sometimes without a profit motive. For instance, the Global Solidarity Forest Fund owned by Swedish and Norwegian churches has invested in half a million hectares in Mozambique for tree plantations.[731] While the fund has a noble cause this is still a form of land-grabbing and has been subject to much criticism.

However, if we look at total investments in agri-business we find that most investments, including in farm land, are in North and South America (together accounting for more than three quarters of all investments) and the former Soviet Union. There are more than 170 investment funds and other investment vehicles that focus exclusively on agribusiness, with combined assets in excess of US$33 billion: farm land accounts for a third of this (US$11 billion).[732] There are many reasons why investments are higher in the Americas than in land-abundant Africa; land is available, the legal and commercial situation is not too messy and the land has a good development potential.[a] Instability and unclear ownership are limiting factors on land deals in Africa, while in most of Europe and Asia there is little land available, and almost none for large scale agriculture projects.

In most countries most of the land is owned by a very small minority of people. For example in Britain, 36,000 individuals, just 0.6% of the population, owns half of all the rural land. Most is owned by a group of just over one thousand aristocrats, such as Richard Scott, the Duke of Buccleuch, who owns 240,000 acres. There has been some

---

[a] The NCREIF Farmland Index, which measures the investment performance of agricultural properties in the United States, has generated an 11.83% compound return since 1992[a]

quite rapid growth in new public or common forms of ownership; the National Trust owns 630,000 acres, pension funds own 550,000 acres and the Royal Society for the Preservation of Birds 320,000 acres.[733] According to the Land Report 2013, the biggest land owner in United States is businessman John Malone (nicknamed the Darth Vader of business) and his wife Leslie, who own 2,200,000 acres, more than the total area of Delaware. In one year they bought a historic Irish castle just outside Dublin and two properties in Wellington, the center of South Florida's equestrian community.[734]

Land and top soil are essential for human survival on the planet. Strangely enough there are no international treaties or agreements to protect the soil, and few countries have a soil policy. It is high time that we pay tribute to the soil and recognize that our management of the soil will determine if the soil will be good or bad. The way we treat our soil has a bearing on how we nurture ourselves, but the impact is more far-reaching. Taking care of the soil is also taking care of ourselves. The way we relate to the soil says a lot about our society.

Frederick Kirschenmann, an organic farmer and philosopher from North Dakota sums up these dilemmas: "until we heal that divorce and become lovers of the soil again, relate soul to soul, many or our social problems will go unsolved – including our food safety and environmental protection problems. We cannot be sustained as a people and a culture divorced from the soil."[735]

"I don't think about the future, I just think about each day and how to survive. I have to put my faith in God, there is nothing else I can do". Rajput Ramjibhai Khodabhai has a proud posture and a steady gaze. He is a 'big man' who has influence in the village of Jaloya in Gujarat, India. But, when asked about the future, he has no answers. And the reason is the lack of water. He has farmed for thirty years, his father was a farmer and his three sons farm close by. Today, his thirty buffaloes are drinking water that is piped for 110 km to his farm because his two 1000 feet deep wells have become saline and useless. As are all other wells in Jaloya. The desert here, on the border between India and Pakistan, advances by the day. The young people want to move away – because without water there is no future. Jaloya is in no way unique, in Gujarat, one needs to tap more than 1000 feet under the surface to find sweet water, and 40% of the ground water is saline.[736]

The drawing of water leads to rapidly falling groundwater tables; in many parts of China and India groundwater levels are falling by between 1 and 3 m per year.[737] Some 300 million people in these two countries live on grain that is produced with unsustainable irrigation practices that pump water at a rate that surpasses natural recharge.[738] Globally, water demand is projected to increase by 55% between 2000 and 2050. The increase in demand will come from manufacturing, energy and household use. "In the face of these competing demands, there will be little scope for increasing water for irrigation", says the OECD. It projects that the number of people living in river basins under severe water stress will reach 3.9 billion, more than 40% of the world's population, by 2050.[739] And it is not only a problem for developing countries. In Australia, the situation is also precarious and the government's program 'Water for the Future' has allocated some A$ 12.9 billion to secure water resources for all Australians and ensure environmental integrity. In the Murray-Darling basin alone, A$3.1 billion will be used to buy back water rights from farmers so that the water can be used for other purposes, mainly to maintain fragile and threatened ecosystems.[740]

Each human being needs a few liters of water for drinking and cooking, and an additional 25-50 liters for hygiene and laundry. The average American was reported to use 350 liters per day and the Australian 570 liters in 1995, ironically given that Australasia is the driest continent of all.[741] Meanwhile, 783 million people were without any reliable supply of clean water in 2012.[742] I have seen women in Mozambique doing their laundry in potholes in the road after a rain. Worse still, many people also have to drink dirty water.

Seventy percent of all humanity's water use is for farming. The irrigated area has increased from 210 million hectares in 1979 to 277 million hectares in 2003, an increase of more than 30 percent.[743] Approximately, two-thirds of all rivers in the world are used for irrigation or hydroelectricity; in the United States, only 2% of rivers flow freely. Great rivers such as the Colorado, the Nile and the Ganges have almost no water left when they reach the sea and great lakes such as Lake Chad and the Aral Sea have shrunk tremendously.[744]

Irrigation plays a very big role in food production. Probably no single investment in farming so clearly 'pays off' both economically and in terms of increased productivity. At the end of the 1990s, around one-fifth of all agriculture areas were irrigated and they produced around two-fifths of all crop and almost three-fifths of all grains. The FAO estimates that 402 million hectares of land in developing countries can be irrigated, of which only half of it is irrigated today. In Sub-Saharan Africa only 4% of farmland is irrigated and this area has hardly increased in the last 40 years.[745] There are several limitations to the expansion of irrigation. One limitation is simply access to water; another is the loss of biodiversity from the lands that can be irrigated, which today mostly are swamps or other wetlands. If wetlands are drained they will normally also be converted from carbon sinks to carbon emitters, thus accelerating climate change. In areas of high evaporation, salinization can be an additional problem. So there are many reasons why irrigation will not expand as much as is theoretically possible. There are also many opportunities to improve water stewardship in existing irrigation schemes or to introduce small-scale technologies, such as rainwater harvesting[a] in farming systems.

In most countries the price of water embodies a subsidy to farming that other sectors do not enjoy. This reduces farmers' interest in water conservation. At the end of the 20th century, global water subsidies were estimated to amount to US$33 billion.[746] Of twelve OECD countries, only the Netherlands and Austria priced water at a what could be called a commercial rate. Households and industries paid between US$0.5 and US$3 per cubic meter, whereas farmers paid a few cents or even fractions of a cent. And, even though irrigation water and drinking water are two different things, with different qualities, the difference in price is not representative of that quality difference. Even in a dry country like Australia, households paid almost 100 times as much as farmers for their water.[747] But it is not only the rich countries that subsidize farmers' water use.

One key element of the so called Green Revolution was to expand irrigation; Indian farmers, such as those in Jaloya, installed tubewells, whose energy costs have since been subsidized by the government. India spends over US$6 billion on energy subsidies annually, and it is estimated that farmers pay only 13% of the true cost of electricity.[748] Water subsidies are not sustainable for the environment or for economic reasons. Irrigation accounts for ca. 15-20% of total electricity use in India and aquifers are being pumped out faster than they can be replenished, which, at the same time, taxes the electricity grid.[749] The end result is Rajput Ramjibhai Khodabhai's empty wells.

I was invited to make a plan for organic agriculture by the government of Dubai in the early 2000s. They wanted to grow irrigated vegetables. I found the assignment quite challenging for the simple reason that farming of the kind the Emirate wanted was not really sustainable, regardless of whether or not it was organic. The traditional farming system on the Arabic peninsula, based on dates, combined

---

[a]   Rainwater harvesting is the collection of rainwater to provide drinking water, water for livestock or for irrigation.

with camels and sheep-raising, developed for good ecological reasons. My conclusion was that it would be more sustainable to ship in food than to grow it with desalinated sea water, which was the only possible water source as the recycled waste water was already used for the golf courses.

Others have drawn similar conclusions, on a larger scale. In the 1970s, Saudi Arabia subsidized irrigation in order to support a massive expansion of grain production. It was, by and large, very successful and the country became self sufficient in wheat. However, by the 1990s, it became clear that this wasn't sustainable. In 2002, the Ministry of Agriculture announced that it would cease animal feed production altogether because of its negative effect on water resources.[750] Since 2008, the government started reducing its wheat purchases from local farmers and from 2016 onwards, the kingdom is expected to import all its wheat.[751]

The word 'rival' comes from Latin *rivalis*, a person sharing the same stream (water). Thirty-nine countries currently get most of their water from sources outside their territory.[752] In many cases, there are tensions between countries that share the same water resources, and conflicts over water are likely to increase. For farmers, in places where water rights can be traded (which is not the case everywhere), it can be much more profitable to sell water rights than to farm. In 2010, two farmers in San Joaquin Valley, California planned to sell their rights under the California State Water Project, to draw up to 70,730,000 cubic meters of water (it takes 2,500 m^3 fill an Olympic size swimming pool, so we are talking 28,300 swimming pools here) per year. Under this sale, the farmers would be paid a total of US$11.7 million dollars a year, selling the water at a price of US$165 per thousand cubic meters.[753] The oil tycoon and investor T. Boone Pickens bought up water rights for the Ogallala aquifer near Texas in the United States for some US$100 million and expects to sell the water for some US$165 million per year as the thirst of Dallas grows. Not surprisingly, this has triggered public outrage, regulatory responses and lawsuits.[754]

Water supplies are being increasingly privatized. Two French water corporations, Suez and Vivendi control about 70% of the world's private water supply sector. In Spain, Aquagest and Aqualia together control 80% of the private water supply sector, which supplies half of all Spain's water.[755] In parallel to this, the maintenance of the water catchment areas is rapidly turning into a commercial service by means of 'watershed service payments'. In 2008, there were some 300 schemes worldwide with payments reaching a total of US$10 billion.[756]

There is an increasing competition for water resources. Eagle Ford in Texas is one of the fastest-growing shale oil and gas plays (a group of fields in the same geological zone) in the United States. It is also located in one of the driest parts of the country. Following the severe drought of 2011, concerns are mounting that oil and gas extraction is competing with irrigation for scarce water supplies. Drilling and fracturing rock formations to release oil and gas (fracking) uses enormous quantities of water: according to most estimates, each well in Eagle Ford consumes between fifteen to nineteen million liters of water. The economic returns from using groundwater for fracking are enormous and easily outstrip the returns of agriculture, so frackers can easily outbid farmers. If the groundwater owner can claim royalties on the output from oil and gas wells, using groundwater to frack wells could earn more than two thousand times more than growing maize.[757]

Not only oil and gas extraction needs a lot of water. Thermal power plants – fossil fuel-based and nuclear – require water, primarily for cooling. Per unit of energy produced, they are the energy sector's most intensive users of water.[758] In Europe, the repeated shut down of river-water cooled thermal power plants, in particular French nuclear reactors, during extended heat waves is a potent reminder of the water-energy nexus.[759] Also, irrigation itself consumes a lot of electricity. Moving and treating water in California accounts for almost 20% of the state's electricity.[760] In 2011, China had to make the tough choice between using water in the Three Gorges Dam to irrigate food crops or for energy. To safeguard food production the government released enough water to fill 2 million Olympic-sized swimming pools for irrigation by June 10. China's oil demand increased by 300,000 barrels a day to make up for lost hydropower generation from the water used for crops.[761] The International Energy Agency notes in its 2012 *World Energy Outlook* that energy production uses some 15% of the world's water withdrawals and that access to water is an important criterion for assessing the viability of energy projects. The availability of and access to water could pose severe limitations for shale gas development and power generation in parts of China and the United States, India's power plants, Canadian oil sands production and for reservoir pressures to support oil output in Iraq.[762]

In this chapter I have discussed land and water at a global level – but let's take it back to the choices of enterprises and individuals. "We just want to get enough money to get the bank off our back," Mark Shannon a farmer in California's Joaquin Valley told the New York Times in 2010. "We would love to stay here because this is some of the best dirt

in the world. But I can't farm myself out of this water problem."
Instead he has to let his land be converted into a solar power
field.[763] This is a very vivid illustration of how shortages of resources
will be a permanent feature in the future, and how land, water and
energy interplay. In a 'free' market economy such a choice is simple.
Has the potential energy in the water a higher market price than the
food that is produced? If so use it for energy production – and let
people starve.

The global water supply is under strain and, in many places, water
is already now a limiting factor for development. There are many ways
to improve water management and the efficiency of water use, ranging
from simple solutions, such as rainwater harvesting to the high-tech
recirculation of irrigation water in greenhouses. To reduce wasteful
consumption, subsidies should be abolished and water use itself
should have a price tag. Further privatizing our limited water resources will inevitably exacerbate inequalities and divert water to rich
people's swimming pools or cars rather than the production of food.

21

Efficiency and productivity– deceptive words

We often hear that 'productivity in farming has increased tremendously', 'the farmer of today is much more efficient than her ancestor' and similar expressions. But those are deceptive words. They come with an air of being measurable and objective. And while they can be measured, the yardstick we choose to measure them against already predetermines the outcome. One has to also reflect over who benefits; what is productive or efficient differs depending on who asks the question.[764] Most choices are made on the basis of the profitability for the person or entity that has managed to, with whatever means, control that piece of nature.[765]

Throughout modern times the prevailing measure of grain productivity in Europe was the 'yield ratio', i.e. the quantity that could be harvested from a certain quantity of seeds. This ratio was often in the range of five in Scandinavia and Germany, reaching ten under good conditions in England and the Low Countries.[766] For a grain-based culture, with access to rather abundant land and labor resources, this way of measuring makes some sense. And this also explains quite well why the Asian rice based cultures were more advanced than the Europeans, until the industrial revolution; the seed ratio of paddy rice is normally very high. Today, seed is only one of many inputs in farming and most farmers would find it strange to measure productivity in terms of seed use even if it still prevails in some places.

The size of the area unit itself was often dynamic and linked to the land's ability to support people. Around the world, the amount of seed that had to be sown to feed a family from the harvest provided a basic measurement of the land. Even in the 20th century, fields in Guangdong Province next to Hong Kong continued to be measured in *dou*, roughly equivalent to seven kg of rice seed, while up the mid-19th century land in New Mexico was computed by the *fanega*, approximately fifty kg of wheat seed. I have also encountered land measurements based on how much land a man could 'open' in a days work, common in cultures with swiddening farming. And 'acre' has similar roots; an acre was the amount of land that could be ploughed in one day with a pair of oxen. When land, labor and food become commodities, most of these localized and subjective measurements fell into disuse.[767]

These examples are good to remember when we discuss productivity and efficiency. Productivity in farming can be measured in many ways. Per area unit; per person-hour; per unit of deployed capital; per energy input or; per water unit. The comparisons can consider total biological production, ecosystem services or only what is directly useful to human beings in the form of food, fiber and fuel. And the results, the useful resources, can also be expressed in different ways, for example, as kg (tons or bushels), as calories, as proteins or simply as money.[768] We can also ask if the productivity is serving to maintain the productive resources or if it is based on extraction of non-renewable resources, resources which perhaps were abundant but now are increasingly scarce? Can we even talk about productivity if the production is based on the unsustainable use of irrigation, fossil fuel and soil management practices which erode the soil?

We can also compare farming with 'nature'. For example, the biological production (mass, energy or protein) in a farmed system can be compared with that in the natural system before farming. 'Productivity' can have a completely different meaning if we counted the impact on ecosystems and the external costs caused by farming. Studies of a wetland in Canada, a forest in Cameroon and a Mangrove forests in Thailand showed the total value of these ecosystems was much higher than the value of the farming systems to which they were converted.[769] But, importantly, the benefits of the systems accrue to different people.

In the long term, it is more interesting to increase the productivity relative to a resource that is limited rather than relative to a resource that is abundant. From this perspective, the contemporary obsession with labor productivity is strange, as we never had so many people on the planet and so limited natural resources. But if we look at monetary value we understand why we always try to save on labor as labor is costly and nature is 'free'.

The total energy harvested per hectare can increase with increased use of ancillary energy; in many situations one can increase yield per hectare fivefold (or more) by using more energy. This energy can be used for better (and timelier) soil preparation, irrigation, fertilizers, etc. The ratio between energy output and energy input (i.e. efficiency in the use of energy) seems to be fairly constant up to a certain level, after which it rapidly deteriorates. Industrial farming systems, have long since passed the optimal energy use level.[770] According to FAO, industrial farming methods require 6,000 MJ of fossil energy (corresponding to a barrel of oil) to produce a ton of maize but traditional methods in Mexico only require 180 MJ (corresponding to 4.8 liters of oil) to produce the same. This calculation includes the energy needed for chemical fertilizers, irrigation and running machinery, but not the 'shadow energy', the energy used for making the machinery, for transporting products to and from the farm and for constructing the farm buildings. The energy ratio is below one – i.e. more energy is consumed than produced – for modern rice farming and just above one for modern maize farming, whereas traditional production of rice and maize gives a 60-70-fold return on energy used.[771] In light of this, to make statements that 'productivity has increased tremendously in farming the last hundred years,' is simply misleading.

Yield per area unit has increased considerably, both in developed and developing countries. For example, in the United States, maize yield increased from around 3,700 kg per hectare in 1961 to around 9,500 kg in 2011. Wheat yields in Sweden tripled between 1900 and 2000. Global rice yields increased by one third in the twenty years between the end of the 1970s and the end of the 1990s. The most dramatic increases can be accomplished in highly regulated systems. In greenhouses with climate and water control, productivity per hectare is up to more than ten times that in an open field. The more advanced producers in the Netherlands take more than 60 kg of tomatoes per square meter, whereas open-field production may only reach some 5 kg per square meter. Still, the profitability of Dutch greenhouse tomato production is very low and largely rests on them getting very favorable gas prices. One should not forget that in many cases yield per hectare is low just because it doesn't pay to increase it.

Land price is a factor that greatly influences productivity per area unit. To some extent, it works both ways. Land with high yield potential has a higher price than land with low potential and when you pay a lot for land you have to get a high yield per area unit. But in many countries and places, the correlation between land productivity and land prices is weak and land prices are influenced also by alternative uses (conversion to forest, industries, and housing), status and culture.

Farming today is very capital intensive. In Sweden, it comes only after utilities and real estate in capital intensity; car-making has less than half the capital costs for a full-time job,[772] and in United States US$1.2 million is invested in each full-time agricultural job.[773] Yet at the same time the return on invested capital in farming is mostly low. The real return is often realized when the farm is sold. As the saying goes 'farmers live poor and die rich': they reinvest most of their profits in their farms. For most farms, especially family farms, the concept of return on capital is somewhat alien. Families invest their capital and their labor on the same farm and there is no distinction in their way of thinking or in their books (if they have any) between the return on capital and the return on labor. One way to assess return on capital is to look at land rents. In the highly commercialized agricultural sector in the Netherlands, land rents are administratively defined on a level of 2% of the calculated production value of the land. If this was not the case, if the farms had to render a commercial rent of say 4% of the land price, farming would not be profitable.[774] Land rents in the United States have fallen from around 7% of the productive value in the 1970s to a low of 3.4% in 2008.[775]

A lot of the support to farms in high-income countries is 'capitalized' in the form of higher land prices. This means that the subsidies increase the cost of the land and this makes it more difficult for new farmers to establish themselves. Depending on the nature of support other production factors can also be affected. In 2006, milk quotas (if you produce more you face a levy) in the Netherlands were valued at an astonishing €20 billion, whereas the gross annual value of milk production was around €3 billion. The right to produce milk thus became a commodity, more important than actual milk production[776] (due to changes in EU agriculture policies the prices of the quotas have dropped recently, and they are about to be abolished in the future). The right to direct support from the EU's CAP (the 'single farm payment entitlement') has also become a tradable commodity. Buying and selling these rights has become a business in itself; 'buying an entitlement to a stream of future payments is an investment decision', according to one analyst.[777]

Contrary to what many may believe, return on capital in farming in developing countries is high. There is very little available capital and even less is invested in farming, but that which is invested is often borrowed at rates of 20-40%, a return on capital which few investors in high-income countries can dream of. Despite this, international capital is not rushing to support the farming sectors in developing countries, at least not in the shape of credits to small farms. The risks involved are also high; farmers can be unreliable borrowers who often can get away with not paying their debts, or delaying payment for years.[778]

While a human being needs a few liters of water to drink, at least one thousand times as much water is used to produce food.[779] The water needed for different foods varies tremendously and even varies for the same product grown under different conditions. Often the figures used mix different kinds of water with no clear distinction. There is 'blue' water – water in rivers and lakes, 'green' water – water in rainfall and in the soil, and 'grey' water – the water that is needed to absorb or purify the waste. Together these make up our 'water footprint'. The Water Footprint Network broke down the water footprint of a margherita pizza (one topped with tomato, mozzarella and basil). They found that it takes 333 gallons (1,260 liters) of water, enough to fill almost ten bathtubs to make a single pizza.[780]

But statistics can be presented in many ways. The water footprint of beef is big, ten times bigger than for grain and fifty times bigger than for (some) vegetables. On the other hand it is smaller than the water footprint of sesame oil, olive oil, coffee, cocoa and a number of other crops. Rainfall is also not the same as the water in lakes or wells. In all dryland areas, except where there are irrigation possibilities, livestock keeping has been the traditional way to get food from the land. And this for very obvious reasons; it is more water-efficient to raise livestock than to try to grow crops that don't get enough water. In Namibia – one of the driest countries on the planet – most of the water falls on the dry rangeland as rain and only a small part is supplied as drinking water for the animals. A borehole for cattle with a solar pump and a capacity of 2 m³ per hour (20 m³ per day) can service some 250 cattle. They will produce in the range of 20 tons of meat per year. The same quantity of water would be enough to irrigate approximately a hectare of farm land, which would produce considerable less food (say 3-7 tons of maize) and a lot less money. If we calculate the total water use of the land and include the rainfall, we arrive at a high water foot print. But this rangeland cannot be used for cropping as the rainfall is to low. The only other alternative use of the land would be to have game roaming there.[781] Therefore, we cannot conclude that cattle-breeding, under those conditions is wasteful of water.

Also, water footprint *per kg* is a dubious measurement. We eat very different quantities of food, and the concentration of useful nutrients that they contain differs widely. As an example, we have to eat 10 kg of broccoli for our daily calorific needs, but only 0.5 kg of bacon. If we look at the use of blue and green water *per calorie*, nuts have the lowest efficiency in water use and root crops the highest, according to researchers Mekonnen and Hoekstra. Most vegetables and meat rank quite similarly. In terms of blue and grey water use for protein, oil crops are the best, followed by milk, lamb, root crops and grains. Nuts and vegetables are the least efficient.[782] Seen on a larger scale, attempts to increase yield per hectare mostly also increase water productivity.

An unirrigated hectare of wheat uses more or less the same quantity of water when it produces 1500 kg as when it produces 5000 kg.[783] If irrigation is introduced into the systems, the effect is, perhaps surprisingly, that water productivity increases; that is, the increased yield resulting from irrigation uses less water per kilogram than the original yield based on rainwater. In a situation where the annual rainfall is around 400 mm, water stress poses a real limitation to crops, adding some 100 mm of water at critical moments can easily double yields.[784]. According to researchers at the Stockholm Environment Institute there is a large potential to improve water productivity through using improved, existing, water management practices. They predict that, globally, we will need to increase water usage by around two thirds of present levels (7000 km3/yr) in order to feed the world in 2050 but that water productivity improvements could save up half of that quantity.[785]

Because labor costs represent a very high share of farm costs, productivity per person-hour or per person-day has been central in leading to the increased mechanization of farming. Labor productivity is also very important from a broader societal perspective as increased productivity of agricultural has released people to work in other sectors. Industrialization could not have taken place unless labor had been released from farming. One person in the United States occupied in farming can now produce food for some 300 people, in some developing countries one farm worker can only feed a few. Another way of looking at labor productivity is to see how much grain can be produced per person-year. Grains are the most important foods in the world, are grown in most places and as such are used as a proxy for general agriculture development. In the areas with lowest productivity, one person can produce not even 1 ton of grain per year, whereas the most productive farms produce up to 5000 tons per person-year as is the case on Bob Stewart's farm in Illinois.

Of course, these comparisons mask the fact that a modern farmer doesn't even 'feed' him or herself or the family or their animals. A modern farm is a company where other people's goods and services are bought and sold. There are accountants, repairmen, consultants, machine operators, computer service technicians and meteorologists, all in the service of the modern farmer. All this work is embedded in the farm produce. Earlier generations of farmers, and still many farmers in developing countries, produced not only food and fodder for themselves and their animals, but also fiber for clothing, leather for shoes and most of their own tools and medicines from their farms. But even when we have taken that into account, the difference in labor productivity between farms in high-income and low-income countries is still staggering. Energy use is the single most important determining factor here as there is a very strong correlation between the energy resources commanded by one person and that person's productivity.

Productivity, measured in added value per worker, is quite naturally much higher in high-income countries than in developing countries. For instance, a farmer or farm worker in Malawi produced an added value of just US$130 per annum in 2001-2003, a Chinese farmer US$368 while their French and American colleagues produced US$39,000 and US$36,000 respectively. Even more worrying is that this gap is widening. The OECD countries had an agricultural labor productivity that was 25 times higher than that in Sub-Saharan Africa in 1971. By 2005 this had increased to 68 times.[786] A report to the FAO projects that revenue per agriculture worker in Sub-Saharan Africa will increase by a meager 50% between 2010 and 2050. Growth in productivity in South Asia (India and its neighbors) will also be slow, and Latin America is the only region likely to catch up with developments in the OECD countries.[787]

Those figures come close to what farmers earn and give an idea of what farm workers are – and can be – paid. It works both ways; if workers are productive they can get a good salary which in turn means that there are incentives for saving labor, which in turn means that income per worker will increase. In addition, if wages in other sectors are high, agriculture wages will follow (even if they mostly stay comparatively low). A particularity of farm labor is that, in most parts of the world, it is markedly seasonal. When it is too cold, to dry, too hot or too wet, there is simply not much to be done in the fields. This means that farm labor often is underemployed, or that seasonal workers take up the jobs. Farm work is also considered to be 'unskilled' even though I personally object to this categorization. In my former role as farmer and employer I can assure the reader that the productivity of people weeding or making bundles of parsley can easily differ by a factor of three or four, depending on their skills. Taking good care of animals also requires a huge amount of skill, know-how and ability. And modern farm work is certainly highly sophisticated.

It is somewhat puzzling why most agronomists and institutions focus so much on yields of crops per hectare as the main measure of agriculture productivity, when in reality that is not a driving force for farmers who look more at productivity per labor unit, or if they are modern agri-business operations, the productivity of capital invested.

If we compare farms globally the farms with the highest yields per hectare are rarely the most competitive. European farmers generally have much higher yields per hectare of wheat than their Argentinean, American or Australian colleagues, still they cannot compete and are dependent on support programs of the European Union, because their general cost levels are higher. Similarly in the dairy sector, the world market is dominated by a country with a low milk yield per cow. The dairy industry in New Zealand is still primarily built on grazing cows and production per cow is low by international standards. The average production per cow in Israel was 12,500 kg in 2007, while it was less than 4,000 kg in New Zealand,[788] but New Zealanders produce milk a lot cheaper than Israelis.

If we compare efficiency in various systems, e.g. in farming or food processing, in most cases this will show that the bigger and more technological advanced system is more competitive. But are they more efficient and productive? Often, small farms have a higher yield per hectare than large farms, but large farms are still gradually squeezing smaller farms out of the market, because of market access, possibilities for rational specialization, economies of scale, better access to credits or governmental policy distortions.[789] Larger crop farms perform better financially, on average, than smaller farms. This is not because the larger farms have higher revenues or yields per area unit, but because they have lower costs. As expressed in the report *Farm Size and the Organization of U.S. Crop Farming* from USDA: "larger farms appear to be able to realize more production per unit of labor and capital. These financial advantages have persisted over time, which suggests that shifts of production to larger crop farms will likely continue in the future." Their yield per hectare is mostly the same as on smaller farms but USDA's research shows that farms with more than 2,000 acres spend 2.7 hours of work per acre of maize and have equipment costs of US$432, while a farmer less than 249 acres will spend more than four times as much labor and twice the amount for equipment per acre. In this limited sense the larger farms are indeed more 'efficient' and 'productive'.

There are many different ways to look at farm productivity and, depending on what and how we measure, we can draw different conclusions. In principle, the factor which is scarcest will, and should, be the most important. Farms in high-income countries are character-ized by a high input of energy and a low input of human labor. They have no shortage of labor but it is costly and therefore productivity per work-hour has been the strongest driver of change. Close to cities, or in very densely populated areas, land is scarce and farms are more shaped by high land prices. At a certain land price, grain farming is no longer viable and farming will move towards higher value crops, or will become a playground for the rich, golf courses or paddocks for race horses.

Economists talk about 'total factor productivity', a rather opaque measure which has a scientific air. It does sound like a good idea to combine all the factors of production in one measure. But as this is measured in monetary terms it will just value things by their market value. So if labor is 200 times more expensive in one country than in another you have to produce 200 times more per hour to achieve the same productivity. And if water is free, water productivity will not be reflected at all. In this way, productivity comes to mean more or less the same as profitability and becomes a circular form of reasoning that is of little value in discussing the big picture, even if it does reflect quite well what guides a modern commercial farmer.

We need to redefine productivity. But it is not sufficient to theoretically redefine productivity, we also need to redesign the economic system which has created a distorted view of what is productive and what is not. Today, productivity is measured by how many trees one person can cut down with her chainsaw or how much fish a fisherman can scoop up from the sea. But as natural resources dwindle, the real productivity lies in how these resources re-generate. We are productive if there is more forest next year than today, if there are more fish and if the soil becomes more fertile by the years instead of being exhausted and eroded. In a similar way we are efficient if the food we produce and consume is healthy rather than if it is cheap.

22

The food puzzle

The World Food Congress, held more than fifty years ago in June 1963 in Washington, DC, drew the world's attention to the problems of hunger and malnutrition and called upon governments and international organizations to make the challenge of eliminating hunger the primary task of that generation. Major shortages of food were predicted by the year 2000. We can see in retrospect that those predictions were wrong. For sure there are (many) hungry people today and some people still starve to death, but proportionally they are fewer than in 1963, and no one can seriously claim that this is caused by a generalized, global, food shortage. This Congress was certainly not the first time people feared global mass starvation; almost all the authors writing about this theme go back to the projections of mass starvation made by Malthus more than two hundred years ago. Malthus was wrong in the short term, as were the world leaders gathered in Washington 1963. I join those who say there is no cause for panic, but that should not be mistaken for saying that it will never be a problem or even that it could not be a problem also very soon, should certain conditions change.

I have mentioned Fred and Susan Mkandawire, a Zambian farm family who harvest less than a ton of maize. The same day in April 2012 when I visited them, I also visited two other farmers. After the Mkandawires I went to Godfrey and Katherine Boma, who have been farming for fourteen years, the same length of time as the Mkandawires. When Godfrey stands next to his tall sunflowers, beaming like them, it is hard to believe that he is 81 years old. After all, life expectancy in Zambia is around 40 years. Godfrey is a former miner and small business man who became a farmer at the age of 67. He and his wife farm nine hectares, of which four hectares are arable land. They use their own oxen for plowing. A better – and more timely – land preparation, better weeding and higher use of chemical fertilizers all contribute to them harvesting around 5 tons per hectare of maize – more than twice the national average and almost three times as much as Fred and Susan. The Boma's have also started with organic maize and they get the same yield from that: "it is fifty-fifty", Geoffrey says, "there is more work with organic but less costs for inputs".

The maize towers over a sea of vigorous weeds. In some cases the greenery has pulled down the stalks and it is almost hard to believe there will be any harvest from that field. Sebastian Scott, the last farmer I visit that day, assures me that his maize will yield some 7 tons per hectare. The 'weeds' are intentionally planted Lablab beans (Dolichos lablab). Seb, as he is called, grows maize without machinery; he and his partner hand-hoe the fields or just sow by hand directly in the mulch with an ingenious piece of tubing. They grow organically; instead of using government-subsidized fertilizers they uses green manure crops to supply nitrogen to the plants. They demonstrate that it is possible to reach high yields, and profits, also with simple tools and intensive organic methods. Notably, the Scotts are young, well educated and healthy, and come from well-off circumstances – I hear afterwards that Seb is the son of the Vice-President.

The three visits show that it is possible to increase yields a lot even in similar circumstances. This can be done using conventional methods or organic ones and it is possible to do it on a small farm or a larger one. The visits also strongly suggest that poverty, in the sense of limited access to resources, such as the Mkandawires face, is more likely the cause of low productivity in farming, rather than low productivity being the cause of poverty. These examples are in no way unique, I have seen them all over the world. Historically we can discern the same pattern. Studies of Swedish milk production in the later half of the 19th century show that poor households had cows for self-sufficiency which gave just some 500 liters of milk per year when fed on straw, moss, hay and waste products. By contrast the commercially oriented farmers fed their cows with oilseed cakes, root crops and good quality hay and had production levels that were five or six times higher.[790] The poor farmers knew how to increase productivity, but didn't have the resources to do so.

The story of food and who gets it and who doesn't has very little to do with agronomic issues, such as the use of more GMOs or more fertilizers. When it comes to food, distribution is a bigger challenge. And distribution, in turn, has a lot to do with markets, which don't distribute food (or agricultural inputs) to those that have no money to buy them. Or as expressed in a report from the United Nations:

> At the country level, food security does not depend on whether countries are able to cover domestic food consumption through domestic food production, but whether they are able to generate sufficient financial resources to finance necessary food imports. Similarly, at the household level, food security is determined by household income more than anything else.[791]

Hunger is the largest single contributor to maternal and child mortality worldwide, with 3.5 million people dying every year of hunger-related causes.[792] In total, the number of malnourished people has been fairly constant over the last 20 years, fluctuating at around 850 million. The optimist notes that, taking into account population growth, the proportion of malnourished people decreased from 16% in 1990 to 13% in 2005. Perhaps surprisingly to some, the majority of hungry people live in rural areas; many of them are farmers, others are landless laborers. According to the FAO, 50% of those suffering from hunger and malnutrition are small-scale peasants, 20% are landless, 10% are pastoralists or fishermen and 20% live in city slums.[793]

But, don't we have to increase production to supply the hungry with the food they need? On the surface, this seems the most obvious solution. But this kind of question obscures the real causes for hunger and malnutrition. The real causes are war and civil unrest, poverty and inequality, unequal terms of trade between rich and poor countries, and bad agriculture and trade policies. It is mainly in low-income countries where people starve or are undernourished. And, except for in very brief periods, rich people have never starved even in countries devastated by famine. There are also many low-income countries where hardly anybody starves, mainly as a result of good food distribution and relative equality. Globally, there is simply no shortage of food; the poor just cannot buy it. Or seen from the other perspective, rich people don't starve. Even countries that import the bulk of their food, such as Japan, are food secure, because they have the money to buy the food they need.

As a nine-year-old, Nobel Laureate Amartya Sen witnessed the Bengal famine of 1943, in which three million people perished. "I was upset by what I saw. My grandfather gave me a small cigarette tin, and said I could fill it with rice and give it to the starving, but only one tinful per family," he told *The Guardian* in an interview 2001. He observed that only people on the lowest rung of the economic ladder, such as landless rural laborers, were hungry. The memory stayed with him, prompting him decades later to make a famous case study of the Ethiopian famine in Wollo in 1973 and the Bangladesh famine in 1974. The opening lines of his study are classic: "Starvation is the characteristic of some people not having enough food to eat. It is not the characteristic of there being not enough food to eat."[794] Sen has shown that most famines have occurred in situations where there was food available but social and economic conditions prevented people having access to that food. Many countries with hungry populations export food at the same time as some of their people are starving to death.

The effects of prices on food production and its distribution is a complicated matter and the effects differ for the urban and the rural poor, between different groups of rural poor and differ in the short and the long term. Increasing production when there is no demand leads to falling prices, which paradoxically can lead to an even worse situation for the rural poor, who make up the majority of those hungry. Most of them are dependent on farm incomes, either as smallholders or as landless individuals seeking employment by farmers. A surplus of food, with falling prices, creates a bigger problem as it drives small farmers off the market so that they cannot buy the things they need for production or for their families. Better prices enable farmers to respond by expanding production, something that was very visible in the period 2004-2009, when global food prices doubled (but thereafter fell again).

Even if poverty itself is the main reason for hunger, more food will have to be produced because of increasing population, increasing consumption per capita and increasing meat consumption. So where will that food come from? There are a number of ways. First we can increase the area used for food production. Second we can increase productivity from existing agricultural land. Third we can reduce waste. Fourth we can employ novel ways to produce food and fifth we can change our consumption patterns to eat things that require less land and other resources.

According to calculations by the FAO as much as 26% of the world's land area could be converted to arable land; which would give us 3.3 billion hectares of arable land, compared to today's 1.5 billion hectares.[795] Most of that land would be in Sub-Saharan Africa and Latin America. In Africa less than 8% of the land is arable land, and the continent is quite sparsely populated. The biggest unknown is how much of the 3 billion hectares of pasture land could be converted to arable land. Most permanent grasslands are not suitable for farming. In densely populated areas one can more or less safely assume that permanent grasslands have been plowed whenever it made sense, as arable farming usually generates much more food and money than livestock. Even in a country with vast land reserves as the United States, most of the land now grazed is simply not good enough for farming. Part of the reason for the disastrous Dust Bowl was that farmers tried to plow very dry lands, that were essentially unsuitable for cropping. In Latin America and Africa, there are lands used for extensive grazing which could be converted to agriculture, this is what has happened recently in Mato Grosso and in Argentina, where the

Pampas is being converted from grass to soybeans. But by and large, one should not expect too much from the conversion of grasslands to arable land. It might even be that in some cases we would produce more food by doing the opposite (more about that later). Most 'new' agriculture land would come from the conversion of savannahs, forests and wetlands.

It is entirely possible to convert large swathes of land to agriculture. We can see that in densely populated parts of Europe and Asia. Perhaps, perhaps it is possible for human beings to convert the whole planet to an agricultural landscape. But that would be at the cost of massive destruction of other species. We already are creating problems by farming just a third of the planet's land area. If we increase the share of agriculture land, we would cause even more dramatic changes in the global and regional cycles of life supporting elements such as nitrogen, phosphorus, methane, water and carbon. The big areas of the planet that are not yet farmed, even if few of them are entirely wild, act as giant refuges and buffers. They control and manage functions that are absolutely essential for us humans. Even expansion of very good farming systems leads to habitat destruction and species' extinction. The more of the biosphere that we convert to farmland, the more we will have to internalize the functions of these ecosystems within our farming systems. It can be difficult, costly and in many cases is still not (and possibly never will be) possible. It assumes an almost perfect knowledge of all those essential functions – while our actual knowledge is very far from complete; it is partial and ephemeral. This is the main reasons for why it is not a good idea to convert more 'nature' to agriculture lands.

It is a paradox that at the same time as 'the need for more food' is discussed, in Europe arable land area has gone down from 373 million hectares in 1961 to 276 million in 2011. North America lost 20 million hectares in the same period. Even more dramatic has the decline been in pasture lands: Europe has lost more than half of its pastures since 1961.[796] Some of the agriculture land has been lost for development or returned to forest or wetland, but some of it could quite easily be farmed again. Notably, much of this land is not very productive, which why it was abandoned in the first place. This is also the case for the 30 million acres in the United States Conservation Reserve. Abandonment mostly occurs because farming a patch of land is no longer profitable – which can happen for a multitude of reasons. It has occurred throughout history in all parts of the world. For example, in Moldova almost one-fifth of the arable fell into disuse after the fall of the Soviet Union, and the country's irrigated land dropped from 308,000 hectares to just

16,000 hectares in 2005. Moldova has excellent conditions for farming, but the Soviet 'market', where goods were distributed according to political decisions, collapsed and the Moldovan agriculture and food industries where not ready for the harsh competition and capital needs of the capitalist market economy.[797]

There is an increasing mismatch between where the agriculture land is and where it is needed and who owns it. Many countries with a rapidly increasing need of food lack water, e.g. most of North Africa and the Middle East, parts of India, Pakistan and China, and therefore they become structurally dependent on food imports. This has major economic, social and ecological implications: As long as world trade and economy are working smoothly and are oiled by petroleum this can work well, but once there is an economic or political crisis, it is apparent that being reliant on global trade for supplies can be risky.

There is also increasing competition for agriculture land for urban development, hydro-electricity, roads and golf courses. Soils are also depleted by erosion. This means that new lands are needed just to maintain the status quo. Finally, there is competition over agriculture land between food, feed, industrial crops and energy, which I will discuss in next chapter. The largest increase of food production the last century came not from plowing more land but from getting more harvest out of the land, as the examples from Zambia show. The question is if this trend can continue.

From 1700 to 1993 there was an 11 fold increase in human population but only a 5.5 fold increase in cropland area.[798] This was possible because yield per area unit increased rapidly. FAO estimates that, between 1960 and 1999, 78% of the increase in food supply came from higher yields per area unit, 7% from more yields by taking two or even three crops per year instead of one and only 15% came from an increase in area. A very important driver of increase in yield is irrigation. On our farm I think putting in an irrigation system was the most profitable investment we ever made and we farmed in an area with rather good rainfall. Increased cropping intensity has also been very important. In slash and burn cultivation land is only used for one or two years in every twenty, in the old European production systems land was used every one or two years out of three. In Asia today many fields give two crops per year, facilitated by a longer growing season than in temperate climates. A major reason for the yield increases in China in recent decades is this higher intensity in land use. In rare cases one can take three major crops per year, and for specialty crops that grow rapidly, such as lettuce, five to six harvests per year can be possible.

Different parts of the agriculture sector claim credit for yield increases. In reality there are many interlinked factors within the technological and socioeconomic complex in which access to energy and the integration of farming within markets are key drivers.[799] According to the World Bank's *Development Report* 2008, seed breeding has been central; hybrid rice is supposed to explain half of the increase in yields in China from 1975 to 1990 and improved varieties are said to explain 53% of the increased productivity in Punjab (Pakistan). But there can be many other reasons for improved productivity, some of which may not be obvious at first. Roads (!) are said to have improved farm productivity in India by 25%. Better nutrition meant a lot for productivity among African farmers, shedding light on the vicious circle of low yields, low income, little food of low quality, illness, low labor availability, low yields, etc. Twenty percent of the increase in yields is attributed to the use of chemical fertilizers, perhaps a surprisingly small figure considering how often they are said to be so important and even more surprising in the light of the tremendous increase in the use of chemical fertilizers in the same period.[800] One factor which is often overlooked is that when farmers retire their land, such in the set-aside programs of the European Union or the Conservation Reserve Programme of the United States, they will set aside the least productive land: as such average yield will increase even with no progress whatsoever.

It is still possible to increase yields per area unit in many parts of the world. There was, at the end of the last century, a substantial scope for increasing yields in Argentina, Australia, Canada, Hungary, India, Italy, Poland, Romania, Turkey, Ukraine and the United States. If these countries increased their yields just half-way towards the theoretical optimal, this would generate a 23% increase in the world's wheat harvest.[801] In most parts of Africa, small holder farmers harvest 1-2 tons per hectare of maize. They could quite easily double this even without using chemical fertilizers or GMOs.[802] In the article *Possible changes to arable crop yields by 2050* researchers from the Rothamstead write "If this [yield gap] is closed and accompanied by improvements in potential yields then there is a good prospect that crop production will increase by approximately 50 percent or more by 2050 without extra land." Interestingly they also project that the yield of most crops will increase by 13% as a result of increase of carbon dioxide in the atmosphere.[803]

But the picture is complicated. Lester Brown from the Earth Policy Institute notes that yield increases have tapered off in the more developed parts of the world, and that globally grain yields grew by 2.2 % per year 1950-1990 but only 1.3 % per year in the period 1990-2011.[804]

Three researchers from the University of Nebraska caution us, in an article in *Nature Communications,* against believing in continued yield increases. In several parts of the world yield increases have reached a plateau, "this seems to be the case in high-yield systems for rice in East Asia (China, the Republic of Korea and Japan), wheat in Northwest Europe (the United Kingdom, France, Germany, the Netherlands and Denmark) and India, and maize in South Europe (Italy and France).[805]

Progress in maize yields in United States have not decreased, however, notes a report from the USDA; "for example, trend growth rates in Illinois maize yields shifted from about 1 bushel[a] per acre per year from 1940 to 1959 to 1.7 bushels from 1960 onward.[b]" But the authors also caution that "extrapolating past yield trends may help to forecast crop yield growth, but trends differ based on starting points and are not necessarily linear over time."[806] Many farmers in United States regularly harvest 10 tons maize per hectare. But wheat yields in the United States have not increased so much as maize: wheat yields increased three fold since the 1940s while maize yields increased five fold. This might be because maize has pushed wheat towards colder, drier and less productive lands. Wheat yields in Unites States are lower than in many other countries, less than half that in Germany, the United Kingdom and France and well below China, Zimbabwe, Uzbekistan, Poland and Mexico. And while maize farmers in United States harvest five times more than their Zambian colleagues, Zambian wheat farmers have more than double the yield of the United States.

The discussion about yield increase, often based on agronomic considerations, tend to largely overlook the effect of economic conditions on yields. While there are certainly biological limits to yields, in most parts of the world economic factors limit yields more than biological factors. Just look at the pepper greenhouse I discussed in the beginning of the book. They produce 30 kg of peppers per square meter, about ten times as much as the average yield in China, the biggest producer of peppers in the world. They do this because they are good growers but also because they invest massive resources into farming, for

---

a 1 bushel of shelled maize is 25.4012 kg.

b The reader should be aware that an increase by a fixed quantity per year means a decline in yield increase as the increase over that of the previous yield will be smaller every year. These differences can, to some extent, explain how different experts reach different conclusions–or how their results are reported by media. 'Stagnating yields' in this sense means that the rate of increase (in percentage terms) is stagnating.

example they use natural gas equivalent of one liter of oil for every kg of peppers.[807] Ironically they can barely make ends meet, because the highest yield is not necessarily the most profitable. They are an extreme case, but ultimately farmers all over the world are continually making choices about how much to invest. Susan and Fred Mkandawire in Zambia sacrifice maize yield by reducing their weeding or by not applying more fertilizers. They do it knowingly. It simply doesn't pay to increase their investment; or as expressed by scientists in Nature Communications, "such fine-tuning [to further increase yields] is often difficult to achieve in farmer's fields, and the associated marginal costs, labor requirements, risks and environmental impacts may outweigh the benefits".

A problem I already discussed is that high yields often come with high energy input and a high price in the form of eutrophication, pesticide use, the depletion of water and phosphorus and increased erosion. And the question is 'can we afford this in the long run?' We should not reduce intensity, but we should replace input-intensity with management-intensity and use more diverse biological systems. By mixing crops and by mixing crops and livestock we can use all of the ecological and biological niches in our production system and thereby increase production. In most cases, this requires more careful management and more people – but people can hardly be a limiting factor on an over-populated planet. Ultimately there is not one recipe for all as conditions differ considerably.

Most of the agricultural establishment and, in particular, agri-business promote genetic engineering as a main solution for future food production. However, you rarely hear such bold statements from those actually engaged in farming. For sure, the uptake of genetically engineered crops (GE crops, GM crops or GMOs) in the United States and a few other countries has been very rapid, undoubtedly because it offers farmers some advantages. But we are not talking about any break-through technologies here; we are talking about technologies that can save farmers a few dozens of dollars per acre, in the same way as the use of pesticides. The reality in the field is far, very far, from the discourse about feeding the world that is propagated by the proponents of GMOs.

According to advocates of GMOs, growing herbicide resistant crops reduces (or should reduce) the use of herbicides. But this is simply not true. In Brazil, the use of herbicides has increased from 7 kg per hectare to 10 kg since the large-scale introduction of GMO crops and a survey in the state of Paraná showed that farmers growing GMO soybeans use more pesticides than farmers who don't grow GMO soy.[808] There is a growing problem with weeds that have become resistant to glyphosate, the most common herbicide used by American GMO maize, soybean and cotton farmers. New strategies are needed to combat them, according to David Mortensen, professor of weed ecology at Penn State University. Since the introduction of glyphosate-resistant crops, the number of weedy plant species that have evolved resistance to glyphosate has increased dramatically, from zero in 1995 to twenty-one in 2013. According to Mortensen the acreage infested with glyphosate-resistant weeds rose from 32.6 million acres in 2010 to 40.7 million acres in 2011 and 61.2 million acres in 2012.[809] When I visited farmers in Illinois and Mato Grosso in Brazil 2012, I realized that the 'new strategies' are to combine Roundup with nastier herbicides such as paraquat in Brazil or atrazine in United States. Paraquat has been banned in the European Union since 2007. It is exported from Switzerland, where its use is also forbidden. People who ingest larger quantities of paraquat are not likely to survive.[810] If a person survives the toxic effects of paraquat poisoning, long-term lung damage is highly likely. More than 3 million liters of paraquat are used in Brazil, mainly on GMO soybean plantations. Atrazine, which is commonly used in United States to deal with glyphosate resistant weeds in maize, is also prohibited in the European Union. It is an estrogen disruptor and is suspected of causing birth defects. Atrazine was found in 80% of drinking water samples taken from 153 public water systems in United States.[811]

When it comes to 'feeding the world' GMO technology has a limited potential to radically increase yields; there is simply no 'high-yield' gene that can be inserted in the various crops. If there were such genetic traits, they certainly would already have been developed through the normal process of evolution. High yields are a result of many synergetic factors, of which genetic factors are only a small proportion (and the genes involved are many). The same is the case for many other GMO promises. Frost tolerant potatoes have been talked about for decades, but are still far away. There is reportedly some progress in draught-tolerant maize, but the size of the challenge is perhaps best understood when realizing that the giant Monsanto has had to team up with its competitor BASF in order to have the muscle to accomplish this. And again, there will be trade-offs. Draught tolerance will come at some kind of 'cost' for the plant, or for the farmer.[812]

GMOs have the potential to solve certain technical problems, but in most cases there are also other solutions. And GMOs are diverting research funds and attention away from these other solutions. GMO research has a massive outcrowding effect: BASF invests around €188 million annually in plant biotechnology research[813] and Monsanto invested more than US$1.5 billion in 2012 on research most of which is based on proprietary biotechnology.[814] GMO research can much more easily attract funds than solutions based on local resources and on-farm solutions, as there is no money to be made from such solutions while the GMO solutions are based on proprietary technologies. The biggest dangers with GMOs are perhaps not the health effects or super-weeds wrecking havoc with nature. Concerns over these some-time seem a bit exaggerated in my view. The bigger danger with GMO is the increased reliance of farmers on purchased proprietary tech-nology. In addition, because of very high development costs, GMOs will lead to a reduction in the number of varieties and lead to more monocultures. It may also make people complacent in facing the problems we actually have. If the knee-jerk response to any agriculture challenge is that we will fix it with GMOs we are in serious trouble.

Lately GMO proponents have started to promote GMOs as a solu-tion for poor farmers in developing countries. In this way they use moral arguments against their opponents, making it look like that those who are against GMOs are contributing to people starving or going blind because of vitamin A deficiency. Some proponents of GMOs dismiss their detractors as being more opposed to capitalism, privatization and globalization than concerned about the environ-mental or human health aspects of GMOs. There may be some truth in this claim I personally don't exclude the possibility that GMO tech-nologies could produce some useful traits in the future. But I am not convinced that this possibility can justify the risks and the enormous investments. And in general I believe that the patenting of genetic materials, GMOs or not, is fundamentally wrong, unjust and yet another step towards the full privatization of nature. The choice about whether or not to employ GMOs is essentially a political and ethical choice not just a mere choice between technologies.

Our knowledge of the soil and the interactions between plants and the soil and with each other is still very limited. There are huge opportunities to find new methods for increasing yields and protecting crops. "Mustard can clean soil from pea-root rot"; "Poo-eating mag-gots can be animal feed"; "Aphids avoid ladybugs" and "Variety mixtures to reduce pest problems" are just four headlines from the latest issue of a research magazine from the Swedish University of Agriculture. Exploring how mycorrhiza binds all plants together in a living web with constant interactions and exchanges of substances and information will certainly give us new ideas about how to farm more intelligently in the future. But, the more money we spend on GMO research, the less will be available to spend on understanding the fascinating underworld which is the basis for our survival on the planet.

Many promote increased use of chemical fertilizers, and sometimes GMOs and pesticides, as the recipe for improved food security. The Alliance for Green Revolution in Africa headed by the former UN Secretary General Kofi Annan and the Millennium Village Project under the leadership of Jeffrey Sachs, and influential policy makers promote subsidized fertilizers. Such schemes in Malawi, Zambia, Ghana and Tanzania have been evaluated and show, with a limited certainty, that increases in productivity per unit area are possible. However, the costs are very high and there is very little convincing evidence that benefits will persist after the programs came to an end. As my visit to the three Zambian farmers show, there are already good opportunities to increase harvests, even without using chemical fertilizers. The Green Revolution increased yields but it did not create food security. India is often a 'poster child' for the Green Revolution and it has more hungry people than the whole of Africa.

Overall, it is a diversion from the real problem to discuss agriculture methods as a solution to hunger, be it fertilizers, pesticides or genetically modified organisms. The solution to the problem of hunger lies in economic and social conditions, in securing the right and access of the poor to critical resources such as land and water. Or, as expressed in a recent report from the United Nations Conference of Trade and Development:

> In fact, only few problems in agriculture are mainly caused by a lack of technology, many are related to social, economic and cultural issues that require structural changes, not techno-fixes. It is therefore critical to first of all define what problems are best solved by changing legal frameworks, trade policies, incentive structures or human behavior and, second, what contribution technology could make within this very context.[815]

In the early 2000s there was a fad among rich Swedish brats to 'sink' champagne, to order two bottles and ask the waiter to pour one away. This way of displaying wealth is perhaps an extremely absurd example of what is called food wastage, our third target for increasing food availability. But even common people waste food now and then. In the 1940s a few friends started a tomato battle in the main town square of Buñol (Spain). From then on, *La Tomatina* has been held at the end of August with tens of thousands of participants coming from all over the world to hurl more than one hundred tons of over-ripe tomatoes at each other.[816]

It is hard to measure food waste, in particular in the first and the last stages of the food chain, the field and in the kitchen. Therefore we should be a bit careful when trying to assess the situation. FAO's *Global Food Losses and Food Waste* (2011) estimates that that 1.3 billion ton of food is lost or wasted globally. This corresponds to one third of all the food we eat. In developing countries most food losses occur at post-harvest and processing levels, while in industrialized countries, most losses are at the retail and consumer levels. The report estimated that consumers in Europe and North-America waste around 100 kg per year on average, while waste at the consumer stage in Sub-Saharan Africa and South/Southeast Asia is one tenth of that. In industrialized countries as much as a half of the production of fruits, vegetables and seafood is wasted.[817] Simply put, people in rich countries waste food because they can afford it, while in poor countries people waste food because they cannot afford to keep it.

Atwater paid quite some attention to food waste and claimed that between one sixth and one tenth of the food in the late 19th century United States was wasted. He even inspected waste bins in New York and concluded that where the upper classes lived a "considerable proportion of the food purchased was literally thrown away by careless servants" (interesting to see that the servants were the ones blamed) while there was much less waste in middle-class neighborhoods. Households in the United Kingdom waste one quarter of all the food they buy.[818] Households and retail operations in United States together lost 60 billion kilograms of food in 2010, almost one third of the total retail-level food supply in weight and one third measured in calories. Of this waste, two thirds of the waste is by consumers.[819] In food services 'plate waste' is a result of oversized portions and undesired accompaniments. On average, American diners leave 17% of their meals uneaten, and few take this home with them. But finishing the meal can also be a form of waste; over-eating is a form of waste that doesn't end in the garbage, but in body fat and illness. And part of it can be blamed on gargantuan portions in eateries. From 1982 to 2002, the average pizza slice grew 70% in calories, the average chicken Caesar salad doubled in calories, and the calories in an average chocolate chip cookie quadrupled, contributing both to waists and waste.[820] I sometimes hear that the food industry is responsible for a lot of waste. One can accuse food industries for many things, but waste is hardly one of those. Already Upton Sinclair noted in *the Jungle* that the meat packing industry used every part of the animals including feet, hide clippings, tails and entrails; "they use everything of the hog except the squeal".[821]

Ultimately, waste is also about showing off, about abundance, about spending money on luxury goods and services to publicly display economic power, of which the sinking of champagne is an extremely provocative example. Use of food to show off goes back to traditional societies. Offerings to gods and other rituals historically also involved the wasting of food, e.g. by burning. The epic *Mahabharata* describes how Krishna and Arjuna burned the great Khandava forest with all its creatures in it as an offering to Agni, the god of fire.[822] The nobles in Medieval Europe had dinners with twenty or more courses, clearly not with the intention that all should be eaten. So called *Schauessen* (German, food to show, to see) were creations of food sculpted into buildings, animals and statues and not intended to be eaten.[823] Some food is decoration in a similar way as the flowers on the table. I remember seeing delicately sculptured vegetables and fruits at functions in Thailand and Malaysia. Nobody cries when the tulips are thrown away, but when fruits which were mainly decorative are thrown away it is seen as an abomination.

As I showed earlier most energy in the food chain is used after the farm gate. To have food going through the whole system and *then* be wasted means that a lot of energy, work, water and other resources have been wasted. 'Waste' at the farm level may to some extent feed wildlife (it is not only rodents that steal food from farms, but also birds, monkeys, elephants, squirrels and deer). Waste at the farm level (say rotten potatoes or moldy grain) can also often be recycled to the chickens or to the soil and is not lost from the food system in the same way as food waste from households. No doubt there is a potential for saving, but perhaps not as big as many believe.

So we can intensify production, we can expand acreage and we can waste less. Now I turn to the discussion about new ways to produce food. Many such ideas abound; synthetic food, algae, aquaculture, hydroponics, insects, wild foods, vertical farms and urban farming are the ones I will discuss here.

"It will be functional, natural, designed food," Vladimir Mironov says. "How do you want it to taste? You want a little bit of fat, you want pork, you want lamb? We design exactly what you want. We can design texture." In a small laboratory on an upper floor of the basic science building at the Medical University of South Carolina, Mironov has been working for a decade in 'growing' meat. He envisions football field-sized buildings filled with large bioreactors which he calls carnaries.[824] And as I write this text Mark Post, sponsored by Google co-funder Sergey Brin to the tune of US$300,000, has just presented the first synthetic hamburger to the world's media. There are many issues around these synthetic foods. With genetic engineering we certainly will see more of them in the future. There are reasons to be cautious about the health effects of eating them. Some of them will probably turn out to be harmful, some might be perfectly safe. We will realize this by the same crude process of trial and error that humans have used all along and sometimes, 'shit happens'. But by and large I doubt that synthetic foods will generate more than research grants, newspaper headlines and bankrupt companies.

Yeast biomass was used as human food in Germany during the First World War. The development of large-scale processes for the production of commercial protein began in earnest in the late 1960s, against the backdrop of looming food crisis. Most of the initiatives failed due to technical or economic reasons. The ICI Pruteen process for producing bacterial single cell protein for animal feed was a milestone in the development of the fermentation industry. This process utilized continuous culture on an enormous scale.[825] However, even if the production worked it was never economically viable – it could simply not compete with soy and fish, and the site was eventually blasted with dynamite. On the same site in Billingham, England there is now a much smaller factory that uses a continuous fermentation process to produce a *Fusarium venenatum* biomass, marketed as Quorn, a vegetarian alternative to meat, with a price higher than meat.

Few people seem to realize that these lab-food need a feedstock. Energy cannot be created out of nothing, and the same is true of proteins and other complicated life molecules. All synthetic foods are grown using biologically derived materials as feed stock. It's not as if you can take oil, nitrogen from the air, phosphorus from the soil crust, shake them up together and get a high quality food. I am sure that there are technical possibilities to do something like that, with massive investments (Mironov in South Carolina wants a billion dollars to develop the process). But nature already does the job for us. And there are few signs that our labs can do it better. To grow maize as a feedstock for artificial food or to produce chicken is not so very different. Chicken production, in many parts of the world, is already landless production, a kind of feed converter factory. And it is obvious that you can do a similar thing with fungi or bacteria. It is not obvious, however, that the process will be much more efficient. Perhaps more appealing for vegans; the only argument for synthetic meat that holds to date is that one wouldn't have to kill animals. Personally I believe there are enough natural plants to satisfy vegans, and if I were a vegan

I would not like to eat a product that mimics what I don't want to eat. In a last data check for the book I look up if Mironov has been successful with his carnaries, and see that the University locked his laboratory in 2011. The latest recording I find of him on the internet is from September 2013, where he promised to develop 3D printing of human organs in Russia[826] – another rabbit to pull out of the hat.

Aquaculture of fish, shellfish, aquatic plants and algae is increasing and will continue to do so. But there are also reasons to be somewhat skeptical of its promise. Aquaculture can capture nutrients that are lost from the soil and carried to the sea by sewage and recycle them into the food system, for example, cultivating mussels. Algae can be eaten, but can also used as a fertilizer, feed for animals or be used for bio fuel. The difficulty is to find practical ways to grow them. As one industry magazine notes: "Though the cultivation of algae using man-made or natural ponds was initially simple, turning it into a viable feedstock has always been problematic. So our industry has always needed a system that could enable higher production levels, lower capital and operating costs, greater biomass density, better environmental control, and above all, industrial scalability."[827] I followed up another article, that claimed that the technology of a company will feed the world – and the cars – in the future, all the way back to the source and realized that the company were producing food supplements for a price ten to hundred times an affordable staple food and totally unrealistic for bio fuel. For sure, algae are already interesting for the production of omega 3 and some other special products and macro algae have been cultivated and eaten for millennia. But some caution is recommended. Perhaps fishing remains the easiest way to use algae.

Much aquaculture today is based on predatory fish, such as salmon, which are fed on (undersized) caught wild fish and fodder from agriculture, a somewhat absurd production system, and surely not a recipe for producing 'more' food. There is not a very dramatic difference between modern fish farming and broiler production. Both are based on keeping a population in a confined space, feeding them with bought-in feed composed of maize, soy and fish[828] and adding minerals, vitamins and antibiotics to keep them alive in bad conditions. A comparison between Norwegian salmon production and chicken production concluded that chicken production was less-resource consuming than salmon when salmon is fed wild caught fish.[829] There is a transformation taking place in the salmon industry to replace fish meal with plant sources, but salmon is a predatory fish evolutionary adapted to eat fish: not maize and soybeans. For aquaculture to really play a meaningful role in feeding a growing population in a sustainable way, we need systems that integrate aquaculture and farming, building on systems that have developed over a long time in Asia where rice, fish and vegetables have been grown in the same system, sometimes also including ducks or pigs.

Foraging, using wild products has undergone some kind of revival lately – although mainly as a hipster fashion. As I discussed earlier some cultures, such as the native North Americans, were sophisticated managers of wild life. Agricultural and forager communities in twenty-two countries in Asia and Africa use an average of 90-100 species. Despite their value, wild foods are not included in official statistics on the economic values of natural resources. In an article in the Philosophical Transactions of the Royal Society, Zareen Bharucha and Jules Pretty conclude that wild plants and animals continue to constitute a big proportion of the global food basket, and that their importance may increase in the future.[830] We can, once again, utilize wild food better than we do. Many wild foods are underutilized. For example despite large scale commercial extraction, only a fraction of the wild berries are collected from Swedish forests. Game is on the rebound in most industrial countries, and deer are now common in urban landscapes. Americans spend more than US$33 billion per year[831] and some 220 million days[832] on hunting an estimated hundred million kg of meat. That means that they spend two days and more than three hundred dollars per kg of game meat…

There are many calls to 'rewild' the landscape. In Montana, Sean Gerrity, a private entrepreneur has established the American Prairie Reserve in an effort to reconstruct the prairie. He plans to replace ten thousand cows with the same number of bison, a keystone species (that is a species that is of fundamental importance for the whole biome) for the prairie. Sean Gerrity's interest is primarily in producing a landscape, but the bison will also be culled. It is not yet clear if they will produce the same, more or less meat than the cows.

Fisheries and whaling are other examples of managing wild resources. I will not go into detail about this complex topic, but just conclude that humans have not been particularly successful in the management of fishery resources. Nevertheless we could have a long-lasting harvest of fish, sea food – and even whales (if we wanted to). We can also forage further down the trophic level (that is lower in the feed pyramid) in the sea - instead of catching predatory fish, catch their prey or even plankton. The total biomass in the sea is very high. One square meter of the ocean can support 11 grams of a predatory fish, 37 grams of an herbivore fish and a staggering 807 grams of plankton. This gives a pretty good idea of what there is to gain from feeding further down in the energy pyramid of the sea.[833] But collecting all those dispersed energy units also takes a lot of energy.

Insects have been consumed by many people for millennia, and some insect food has been held in high regard. More than 1,900 species have been consumed in the world.[834] The most famous cultivation of insects is silk worms which breed on mulberry leaves. *The Insect Cookbook*, released March 2014, features recipes and interviews with top chefs, insect farmers, political figures, and nutrition experts, including chef René Redzepi, whose establishment in Copenhagen has for three years running been selected as the 'best restaurant in the world' and Kofi Annan, former Secretary-General of the United Nations. Perhaps I am a bit cynical, but when I see the array of celebrities 'on stage' to promote insects as our future food I think something must be amiss. Do we need all these hotshots to convince us to eat bugs? I have nothing against eating insects; I have eaten my share of known and unknown insects, not only the worm I swallowed to show off as a young boy. I have been offered, and enjoyed, flying white ants (termites) in Uganda and ant eggs in Thailand, both regarded as special treats. Since 2003, FAO has been working on issues related to insects in many countries around the world. It says "edible insects contain high quality protein, vitamins and amino acids for humans. Insects have a high food conversion rate, e.g. crickets need six times less feed than cattle, four times less than sheep, and twice less than pigs and broiler chickens to produce the same amount of protein."[835]

Various waste materials, including manure and our own faeces can be used as feed stock for insects. However, if insects were to become a big part of the food system they would certainly have to be raised on cultivated crops. In this way we should ask if they are more efficient than chicken, carp or salmon in converting food crops into new food. Farmed insects will most likely play an increasing role in our food system in the future. But I wouldn't bet on them becoming a substantial part of our diet for many decades, not mainly for gastronomic reasons but because of practical and economic constraints. The FAO acknowledges that the cost of production is currently far too high and while promoting insect rearing as an interesting option for small scale production they also advocate increased mechanization to drive down costs, which will not favor small scale production, rather the opposite.[836]

Hydroponics (the growing of plants in water with drip-fed nutrition) is another much-hyped technology. There are some traditional hydrocultural systems that work well, where people farm on floats in rivers or lakes, e.g. in Bangladesh and Burma, and of course there are edible aquatic plants. In its modern scientific form hydroponics was developed by several researchers at Berkeley University in the 1930s and William F. Gericke published *The Complete Guide to Soilless Gardening* in 1940.[837] In 1937 Time Magazine reported that "his tanks have yielded some remarkable results".[838] At least the magazine is persistent in its acclaim as they elected a hydroponic system (this time vertical to add spice) to one of the 50 best innovations in 2009, "a hydroponic-farming system that grows plants in rotating rows, one on top of another. The rotation gives the plants the precise amount of light and nutrients they need, while the vertical stacking enables the use of far less water than conventional farming."[839] Time Magazine and many others severely underestimate the challenges for hydroponics. As with algae production, hydroponics may certainly can play a role, but I suspect a marginal one, at least in my lifetime.

Superintensive farming systems are also said to be relevant for feeding the world. As I have shown with the examples of Pudu Peppers, it is indeed possible to get very high yields from a limited space. 'Can this technology be used to produce food as well?' I ask Leilah Thiart, communication manager in Grodan, the company that produces the mineral wool slabs in which Pudu Peppers grow their capsicum. She looks first surprised and then a bit offended when I point out that Grodan has 'feeding the world' as quite a prominent part of their marketing message. From what I can see only tomatoes, capsicum and cucumbers are grown with the technology, and while they are appealing and commercially interesting crops, they are only marginally relevant for human nutrition; 'feeding the world' has very little to do with tomatoes. 'Is there any production of staple food, like potatoes or grain with this technology'? I ask and I am told that the only such application is growing seedlings for rice production in Japan. It is of course possible to grow potatoes or grains in superintensive systems and if we were to do that we certainly could feed even 20 billion people. But the costs and competing demand for resources make it uneconomical.

There is also considerable current hype around vertical farms in the city for food production. We see sketches of green skyscrapers feeding the people with clean and nutritious food. Yet, vertical farms are totally dependent on inputs that will need to be transported in, they are not part of any ecological context in the city, and if they are large, the crops will be put into the normal food distribution networks. So they are like any other assembly plant. And, like most other assembly plants, they are better located outside of cities. But then the rational for stacking crops on top of each other is gone where land prices are lower. Pudu Peppers in the Netherlands are already employing the technologies needed for superintensive farming. To stack their greenhouses on top of each other would provide very few benefits. It would necessitate the use of artificial lighting and it would increase construction costs tremendously. For sure, it is possible to produce lettuce in high towers with automated systems, I have seen it. But the fact that it is possible doesn't mean it is viable on a larger scale. Most such plans remain on the drawing boards for very simple reasons. Land prices are very high in cities and farming is basically a land based activity, which makes it uneconomical to locate farming in cities, which is the reason why cow-sheds and market gardens have largely disappeared from cities. It can of course be a cool marketing gimmick for a supermarket to grow its own lettuce on the roof of the outlet, in the same way as they have an in house bakery. And it can, of course, be an interesting architectural and engineering challenge to have green skyscrapers, but it has little relevance for feeding the population.

Guerilla farming in London, rooftop farms in Brooklyn, green walls in Milano, community farms in Berlin – urban farming is hip and cool. Meanwhile many hundred million people in developing countries are growing crops and vegetables alongside railroad tracks and highways or in polluted swamps in the megalopolises of developing countries. In many cases the poor grow their crops in lands that often flood and the hygiene status of the produce is questionable. Sometimes they keep chicken and goats as well. Is urban farming a realistic alternative to feed growing urban populations?

To answer that question it is worthwhile looking back at the reasons for urban farming and why it disappeared. Farming in cities is as old as the city. Most cities have had some gardens within the city walls, and almost all of them, except for pure trading seaports have had a close relationship to the rural hinterland. This continued as long as ecology and economy belonged together. In Paris in the 19th century and well into the 20th century, there was a substantial production of early out-of-season fruits and vegetables. The market gardens were highly labor-intensive, employing 9,000 gardeners on 1,400 ha of land, much of it within the city walls. They reached yields of up to 100 tons per hectare, with massive applications of manure (much of it provided by the horses that they used to market their produce and plow the land). Between three and six fruit and vegetable crops were taken annually from each plot made possible by a build up of fertility in the soil and because 25% of the land was under glass. In some cases the greenhouses were heated with stoves or steam boilers.[840] This is just one of many examples of how farming took place in cities. I previously discussed London's cow-sheds and the extent of suburbian production of luxuries in Rome.

In some places of the world cities were not very dense or big, and therefore they could produce a lot of food on the land of the city. For example in Sweden, most cities had their own farm land within the city perimeters, and this land was managed by city people. In the 17th and 18th centuries, the city of Uppsala not only produced all the grain it needed, but often produced a considerable surplus. Farming was the main activity and other crafts and trades were a side business for many townsfolk. Professors at the university had an average 3 hectares of land for their use. More than half of the households had access to the city farm land for grain production. In addition there were private garden plots and animals within the city perimeter. The urban farms were also part of a social welfare system, providing income and producing food for the needy; a large proportion of the city farms were managed by widows.[841]

Despite the hype and attention given to urban farming in modern wealthy cities, most urban farming takes place in developing countries by poor people. The FAO estimates that 800 million people are engaged in urban or peri-urban farming. Almost half of them also sell some of their produce. In Hanoi, the capital of Vietnam, more than 150,000 tons of fruit and vegetables are produced and one of four households are engaged in urban farming. In many cases it is a necessity rather than the fashion statement it has become in developed countries. I visited an urban farming project in the shantytowns of Cape Town, South Africa. It was established to provide employment to unemployed urban youth, but at the time of my visit the only people engaged were four elderly women who came from rural areas. They appreciated the irrigation, the free seeds and the working equipment, while the youngsters saw cultivation as a meaningless toil.

Farming in the cities had as much to do with using the cities' waste as with the city as an outlet of production. Most big cities had well developed systems for collecting human waste and bringing it back to the farm land, 'the more the city stank the richer it was deemed to be'. The city of Gothenburg in Sweden had its own swine farm up to 1927, which fed the city's waste to thousands of hogs every year. In Gennervilliers, outside Paris, the first municipal sewage treatment plant in 1869 was based on recycling nutrients. Forty farmers were invited to farm on the land irrigated by the sewage water. It was a great success and farmers fought for the contracts and by 1900 there were 5,000 hectares irrigated by the sewage water. Berlin followed Paris in 1878.[842]

London chose another way, unfortunately the one that would dominate the century to come. The man who discovered the basis for artificial fertilizers, Justus von Liebig, understood well that the waste from the cities needed to be recycled to the fields to ensure their long-term fertility and he engaged in the debate on how to make a sewage system for London. This was long overdue, cholera epidemics ravaged the city in 1832, 1848 and 1849, killing tens of thousand and during the infamous Great Stink of 1858 the smell was so intrusive that Parliament had to adjourn for a week.[843] His arguments lost, however, and the choice was made to flush out the sewage water into the Thames.[844] This continues today. Before being released the solid fraction is separated and, for a long while, was dumped in the North Sea. Today it is dehydrated and burnt since the European Union prohibited sea-dumping. The irony here is that von Liebig's discovery led to the production of artificial fertilizers which were needed to replace all the nutrients lost to the sewage system, an invention that enabled this system to be accepted and work. Increased attention to hygiene, the development of cheap artificial fertilizers and water toilets broke the system of recycling in most places.

In the modern city, there was normally little space for livestock but in Europe allotments were common and popular (and are undergoing a revival – in some London boroughs the waiting list for an allotment is 40 years[845]). During the two great wars they played a key role in feeding the populations. By the end of the Second World War there were more than 1.4 million allotment plots in the United Kingdom and parks and other public spaces were being used to grow food and eliminate dependence on imports.[846] This was largely a result of the public *Dig for Victory* campaign. Cuba, after the crash of its favored trading relationship with the Soviet Union, and facing a continued American embargo also turned to urban farming with much energy and some success in the 1990s.

We need to have realistic expectations of what can be produced in the city. I visited Cuba in the early 2000s and was not as impressed by what I saw as many other 'food movement' writers. In the semi-deserted and bankrupt city of Detroit it is estimated that almost 5,000 acres could be allocated to urban farming. Depending on the intensity of production this could supply Detroiters with between one third and two thirds of the vegetables consumed and between on sixth to two fifths of the fruit. This seems impressive – but fruit and vegetables play a minor role in feeding people. The same area could perhaps give 10,000 tons of wheat, which sounds a lot, but equals the calorific needs of 30,000 people, just a few percent of the population of Detroit. In

Oakland, California, researchers estimate that urban farming could only contribute between five and ten percent of the city's vegetable consumption, and this is based on the assumption that the production would be professional in character. If the project would be left to amateurs the production would be considerably less.[847] Research in Bristol show similar results.[848] The production of vegetables in the cities could contribute to considerable lower energy use as transporting and cooling fruits and vegetables are particularly demanding – which was the reason why market gardens were located in city perimeters in the first place.

Meanwhile, urban farming has a role to play in reviving community spirit, for recreation, for green therapy. It is also a good way to engage people in food production and in appreciating food quality. For many the allotment is a space for contemplation and/or solitude. It can also offer an opportunity for excluded groups or individuals to participate and become involved. Urban farming as it is practiced in the developed countries today is more about empowerment and participation than actual food production and that has its own value.

If we are serious about feeding the cities more locally, we should look more to the perimeters of the city and to the interplay between cities and their hinterland. That connection is almost gone in modern food systems and it is here that there really is a potential to feed the cities. As area increases by the square of the distance, a city with a radius of 1 km occupies 3.14 km^2 but the area within a 10 km radius contains 314 km^2, that is one hundred times as much land to produce food from.

In general, the most-hyped new ideas which are promoted in the media and by scientists seeking funds are often the least realistic alternatives. High-tech solutions inevitably attract attention. But mostly they stumble on practicalities or economics. There are very many 'good ideas' out there, but they usually do not materialize into real life technologies, because they are simply not viable. Just because it is *possible* to do something doesn't mean that it is *feasible*. The steps from a developing a prototype to full-scale production and adoption are often many more and much bigger than we give credit for. The ancient Greeks knew how to use steam for mechanical movement and they also knew electricity, but it took more than two thousand years before that knowledge was put to practical use. It took two hundred years to refine cooling technology so that it became an everyday technology. The unglamorous, and some say unhealthy, grain will still form the backbone of human nutrition for decades to come. Grain is equally important as a porridge, pasta, bread or whole grains, and some of it will feed animals. In addition to grains we will be fed by oilseeds, root crops and grazing animals and to, an increasing extent, the products of aquaculture.

There is no silver bullet that in itself can guarantee food security. It seems clear to me that food security, poverty and equality are intrinsically linked, and that the root cause of food insecurity is found in an unjust society and unequal access to resources. As such, the main path to food security involves correcting those injustices. There is a growing discourse that seeks to reframe hunger and access to food into a human rights context, and another that seeks to redefine basic foods as commons rather than as commodities,[849] something that I will discuss more in the last part of the book. John F Kennedy told the delegates at the 1963 World Food Congress that "we have the ability, we have the means and we have the capacity to eliminate hunger from the surface of the earth. We only need the will."[850] Things have not changed much.

In this book I have, on several occasions, claimed that the risk of global food shortages is perhaps not the most imminent problem facing humanity. But it is prudent to qualify this claim. First, it is based on the assumption that we will arrive at a peak of world population of below 10 billion persons. Equally I have discounted the (ever-possible) questions of large scale instability and insecurity. Financial collapse, wars and other security problems could rapidly change the situation, undermining production and / or trade. We have seen how an extremely import-dependent country such as Britain successfully managed to feed its population during two world wars (of course as a seafaring nation they were never totally cut off from food supplies – but they were considerably diminished). However, modern food chains are really a quite different kettle of fish. They are too few people in the countryside, and too few of them with the required agricultural skills to ramp-up food production in the same way. And where are the shovels and wheelbarrows? When the barn was converted to a spa, stables or an atelier, they were dumped. We also face the threat of climate change. If greenhouse gases continue to rise, or even if we stabilize them, we will have a warmer and less predictable climate, and sea levels will rise, inundating large areas of fertile lands. But productivity can also rise due to higher levels of carbon dioxide. How that will play out for global food production is anybody's guess.

My main fear in the medium term is energy costs and energy shortages. Few people realize how incredibly dependent our whole food system is on the supply of external energy, in particular fossil fuels. The five main uses in agriculture are the production of chemical fertilizers, irrigation, the driving of tractors and other agricultural machines, the whole transportation network and the cool chains and storage. This should also seen in the light of the huge disconnection between where people live and where food is produced. Even the primary production of meat in China and Europe is hugely dependent on massive imports of feed stuff from other continents. While there are many surveys showing that organic production can be fairly productive, there is no doubt that a dramatic increase of prices of chemical fertilizers and a corresponding decrease in their use would, certainly in a short term, lead to a drastic reduction of output and this would require a fundamental reshaping of the whole global production model. While that would be largely positive in the longer term, if the transition were forced upon us too quickly it would, inevitably, lead to reduction in food supply. We cannot lose the massive energy subsidy that we have given ourselves (with the tractor) and the plants (via nitrogen fertilizers) without major repercussions. Sometime they will have to go, but it will be hard. In the longer term, higher energy prices will affect population patterns as well. In the same way as cheap energy allowed us to congregate in mega cities, the loss of cheap energy will make it less possible and less attractive, so we may well experience a re-ruralization and a relocalization of the food system. But that's enough with projections for the future, for now.

23

Cars, animals or people?

The global energy market is worth about US$7 trillion per year and the agricultural/biomass sales reaches at least US$7.5 trillion. "The potential profits from merging fossil carbon and living carbon are huge", says the action group on Erosion, Technology and Concentration, an NGO that monitors corporate power in the food sector.[851] They, as many others, see a convergence between the energy and food sectors, with biofuel, as the most prominent example. As I discussed earlier there are many interactions in the land, water and energy nexus. Should we feed people, pigs or cars? Will hungry people get less food because you drive an ethanol-powered car? Those are leading questions. The global food system is indeed one system and it is an illusion to believe that what is done with maize in United States has no implications for the global food markets. But the food system is also very complex and the effects of a change in one place can cascade through the system with opaque feedback loops and interactions.

Before plunging into the debate, let us remember that bio-energy is nothing new, it was there in various forms before fossil fuels, and traditional biomass still globally plays a more important role than biofuels. In the United States it is estimated that, by 1960, the tractor had replaced 23 million draft animals, and the 79 million acres of land used to grow feed for them could be reallocated to other uses.[852] This equals the average total area used for growing maize up to the year 2007 (after which maize expanded further). Some 140 years ago Sweden had an export boom in oats, not for making muesli or oatmeal porridge but for driving Britain's transport system. While the British trains were driven by steam engines, other ground transport, including trams, were still horse-powered, and the increase in transportation necessitated more horses and thus more oats, a favorite feed for hard-working horses. From a global perspective, the use of animals for traction is certainly not something of the past. Still today, half of the world's agricultural land is tilled with the help of animals and many people rely on them to transport themselves, their produce, or sup-plies. Even cell phones and widescreen TVs reach people by mule or camel. Light, in the form of candles and oil made from animals, whales or plants has been with us for several thousand years. Wood, the most important bio-energy there is, still heats the homes of many people and it is the main cooking fuel for most of the world's poor. And humans have used ethanol alcohol, made of grain, banana, palm or tubers to keep themselves warm and somewhat happy for millennia.

There are several types of biofuels: ethanol from maize, wheat or sugar cane; biodiesel from rape seed, palm oil or copra; methanol from wood, and; biogas from fermenting various waste materials or manure. In the agriculture context ethanol and biodiesel are by far the most important. Global production of biofuel grew from 16 billion liters in 2000, to an estimated 110 billion liters in 2012. More than 80% of the biofuel is ethanol, mainly made from maize and sugar cane. United States and Brazil dominate ethanol production. The United States produced some 50 billion liters and Brazil 28 billion liters, with China producing 2 billion liters. The United States use of maize for biofuel fluctuates with the yield, but it is in the range of thirty percent of the total harvest.[853] Biodiesel production is smaller and spread in more countries with the United States, Germany, France and Brazil being the main producers.[854] Between 2004 and 2007, investments in the biofuel sector increased substantially. In 2007-2008 when agricultural commodity prices rose sharply this led to a global discussion on the impact of biofuels on food prices. This discussion and the reduced profit margins, because of higher costs for the feedstock crops, led to a sharp drop in investments and biofuel expansion.

Sugar cane ethanol is the most competitive biofuel, but it is still more costly than gasoline and biodiesel costs typically twice as much as petroleum diesel.[855] You need some 5.6 kg of soybeans to produce a liter of biodiesel, 2.7 kg of maize or wheat for one liter of ethanol and 12 kg of sugar cane to produce one liter of ethanol. Approximately 111 million tons of soybeans, rapeseed and sunflower, 157 million tons of maize and wheat and some 370 million tons of sugar cane were used for biofuel production in 2010. The brut calorific energy of this total is around 1.27 quadrillion calories, just under one tenth of the total calorific production from the global agriculture system. Expressed per person, it is 480 kcal per day.[a] The interested reader can find more details in the annex, table 12.

In theory, energy production from food crops only takes away the energy, the calories, from the food system, leaving all the other nutri-

---

[a]   Calculations based on EIA international biofuel statistics.

ents, such as proteins and minerals, for animals and people.[856] The residual products of ethanol production from grain and from oil-crushing provide very good feed stuff, so not all the calories are 'lost' from the food system. The amount that comes back depends on the conversion ratios in livestock production. Distillers grain, the main by-product of maize and wheat ethanol production, is a good animal feed containing 27% protein. For each 10 kg of maize used for ethanol, 3.3 kg of distillers' grain is produced.[857] In the United States it is increasingly displacing soybeans and maize as an animal feed. As ethanol production increased the distillers' grain business has evolved its own market, in a similar way that soybean meal went from being waste, to a by-product to a valuable commodity. One study from the FAO expresses the evolution in the questions that livestock producers in the United States have being asking as the ethanol industry and production of distillers grain have increased. Starting from 'Can we use distillers' by-products in animal feeds?' they moved to 'How much distillers' by-products can we use?' and then 'Can we use more?'[858] The United States also exports increasing quantities of distillers' grain to more than fifty countries around the world, including Canada, China, Mexico, South Korea and Vietnam, for use as swine and poultry feed and also in aquaculture.

Very few biofuel initiatives have emerged on pure commercial grounds as profitability is low. Biofuel production is subject to even more political interventions than food production. For example, the European Union and the United States have (fiercely debated) mandates to utilize a certain proportion of biofuel. There are a multitude of political drivers for biofuels. One is based on the desire for energy independence (or at least reducing energy dependency). Many countries had ethanol and methanol programs during the Second World War, but the flush of cheap oil after the war led to them all closing down. With the oil price hike 1973, there was a new interest. The Brazilian government mandated the blending of gasoline with ethanol, with a proportion fluctuating between 10% and 22% from 1976 until 1992. Both Brazil and Argentina have policies that require that biodiesel is blended into diesel at specified levels.[859] A more recent driver is the desire to reduce greenhouse gas emissions. A third, very strong, driver is the need to offload the constantly-increasing production of farmers, which has led to vast subsidies for producing biofuels. Globally, biofuels received some US$11-12 billion in subsidies in 2006.[860]

Some claim that it is unethical to produce biofuels. Others support it so long as these are made in a sustainable way; some promote certification to safeguard this. For some reason, nobody argues that all fuels be subject to the same criteria or to certification. This would imply applying the same sustainability criteria to petrol (gasoline) which obviously would not make the grade. This is because our global energy and transport systems are not sustainable, due to excessive demand, regardless of where the fuel comes from and from what it has been produced.

A report for Friends of the Earth calculates the realistic bioenergy potential of cropland and grazing land in the year 2050 to be around 70–100 EJ per year.[a] The current global use of fossil fuels stands around 450 EJ/yr. The bioenergy potential from cropland and grazing land is estimated to be in the order of magnitude of 15-22% of current fossil energy use."[861] Another report by four Swedish researchers at Global Energy Systems, Uppsala University gives similar results.[862] Both reports, optimistically, assume that a large share of crop wastes can be converted to biofuels. This can only be done commercially with new technologies and, if more biomass is diverted from soils to cars, this could have severe side effects on soil fertility. Most papers I have reviewed have exaggerated expectations of the potential yields of biofuel crops, especially given that the authors expect biofuels to expand into marginal lands. While the quantities involved are huge, biofuels accounted for only 2.3% of global transport fuel demand in 2011; Brazil, the United States and the European Union had considerably higher shares, at 20.1%, 4.4%, and 4.2% respectively (2010 figures). According to Lester Brown, if the entire United States grain harvest was turned into ethanol, it would still only satisfy 18% of current United States gasoline demand.[863] This isn't an argument against biofuels by itself, rather an argument for the need to totally redesign our transport systems. As such, biofuels present a rather limited option for reducing our dependency on oil, even less so if consumption rates in emerging economies are catching up with those in rich countries.

Any reader who has ever been moonshining will be aware that huge amounts of energy are needed in the process of making maize or wheat ethanol. Through the fermentation of the grain mash, sugars are converted to alcohol, but the resulting beer soup has to be distilled and the water and ethanol have to be separated by boiling. In a similar way the extraction of oils for biodiesel is also very energy consuming. This

---

[a]   EJ stands for Exa Joule; 1 EJ=10^{18} J.

is one reason why biofuel production often has a bad energy ratio. Another reason is that much energy is used in producing the grain in the first place, something I discussed earlier in the chapter on energy. In some cases when added together the energy ratios are less than 1, meaning that the production of biofuel uses more energy than the energy content of the fuel itself, something that can only happen when massive political and economic distortions exist. For grain-based biofuels, the energy ratio, expressed as energy return on energy invested (EROEI), in a number of case studies ranged from 0.7 to 2.8.[864] In comparison, EROEI from wind energy, hydroelectricity, coal and oil (not shale) are mostly far above 20.

A low energy ratio is not the only reason for questioning the value of making ethanol from grain. It also leads us to question the extent to which ethanol helps cut greenhouse gas emissions. According to a report from the United States Congress Budget Office, driving cars exclusively on ethanol only reduces greenhouse gas emissions by twenty percent. And, if the ethanol factory is powered by coal, the ethanol will have higher greenhouse gas emissions than gasoline. If biofuel production expands into non-agricultural lands, such as forests or savannah, there will be huge emissions of carbon dioxide as a result of the changed land use; the expansion of biofuels into productive tropical ecosystems will lead to net carbon emissions for decades, possibly centuries.[865] Research from the United States points out that it can take more than 50 years of ethanol production from switchgrass to offset the emissions caused by plowing the land to grow switchgrass: even longer if the land it taken into maize production.[866] Of course, this is not unique for biofuel crops, it is the same for any expansion of crop land, but clearly if the motive to grow biofuel is to limit emissions, it is self-defeating if it causes a lot of emissions. The low energy ratio is also reflected in low profitability of producing ethanol and biofuels, which is dependent on subsidies.[867] This is not just a case of bad economics or a failure to reduce greenhouse gas emissions, it is much worse. Low energy ratios mean that the global calculations of energy needs are grossly misleading. If the energy ratio is as low as 2 this means that, in order to replace 10% of fossil fuel currently used, biofuel corresponding to almost 20% of current fossil fuel use will be needed.

Many proponents of biofuels point to the 'second generation' of biofuels, biofuels made from cellulosic materials. Instead of using the 12 percent sugar that is found in sugar cane, the whole stem could be converted into feedstock for ethanol. The technology for this already exists, but the costs of production are high, making it even less profitable than normal biofuels.

Biofuel is often grown in monocultures, which use a lot of agrochemicals and can be a motivation for 'land-grabbing'. Many proponents of biofuel promote the idea that marginal lands and unproductive pastures should be used. But most grazing areas are left for grazing for a good reason; because they are not productive in the first place. For marginal lands this is even more apparent. There is no reason to believe that it will be profitable to grow maize for ethanol on marginal lands when it is not-profitable to grow maize for food. The same applies for wheat, sugar cane and palm oil. In addition, while many so-called marginal lands may not be media darlings like a tropical rainforest, they do contain very high levels of biodiversity. Very often when land is said to be unused, it is used in some way by pastoralist or marginalized communities.

But there are many nuances in the arguments for and against bio-fuel production. Small-scale biogas plants running on manure and other waste fuel the cooking of many millions of people around the globe. Several hundred million animals provide the power to pull farm implements and transport goods all over the globe – and their 'fuel' all comes from agriculture land. It can be very interesting for farms to produce their own energy, individually or collectively. They largely had to do this until the tractor and electricity took over from the horse and wood. Heating needs are the easiest ones to take care of as there are biomass residues that can be burned. Biodiesel or just plain vegetable oil (which can be used to run some types of engines) are the easiest to produce on a small scale. There are small oil mills that can run continuously. Depending on the climate they can be fed with canola, sunflower, soybean, oil palm, coconut, jatropha or any other crop with a high oil content. While small scale biogas plants for cooking and heating are widespread and cheap to install and run, the biogas needed to drive a tractor needs to be cleaner and to be compressed, which can only be accomplished with expensive technologies, which means it is unlikely to be profitable at the scale of individual farms.

The same is true for producing ethanol from grain and it is even more complex to make ethanol from straw or other cellulose rich materials.[868] A study from Sweden found that using land to produce wheat and potato for ethanol to be used on the farm itself (instead of conventional diesel), lowered food production significantly, by 23% and 18%. This could partly be off-set by changes in the cropping system which could take food production to up to 90% of the reference scenario. The least impact on food production would be achieved by combining a draught horse and on-farm cold-pressed rapeseed oil.[869]

In the scenario the main constraint would not be the need for feed for the horse from the land but higher labor costs. All of these biofuel and bio-energy solutions share a common feature: they are integrated within a production system whose primary purpose is to produce food. This gives a very different logic than scenarios in which biofuels are produced as market commodities. In this way there are many similarities between the debate over biofuel and the debate over meat.

There are many arguments, valid or not, in favor of reducing meat consumption, about greenhouse gas emissions, other environmental issues, animal welfare and health. I already discussed methane emissions in the chapter about greenhouse gases. I have also discussed how the industrialization of chicken and other animals has lead to problems with antibiotic resistance and animal welfare. In this book I will not delve on the health aspects of eating meat. I will also only briefly discuss the ethics and acceptability of killing animals in order to eat them. But I want to discuss how (and if) meat production competes for land and resources which could be used for more efficient food production, a discussion that is quite similar to, but even more complex than, the biofuel debate.

Between 1983 and 2005, global meat consumption per person doubled. As the global population also increased by 2 billion people, the total meat consumption increased by much more. It is estimated to double again between 2000 and 2050, the biggest increase being in developing countries, assuming that economic growth will continue (an assumption which may prove wrong). Livestock products, such as milk, meat and eggs provide 17% of all energy and 33% of all protein for human nutrition. Meat consumption ranges from 5 kg per person per year in India to 123 kg in the United States.[870] In some European countries and in the United States total meat consumption has dropped slightly in recent years, e.g. in Germany it dropped from 64 kg in 1991 to 60.5 kg in 2009.[871] China today is both the biggest producer and consumer of meat.[872]

Even if reliable statistics for historical meat consumption are scarce (and it is also not always clear if bones and entrails are included), it appears that as early as the 19th century common people ate considerable quantities of meat in London, Paris and Berlin. Already at the end of the 18th century, the average annual consumption of beef and mutton in Paris was estimated to be 60 kg. Berlin's consumption of meat increased from 45 kg per person in 1845 to 73 kg in 1894. As table 5 shows, a working class household in 1848 in Stockholm ate 2.5 kg meat per week and much bigger quantities of fish. And at that time

Sweden was still a very poor country. In a similar survey a hundred years later, meat consumption in an average Stockholm household was lower, at 1.8 kg, but the family size was smaller as well. [873]

Table 5 Weekly intake of food in a working class household in Stockholm, 1848

	Quantity in kg	Energy in kcal
Bread	14.9	44,700
Salted meat	1.7	3,400
Fresh herring	4.25	7,172
Salted herring	1.3	2,195
Pork	0.85	2,050
Potatoes	18.3	12,810
Sum		**72,300**

Source: Pettersson, R (editor) 2008, Bekvämlighetsrevolutionen. This survey does not include any beer and liquor consumed or any food eaten out of home.[874]

The increase in consumption is often explained from a demand perspective, but can actually be better understood by the industrialization of livestock production and the gains in efficiency, measured as output per kg feedstuff used. This has been coupled with the large-scale monocultural production of soybeans and maize and other feedstuffs. This industrialization is not just restricted to rich industrial countries: Brazil, Thailand and China are going through this process at a rapid pace. The model includes large farm units, bought-in feedstuffs, modern breeds and other technologies and generally some kind of 'vertical integration' such as contract farming.[875]

Of the forty-one most important crops in the world,[a] 24% of the *weight* is used for animal feed, 67% for food and the rest for industry and fuel.[876] According to the USDA, it takes a less than 2 kg of grain equivalents to produce 1 kilogram of chicken, 5 kg to produce 1 kg of pork, 12 kg to produce 1 kg of beef and just 0.7 kg to produce 1 kg of milk.[877] However, to compare kilograms of (dry) feed with kilograms of (wet) chicken or (very wet) milk is a bit too simplistic. It is more interesting to look at how much protein and calories one gets from the

---

[a] In the United States 57% of these crops are used for feed, compared to just 4% of the major crops in India

feed and the animals respectively. Researchers from University of Minnesota concluded that 36% of the calories produced globally went to animal feed of which 89% 'got lost' in the conversion to meat. In theory, those calories could suffice to feed another 3 billion people.[878]

These, and similar calculations, have led some to conclude that animal products should not be consumed at all. However, things are not so simple. The same researchers found that milk is by far the most efficient way to transform feed to food with a 40% efficiency for calories and 43% for protein. Egg production converts 22% of the feed calories and 35% of the protein to egg calories and protein, chicken meat production converts 12% of the calories and 40% of the protein, and pork 10% of both.[879] The main nutritional reason for consuming animal products is for their protein and not for their calories. Increasing consumption of animal protein is one of the easiest – admittedly not the only – methods to rapidly improve nutrition and avoid the long-term damage caused by the malnutrition of children, who may never develop to their full bodily or intellectual potential. Yet while the figures quoted above are correct they are also misleading. There are also 'gains' in the process, especially from ruminants which convert grass to edible calories. The researchers' calculations are based on the assumption that all livestock products are derived from feeding them on cultivated crops. But this is only the case for industrially-reared livestock and not the case for small-scale or pasture-based livestock systems, or for systems that combine grazing with some supplementary feeding. If we look at the global figures, one-third of the calories in feed come back to us as calories in animal products. Around 48% of the protein in all crops is fed to livestock, but animal products supply us with about 40% of the protein we need, so the net loss of protein is smaller than the loss of calories, and the quality of animal protein is very high. I have not managed to separate out ruminants from other animals, but considering that pigs and poultry are the main consumers of crops fed to livestock, it is likely that milk from ruminants, demonstrates a net gain of protein rather than a loss. This is clearly the case for animals which are largely fed on grass with just supplementary feeding of crops and crop wastes, such as the Indian cow.

Vegetable oil consumption is the most rapidly growing segment in the food sector. And even if some people over-consume fat, on a global scale consumption falls short of people's needs, so the consumption of vegetable oil is likely to continue to increase. If we avoided consuming animals (and all their products, as is the case with veganism) altogether we would need to considerably increase vegetable oil production, as animals contribute one third of all dietary fats. Here there is a paradox. Almost all vegetable oils give a nutritious residual product (palm oil has the least quantity of by-products) which together with residual products from ethanol (distillers grain), cotton (cotton seed) and sugar beet (molasses and beet fiber) production represents more than one third of all global crop protein. This protein is recycled back into the human food chain by being used as animal feed.[a] The same goes for hulls, husk, bran etc from grain, most of it which would be lost without the animals. Even the iconic tofu have a rest product which is used as pig feed. It is simply not correct to look at what is fed to animals and what we get back and call the difference a loss. Much of it would be lost even if we ate no meat or drunk no milk. Some valuable animal products are also disregarded in this discussion. Leather, wool and skin are important clothing materials and there are important medicinal and industrial uses of animal products.

Ultimately, one can count in many different ways, per kg, per calorie or how many people could be fed, if feed was consumed directly by humans. But all these ways of counting have their weaknesses. How do deal with grass and hay? Most farmland in the world is grassland, but most of that grassland cannot be used for arable crops unless there is irrigation. Almost all natural grassland is also very low in productivity, so one cannot take average yields from farming and assume that they could be achieved on grassland. There are some permanent grasslands, which are on arable land and could be used for arable crops, such as in the Netherlands and in New Zealand. However, some of these lands are very productive, and growing grass is comparatively more environmentally benign than growing grain, so the advantage of converting them to maize fields is not apparent.

There are also socio-economic aspects of livestock production. Livestock is an important buffer of food and provides livelihoods for people who otherwise would have no income. Today, 600 million people are engaged in small-scale livestock production perhaps 200 million people live from pastoralism. This kind of animal production uses ecological niches that are not suitable for crop production. In addition, 400 million head of livestock are used as draught animals, and their role is mainly to help human beings to grow more food for themselves, even if they mostly also end up on our plates.

---

[a] I can not exclude the possibility that it will one day be possible to make a protein-rich food from soybean or rapeseed cake, which would break this link between vegetable oils and animal-rearing.

Small-scale pig or poultry rearing has traditionally been based on waste products from the field or kitchen, sometimes from food processing (such as whey or distiller's wash). Such feedback loops have been of huge importance for human nutrition. Cultures with limited food resources have used these animals in these roles. Until the 1990s, commercial pig feed in the United Kingdom consisted of 50% food waste.[880] This kind of livestock production doesn't really compete with producing food for human beings.[881 882 883] Industrial production systems have led to the demise of these ecological roles of pigs and poultry. Part of the reason is a fear of disease, which has led to severe restrictions on the use of waste. Even more importantly, feed has become much cheaper and, as production has intensified, waste is not sufficiently standardized and controlled for modern breeding systems. Still, as noted above, these animals are to some extent fed with industrial waste products such as distillers' grain and oil cakes. Clover grass and alpha alpha are often grown in traditional European crop rotations: they produce very good feed for ruminants(in the form of hay or silage) and also stimulate higher yields of grains and other foods on the land in subsequent years. They sequester nitrogen which can be used by the grain crop, and the manure from the animals can be used for demanding crops at the right time.

Finally, while the aggregate maths might suggest it, there is no evidence that livestock production currently diverts food from those who currently go hungry[884] even if there are theoretical possibilities for this to happen. Once again, we need to look at the whole system and not discuss one component in isolation.

Industrial livestock production is, however, the opposite of traditional systems; it absorbs a lot of capital and natural resources, is largely grain-based and demands high quantities of water. It's energy use is also high; it takes thirty-three times more energy to produce a calorie of industrial beef than one calorie of potatoes. Large-scale ranching might perform better in many of these respects, but raises other issues, for example, posing a threat to other valuable ecosystems, such as the forests that are cleared for grazing. A large share of the increase in meat production in Brazil is from the rainforest zone.[885 886] From this brief overview, it should be clear that one cannot make general statements about the effects of eating meat or keeping livestock. This notwithstanding, the total increased pressure on natural resources caused by the combination of the growth of the human population and the growth of meat consumption is worrying. And it is unlikely that freely-grazing ruminants and waste-eating chicken and pigs could meet an ever increasing global demand for meat, even though I have seen no serious effort to actually calculate this. From the perspective of food availability and our environmental foot print, there is nothing wrong in drinking milk or eating meat in reasonable quantities. But we have to ask how they are produced. If chemical fertilizers and pesticides were abandoned, monocropping ceased and livestock production was humane, the price for meat would be much higher than it is now and most people's consumption would be much lower. Chicken would once again be a Sunday dish.

Plants and animals are complementary. They use and need each other. There are no natural ecosystems without animals, and there has never been a sustainable intensive agriculture system without some livestock production. We saw, in the case of the first agriculture revolution in Europe, that the integration of livestock within farm production, including the growing of fodder on arable land, increased production, of both feed and food, tremendously, It also increased people's consumption of livestock products. One should also not forget that much of what is said to be 'lost' by raising animals is recycled to the land as manure and contributes to improving the land and supplying it with nutrients[a] and humus. The benefits of integrating animals is somewhat reduced when chemical fertilizers are used in the fields, but as I have demonstrated elsewhere, chemical fertilizers have other serious drawbacks.

A vegan system of farming, while needing less total land area for production would need more plowed, arable land than a mixed farming system where ruminants are largely grass-fed and pigs and chicken are largely fed with waste products from the food industry. It is too early to draw far-reaching, negative or positive, conclusions on the viability of a full vegan production system. Veganism is largely based upon ethical misgivings about humans having the right to keep animals in captivity for their own benefit. It raises issues about whether animals have 'rights' and whether we have special obligations to those animals that have now adjusted themselves to live with us (few of them would survive in the wild). My view is that we are bound to these symbionts by ten thousand years of farming. Modern market based farming systems treat these symbionts awfully and this cannot be justified. I believe there are systems where we don't see them purely

---

[a] Animal manure doesn't provide any new nutrients to the system, as all the nutrients in the manure comes from the soil in the first place, but there is no doubt that animal manure has very good soil building properties and also has the benefit of being possible to use where and when it is most needed.

instrumentally (valuing them solely for meat, milk or skins) but as living creatures, worthy of respect and a life reasonably adjusted to their innate needs and natural behavior.

Biomass is not solely used for fuel or feed. Industrial biotechnologies use agricultural rather than petroleum-based feedstock to produce chemicals and plastics – the more so if they can claim that they are 'sustainable' or 'green.[a] The value of biochemicals (excluding pharmaceuticals) could increase from 1.8% of all chemical production in 2005 to between 12% and 20% by 2015 according to the OECD. Not even one percent of plastics produced are currently from biological materials, although in the not-too-distant future most of them could be made from such raw materials.[887] For example, by the end of 2013, Coca-Cola had used 18 billion 'Plantbottles', partly made from sugar cane from Brazil and India.[888] In Japan, the 'Biomass Nippon Strategy', established in 2002, requires that 20% of all plastics consumed in the country are renewably sourced by 2020. This prompted Toyota, NEC and others to accelerate their R&D activities into biobased plastics and to raise the biobased content of their products.[889] Using the sophisticated molecules made by photosynthesis for this purpose seems to be more interesting than burning them as bio-fuels. Nevertheless, a bio-refinery industry would further increase pressures on land.

The discussion about changing consumption patterns is the part of the food puzzle that attracts most attention. I think the attention it receives it is a result of several factors. One is the neo-liberal dogma that the market is the main play ground for all sorts of human interactions. This, combined with many people's despair that politics, policies and politicians change very little has given rise to the ethical consumer movement, premised on the idea that our purchasing decisions determine what kind of society we live in. These discussions are also used as a proxy by people having a wide range of ideas about nutrition and/or ethics. I find that this discourse is disconnected from the realities of farming, and the factors that determine farmers' choices.

In a global food system, which land is plowed for which use is often difficult to ascertain. The chain reactions in the food system are immense. What would the implications be if there were no palm oil production in Indonesia and Malaysia? Would there be less vegetable

---

[a] I believe there are reasons to be quite skeptical about the real environmental benefits of many of these.

oil consumed or would soybean production expand even further into the Amazon? Considering that oil palm gives almost ten times more oil per hectare than soybean oil, would we save 1 hectare of rainforest on Borneo by cutting down 10 hectares in the Amazon? Or, would there be an expansion of rape seed oil production with a massive increase in the use of pesticides, causing bee-death, and of chemical fertilizers. If people stopped eating beef and lamb, what would happen to the enormously biodiverse mountain pastures kept open by their snouts? If more maize were diverted to biofuel production in the United States, and the protein-rich by-product is used for animal feed, would it replace soybean production and thereby reduce deforestation?

Cotton is grown on 34 million hectares, rubber, coffee and cocoa on another 10 million hectares each, tobacco and tea on more than 4 million and 3 million hectares respectively. Wine, beer and liquors are all produced from agricultural crops which occupy more than 20 million hectares. The United States has 9.2 million horses, almost all of them for hobby.[890] Golf courses take up much (potential or former) agriculture land, one estimate is that they use 5.3 million hectares globally: much, but not all of that, is on former agriculture land.[891] If there were a generalized, real, food shortage this land could, of course, be turned back to food production – particularly the golf courses which have abundant irrigation – though whether the returns on crops would match those of membership subscriptions remains to be seen.

At the time of writing, there is a fierce debate within the European Union about the limits to biofuels made from food crops. The European Union currently plans that 10% of transport fuel should be renewable (read biofuel) by 2020. But there is a lobby against converting food crops into biofuels. While this position might reflect genuine concern for the hungry of the world, the 'biomass market' has no such qualms. Food, feed and energy compete with each other for land, water, investment and research funding regardless of the European Union's goals. If the European Union really cared about the poor and the hungry in developing countries, it might first turn its eye to look at the effects of its own agriculture and trade policies.

Many of the criticisms of biofuels and animal feed production seem to be based on a limited understanding of how global food and agriculture markets work in practice. The food sector has historically been a buyer's market. Increased food prices and emerging alternative uses for farmland are a boon for farmers, and generally positive for rural areas, and those who live there. Most hungry people in the world live in rural areas and even those who are net buyers of food, such as agriculture workers and small farmers, will mostly benefit from increased incomes in the area as this means more employment, more demand for services and labor and better infrastructure. If biofuel production in the United States, the European Union and Brazil were to cease, or people were to stop eating meat, there would be a massive fall in global agricultural prices. For a short while, poor people in the slums would get cheaper food. But within a few years, millions of farmers, in both developed and developing countries, would have been forced off the land and, in developing countries, most would become dirt poor. They and the people working for them would be worse off than today, and hungrier. Welcome to the global market economy. Welcome to the treadmill.

24

The agricultural treadmill

The commercialization of farming means bringing more farmers into a mainly cash-based and market-based economy, both on the input and output side. Almost all farms are today linked to the world market, in one way or another. Even if they don't produce *for* the world market, the prices for the staple foods they produce are affected by world market prices. If local prices drop, exports commence and prices move towards world market prices; if local prices rise, imports press prices down. In this way, the global market can have an impact on prices all over the world, even if rather small quantities are actually traded, such as is the case with milk. The market for the products is mirrored in the operations of the farms, where commercial farmers are, directly and indirectly, increasingly dependent on commercial seeds, fertilizers, pesticides, specialized machinery, credits and external expertise.

When traditional farming systems are brought into the market economy, the change is not only technical or economic but the whole social context is disrupted. As commercial relations become more dominant they weaken other relations, so that farmers become more inclined to harm ecosystems, labor, village communities, commons and other institutions. This was certainly the case when farming was brought into the market economy in Europe and the same pattern is seen everywhere. This disruption was not only a negative thing, it was also a pre-condition for breaking down crippling traditions, prejudice and discrimination. In some places it also contributed in bringing down the feudal system. This tension between the capitalist market and traditional farmer and community values is one of the reasons why farmers often are depicted as a conservative force, embracing traditional values, community and family as opposed to commercialism. This remains the case even in countries where farming is totally submerged in the capitalist market economy. As one study from the United Kingdom in the early 1990s puts it "The family farmer has sought and in large measure achieved political legitimacy by seeking to distance himself from 'capitalism' at the ideological level, whilst fully embracing it at the economic level".[892]

When discussing the effect of the integration of farming and food into the market economy, it is important to differentiate between commercialized farming and farms that bring a limited surplus to the market. This is also mirrored in the role of markets in society at large. One should not equate the existence of markets in most human societies for some thousand years or more with the existence of a 'market economy' or, still less, a globalised capitalist market economy. Does this global market system produce good food? Does it produce quality? Does it promote land stewardship? Well, I hope that by now readers of this book will agree that the market system certainly has produced cheap food, but not necessarily good food. True, if you are wealthy enough, and have the time and knowledge, the market can also supply you with exquisite organic or artisanally-produced foods which are fairly-traded with small-scale producers. The proponents of the free market as the best way to organize food – and all other production – will argue that this is exactly the beauty of the free market. If people are interested enough they will spend their money on such high quality items, and if not they will buy junk food. What's wrong with that liberty?

But this argument misses out a lot. First, the externalization of costs in the market system grossly favors those actors in the food chain who can let the bill be paid by someone else, whether it is nature, future generations or workers in distant countries. Secondly, the high-quality of life style enjoyed by the rich is built on the backs of the poor. It is because a hand seamstress who makes haute couture dresses herself in cheap confection that the rich can afford boutique clothes. In the same way as the attendant at the delicatessen desk in the super-market cannot afford to eat any of the stuff she sells to her well-heeled clients. And this ignores the huge disparity in affluence and market power between wealthy consumers in developed countries and small-holders and slum dwellers in developing countries. Therefore, inequality is a precondition that allows the rich to enjoy exquisite food provided by the market. At the opposite end of the spectrum we have all the poor people who go hungry, and for whom choice in the global market is just a cruel joke.

The unlimited competition in the free market also has profound effects on how we farm. Large farms now dominate crop production in the United States. In the 1980s most cropland was held in units of less 600 cropping acres. Today it is mostly on farms with at least 1,100 cropping acres, and many farms are five and ten times that size. In 1987, the half of America's cows were in herds of 80 cows or less, by 2007, it was 570.

The change for hogs is even more striking; in the same period the scale of operations increased twenty-five fold. This long-term shift in farm size has been accompanied by greater specialization – beginning with a separation of livestock farming from crop farming. For instance in 1900, three quarters of farms in the United States had dairy cows and hogs, while by 2005 only one farm in twenty had either hogs or dairy cows. This allowed crop farmers to devote more time to and invest in crop production and gradually increase yields and acreages.[893] As I noted earlier, larger crop farms in the United States don't producer more per area unit than smaller farms, but they have lower costs for most necessary inputs including labor and capital.

By and large, similar developments are seen in other parts of the world. For example in Sweden in 1927 there were 350,000 farms which had an average of 4 hogs, while 2010 there were only 1,700 farms that kept hogs: and they had an average of 1,900 hogs.[894] In the United Kingdom the average dairy herd size went from 78 cows in 1997 to 113 in 2012, and the number of producers more than halved in the same time.[895] And these developments are not solely reserved for industrial countries. In Rio Grande Do Sul in Brazil, the number of specialized pork producers fell from 85,000 to 10,000 between 1995 and 2008, and when the multinational company Smithfield expanded its business into Romania in the past decade, the number of Romanian pig producers declined by 90% within four years.[896] Evelyn Mathias concludes in the report *Livestock out of balance* that there is a global technology race in the livestock sector. To join and stay in the race, farmers are investing in new technologies and improved animals. But for many, the long-term prospects are depressing; "their livestock threatens to turn from a multipurpose asset into a financial liability, driving them into continuous investment and a debt spiral".[897]

Agriculture suffers from a paradox which few outside of the sector are aware of and even fewer understand. The Secretary of Agriculture of the United States wrote in the annual report 1910 that "year after year it has been my privilege to record 'another prosperous year in agriculture'". What has been called a golden age for American agriculture, the period between 1900 and 1914, was a period of almost no growth in the sector. Output per worker increased by only 1% between 1900 and 1910. And total farm output by only 8%. Meanwhile the population increased by a whopping 21%. The result of this was better prices for farmers and thus the prosperous years.

Conversely in the 1950s, agriculture output increased at a rapid pace as a result of increased agriculture productivity. However, the decade is remembered as a time of hardship for most farm families.

Input prices went up and farm product prices fell. A million and a half farm families gave up farming in this decade as they couldn't make ends meet. Those that survived were the more advanced and commercially successful farmers, who could buy up the land from those that lost out. A similar pattern was repeated in the 1980s when productivity grew by 3% annually, product prices fell and input prices and interest rates soared. "In terms of agricultural development for the national economy the decade of 1980s was a huge success; in terms of the financial well-being of most farmers it was an economic nightmare" writes agriculture economist Willard W. Cochrane.[898] By and large farmers are stuck on a treadmill. They are forced by competition to increase productivity, and the increased productivity leads to lower prices. The fact that 'people will always need food' is a small comfort for the farmer who cannot compete. Product development and innovation, which allows industrial companies to stay away from a similar treadmill, takes place further down the food chain, among food processors and retailers. As a consequence they capture an ever-increasing share of the food dollar. This treadmill is the reason for the enormous pace in the increase in size and productivity in farming.

Vanguard farmers will constantly develop and improve and mostly increase in size, at the expense of their less successful colleagues. They will establish a new level of costs and prices each time racking up the notch for the minimum efficiency needed to stay in business. For farmers who cannot participate in this stiff competition there is no way out except to get out! Some production disappears all together. In some parts of the world the available natural resources clearly limit the possibilities for large-scale farming. Compare for instance the conditions for a farmer growing grain in a traditional agriculture area of Europe. The landscape is varied and roads, rivulets, hills, settlements and cultural and archeological remains mean that fields cannot be expanded. Because of land scarcity, land prices are also high and not primarily determined by agricultural productivity. The farmer will end up with a small farm and the size of machinery he or she uses can never be the same as on the Great Plains. Those farmers cannot produce grain at the same price as their competitors in United States, Russia or Argentina, even if they can intensify production and get higher yields per hectare.

The same obviously applies to the relationship between Bob Stewart in Illinois and Susan Mkandawire in Zambia. The use of fossil fuel by big farms has increased their productivity tremendously, i.e. it lowered the costs and thus the product price. The same cheap energy also radically increased the level of competition, as transport costs today are a small part of the final product price. Farmers all over the world compete in the same market. Even if Susan's labor cost is set at zero, she can not compete as her costs of production (seeds, transport, soil preparation, credits, and fertilizers) are mostly higher per unit. Under those circumstances low labor cost is no competitive advantage. She and millions of smallholders operate far below their ability to renew or invest in their farms. That is the reason why more than 80% of the farmers in sub-Saharan Africa and around half of the farmers in Asia and Latin America still farm manually.[899] Agriculture historians Marcel Mazoyer and Laurence Roudart conclude that such farmers would have to devote *all* their monetary income over a whole life to upgrade to ox-plowing.[900] However, they are still, mostly, (just) above the threshold of survival, which mean that they will continue to farm as long as there are no more promising alternatives beyond agriculture.[901] But it also means that, apart from producing their own food, they will prefer other income-generating activities to agriculture.

The treadmill is driven by specialization and – in turn – it drives further specialization, filling each area with just one or two crops or huge livestock operations. The economic and social implications are huge, but the environmental implications are even bigger. Large-scale landscapes are stripped of variation and biodiversity. They no longer produce the required ecosystem services which have to be produced elsewhere at high costs. In, addition these forms of production also cause direct and indirect damage to nature which have to be compensated for. This specialized, industrial, model of agriculture is replacing more and more local and varied regenerative systems. It is a key reason why agriculture produces cheap food but is also the chain that ties farmers onto the agriculture treadmill. Unlimited competition in agriculture will never be sustainable, ecologically, economically or socially. It only leads us further away from sustainability.

The solution sought by farmers who cannot run faster to keep up is to find market niches, local food, gourmet foods, organic and the like. And as the treadmill is spinning quicker and mainstream agriculture becomes bigger and more industrialized there is growing demand for these alternatives. But we must also realize that this is only possible because other farmers and other landscapes have taken over the production of carbohydrates for the billions; following the same kind of logic that led to the colonization of faraway landscapes for growing sugar cane some four hundred years ago. Also once niches become important enough they also become subject to the treadmill logic. This is clearly visible in the organic sector where agribusiness has staked real claims. I will discuss this a bit more shortly.

The other solution is governmental support to the farm sector. But we have enough evidence from the United States, the European Union and Japan to see that support policies often fail to deliver their intended objectives and often cause harmful and unforeseen effects. When I visited Japan in 2011, a number of policy failures were apparent. Japan is a major food importer and provides very high levels of support to farmers, yet there was plenty of fallow land. As a result of the very high levels of support to paddy farmers there was overproduction and some of the rice – at a price many times the world market price – went for animal feed. In addition, as a combination of the westernization of diets and the very high domestic price for rice the Japanese are switching away from rice, in fifty years consumption per capita has halved.[902] It is well known that both in the United States and the European Union most support goes to the largest farms. Clearly support that is based on volumes produced (or land holding size) will have no effect in the long run on the cannibalistic nature of the sector. The same process will continue, the main difference being that the support will be capitalized in land prices. Other subsidies to the farm sector tend also to be capitalized by other less direct processes. Further, poor countries, where a large share of the population is engaged in farming, could not subsidize their farmers in the same way, even if they so wish.

The forces of competition mean that people directly involved in the food chain are not necessarily rewarded for the immense gains in productivity they achieve. Often the opposite. This holds true all the way through the food chain: from the farms to the shops and the fast food outlets. Farm workers in all parts of the world are a low status group and they mostly have a very weak bargaining position towards the farmers – and farmers themselves are not usually in a position to offer better conditions. Farm workers are treated like the dirt they till. Despite so much mechanization, some 85% of the fruits and vegetables in United States are harvested by hand. Farm workers are often 'illegals' and even when they are not, the conditions are often deplorable. Bakersfield is a city near the southern end of the San Joaquin Valley in California. It is the county seat for Kern County, the fourth most productive agricultural county in the United States. Its major crops are grapes, citrus, almonds, carrots, alfalfa, cotton, and roses. Bakersfield is the home for corporate and regional headquarters of companies in these industries. Still, or perhaps because of this, more than one in four households in Bakersfield's metropolitan area experience food hardship. [903]

Two thirds of all farm workers in the United States earn less than US$20,000 per year and more than a fifth less than US$10,000.[904]

Working conditions are also often sub-standard. Many children are engaged in farm labor and farm laborers are regularly exposed to pesticides. And it doesn't stop at the farm gate. Workers in slaughtering and butchering industries work at break neck speed with accident rates three times the average rate in other industries. No wonder when the five largest pork plants in the United States slaughter between 18,000 and 32,000 hogs per day.[905] The fast-food industry is also notorious for deplorable working conditions. Median pay for core front-line fast-food jobs in the United States was (in 2013) US$8.69 an hour, with many jobs paying at, or near, the minimum wage, according to a report from the Labor Center of University of California. More than half of the families involved were enrolled in one or more public welfare programs; fast-food workers' households receive an annual average of US$1.04 billion in food stamp benefits. Even full-time hours are not enough to compensate for low wages.[906]

So, does the market system work or not? The answer to that question depends of course on where you are standing. In my view, the market works as intended, as described in the text books. Greater efficiency and competitiveness in each part of the food system drives each individual actor to cut labor costs, and constantly seek to rationalize and externalize costs. This process started long ago, even if farming culture has mounted considerable resistance to it. It is just that, with super-efficient logistics, fewer political hurdles and other technical barriers the system is too efficient and too competitive, driving the food system to a place where most people don't want it to be. The monocultures of the field are reflected in the food industry, in the supermarkets and finally on our plates. Of course, for economic development at large, this constant productivity increase in farming frees-up resources that are used in other sectors. It is quite clear that reducing the proportion of workers in the farm sector from eighty percent to, say, twenty percent was a pre-condition for industrialization and many other aspects of modernization, both good and bad. But one can wonder if it is advantageous to continue this process in an endless treadmill? Especially as the manufacturing sector also doesn't need more workers anymore and when we see the adverse effects of large-scale farming on biodiversity and animal welfare. 'Enough' is a word that doesn't seem to exist in the language of economists or, for that matter, politicians.

'Free' trade sounds like a good proposition, and it certainly has some advantages. But there are also some serious disadvantages. Unlimited competition means that it pays to – indeed is necessary to –

cut out all slack in the system. Slack (or redundancy) might sound like a bad thing, but it can also be understood as buffering capacity, giving people flexibility, options and resilience. Historically, there has always been redundancy at all levels. First and foremost among farm households and herds of cattle. They were stores of much food (which could be drawn on in hard times) and there was a lot of 'surplus' labor which, when needed, could attend to food production. Governments also kept food stores, for strategic reasons.

Today, the expectation is that the international trade system will supply us with food, with one hemisphere feeding the other one in the off-season. Redundancy is a valuable ecological principle, applied by all species. But it doesn't match with modern economic principles of efficiency. Those who try to keep some slack will lose out to the competition. Today's agriculture system has removed most of this slack and has also seriously diminished the slack in the nature that surrounds it, upon which it is still dependent.

Another important consideration when discussing the food system is 'who benefits?' A proportion of the world's population live in a middle-class environment and are in economic terms at least, the 'winners' of globalization. They (and I should include myself here) can afford to access interesting foods from exotic parts of the world (albeit within certain limits). They can often afford trips to exotic places (within or beyond their own countries) where they can find new recipes á le paysan and ingredients to tempt their palates. Failing that the chefs come to them. In most European capitals, one can eat the cuisine of every European country (often regionally differentiated) and besides the normal choice of Thai, Indian and Chinese, one can eat Cuban, Argentinean, Tuareg, Ethiopian, Cambodian or Tibetan).[a] These people were (mostly) not brought up on soda and sugar candy. It is quite clear that only a small proportion of people in the world benefit from this system – and only a small number will *ever* be able to do so. How many white table cloth restaurants would there be if the waiters, the cleaners and all the people in the food chain – down to the farmers – could earn the same salaries as the patrons? Is the glorification of artisanal food anything more than the social marker it always has been? Are the poor stuck with the tyranny of industrial foods: deprived of the opportunities to eat varied and good food?

---

[a] Conversely, for millions of upwardly-mobile Asians or Latin Americans a trip to McDonalds or Starbucks represents the heights of urbanity and sophistication.

Most books, movies, comics or art that deal with the problems of our food system conclude with a nice little 'what to do' list for these issues. In most cases this is a (non)-shopping list of 'dos and don'ts'.

> People who reject the increasing use of chemicals in the production system, can chose organic foods.

> People who reject long distance transport or want to support the local economy can buy local.

> Those concerned about unfair power between rich consumers in the West and poor people in most of the rest of the word can by Fair Trade.

> If you object to the widespread cruelty to animals in industrial animal production you can become vegetarian or vegan or buy organic or humanely raised meat.

> If you are concerned about the development of our eating culture you can join Slow Food and reject fast food joints.

> If you want healthy foods (depending on how you define what is healthy) you should reject highly processed industrial foods made of the 'big five', maize, soybeans, palm oil, wheat and sugar.

This list can be expanded *ad infinitum*. There are specific market schemes today that allow you to eat 'vegetarian' chicken (surely a contradiction in terms), sustainable palm oil, or protected regional specialty products. But can we cure the market's ills through the market? After all, it is the dictate of the allegedly impartial and rational market – guided by the not-so-invisible and cooperating hands of profit-seeking and government manipulation – which has led us to the system we now face.

It is more than a coincidence that almost all those schemes mentioned above are actually responses to certain aspects of the global market that is built on unlimited competition and controlled by a limited number of corporations. While 'organic' can be seen as a protest against agro-chemicals it can equally be seen as a protest against a linear input-based production system removed from any ecological context. And if you support local production, it is because you have some awareness of the effects of unfettered competition on (agro)biodiversity or of finding that only a small fraction of your food comes from people you know or having an economy where money circulates locally.

But the global food system perverts most of these efforts. When I recently visited a convention for artisanal food producers in Östersund in the north of Sweden, I realized that most of them sell most of their produce to the bigger cities and luxury restaurants; some are exporting or had that as a goal. Champagne, perhaps the archetypical regional product was in fact a creation of Wall Street and the City of London. Ironically, it shares this globalised history with port, parmesan cheese and other regional specialties. In Italy there is a high profile scheme to 'Adopt a sheep' within the Abruzzo National Park. In this scheme more than thousand subscribers pay 190 Euro for a certificate of adoption, an identity card, a photo of 'their' sheep, two kg of pecorino cheese, two kg of juniper-smoked ricotta, one pair of trekking socks, one kg of *salamelle di tratturo* (sheep salami) and five liters of olive oil. These packages are sent by airmail all over the world.[907] This presents us with a paradox: on the one hand it is a scheme that allows people to buy high quality artisanal food and helps the maintenance of a living rural landscape and community, on the other hand it is based on air-freight, global markets and long distance relationships.

Surviving within the market economy requires one to submit to the logic of the market; it leads to an increased use of inputs in production, externalizing costs, business-as-usual approaches and exposure to corporate take-overs. I have spent thirty-two years as organic farmer myself and know how this plays out in daily life. Most organic farms today follow the same business model as conventional ones. In France, organic farms have followed the conventional pattern of de-coupling livestock and crop production,[908] despite the integration of animals and crops being strongly recommended for good organic management. In many countries organic farms are now bigger than non-organic farms. Organic dairy farms in Scandinavia are more reliant on robotic milking than non-organic ones and they are highly mechanized and use considerable quantities of fossil fuel. In Denmark, the quantity of organic milk produced was stable between 2001 and 2012, but the number of farms involved halved in the same period.[909] Huge multinationals buy up pioneering organic companies and, in the words of Michael Pollan, it took them less than a quarter of a century to turn organic bagged salads into 'a cheap international commodity'.[910]

A study of ten organic farms in Denmark show that they too have to focus excessively on short term profits and ever-changing market requirements and have little time, energy or money to develop their farming system into a more ecologically sound system.[911] At the height of his farm enterprise Knud Erik Soerensen, the President of the Danish organic association from 1998 to 2007, had 70 dairy cows and 11,000 layers. Today he raises beef cattle and keeps only eleven chickens rooting freely in the compound. "I can see that this is how you should keep chickens. Organic farmers are becoming too obsessed with size. We should ask ourselves 'is this really the road we want to go down?"[912] This experience is echoed in England and Germany. A German organic farmer explains: 'in the beginning I carried out experimental cultivation of heritage grain varieties. But then I gave up everything that didn't bring in money, because when the business is in the red it doesn't make much sense'.[913] The farmers truest to organic principles are mainly small-scale gardeners who produce for themselves and give or barter their surpluses locally, or lifestyle farmers. They can be true to the organic ideals not because of moral superiority or higher skills, but because of their autonomy from market forces.

If the market economy works as intended and produces a bad result that leaves us with at least two options. Either we regulate markets to take away the 'bads' and reward the 'goods'. Or we find other ways, new relationships, outside the market, to produce and distribute a substantial share of our food. As discussed before (in chapter seventeen) there are enormous challenges involved in internalizing costs and in rewarding farmers for providing environmental services. Such mechanisms have been proposed for more than 50 years and very little progress has been made so far. This leads me to think that it is naive to assume that this will ever happen. There are also reasons to be skeptical about the results if it ever did happen. At this point in time it is more fruitful and stimulating to work on a new system or new systems.

Part IV: Dessert

To bake the bread I wanted, I didn't just need a better recipe, I needed a whole different civilization.
Michael Pollan[914]

25

Looking ahead

The commercialization and industrialization of all aspects of the food system have some advantages and an awful lot of disadvantages. We have to bite the bullet; the food system is not a *smörgåsbord* where we can pick out the bits we like and leave those we don't like. There is no way to produce good artisanal food and biologically diverse landscapes for the masses in a containerized, standardized monopolistic food system. And there is no way that you can combine dirt-cheap food with quality and gourmet food. Agriculture, food processing, food trade and marketing and cooking have developed in tandem with each other, and any alternative must also encompass the whole food chain. But the changes will need to go far beyond the food system.[a] Localized societies with less specialization will inevitably produce fewer innovative technological gadgets. In such a world you would not fly to a sunny beach on the other side of the globe on a whim. Even some environmentally benign innovations or breakthroughs in medicine would not happen. So there will be draw-backs. But in my view, there are already far too many bads in the existing system to say 'enough is enough'.

Four additional drivers may help, or force, us to develop those alternatives. I hope the reader of this book has understood how tremendously important cheap energy has been in shaping agriculture and our current food systems. Historically, farming and forestry have proven themselves to be efficient ways of capturing solar energy, not

---

[a] It is my assumption that it is not possible to localize the food system while the rest of society remains locked into a globalized economy. I can find no evidence from history that different parts of the economy can be based on totally different principles from each other for any sustained period of time. Although this can happen in times of transition: for example, large parts of the agriculture sector were still geared towards self-sufficiency or feudal economic relationships in the early stages of the emergence of capitalist society. But ultimately they were coerced into the capitalist mode.

only using it for food but for building a human society. Fossil fuels reduced the role of farming in building societies, leaving it as a simple producer of food – or so we thought. They replaced most labor with machinery and replaced ecological embeddedness and bio-diversity with fertilizers and pesticides. They have also allowed for far more of our daily needs, including foods, to be provided through markets and distant trade. A break down of energy supply would have profound effects. My best guesstimate is that we will not face a 'break down' of energy supply but that we will face an energy crunch with increasingly more expensive energy. The costs for energy will cascade through the system and make things that today seem 'efficient' or 'rational' seem like lunacy. In this way, many of the fallacies of today's system will 'automatically' disappear, in particular production systems based on chemical fertilizers, mass transport of food and cold chains for fresh convenience foods. This scenario is also likely to lead to increased protectionism as natural resources will become much more precious than they are today. This will further contribute to the reduction in trade already caused by costlier fossil fuels.

This will be closely linked to climate change, and political responses to it. Climate change itself can and will shake up our societies immensely, but probably only in several decades time. The question is if the political responses to the threat of climate change, today or soon, could also trigger a radical shift in energy policies, essentially having the same effect as increased energy prices (described above). Another event that would shake up the board a lot would be a global financial collapse. This would de-globalize the economy quite rapidly, in a rather similar way as an oil price shock, which is not surprising as the constant growth paradigm and constant increased energy supply are part of the same game. A widespread financial collapse would also generate major social disruptions. Such disruptions would also favor the local, the personal and direct over dependence on anonymous global supplies. This can be seen in all societies in crisis. A fourth driver is if people would, to a large extent, downscale their economic life. This can be as a reaction to the other drivers or as a result of a choice of voluntary simplicity driven by the search for personal fulfillment. In many cases this could be linked to efforts to grow and preserve and process one's own food. These four drivers might well support each other and initiate a rapid change. Or, of course, there might also be a 'black swan' which we, by definition, don't know about and will not know about until it is too late.

The measures, new economic relations, lifestyle choices and policies I recommend are probably not sufficient to deal with all challenges of the future, but they will help make us better prepared. They are also an alternative to, or at least a way of mitigating a *rapid* collapse. They could help us achieve a gracious descent rather than experience a full scale implosion of civilization as we know it.

Philip Ackerman-Leist, professor in sustainable food systems at Green Mountain College, writes in Rebuilding the Foodshed: "Modernization certainly was inevitable, but the technological innovations were increasingly geared to national and international wholesale markets and consequently the dissolution of far too many local markets. Our society chose one path and not the other...I am certain that we left a lot of good options behind".[915] I am not advocating a total abolition of markets for foods, agriculture inputs and food processing. But I am advocating a radical re-balancing, where much less of our daily food is sold via anonymous mass markets. Equally, I also do not advocate a Soviet style planned farm and food system, even though a central state may have a role to play, e.g. for food reserves.

Some portray the main political divide as being between those who believe in the market and those who believe in the state. I believe that these two are excellent bed fellows and often have shared interests. The 'Marketstate' dominates everything and everybody today. We have to reach beyond the market and the state. This is certainly not a new idea, throughout history communities have found ways to organize themselves and I discuss some of these below.

In this last part of the book I look at alternative pathways for a better food and farming future. I will discuss 1) technical solutions, mainly about farming; 2) where the food might come from; 3) how we can change our consumption patterns; 4) economic alternatives in a wider sense; and 5) the policies needed to get us there. In the very last chapter I will venture into talking about a vision of land and food ethics as a way to tie all these together. They are all interlinked and in my view they are all essential. Any new system will have to be built on such interactions, with positive feedback loops, where the economic system supports the ethical and cultural, where technology is built on renewable principles and where democracy is extended beyond the political sphere into the economic sphere.

The coming chapters are intended to give sufficient ideas about how such rebalancing could work out, without being overly prescriptive. I don't believe in being too prescriptive for the same reason that I don't have a lot of faith in forecasting. If we cannot make credible forecasts even for how our *existing* systems will develop in a thirty years time, how could we then design *alternative* systems with any credibility? Some say that people will only follow if they know where they are going. This is another version of the opinion that you can only convince people to change by appealing to their self-interest. I simply don't believe that. Many big changes in society were driven more by external factors or by people revolting *against* something rather than having a strong vision about where they were going. As I have repeated several times in this book, you can not change just one thing, and it is almost impossible to make firm predictions about complex systems, so this is more like an exercise in speculating what a new brave world would look like. There is no harm in doing this, but please don't recruit disciples on the basis of detailed blueprints of the future. Another problem with detailed blueprints is that people easily get stuck on some detail which they don't like or understand, when studying them, instead of seeing the bigger picture.

Making all the needed changes will take a long time and involve travelling a long road. And it will not always be easy or comfortable. It can be tempting to sweeten the message by making it sound all fine and dandy. Much of the environmental movement has been doing that, making us believe that we can just shift from petrol to electricity, from waste to recycling, from light bulbs to LED or from NPK to organic at no major cost. But as a report from the Nordic Council[a] concludes[b] "selling sustainability via self-interest may backfire when changes are needed that offer no immediate personal gain. Even the interests of future generations might be difficult to safeguard in a society that propagates immediate wins and prizes ruthless competition at the cost of the environment and social equity". Despite our whole society being built on the doctrine that everybody acts in their own interest, we hardly ever use this rationale to justify what we do, preferring to emphasis the common good. I think that environmentalists and others who want to improve the world should stop using the same methods as commercial marketing when 'selling their messages'. It appeals to the wrong triggers in the first place.

I am sure we have interesting, rewarding and even glorious days ahead of us, but they will be mixed with a lot of dirt and sweat. My biggest fear is that Fred Kirschenmann might be right when he writes,

---

[a] An inter-parliamentary forum for cooperation between the Nordic countries.

[b] This is echoed by the report Common Cause–the Case for Working with our Cultural Values (2010) by WWF, Oxfam and Friends of the Earth in United Kingdom.

"there are limits. Many of us would like to insulate ourselves from those limits. Becoming lovers of the soil puts us back in touch with those limits. The fact is, we don't like being tied to the soil's limits because they remind us of our own limits. Most of us like the idea that modernization insulates us from dirt, toil, flesh and grave."[916]

26

Farming for the future

While I do think that most of the changes needed are in the social, economic and political realms, it is also important to discuss farm and food technologies and systems. The global population is still increasing and as a result we need to produce more food, and find ways for people in need to get that food to eat. At the same time, we need to restore and maintain critical ecosystems.

An overwhelming majority of our crops are annual plants which we have to sow every year often in single stands. This is a situation which suits pioneer plants, but it is by and large 'unnatural' – annual plants are exceptions in most ecosystems. They only emerge in large number in soils that are disturbed, for example by wind or water erosion, floods or fires. Soil that isn't dug or plowed and has a cover of plants will only erode in extreme cases and will usually guard its nutrients. Plants grown in companionship with other plants generally suffer much less from pests and diseases, and if they are attacked, the other plants can make use of the space, nutrients and water. By and large, systems based on perennial crops grown together are likely to be more resilient and could still be productive. Some of them are promoted under the banner of permaculture. The term permaculture is also used in a more specific sense as a defined concept for ecological design (see books written by Bill Mollison and David Holmgren) but here I use it in a more generic sense for production systems based on a high share of perennial crops and grazing.

There are and have been many such systems in the world. The Maya *milpa* system is among the most diverse cultivation systems in the world. Researchers working with the El Pilar Forest Garden Network in Belize looked at nineteen forest gardens and found approximately 370 different species of plants cultivated by the forest gardeners.[917] The forest gardens of Sri Lanka are unplowed, tree-dominated plots that are cultivated year-round. They sustain biodiversity and animal habitats while producing plants to meet many human needs for food, medicine, spices, dyes, ornaments, construction, household products, toys, beverages, rituals, fodder, and more. Similar systems exist in tropical climates in every continent and many are still maintained by smallholders. They are almost entirely maintained with local resources, such as household refuse (compost), organic material (dead weeds and wood), ashes from kitchen fires, and manure, all of which enrich the soil and productivity of the land.

Another old permaculture landscape can be found in the cork oak forests which cover nearly almost 3 million hectares of Portugal, Spain, Algeria, Morocco, Italy, Tunisia, and France. They provide income for thousands of people and support one of the world's highest levels of forest biodiversity, including endemic plants and endangered species such as the Iberian Lynx and the Iberian Imperial Eagle. In this landscape cork is produced from the bark of the cork oak tree (*Quercus suber*) which renews itself after harvesting, cattle graze and pine grow alongside the cork oak trees. In 1989 the *Montados* in Alentejo, Portugal, hosted about 40,000 cattle, 1,050,000 sheep, 149,000 goats, and 6,000 pigs on a grazing surface of 1,356,000 hectares. Up to 130 different plant species thrive on each square meter of land. The *Montados* also plays a role in water regulation and carbon storage, not to talk about its value for culture and meaning of the people living there. A multitude of foods are produced from such a landscape.[918] The grazed meadows of Northern Europe are also example of permanent production systems where nuts, berries, mushrooms and trees coexist with grazing animals. Perennial growing systems are thus old and traditional. They are also mostly highly productive, as all the ecological space is used efficiently. They are, however, in most cases very difficult to replicate or extend. There are obstacles to this, at all levels, but particularly in the very high costs for mechanization of such systems compared to monocultures.

Some people are also engaged in trying to create new systems based on perennial plants. Wes Jackson from The Land Institute in Kansas writes "If we could build domestic prairies we might be able one day to have high-yielding fields that are planted only once every twenty years or so. After the fields had been established, we would need only to harvest the crop, relying on species diversity to take care of insects, pathogens, and fertility". His colleague, Jerry Clover, found that unfertilized grasslands harvested annually for 75 years yielded similar amounts of nitrogen per hectare as adjacent high-input wheat fields. The grasslands, despite being harvested each year also supported a range of valuable ecosystem functions.[919]

Grasslands cover almost one quarter of the terrestrial area, but most of them produce rather little food. Statistics are very weak, but one assessment is that agro-pastoral landscapes *and* system based on extensive grazing produce 24% of the beef, 46% of the lamb and 20% of

the milk in the world.[920] Considering that this area is more than twice
the area of arable land, it not so much food per area unit. Clearly, most
grassland will never produce as much as arable lands because of
climatic, geological or topographical reasons. But, we should not forget
that while they don't produce much food, many of these areas are very
important for biodiversity and other ecosystem services. Nevertheless
there are some very promising developments in grazing, both for
drylands with extensive ranching and intensively managed grasslands.
There are pioneers such as Allan Savory from Zimbabwe and Joel
Salatin on the Polyface farm in Virginia who are promoting various
grazing strategies and claim that these radically increase grassland
productivity and food production. As a bonus, these grasslands can
bind large quantities of carbon in organic matter, which could make a
big difference for our climate.

"I don't believe in arable farming, it takes the fertility out of the
soil. We only have fifty years supply of phosphorus left from
Morocco", says Ado Bloemendal, who has worked for ten years as an
advisor for intensive grassland management in the Netherlands. The
cycles of nutrients are disrupted by plowing and tilling the land but in
permanent grasslands the cycles can be closed, and very few nutrients
will be lost. Under the brand of Pure Graze, fifty farmers are working
with intensively producing grass-fed chicken, pork cattle and dairy
produce. Fifteen of the farmers are marketing under a common brand.
Some of the farms are organically managed and no farmer uses pesticides or chemical fertilizers. There is very little use of antibiotics and if
they are used as a last resort to treat an animal, the meat is not sold
under the brand.

The cows graze very intensively, staying just a few hours in the
same place, mirroring the movement of herds in the wild. Through this
intensive grazing the quality of the grass and the productivity are very
high. In addition, it regenerates the grassland. 'Grassland' is perhaps
not the right term. "The invention of chemical fertilizers and the
dominance of English ryegrass are linked", says Ado. This is because
English ryegrass and the other grasses are favored by nitrogen fertilizers and therefore outcompete other plants; a perfect lawn is a terrible
mono-culture. It is better for both the cows and nature to have more
variety of plants. Pure Graze supplies a few different seed mixes. For
cows they have a mix with eight clover varieties, six grasses and eight
herbs including caraway, parsley, chicory, pimpernel, dandelion and
yarrow. Ado calls it his 'salad buffet', perhaps borrowing from farmer
Joel Salatin on the other side of the Atlantic.

Dairy cows in this system produce up to 20,000 kg of milk per hectare of land. Almost all the feed comes from the grasslands, mostly as

direct grazing, but some of the grass is cut for silage for winter feed.[a] As the cows get almost no supplementary feeding and they are moved around in the pasture, there is very little risk of the pasture being overmanured. To get the right perspective on this productivity: 20,000 kg of milk· has 700 kg protein, 800 kg fat and 12 million calories. This equals the annual energy (calories) needs for some 14-15 people, enough protein for some 40 people and fat for 30 people. You could still feed more people with calories with a bumper crop of ten or eleven tons of wheat from the same area but only with massive investments in fertilizers and pesticides.

There are reasons to look more into these permanent cultivation systems, and try to develop them further in the future. They are, without doubt, superior in the production of biodiversity and ecosystem services, but mostly produce less food per area unit compared to annual crops when the conditions for annual cropping are good. This is because there are trade-offs which make it very hard to maximize early and vigorous reproduction (seeds such as wheat) *and* the longevity needed for perennial crops.[921] That is the reason why the grasses we grow for seeds (grains) are annual while most grasses we grow for pasture are perennial. Trees seem to be more able to combine perenniality with high yields of fruits, as we can see from apples, coconuts and oil palm all of which produce impressive quantities of edible fruit per area unit. One big obstacle to the development of perennial crops is the privatization of seed breeding. There's no incentive in the private seed breeding industry to breed seed that you can sell only once.

As discussed in chapter twenty-one, better management of wild resources, urban farming, insects and aquaculture can all contribute to more food. By and large though, it would be dangerous to give all our attention to these alternatives and permanent cultivation, because, whether we like it or not, farming annual crops in fields will remain a very important way of producing the bulk of our food in the years to come. But there are many different ways of doing it.

I believe this book has made clear that the industrial farming system is simply not appropriate. The best elaborated alternative so far is organic farming. It is not the only alternative but I will use it here it as

---

[a] Dairy cows normally get 2 kg of beet fiber added to the diet for energy and fiber.

a proxy to cover a range of similar approaches, such as ecological farming, agroecology and so on. In my view the term is not the most important thing. After all what is called organic in English is called 'biological' in Romantic languages, 'ecological' in Germanic languages and plain 'natural' in others. Some associate organic farming with foods sold in a premium market to upper-middle class consumers. But organic farming is much more than that. Many people understand organic as meaning free from pesticides and other synthetic inputs. And it is true, but it is a lot more than that. The origin of the word organic lies in the perception that the soil is a living organism, but organic is also more than just the soil; it is about the plants, animals and people. During my presidency of the International Federation of Organic Agriculture Movement (IFOAM), between 2000 and 2005, we developed a widened understanding of organic agriculture by stating the four principles of organic farming:

> the principle of health – that organic farming is about the health of the plants and the eco-system and ultimately of human beings. Our health and the health of nature are forever connected;

> the principle of ecology – that we in organic farming work in accordance with the same principles as most eco-systems, circulating nutrients, diversity, balance;

> the principle of fairness – that our responsibility extends to how we treat animals in the farm, surrounding eco-systems and our fellow human beings, and;

> the principle of care – that we take a precautionary attitude and see ourselves as stewards of the parts of the planet under our responsibility

Organic farming is essentially a reaction to the whole system that is based on the exploitation of nature and of fellow humans. Many in the organic movement, myself included, have recognized the importance of making the farming system more benign without necessarily involving ourselves in challenging the prevailing market paradigm. One vehicle that has been used for doing this has been the 'mainstreaming' of organic produce into mass markets and into government policies. That is a praiseworthy effort and has been very successful – especially if we consider how marginal the organic sector was thirty-five years ago. But it has come at a price: parts of the organic farming sector have changed to fit in with mainstream food system, which inevitably leads to some dilution of the key principles of organic ideals (while adhering to laid-down standards), something I discussed in the previous chapter.

Future agriculture systems need to build on the principles embedded in organic farming and other similar methods. It is quite intentional that I write 'systems' in the plural. Organic farming, as a standardized and regulated way of marketing within an anonymous mass market is just one form, but its strength in this market place, of being clear and standardized is also part of its weakness. Local adaptation and standardization don't go well together. Natural farming systems are dynamic and adapt themselves to the site. We need to 'consult the genius of the place', in the words of Wes Jackson.[922] Biological diversification and ecological intensification are keywords for such systems that include practices such as intercropping, crop rotation, biological nitrogen fixation, perennial crops, soil fertility focus and low tillage. Recently much attention has been paid to conservation farming: a term that is somewhat misleading as this system does not pay much attention to conservation in the system, except that it is based on no or low tillage, i.e. conservation farmers don't plow. This does have the benefit of usually substantially reducing soil erosion. Unfortunately conservation farms are generally large scale farms that use a lot of herbicides. Nevertheless, the ambition of reducing tillage, of which permaculture is the most extreme expression, is a worthy one. In practical farming one usually has to make compromises between ideals and what is practical and economical.

We need a farming system that regenerates its own production capacity and potential. Regeneration and reproduction are as essential in the farming system as production; it is just as important to regenerate the conditions for farming as it is to farm. This perspective makes it quite obvious that crop rotations and bio-diversity are more desirable than buying in 'fertility' in the form of bags of chemical fertilizers or 'pest control' in the shape of plastic drums full of poison. Farms should also have good working conditions, because without people there is no future. There are ample opportunities for producing more foods with regenerative methods, such as organic farming. A meta-review of research made by Claire Kremen and Albie Miles from the University of California concludes that diversified farming systems are equally productive as conventional systems yet they also enhance, rather than undermine, ecosystem services, such as biodiversity conservation, pest and weed control and soil fertility. They are also more drought resilient and reduce greenhouse gas emissions.[923]

While I am a strong proponent of these systems, I am not convinced that their productivity per area unit can always match that from a system using chemical fertilizers. A regenerative farming system has to generate its productive resources from within the farming system or as an embedded part of adjacent and global ecosystems; it takes internal energy and resources to supply some of the needed services. Regenerative agriculture cannot use the shortcuts of industrial agriculture which, by and large, are different versions of fossil fuel. Yet it is also a strength because the system can be truly sustainable and resilient and has to build on local resources. When farmers rely on local resources they will care for and manage them properly. An obvious example is nitrogen. One can supply the nitrogen that plants need from within the system by increased use of leguminous plants, but that comes at a cost. Symbiotic nitrogen fixation needs energy, energy which the bacteria will get from the plants in exchange for that nitrogen. Yet it is not at all evident that people need or want all those leguminous plants in their diets. Inevitably we will also get somewhat lower yields from such a system than when we use fossil fuels to bind nitrogen from the atmosphere. We should also increase the production of other ecosystem services from our farming system, something which is much needed but which, in all likelihood, will also take some space that could be used for our primary crops. Of course, we should put much more research into regenerative systems which can increase their productivity, but it is a realistic assumption that these will never compete on yield alone with a system heavily subsidized by external energy. But that need not be a big problem as the yield gap is also high within regenerative systems; their yields can also be greatly increased. Equally we should shift our focus away from just kilograms and tons and think much more about the quality of the food we eat.

Old landraces and varieties, in particular of the staple grains and tubers and livestock, often have a higher nutrient density. Of course, there are reasons why these varieties and races were left behind by farmers and food industries, and some of the reasons are still valid today. But in many cases the reason was simply that they didn't have high enough yields or the right quality for industrial processing, or often were not homogenous enough. Anders Lunneryd has a rather small organic farm on the south-western plains of Sweden where he grows old varieties of grain. He belongs to *Wästgötarna* an association of like minded farmers that sells some 400 tons per year of 15 different sorts of grains to mills, bakery and end consumers. The products include a number of dinkel wheat (spelt) varieties, old wheat varieties, naked barley, rye and swiddening rye. When farmers move to these crops and this system it involves changing their sense of aesthetics. For a long while, farmers have been proud to point out their big fields of one and the same crop with the same height and color, uninterrupted by any weeds towering above the heads of the grain. "It is really exciting to look out over a heterogeneous field" says Anders Lunneryd who converted to organic farming 1999 and hasn't looked back.[924] Most farmers trying new paths, have also had to change their marketing channels. This kind of production doesn't work with the anonymous mass-markets: the bakers using the crop are mostly artisanal bakers.[925]

Regeneration is also about knowledge and people. We need more people on the land and the whole food sector to manage diversified landscapes and diversified production. I don't see more people in the fields or in the kitchens as a problem, it is more an opportunity. It makes little sense that only a tiny proportion of the population is involved in natural resource management of all sorts, including agriculture, forestry, fisheries and nature conservation, while so many are engaged in commerce, industry, services and a mushrooming flora of intermediation. It is ironic that, in an overpopulated world, the countryside is depopulated to the extent that sustainability is threatened. If we cannot keep people interested in farming we will face serious problems. Apart from making it possible to live from farming and improving its status, we also need to develop the knowledge of farmers. Knowledge generation should be more localized and farmers should be partners in agricultural research and in setting the research agenda.[a] Often, especially in developing countries, the gap between the resources (irrigation, seeds, machinery) available at agricultural research centers and those available to marginalized farmers is huge and the knowledge generated rarely gets transferred.

The large and growing population means that we have to intensify production. But, intensification doesn't have to mean more waste of resources or less biodiversity, although it will mean another diversity. In the same way as capitalism is based on a rapid flow of money – so that profits can be repeatedly generated for each cycle of money use – natural resources such as land, water and nutrients need to be used efficiently, again and again. In each cycle, what is needed can be skimmed off, not eroding the capital but just taking away the surplus.

We also need to look at the food system as a whole. We should close the cycles of nutrients. For example, our sewage systems mix potentially valuable human excreta with all sorts of other waste, many

---

[a] Although obviously this does not exclude cutting-edge research taking place in central institutions.

of them toxic or certainly not fit to use as compost. In the 19th century, Von Liebig noted that we need to recirculate nutrients. His innovation, chemical fertilizers, ultimately allowed us to skip this essential step, and now we are stuck with unsustainable sewage systems that will require substantial efforts to reconstruct.

Apart from finding new ways of managing the food system, we also clearly need to devise systems for maintaining ecosystem services. One is to 'set aside' nature so that it can produce what people need, or believe they need, without human intervention, or rather with limited human intervention. After all almost all landscapes have humans as part of the system; the Maasai are as natural, and perhaps as important, for the ecosystems of the Serengeti as the lions. We need to continue to develop natural reserves, and, reserves in oceans, waterways and coastal zones particularly, need expanding and strengthening. One of the many reasons to include substantial areas of land or water in reserves is that we do not fully understand the effects of human actions and, no matter what we do, we are likely to lose some biodiversity. 'Wild' nature offers buffers and refuges, or 'redundancies', which are of great importance for the stability of a system.

On those areas of land and sea that are not set aside as natural reserves, we need to more consciously produce the ecosystem services required. Rather than focusing solely on reducing negative human impacts on ecosystems, we should also try to increase our positive impacts. We also need to increase the production of ecosystem services in our cities, grow more food there, do more natural recycling, filter water through living roofs and the like. Between these two extremes, the wild and the city, there will be semi-wild pastoralist landscapes or landscapes where wildlife is 'managed' to optimize the yield of meat and other useful resources as well as ecosystem services, and there will be farms similar to the farms of today. There will also be systems that are more intensively managed, more like gardens, many under protective structures and with more people working them.

Instead of the monoculture mindset that has shaped land use since industrialism, humans need to act as 'planet keepers', as gardeners, the land stewards. The *Landcare* movement in Australia is an example of community efforts to take care of the landscape in which they live. The units can be small, sometimes often just a farm, but more often they are organized around watersheds (drainage basins), a natural divider of importance everywhere and even more so in a very dry continent. It originated as a series of soil conservation programs in the south-eastern state of Victoria in the mid 1980s. There are now some 5,000

Landcare groups in Australia, and the idea has spread to a number of other countries. The groups work in a participatory manner with varying levels of support and recognition from the authorities. Some local governments collect local taxes to support Landcare groups. The actual work of the groups varies widely, there are no national rules. Mostly they adopt natural, community-based, solutions to landscape management and solutions that allow for continued productive activities. Tree planting, conservation farming and better pasture management, the protection of native ecosystems and the eradication of many invasive species make up a large part of the programs.[926] Landcare offers an approach to landscape management that is neither dependant on government regulations or the vagaries of the market place.

In addition to questions of what food shall be produced and how we should manage the landscape, there is also the question of *where* the food should come from? Should everybody grow their own food? Should it be primarily local or regional food? Or, should food be fairly traded from other continents, from smallholders or agribusiness? A survey in Britain shows that supporting local farmers and producers and supporting the local economy are the main reason (56% and 51% respectively) for people buying local food, followed by taste and concern over food miles.[927] The push for local is also driven by concerns over food quality, over the landscape and biodiversity, a desire for less dependence on energy and a more resilient food system. In assessing the food economy of the Chesapeake Bay region, Ken Meter found that a 15% increase in local food purchase would bring in three times as many dollars to farming communities than are currently provided by federal subsidies. A Worldwatch study estimated that if the greater Seattle area were to source 'just' 20% of its food locally (I put just in quotation marks, because 20% is already a lot), it would inject an extra billion dollars per year into the city's economy.[928]

The rise of local as a marketing niche inevitably leads to abuse and regulatory responses. The United States government defines local as a place in which the final product is marketed, with the total distance that the product is transported less than 400 miles from the origin of the product or the state in which the product is produced. In similar fashion, the Canadian Food Inspection Agency recently defined local food as "produced in the province or territory which it is sold" or "food sold across provincial borders within 50 km of the originating province or territory".[929] I find the notion of defining 'local' by means of government regulation a rather futile exercise. It seems to be based on the notion of local as a marketing niche concept that needs to be standardized into a market commodity – but commodifying local defeats the purpose even more than commodifying organic.

We can not say that local food is always good. It is not geography or distance that is the most important factor in our relationships, even if geography clearly exerts some constraints. A feedlot is no more humane just because you live next door. On the contrary, it is probably worse as the smell of it will ruin your evenings on the deck and the manure run off has killed all the fish in the nearby lake, and you cannot swim there. Another thing is that 'local' isn't necessarily very local in the sense that it is embedded in the local situation. Some farmers hypocritically urge consumers to buy local, while they themselves buy cheap stuff in the malls in the city or inputs via the internet instead of buying them from local suppliers. The feed for their livestock is imported from another continent in order to save a few percent on the cost.

The same goes for 'national'. I have garnered wrath over the years by asking what is Swedish in a Swedish tomato? The greenhouses are from Holland, as are the seeds, the plants are isolated from the Swedish soil by plastic (possibly made in Sweden from imported oil) and grown in mineral wool slabs from Denmark and the irrigation technology is from Israel. Most of the workforce are from other countries, mostly Poland[a], the ownership, and management, is increasingly also from somewhere else. What is essentially Swedish is where the business pays taxes. I am not at all in favor of nationalist ('we are better because we are in this country') arguments for buying stuff, and it certainly becomes void of any meaning when the production just assembles parts from other places.

Two researchers at the University of Washington, Branden Born and Mark Purcell argue that the attention to proximity or scale is a trap, misguided and a "significant intellectual and political" danger. They challenge the notion that local and small-scale is a shortcut to just and sustainable systems, "we cannot assume that local food systems are inherently more ecologically sustainable than global ones, that locally grown produce is healthier than produce grown elsewhere, or that local control over agricultural decision making is inherently more democratic than, say, national scale control". They claim that many of the arguments used against 'globalization' are actually not based on

---

[a] Polish workers are greatly appreciated in Swedish farming, as in most parts of Europe.

scale but are a reaction to the capitalist system that rules the economy. Corporate capitalism and globalization have been so intertwined that most people can not separate them.[930] I agree with this last point; it is so difficult to challenge the paradigm and hegemony of the capitalist market economy that many people focus instead on the symptoms of what it produces or the conditions that enable it.

However, I still think it is a mistake to go from there to the conclusion that scale is irrelevant. The large-scale agriculture landscapes created in Mato Grosso and the United States Mid West are neither people-friendly nor nature-friendly. There is a distinct difference in terms of the landscape, biodiversity, and the welfare and quality of life of the animals, laborers and local communities between a region with a thousand farms with ten cows each and one with ten farms with a thousand cows each. The many small farms will maintain a diverse landscape with many paddocks and meadows for grazing. If the animals are concentrated in one stable, the area close to the stable will be just mud mixed with manure; a bit further away it is severely overgrazed and filled with parasites, while further away there will be no cows grazing. Giant slaughter houses treat animals like commodities and the people working there will, inevitably, become insensitive to the suffering of animals.

There are optimal sizes for human society and groups, just like ant hills or elephant herds, and part of the problem is that we have created a technosphere and economic system which is not conducive to the human scale. If we look at human society large scale structures basically only emerge under compulsion. People organizing themselves voluntarily don't build factories for ten thousand workers, or housing complexes for a thousand households. These are products of dictators or enormously centralized economic power. That is how the pyramids, medieval cathedrals, the House of Ceausescu, Disneyland, the Great Wall of China and the Great Mall of China were built. Admittedly, the pyramids and Notre Dame are awesome to visit. But if we take into account the enormous sacrifices involved in constructing them it is hard to say that they were worth it. Up to a million people are said to have died in the construction of the Great Wall in China.

Some talk about an 'agriculture of the middle' as the most promising system, that is on a scale which still use fair amounts of modern technology without the gargantuan scale of today. I think the discussion should also be enlarged to include food processing and distribution, as they all belong together; Big buys from Big, and Big sells to Big, with Big processors and handlers in between. The hope is that the middle range would combine mechanization and economic efficiencies with humane and ethical production and a smaller ecological footprint. I think there are reasons to believe that this could be true. The crux is, I believe, to develop the economic and political frameworks needed to stimulate this. Cut-throat competition takes the biggest toll exactly in this middle range, as the smaller often can survive as pure niche producers selling to wealthy people. I have no clear proposal as to how the middle might prevail, but I do believe that the suggestions in this book will at least work in that direction.

One powerful argument against local markets is to ask, 'how will we feed the (mega) cities if everything is local?' But if it is hard to feed a city of 10 million locally, this is perhaps as much an argument against cities of this size as it is against 'local' or 'small-scale'. There is no inherent value in gathering such masses of people in one place. Most of humanity has developed without such big cities, and wonderful cultural expressions have emerged from small towns of just 50,000 people. Today's civilization has such hubris that most people think that 'development' is a linear process that runs in one direction. But there are very few reasons to believe this. Cities are populated and depopulated. Europe is littered with empty factories, mines and shipyards, which a few generations ago were the pride of their countries. In 2010, Detroit, the automobile capital of the world, had a population of 714,000, less than 40% of its peak population of over 1.8 million in 1950. More than 370 cities worldwide are currently experiencing a population decline.[931] Even Las Vegas, Mexico City and Chongqing will crumble, sooner or later.

The changing conditions I discussed previously will greatly influence population patterns. Cheap fossil fuels have led to the creation of the automobile society and suburbia, to the depopulation of the countryside and increased global competition. Increases in energy prices are likely to change that. Authoritarian or unequal societies also seem to drive urbanization, as everybody wants to be close to the power, the glory, the action, or if nothing else, the crumbs from the rich man's table. A more equal society will reduce this tendency.

I envision a renaissance of rural societies. There are clearly some environmental and social advantages of more people living in the countryside; it would contribute to a more sustainable social environment for those who take care of natural resources; it would allow for small-scale (distributed) power generation and establishing closed local cycles of nutrients and materials. For populations engaged in industry and commerce, a more densely populated habitat can preserve resources and reduce the demands on infrastructure. Perhaps networks of small towns connected by rail traffic would be a good solution. This doesn't mean that *all* food has to be locally sourced. There are some strong arguments against local fundamentalism. First is that one can get better and varied diet by sourcing a certain proportion of food from further afield. This allows Northerners to get some fruit, or people living far from the sea to get some fish or seafood. Another strong argument is that climatic shocks may harm some areas so much that they cannot keep their people above the breadline. With a bigger food catchment area local climatic events will have less impact on the food supply.

Ultimately, the conditions under which people live vary greatly as does the carrying capacity of different areas. As such, the solutions for places where there are hundreds, perhaps a thousand human beings per square kilometer will be very different from those for places where there are just a few dozen (or less) people. This can be easily seen in the difference in historical population patterns. Population density and water and land resources are important factors that determine the optimal mix. In the end, people should have the right to live where they like and human settlement patterns will and should change by 'natural processes' rather than by Pol Pot-like policies of localization. There will never be one perfect system, nor will globalized food systems ever revert to being totally local. As in the past, some places will have a very high level of self-sufficiency, others lower. But this should be based on the actual local ecological conditions and not by profit-seeking of a capitalist economy.

The things that 'local' food can give us are relationship and meaning by being embedded in the local culture and landscape. Through local food production we can reconnect with and experience the effects that our consumption has on the landscape and on the people and animals that are part of our local communities. The important thing is the interactions between all organisms. Therefore, we need to expand the redesign of the food system to include food processing and preparation, cooking and even the act of eating; or as expressed by the Slow Food movement 'eating is an agricultural act and producing is a gastronomic act.' They are all a reflections of our relationships. This is but one of many reasons why local should not become a commoditized, standardized category on the shelves of the supermarkets and the menus of fast food restaurants.

27

New relationships

Benjamin Lundy, a Quaker, opened a store in Baltimore 1836 which sold only goods obtained by the labor of free people. This is an early example of ethical marketing which continued up to the end of slavery in the United States in 1865 and beyond. Ethical marketing based on voluntary standards and certification has spread at a rapid pace in recent decades, as a result of converging – and interacting – trends. These trends include a growing emphasis on the market and consumer choice as important tools to achieve ethical, economic, environmental or social goals; government de-regulation which has left the door open to more self-regulation to the industries; and stiff global competition, which makes differentiation in the market place an essential survival strategy to escape 'commodity hell'.

There are well-known labels for organic and fair trade foods that now compete with a plethora of new labels. In the United States a food justice movement has emerged, which seeks to ensure that the benefits and risks of where, what, and how food is grown, produced, transported, distributed, accessed and eaten are shared fairly. This has also been transformed into a marketable concept; the 'food justice certified scheme' guarantees that certain standards are met.[932] Some sector-wide commodity schemes, such as the roundtables on sustainable palm oil, soya and biofuels have the ambition of becoming 'floor standards', standards for which certification is a necessary license to do business. The most notable example is Globalgap, through which supermarkets dictate food safety and hygiene standards which effectively exclude millions of smallholders from the market place. These are the same supermarkets that market fair trade[a] products, intended to help smallholders. These systems mainly emerge in the space between what

---

[a] I write fair trade when referring to any trade schemes of social responsibility, and Fair Trade when referring to the particular scheme operated by the Fair Trade Labeling Organization.

is well-regulated by markets and by governments. Whether they are results of 'policy failures' or 'market failures' or if they should be seen as permanent institutions is an interesting topic for debate, unfortunately neglected by most proponents of the schemes.

When you buy a cup of coffee for US$2 the farmer gets 3-4 cents for the coffee in that cup. If you buy a cup of organic and Fair Trade coffee you are likely to have to cough-up US$2.50 – and the farmer will get 4-5 cents. The farmer's income will increase, perhaps by an impressive 20-25%. Looked at from another perspective, however, you spend an extra 50 cents to increase the farmer's income by 1 or 2 cents. This begs the question of how efficient the market mechanism is in transforming consumers' willingness to pay for the direct or indirect benefits of a product into an increase in producers' income.

In many countries governments say that it is consumer choice, or 'the market' that will determine if farms will farm organically or not. By doing so they make questions over how we farm and what food we eat into a market issue, a question of purchasing decisions and consumption. But governments could prohibit, or impose prohibitive fees, on chemical pesticides if they so wished. They could ban factory farming, it they so wished, and if we demand that as citizens. Denmark has the most advanced organic sector in the world. It has had government support since 1987 and the market share of organic products is above six percent. Knud Erik Soerensen tells me "I don't believe in that we can grow the organic sector by just voluntary means. We need regulations which gradually force the conventional farms to convert to a more sustainable farming system based on nature".[933] Based on my experience from Sweden and many other countries I agree with him.

The environmental and animal welfare benefits of buying organic foods are shared by those who buy conventional food, which means that they are free-riding on the organic sector. Such a situation is typical for things that are inefficiently organized by the market place. The question of whether some consumers should voluntarily shoulder the costs while others can be free-riders is not only a practical one, but also a philosophical and ethical one. It is rather naïve to believe that this system will carry organic production from 1 or 2 percent the market share into the mainstream. And the facts on the ground support this view. Organic production continues to grow world wide, but the pace of growth in the more mature markets is not so high any more. The organic labeling system is a useful tool, but it certainly is not enough in itself to transform agriculture to a situation where organic is simply normal.

Fair Trade has grown a lot in recent years, and it faces some issues in common with the organic sector as well as some that are specific for the scheme. Its idea is to use the normal market, but to tilt the rules in favor of small and poor producers. But this comes with many caveats. To begin with the relationship is still very unequal. Buyers in the North basically dictate most of the conditions, including the standards to follow. Their view of what is fair and just is what is codified; as are their definitions of quality rules, etc. There are no codes for the super-markets to follow, they can and sometimes do mark up Fair Trade products as much as they want and the consumers who buy the products are also not subject to any commitments – they can buy or not buy on a whim. The producers are mainly objects in the marketing of Fair Trade ('meet Juan & Maria, the proud producers of your coffee, see their happy children going to school and marvel over the rainforest that is maintained'), in much the same way as the fake Grandma is on a biscuit-maker's packaging.[934]

Fair Trade tries to use the same market which created inequalities to correct them with some interventions, mostly price-fixing. But in a free market, you cannot fix the price unless you also regulate supply, as a fixed 'good' price, inevitably leads to overproduction. Which is the case with Fair Trade. Fair Trade producers compete with each other on quality, which might well be a good thing. But this also means that only some of them can sell all their coffee on the Fair Trade market, while others sell only a fraction of their coffee as Fair Trade. And, it is generally easier for the better-off farmers to produce a higher quality.

Many of the objectives of Fair Trade could equally and more effi-ciently be addressed by political measures. For example in Ghana, the Cocoa Board sets a fixed national price. This guarantees the price for *all* cocoa farmers. In addition, the government has established a stabiliza-tion fund, which provides a three year pot of funds to be drawn upon by the Cocoa Board to ensure that the fixed price is met when world prices decline. In effect, the government does the same as the Fair Trade organizations try to do – but with more clout and more reach. For a long time the Fair Trade price was actually below the public price in applicable in Ghana.[935]

In all fairness, most organizations engaged in Fair Trade also have a political agenda and work for rules that will promote universally fairer trade rules. But my discussion here is about the use of Fair Trade as a market instrument. In a grotesquely unfair world there is certainly nothing wrong in buying Fair Trade. But to 'sell it' to consumers with slogans like "There's only half an inch between poverty and paradise" (Cafédirect, UK) or "Eradicate poverty over a cup of coffee" (Löfbergs, Sweden) is simply grossly misleading, and lulls people into believing that they really change the world by buying Fair Trade products.

My conclusion after working with voluntary standards and certification schemes for some thirty years is that the market mechanism is inefficient in dealing with the problems that are rooted in fundamental structures of society, the market place and the economy. This was also realized by those fighting against slavery in the United States. The market for products from free labor didn't abolish slavery, it had almost no impact. It was political action, and even the United States' civil war, that led to the abolition of slavery. And why should it be down to us in our role of consumers to decide if there should be slavery in the world or not?

It is a good thing to make educated and ethical consumer choices. It is not only a good thing – it is our responsibility. And movements that promote those choices can send political signals and raise awareness. But in many cases it makes more sense to have those choices made politically; as one researcher into these issues says "confronted with my own impotence as a consumer, I, in the capacity of citizen, plead for arrangements that empower me to act virtuously".[936] Things work best if the two go hand in hand. Our acts as consumers and our acts as citizens can be linked, and one can bear the seeds for the other. For instance for a while ethical consumers in Sweden boycotted eggs from layers in cages, and this led to a public ban on such eggs. Similarly, consumers who buy organic food as a symbolic gesture, may embark on an educational journey which may radicalize them, leading them to demand better policies from their governments or get engaged in building more concrete alternatives.

When asked abstract questions, most people stress the importance of animal welfare or social justice, but when acting as consumers very few act according to these stated preferences.[937] Some believe that this 'market failure' should be corrected by better information which, after all, is a pre-condition for a well-functioning market. However the discrepancy between *citizen* preferences and actual *consumer* behavior is not primarily a result of too little information. After all, you must be both blind and deaf to not know that many vegetables are harvested by badly paid illegal immigrants or that when pork chops are sold for a few dollars per kg that they certainly originate in factory farms. As humans we adapt ourselves to different situations, and when we go into consumer mode, we play that role well. This is an indication that the market is not the appropriate institution for solving these dilemmas. Research in Europe also shows that in the cases where 'the market' has chosen more animal or environmental friendly products, this has mostly been the result of pressure groups convincing the major actors in agri-business to make changes. "It is easier to convince five buying directors than five million consumers" says food and agriculture researcher Stef Aerts from the University of Leuven.[938]

Organic milk is served by basically all schools in Sweden. Some schools began buying organic milk as early as the 1980s. In 2006, the Swedish government adopted a goal that 25% of all publically procured food should be organic. Borlänge, Lund and Södertälje have reached above 40 percent and in total 27 municipalities and 8 counties have reached this official target. Two sizeable towns (from a Swedish perspective), Malmö and Uppsala, have set themselves the goal that all publically procured food should be organic, even if they still have a way to go; Malmö reached 38.7 percent in 2012.[939] This is a good example of political action and also demonstrates that political action can often be more effective than appealing to consumers' willingness to pay. After all, *consumers* in Uppsala don't buy more than perhaps five percent organic food, while the same people as *citizens* gladly support children and the elderly getting one hundred percent organic.

The economic conditions under which farmers, other actors in the food system and consumers interact is the factor that most strongly shapes the food system, and therefore it will be futile trying to change the contents of the system while leaving the economic conditions, structures and relationships intact. What we have got to today is – somewhat simplistically put – what makes sense under the conditions under which farmers, agribusiness and consumers operate. One way ahead is to seek autonomy, self sufficiency. In the most extreme case it means growing, storing, preparing and cooking all your food yourself – nothing could be more local or fairer. And certainly you will be empowered, responsible and accountable if you control all of it yourself, or with your family. While autonomy can be appealing, it also easily leads to both mental and social isolation. If nobody needs anybody else society will dissolve. The reason why we don't talk to the neighbors in our apartment block, but we do talk to colleagues at work is that we don't need the neighbors, while we do need our colleagues. Dependency is a shackle for the individual but also the glue for society.

The idea is also ahistorical, a victim of the same individualism that is so strong in contemporary culture. Some people have a romantic idea of a pioneer farmer, breaking new land producing everything for the family's needs. Breaking new land with what? His (it is often a 'he' in this scenario) bare hands? No: with tools, tools made by someone else. Sowing seeds he got from someone else, rearing cows bought from someone else, and using knowledge accumulated by generations. I have tried quite far reaching self-sufficiency and it can work unless you are totally fundamentalist in your interpretation of self-sufficiency. For every step that you move closer to that ideal, the more stuff you have to drop. Of course you shed all that consumerist crap, the sliced bread, the soda, the marshmallows, the car and the iPhone. But if you want to be really self-sufficient you will have to shed basically everything down to the skillet in which you cook. The dishes you cook may not be so delicious when the variety is limited and fresh food is not there in the winter, or the dry season, or the rainy season (depending on where you live). Designer Thomas Thwaites recounts in the book *The Toaster Project* how he set out to build his own bread toaster from scratch. It took him nine months and cost 250 times more than the toaster he bought at the store, and then he was still 'cheating' using some modern tools, traveling by train to get some raw materials and so on. That gives you an idea. Pursuing total individual or household autonomy is not really a solution to the predicament we face.

Still, *increased* autonomy on the level of the individual, the household and local communities is a good thing. To a large extent this can be labeled the 'peasant strategy'[940], based on the ways peasants have always related to the market, limiting their dependency on inputs for the production and reproduction of the system, such as fertilizers, paid labor and credits. International and regional food systems can still contribute to our diets and the pleasures of eating. But we need to limit the share of food that we source from such systems. These limitations ensure that soils in exporting countries are not mined of their nutrients and that importing countries do not get overloaded with nutrients. Through increased autonomy we can avoid a situation with unlimited competition and downward pressure on food prices, and we will have to take care of the turf on which we stand, and the animals we are dependent on as well as the people who take care of them – for the better and the worse.

In order to get there, we need to build new *economic relations:* systems in the tradition of cooperatives, guilds, communities and villages. Models that break free from the dichotomy between the state and the market which, in any case, represent a false choice.[a] It is about lifting autonomy to another level, from a personal strategy to a community strategy. In the remainder of this chapter I will discuss some of the

---

[a] The interested reader is recommended to read Peter Kropotkin's *Mutual Aid*, the works of Nobel laureate Elinor Ostrom or the mushrooming literature on the management of 'commons'.

initiatives which can play a role in such a strategy. They may be, just ideas, pilots, narrow, nerdy or incomplete. Try to see them as building stones not as completed structures. It remains to be seen how they might fit together, and how they might fit with other, yet to be discovered, initiatives.

The American government nowadays supports farmers markets and, as of August 2013, the USDA's web site, listed 8,144 farmers markets in their National Farmers' Market Directory.[941] In the United Kingdom, the first farmers' market was introduced in Bath in 1997 and by 2012, there were 750 farmers' markets selling produce from 4,000 farmers and 5,000 small scale food producers generating an estimated turnover of £250 million.[942] For sure, farmers' markets are nice ingredients in a town's social life. And, for some farmers they can also be important for their living. Of course, farmers' markets are nothing new at all; nothing modern. On my trips in developing countries I have seen farmers' markets all over the place, a woman selling five chickens and ten pyramids of tomatoes, a man selling a bucket of sweet potatoes. But I don't think farmers' markets will be a keystone for a new food system, even if they certainly can play a role. Their main role is that they are a very good platform for dialogue between consumers and producers, a step towards food literacy. A step to closer cooperation is Community Supported Agriculture (CSA).

CSAs are based on direct person-to-person contact and trust, with no intermediaries. It is usually formalized with a contract between each consumer and the producer, and a commitment to supply one another with money and food. CSAs share both the risks and the benefits of production that is adapted to the natural rhythm of the seasons and is respectful of the environment, natural and cultural heritage and health. Consumers paying a fair price for the produce enables these farmers and their families to maintain their farms and live in a dignified manner.

In Europe there are some 4,000 farms and 400,000 consumers engaged in CSAs. They vary greatly in style, size and the extent to which they are activist or mainly a just way to organize the food supply. Some are farmer driven, some consumer driven and others are organized as cooperatives. The first CSA in Europe, Les Jardins de Cocagne, started near Geneva in 1978. Burschberghof near Hamburg was set up in 1988 and today there are more than thirty-five CSAs in Germany. The first CSA in France was created in Aubagne in April 2001 and now there are more than one thousand six hundred. A French CSA normally includes several farmers and up to hundred and fifty households.[943] Eighty CSAs in England provide food for around five thousand families.[944] Community supported agriculture is even older in Japan, where it is called *Teikei*, which means 'co-partnership'. The Japanese Organic Agriculture Association was founded 1971 bringing consumers, farmers, scholars, public servants and cooperative workers together to promote a system that would benefit them all. "Under the teikei system, relationships are face-to-face, as all products are distributed directly from producers to consumers. There is no middleman or costly inspection bodies".[945]

The term Community Supported Agriculture was coined by Robyn van En in 1985, when inspired by the Swiss initiative and together with a group of like-minded producers and consumers she started a project with a small apple orchard at her Indian Line Farm in Massachusetts. Within four years, the farm's original membership of thirty shares[a] had expanded to hundred and fifty. As word spread about the success of this new concept, Robyn quickly went from being a market gardener to the leader of the CSA movement in the USA. Across the country, she has helped to establish more than two hundred CSAs.[946]

Another CSA pioneer and advocate[b] is Elizabeth Henderson of Peacework in New York State. The CSA started as a combination of a desire to create new relationships with consumers and the direct need to sell products, as her farm was simply too far from any viable market or outlets. Already at this time, 25 years ago, she could see the writing on the wall, how agro-business would twist the emerging organic market to meet its own interests. Stores that sold organic and claimed to support local foods still bought produce from California if a lettuce was one cent cheaper. "It seemed to be really important to have a group of people who were loyal to our farm and interested in keeping it going, and once we started it turned out to be a lot more than that", she tells me when I ask her about her work.

Every member contributes their share of labor at the farm but is not asked to do anything beyond their abilities. Peacework Farm grows hundred different vegetables and cover crops on approximately twenty acres and subleases the hayland to a local producer of beef and grass-fed bison. Over 95% of Peacework's produce is sold to CSA

---

[a] CSAs often use the terms members, shareholders or subscribers to describe the participating consumers, or non farmers.

[b] She has published a CSA cookbook as well as the book *Sharing the harvest*.

members. If and when there is a surplus, it is usually sold to a few local shops. The farm has become a limited liability company in order to lease the land from a land trust. This structure makes it possible for new people to join the farm partnership and old partners to leave or retire without interrupting the lease agreement. "The relationship to the land is that of stewardship, not ownership: this land will never be sold to finance the farmers' retirement, which has been the demise of so many family farms in the United States".[947]

Elizabeth, who now has retired and left the farm to her younger partners Greg Palmer and Ammie Chickering, explains that the CSA is a separate legal entity from the farm so that the farm is not burdened with labor rules or other regulations that constrain the members of the CSA. Members run the organization so that the farmers can farm. When members come to work at the farm, they are not employees; they pick the produce the CSA has contracted for with the farm. "Around 100 families have been with us for more than 10 years, and for them it is part of their way of life", Elizabeth says. Then there is an equally large number of members who stay for a while, move on or shift to another CSA.[948]

In Elizabeth's view a CSA is as much about social justice as about organic farming and local marketing "A CSA is not going to feed everybody, but it is the only form of market relationship where consumers share risk with the farmers." Farmers live under precarious conditions. She, like most farmers, lived on 'poverty wages' her whole life. When the members of the CSA realized that she couldn't afford health insurance, they voluntarily decided to increase their payments to the farm by US$1 per week per share. While it is important that the farmer has decent living and working conditions it is also important that CSAs are inclusive. There are CSAs that have special rates for low-income members and that accept food stamps. Peacework, for example, charges on a sliding scale according to income and provides subsidies to low-income members.[949]

She notes a new interest in CSA the last six or seven years, and notes that the Occupy Movement has brought a flush of new, young, people. "Every new young farmer wants to have a CSA". When asked about how CSAs, or the experiences of CSAs can be scaled up and also reach low-income people Elisabeth tells me about *Corbin Hill Farm*, a network of farms in Schoharie County and urban communities in New York City. It has an educational farm that produces a small amount of fruits and vegetables and serves as a distribution centre where the participating farmers bring their produce for further transport to sites in Harlem and the South Bronx. Shareholders (their term for members) pay in advance to receive their freshly harvested produce. Many of the members are from disadvantaged communities. While the level of direct engagement is not very large, members do make trips to the farm and at an occasion when several farms were flooded, the members contributed financially to the farms, despite many of the members being rather poor.[950]

Over and above the direct purpose of a CSA and the interaction between the farmers and their consumers (I note that Elisabeth still refers to them as consumers), there is a great value in the educational aspect of CSA. "There is a lot of money in the food system but consumer dollars are not shared out fairly among the people who do the hard work of growing, packing, delivering and processing food. The cheap food policies of the United States create externalities – chemical residues food that cause chronic illnesses, the pollution of soil, air and water, the erosion of soil – that industrial agriculture avoids paying and leaves to the tax payer. Many CSA members understand this and can be a core group in influencing the mainstream food system".[951]

Interviews with participants of the Earthshare CSA in Scotland show that although people had many different reasons for engaging in the CSA, over time they became more attuned to the wider values of CSA. The researchers concluded that "consumers' motivations and identities are as much produced through their participation as leading to participation to begin with".[952] I believe this is an essential observation of human behavior. I believe that there is a constant interplay between what we do and how we think about ourselves. As much as we become what we want to be, we also become the roles we play, regardless of if the roles were consciously chosen or not. This is how consumers are shaped by shopping in supermarkets, and how soldiers become killers in an army. Those who share similar values obviously also become more dedicated, "the core group have stayed with Earthshare through thick and thin, right, even when we had a bad winter they were still there"[953] says Pam Bochel from Earthshare.[a] The research suggested that, by being part of alternative food schemes, consumers are encouraged to think about food in different ways, often to cook more, to eat more seasonal fruit and vegetables and to eat in a more health-conscious way.[954] CSAs also contribute to local develop-

---

[a] From the book *Reconnecting Consumers Producers and Food* (mentioned earlier) where the researchers tell the stories of six different alternative food schemes, including Earthshare and 'Adopt a sheep'.

ment and the environment in a number of ways. CSAs in England employ five times more labor per hectare than the agriculture average (a result of a combination of small scale, organic production and orientation to vegetables); 55% of CSAs have planted hedges and 61% introduced new wild life areas.[955] In addition, most CSAs farm organically, whether certified or not.

A simpler version of a CSA is a box scheme, a system by which consumers can subscribe to weekly supplies of food, most usually vegetables. In this way consumers are not directly participating in the farming, but are subscribing to regular supplies. For many farmers, starting a box scheme, much like a CSA has been a way to get out of the commodity trap offered by supermarkets. In the United Kingdom there are 500 organic box-schemes and organic home deliveries were worth £167 million in 2011.[956]

Some try to tackle the issues in other ways. Freiburg lies at the entry to the scenic Black Forest (*Schwarzwald*) in the upper Rhine valley; it is, the sunniest and warmest city in Germany. The city was established in the early twelfth century and is known for its medieval university and progressive environmental practices. It is situated in the heart of a region that has a diverse agricultural production and small-scale farming. Lately, the growth of large-scale, monoculture farms has led to the decline of family and small-scale agriculture, particularly through farm consolidation. Half of the farms in the state of Baden-Württemberg, where Freiburg is located, have closed down in the last 20 years. For those who want to buy a farm it is very hard to secure working capital and land. Despite its good climate and diverse traditions, it is estimated that today only five percent of the food in Freiburg is sourced in the region.

Christian Hiss grew up on one of Germany's first organic farms, started by his parents in 1953 in Eichstetten, not far from Freiburg. At the age of twenty-one, Christian and his wife started a vegetable farm as a private enterprise and in the 1990s he started seed breeding. Christian felt that it was increasingly difficult to include organic values in the enterprise, he tells me when I visit him. Market logic applied to all the needed inputs, seeds, land, operating capital and knowledge and, even in the organic sector, his colleagues were increasingly discussing things from the perspective of whether it was profitable or not. He also experienced the typical problems of farms of today: lack of access to capital and unclear farm succession. He also found that there was poor valuation of the socio-ecological services of farms. When he asked for a loan from the bank to build a new cowshed the bank turned him down and he felt it was time to act. "If it was so difficult for me to raise capital even though I had inherited the farm, how difficult would it be for a new farmer?"

There was a need to find a new structure for doing business, so he formed the Regionalwert AG[a] (RWAG) in 2006. It is a model for what Christian calls *community connected agriculture*, in which people support farms and food business not just in their role as consumers. Farmers should not see society as consumers and society should not see farmers as just producers. It is a question of relationship and dialogue, and "dialogue is about embeddedness" says Christian. RWAG's main point of intervention is to supply organic farms and other actors in the food chain with capital. However, this is not its only activity: the RWAG also helps the organizations they support with market integration and they have established a regional brand.

"It is easier to sell the eggs through other RWAG network partners, such as the Frischekiste (a box scheme)" says Philipp Goetjes at the Breitenweger Hof in Eichstetten, where he and his wife Katarina have an organic dairy and egg enterprise. The cooperation extends beyond markets; Jannis Zentler and a colleague at Querbeet Garden (the farm originally started by Christian), another RWAG partner, grow vegetables on thirteen hectares, but they also have seven hectares of clover grass, which is fed to Philipp and Katarina's cows in exchange for manure. Jannis also tells me about the bio-dynamic association which has been working together with the farm ever since it was established, a long time ago, "they know the place better than we do, and they want to have old varieties and seasonal food". These consumers are very different from most of the newer consumers who just want to buy organic foods.

Five hundred people in Freiburg have invested in the RWAG. All sorts of people are shareholders, the biggest investor has seven percent of the capital and the total capital available was more than 2.3 million Euros in 2013. The RWAG offers food entrepreneurs various forms of investments in business expansion if their business plans are viable. Often RWAG provides capital for a fixed rate of interest of between 3% and 8% for land, machines etc. It also buys land and farms and leases them to farmers at a reasonable rent. RWAG can also be a partner or a shareholders, it has 40% of the shares in *Regionalwert Biomarkt Waage* a shop in Emmendingen. It support sixteen operations, including a

---

[a] Regional Value Ltd

winery, two vegetable farms, a cheese farm, a box scheme, a catering company, a wholesaler, two shops, a mixed farm, a dried fruit operation and an accountant (also part of the food chain!).

RWAG works with a set of 64 sustainability indicators covering aspects such as employment structure and wages, biodiversity and resource consumption, value creation for the region and dialogue within the value chain. These are reported annually for all the enterprises and then compiled in an annual report. The proportion of renewable electricity used by the companies increased from 62% in 2009 to 98% in 2012, although the proportion of renewable energy for fuel is still zero. So far there are no incentives for the enterprises to actually improve their performance on these indicators apart from the pride in doing so. Christian wants to see a system where enterprises are rewarded for this and equally those who harm or destroy the environment have to pay for it, but he recognizes that this will rarely happen in a voluntary market.

"Governments tend to be reactive rather than pro-active; most change comes because people just go on with it and start to live their lives as it had already happened[957]". Originating in the small town of Totnes in South West England, the Transition movement has spread to many countries. There are now some 1,300 official Transition initiatives. According to Rob Hopkins, founder of the movement, whom I interview in February 2014, that is only the tip of the iceberg. Transition Towns are communities that seek to reduce their use of fossil fuels and their carbon footprint and to prepare themselves to cope with the challenges of climate change and diminishing energy supply.

Transition Town Totnes, which was initiated by Rob, was the first initiative and strives to build resilience through a process of 're-localizing, where feasible, all aspects of life'. By using much less energy and resources these communities seek to be more resilient. Many find that the process of relying more on their own resources and communities brings a lot of pleasure. The initiatives start with a positive visioning exercise that emphasizes the things that can be done here and now. Food is one of their main entry points and many actions are very hands-on, e.g. in Totnes there is a community supported brewery. In Slaithwaite the Green Valley Grocer is a community-owned bakery. A group in Norwich started a farm with bicycle deliveries: Our vegetables are grown a few miles out of the city, picked in the morning and delivered by bicycle in the afternoon. What could be better?".

One aim of Transition Town Totnes is that where 'possible and appropriate' food is sourced within 30 miles of Totnes by enterprises and resources owned by members of the community so that the elements of the localized food system create an interdependent web. It deepens the 'buy local' argument by also including *from whom* they should buy locally. In the report *Economic Blueprint for T&D: Our local food economy* they conclude that it is better for the local economy to buy from independent shops than from supermarkets. Buying from independent shops generates 2.5 times as much local income than buying from supermarkets. This is because local shops tend to buy local services, "if our aim is to strengthen our local economy, it's just as important to look at where the money is spent, as well as how much".[958]

I wonder if this also holds for farms. After all, many farms are more like assembly points. For example, a chicken producer buys the chicks, all the feed, the industrial equipment, vaccines, professional consultancy etc, mostly from national or global organizations (there are three broiler chicken breeders that totally dominate the global market), and does all it can to reduce need for labor, or uses migrant laborers. This means that the farm is not particularly embedded in the local community economy or environment. Rob acknowledges this and says that those kinds of farms would typically not engage in the local business in any case.

Some buy local campaigns don't take into account the financial realities of many people these days Rob notes, "if you are on a low to medium income, buying *all* of your food locally is not financially an option". By putting the ambition lower, say at ten percent, it doesn't exclude people. If Totnes could shift to eating ten percent locally produced food that would put an extra £2 million in the local economy every year.[959] With aims at this level, it is also easy to build coalitions with other institutions, such as the local town council. Rob says "ten percent feels achievable, totally re-localizing the entire food economy feels a bit abstract to me".[960]

Transition is rather quiet in big political discussions but while (or perhaps because) there is no (explicit) critique of 'the system' or 'the economy',[961] Rob Hopkins thinks that these initiatives have a big impact on policies. Instead of arguing against growth they argue that building community resilience is a form of economic development. He thinks the Transition movement addresses many of the pressing issues facing us today through positive action, rather than by criticizing the systems or through political action. Community ownership and cooperatives are preferred to private companies as the models for collective actions in transition initiatives. "Transition is a social technology designed to work on a local scale and in order to do this you have to try to stay below a lot of those discussions and focus on doing stuff".[962] While it is important that there are also people who focus on the bigger policy issues, the role of Transition is different, "you need the examples, and you need the stories, and you need the stuff that is already happening and the stuff that just started without waiting for permission[963]".

"We didn't want to stop selling locally but the market dwindled", says one farmer in the Totnes area. A report by Holly Tiffens concludes that a wide range of fruit, vegetables and cereals was grown in the Totnes area in the past, but the producers gave up or scaled down this diversified production mostly due to labor issues and low economic margins. Other disincentives were supermarket competition, limited consumer demand, inadequate processing infrastructure and inefficient distribution methods. The report recommends ways to re-establish a diverse local food production regime including the formation of co-operatives, improvements in supply chain infrastructure and distribution efficiency, as well as investment in consumer education to strengthen local markets and enhance demand for locally grown products.[964]

I think that is all good. I and my friends did this in our first organic marketing cooperative back in 1983. But while it is good, it is not sufficient to roll back supermarket domination and farm consolidation, unless the underlying economic rules are changed. These new local initiatives still have to pass the test of time and it is hard to assess how much uptake they will attract. And it isn't easy. 'Tolly', Iain Tolhurst, a renowned organic grower at the Hardwick Estate in England tells me that only eight or nine clients for his organic boxes are from the thousand affluent households in his immediate vicinity, and that marketing remains his biggest problem after forty years of farming. And the person talking is a showcase farmer with high credibility and standing. Barbara, the manager of the RWAG shop I visit notes that some consumers are interested in the regional, but most prefer the wider offer that a globalized market can offer. Elizabeth Henderson tells me there are now so many CSAs that they compete for members. The expectations from farmers and consumers have in many cases diminished and there are many different ways that people can get local organic foods – from farmers' markets and other sources. In addition there are commercial middlemen, 'aggregators', which are not CSAs, but operate under that flag. But as she points out, if there is anything that distinguishes a CSA it is that it is direct, there is no middle man. Taken together these recent developments discourage farmers from 'asking too much' from the members. Do people even want to partake in these projects or do they prefer to place their trust in governments and retailers, thereby avoid taking responsibility?

Tim Deane, of Northwood Farm in Somerset describes their marketing journey since 1984 – quite similar to our experience at the Torfolk farm. He and his wife Jan were co-founders of a marketing cooperative for organic producers. The main clients were supermarkets. Increasingly, the clients squeezed returns and upped the grading specification. And when competition from other growers drove down the prices, they had to re-orient themselves to direct marketing and started a box scheme. Tim summarizes the benefits with "better returns, no bad debts, human contact and appreciation and thus more job satisfaction". Also, because it allowed more diverse production it fitted in better with the underlying principles of organic production. But there were also some disadvantages. While they got more contacts with consumers, they got much less contact with other growers and become more inward looking, and less likely to improve their productivity and efficiency. "Direct marketing enables the grower to forget about much of the bigger market in the wider world and from a personal business perspective that is an advantage, but those people are still there to be fed. What can a model offer them which at its extreme end is largely dependent on hand work?" Tim ponders and continues, "I don't know, the choice between dealing with the world as it is or seeking to step outside is not straightforward".[965]

Lately, box schemes have also become subject to increased competition. Some box schemes in Europe today serve tens of thousands of consumers, and consolidate products from many producers, and often also include imported products. The first box from Aarstiderne in Denmark came into the world in 1999. Today they deliver vegetable and fruit boxes to around 40,000 households in Denmark and 5,000 in Sweden. The Riverford box scheme began when Guy Watson started delivering vegetables locally to 30 friends in Devon. It now delivers around 47,000 boxes a week to homes around the United Kingdom.[966] In addition to box schemes there is a surge of internet-based food options. *Ooooby* in Auckland and Sydney aggregates products from many local suppliers and delivers to customers' doorsteps.[967] These tools may be useful for taking more possession of the food chain, but at the same time there might also be risks that they displace the relationships of a farmers' market or a CSA.

It is important to realize why things have developed as they have. Why has large scale, monoculture farming outcompeted small-scale diverse farming? Why does consolidation in the food industry continue and why do supermarkets and fast food chains expand at the expense of independent local business? I believe I have explained the drivers behind these developments. And if we don't change those drivers – or they are changed by physical realities such as an energy shortage – it is hard to believe that there will be any fundamental shift to a more local food system, as the logic of the system will remain the same. The agricultural treadmill (discussed before) will continue to turn, even if we try to support local and organic. As one farmer says "back in 1977 we were selling cauliflowers at about 25p each, and today we sell them for about 30p each, so in that time they've only gone up by 5p. But in comparison the prices of fuel, sprays and labor have all gone up dramatically so we were getting less and less profit. We essentially have to run faster to stay in the same position."[968]

It will not be easy to achieve a transition of the food system. I do agree with the Transition Movement that it is important to change things here and now. But it is equally important to try to change the macro-economic structures which nudge both producers and consumers into the logic of the competitive market. It is not a question of either or, but both. They also have to be combined with a change in values and paradigms that establishes an economy in which man's wealth does not result in nature's poverty or the poverty of other people. As Peter Volz, a researcher who accompanied me on my visits to the various businesses which are part of the RWAG says "the moment of social transformation is when people look each other in the eyes." The problems begin when people act based on their place in an abstract system instead of as humans beings.

Agricultural cooperatives have strong market positions in many countries. Their starting point was one of social and economic betterment for producers, often in fierce competition with private agribusiness. In recent decades, we have witnessed significant changes in competition, distribution of market power and governance structures of food chains. Cooperatives have adjusted to this new environment with new governance structures, employing CEOs from the corporate sector, using new financial instruments, and inventing novel organizational set-ups. Consequently, many of the traditional cooperative traits are fading, being left only on the surface.

Consumer cooperatives have experienced much the same process of transformation. In European countries where consumer cooperatives have been strong for more than hundred years, it is hard to see much difference between their shops and purchasing policies and those of privately owned supermarkets. They also have not had a very farmer-friendly attitude because of their middle class and working-class, urban, origins. Even today, they are generally more keen to support Fair Trade in coffee and bananas from the third world than to pay local farmers better, or even to buy from local farms. The consumer cooperative movement of Sweden, with roots in the 19th century, was also not friendly to small shops or food processing companies as their small scale stood in the way of modernity, hygiene and cheap food, which were their main concerns. Newly established cooperatives, be they farmer or consumer cooperatives, mostly have a strong ideology. Unfortunately, as years go by they tend to mimic prevailing market practices. It is likely that the pressures of the market, the imperatives of competition and constant innovation, drive cooperatives to act like corporations in the end. This means that it is the market that ultimately determines what actors do, and how they do it, rather than the actors' organizational form. If that is the case, we have to change those relations in a profound way.

I think solutions could be found in cooperative platforms built on the notion of food and the landscape as commons to be commonly managed, rather than on that of producers or consumers. They would include many of the aspects of the examples above, but most importantly they would transcend the categories of the capitalist market. This doesn't necessarily mean that they would not use markets at all or that they would not use money at all. Perhaps they will shun both, perhaps not. The focus would be on relationships and stewardship and not primarily on the exchange of products. Thereby they would avoid some of the pitfalls of earlier cooperative attempts.

In the United States a group of researchers, farmers and food activists are working with the concept of the Food Commons to build a network of regional food systems. The ideas are still in the trial and testing stage but center around three building blocks. The Food Commons Trust will be a non-profit entity that acquires and stewards critical foodshed assets, such as farm land. The community-owned Food Commons Bank, shall provide capital and other financial services to the enterprises in the network and the distribution will be managed by Food Commons Hubs. They should also act as service providers to the actors and as incubators for new small food businesses. Pilots are taking place in Fresno and Atlanta.[969]

The RWAG and many, many, others employ more or less sophisticated systems of social and environmental indicators as the basis for measuring their performance rather than solely relying on the usual financial balance sheets. Many others also promote measurements other than GDP to guide societal developments. While I support the development of these alternative measures and indicators, I do not think their role is so important, because in the end they are just meas-urements. It is not the measuring of GDP that gave us growth or drive growth. There was no GDP measure at the time of the most intensive growth of western economies. Growth is driven by human aspirations and a number of functions built into the economic system, profit-seeking, interest rates and competition. 'Triple bottom lines' and environmental and corporate social responsibility indicators don't really change the treadmill logic under which companies operate. It is very hard to build in rewards for non-economic factors in the market price of products.

The sustainability of the efforts briefly described here will depend on us going far beyond the hype that now surrounds many of the alternatives, and also acknowledging the huge complexities involved. At a certain time such movements might even become strong enough to capture political power to further their endeavors. As with earlier societal transformations there will be struggles. Whether or not these will be peaceful or not depends on the actors in the play, and particu-larly whether those who stand to lose some of their dominance and power will accept their losses, or even better see it as an emancipation of themselves.

28

The political strategy

I fully agree with Rob Hopkins that governments are mostly reactive and that most things happen because people take things in their own hands. I would add that external (for example access to fossil fuels) and endogenous (for example population growth or financial booms) factors also play very big roles in driving change. Financial crises and the sky-rocketing of energy prices have done more in recent years to curb climate change than endless UN-led negotiations. Nevertheless, there is a constant interplay between the public sphere and the economic, cultural and ecological spheres and peoples' daily lives. And there are also those pivotal moments and situations when people hit the street and say 'enough is enough' and change becomes inevitable. By and large, any transformation will be more successful when political, economic, social, cultural systems and trends are synchronized. We will only rebuild our food system if we also dare to move beyond our roles as consumers and volunteers and take on roles as political citizens. I mean political in the wider sense, influencing those public institutions that are charged with managing our social commons, regulating markets and driving research. This includes governments, municipalities and a whole range of public institutions from schools to utilities, pension funds and universities. But it also includes building new institutions that will usurp power from states and corporations, when needed.

Even the most convinced proponents of a free market realize that there are things that cannot be left to the market to sort out. Human rights, law and order, security, and basic social security have, in almost all societies, been regulated by non-market institutions, often by the state. And even for those things that are regulated by markets there are many governmental rules, some stupid and others very much needed. The more central an issue is to our society, the more regulations there are. For example, all countries have labor regulations. They are there because we realize that the workers are a weaker party in the supposedly 'free' labor market: they need some kind of protection by society. It is also apparent that *Nature* needs protection: far more than we extend to her today.

Food production and consumption are also subject to myriads of regulations in most countries. Throughout history, the food supply has been subject to political intervention. The Romans tried to regulate prices, although they failed, like most other subsequent efforts – the record of government interventions in food markets is rather poor. The fact that we have major famine in several places in the world while lots of food is wasted in other parts of the world is also an indication that markets in food don't work very well in safeguarding the survival of fellow humans. We cannot deal with food mainly as a marketable commodity – very few societies ever have. If things get rough, governments, civil society and groups of people will step in and regulate, distribute and produce outside of the market system. The market system also has very few levers that guide it to supply food that is nutritious.

The market in food is totally dysfunctional for shaping the farming system in the best way for its role of planetary stewardship, a role that is increasingly important as agriculture occupies more and more of the surface of the planet and natural resources are under immense pressure. There are almost no market mechanisms in place for undertaking this important task, and there is a limited potential for them to emerge. Even if they did they will never reach the extent required, considering that the value of agricultural ecosystem services might well be as high as the total value of agricultural production. At present the market is still driving farmers the other way; into more and more specialization and monocultures and less stewardship of nature resources. Already today massive government interventions are directed to compensating for market failure. We need to look in other directions if we wish to sustainably manage the agriculture landscape.

'Agriculture and food systems, with their associated nature and landscapes, are a common heritage and thus, also a form of common property' according to Professor Jules Pretty[970] at the University of Essex. Stepping away from market imperatives frees our minds and thinking about food and farm production. This of course has implications for land and other resources needed for farming and food production. The more food is viewed as a public good, the less appropriate it is that the productive factors needed to produce foods, seeds, land, water etc, are provided by the market. When food is a right, and the production and distribution of food takes place in the commons instead of in the market, new ways of addressing the unfair distribution of food can emerge.

The *Universal Declaration of Human Rights* of 1948 already defines food as a human right: "Everyone has the right to a standard of living adequate for the health and well-being of himself and of his family, including food, clothing, housing and medical care and necessary social services, and the right to security in the event of unemployment, sickness, disability, widowhood, old age or other lack of livelihood in circumstances beyond his control" (Article 25). The right to food has been re-asserted ever since, for example at the 2009 World Summit on Food Security in Rome. There, world leaders agreed on 'the right of everyone to have access to safe, sufficient and nutritious food'.[971] The new constitution of Kenya, approved by a popular referendum in 2010, states the right of every person "to be free from hunger and to have adequate food of acceptable quality" and imposes a duty on the State to respect, protect, promote and fulfill that right. A study in 2011 identified twenty-four countries in which the right to food was explicitly recognized, many of them in Latin America.

Of course, it is one thing to proclaim a right and another one to enact it. Rights need a guarantor, duties and obligations, and an enforcer of some kind. Increasingly courts are using the constitutions or international treaties as a basis to safeguard people's right to food.[972] The Special Rapporteur on the Right to Food for the United Nations, Olivier De Schutter, writes in the report to the General Assembly in August 2013: 'The right to food has come to the fore as Governments realize that their efforts to combat food insecurity and hunger have been failing and realize the urgent need to strengthen national legal, institutional and policy frameworks'.[973]

Brazil has been successful in the fight against hunger and in promoting the right to food. The *Fome Zero* (zero hunger) program was initiated during Lula's presidency. Its most important component is *Bolsa Família*, whereby poor families get a basic income tied to conditions such that the children go to school and are vaccinated. The cost of the whole program is just 0.5% of Brazilian GDP but it reaches 44 million people, more than a fifth of the population. Malnutrition in Brazil decreased from 13% to below 2% between 1994 and 2006. The program also includes the purchasing of local food, often organic, to schools and other support measures to small farmers.[974]

Rethinking food as a right, farming as a management system of the planet and the food system as a commons necessitates the building of new institutions fit for these purposes; Jose Luis Vivero Pol, a food governance researcher describes these as "a third force of governance and resource management by the people as a compliment to the market and the state".[975] This will require experimentation at the personal, local, national and international levels. This doesn't rule out markets as one of several mechanisms for food distribution, but does it reject market hegemony over our food supplies, and rejects the view that market forces are the best way of allocating food producing resources, such as land, water, knowledge and seeds.

Political actions to reform the food system can take many forms and happen on many levels. Citing America's Declaration of Independence and the Maine Constitution, the one thousand or so citizens of Sedgwick voted in 2001 in favor of a local ordinance stating that "Sedgwick citizens possess the right to produce, process, sell, purchase, and consume local foods of their choosing." These local foods include raw milk and other dairy products and locally-slaughtered meats. The ordinance also states that, "It shall be unlawful for any law or regulation adopted by the state or federal government to interfere with the rights recognized by this Ordinance".[976] Of course, this is mainly a provocation, rather than a practical policy. But the system certainly needs provoking. In similar ways many municipalities and counties in Europe have declared themselves to be GMO-free zones. Austria banned GM maize and rape seed in 1999. The European Commission has tried to overrule the Austrian ordinance on genetically modified seed, but the member states have twice backed the ban, so Austria remains a GMO-free zone. All the Austrian Bundesländer (states) have declared their intention to remain GMO-free and more than hundred municipalities have signed resolutions to the same effect.[977]

In the United States, Food Policy Councils act as forums for food issues and platforms for coordinated action. The first Food Policy Council started in 1982 in Knoxville, Tennessee. Since then Food Policy Councils have been established at state, local and regional levels across the country. Some have remarkable success stories. Others have failed, disbanded, or spun-off into other services and non-profit organizations. According to a report from California-based *Food First* (describing itself as people's think tank and education-for-action center), the councils serve as forums for discussing food issues, coordinate between sectors in the food system, influence policy and support programs and services that address local needs.[978]

In 1995, the agreement on Trade Related Intellectual Property Rights (TRIPS) came into force under the WTO framework. Through that agreement (and corresponding national regulations) cells, genes, plants, sheep and cow breeds became intellectual property. The effects of this are still working their way throughout our food system and are still the subject of a lot of controversy and opposition. Indian researcher and environmental activist Vandana Shiva says that the agreement doesn't only open up the possibility that life *can be owned* but that it stipulates that it *has to be owned*. [979] We need to defend and develop biodiversity and common knowledge as commons rather than as privatized intellectual property. An American company patented the use of the neem tree as a fungicide, despite neem having been used as a pesticide for 2000 years. A coalition of the Greens in the European Parliament, Shiva's Research Foundation for Science, Technology and Ecology and the International Federation of Organic Agriculture Movements (IFOAM) sued the company at the European Patent Office. After a 10-year-long process, to a large extent driven by Linda Bullard, the President of IFOAM at that time, the patent was declared void.[980] But this success is a rare exception. The fundamental problem lies in the rights of ownership to life, which needs to be rolled back. And many are working on this issue. The *No Patents on Seeds* coalition is supported globally by over 300 NGOs and farmers' organizations, and has collected about 100,000 signatures against patents on plants and animals.[981] But the forces in support of intellectual property rights of all kinds are very strong as patents and licensing are major sources of profit in contemporary capitalism, where trade and manufacturing have been so commoditized that they provide very low profit margins.

In general the private ownership of resources needed for the production of food and ecosystem services is a key target for policy reform. Ownership should not be confused with customary rights to use a certain resource. The latter has been the norm in human history, while private ownership is the anomaly. Already today, the status of private property is quite different under different legal systems, and property rights can often take a second place to the public interest. For instance, the German Constitution says, 'Property entails obligations. Its use shall also serve the public good'.[982]

Free market proponents believe that 'the economy' should be free from political interference. In reality the whole framework of the economy is defined by political processes. Private property, limited companies, the right to charge interest, money, the relationship between capital, employer and labor, patent rights, trade agreements are all politically determined, and are necessary for the economy to work. Even the abstract market and its most important tool, money, are commons, social institutions upheld by government regulations and judicial systems. The notion that the economy is something separate from society and from nature is part of the problem. In essence this view makes society and nature into sub-systems of the economy instead of the other way round. This can be noticed in current political discourse where the role of public policy is mainly seen as being about strengthening countries' competitiveness in international markets. As an example of this distorted perspective, the current political discussion about climate change is about how we can afford to mitigate it, while the real question should be how we can afford to be driving the cars that cause the emissions in the first place. Reducing emissions is no more a cost than it is a cost to eat less.

To quite a large extent, politicians have taken a back seat in discussions on how to transform our food system to a more sustainable shape. By and large, they have put their faith in a 'sustainable development' paradigm originating from the 1987 Bruntland report, *Our Common Future*. Big businesses and many of the major environmental NGOs have also endorsed this approach, which puts faith in market-based solutions, corporate responsibility and green consumerism. These mechanisms have failed to deliver over twenty-five years but were still re-launched at the UN Environmental Conference in Rio 2012 under the slogan *'The Green Economy'*. A 2013 expert report for the Nordic Council of Ministers challenges the prevailing orthodox belief in sustainable consumption. "It is unrealistic to expect a sustainable society to materialize from current political strategies on sustainable consumption." Governments need to lead the shift to sustainability by creating the structures and regulations that make sustainable living the default option. The emphasis on green consumption is based on a "falsely optimistic view that technological solutions will be sufficient to achieve sustainability".[983]

Political action should address the immediate deficiencies of the food system in fields such as food safety, biodiversity, environmental protection, climate change, animal welfare, social justice, health and food security. Those actions should include taxes, fees or limitations on 'bad' methods or technologies. It is equally important to support the development of new solutions. The actions should be geared towards resilience and increased local consumption. There are already people out there building a new food system, or wanting to build a new food system. Governments on all levels can take the decisions needed to remove the obstacles or roll out the red carpet for them. This includes supporting efforts to strengthen local economic networks. This can be in the form of direct support, letting local initiatives use public resources or favoring local foods in government procurement. There is a need to develop new legal forms for the management of the commons and for social entrepreneurship and simultaneously abolish the right of corporations to privatize profits while socializing losses. There is also a need for support to relevant research in all fields, particularly in the socio-economic field and to allocate space in cities for farmers' markets, urban farming and other forms of collective production.

Policy actions should also address the macroeconomic drivers and tax systems that shape the food system. Profit-making, competition in open markets, the availability of cheap energy resources and throw-away technologies are among those most prominent. To tackle them, states need to throw sand in the machinery of the international trading system. This can range from opting out of the WTO or free trade agreements, obstruction or other ways of favoring local industries as well as prohibiting import of livestock products from industrial livestock operations or products causing too high greenhouse gas emissions. It can also include rolling back agreements that open up natural resources for private ownership or the introduction of carbon taxes. Countries should set serious food self-sufficiency targets and establish reasonable food reserves. On an international level countries should agree on mutual food security guarantees in the same way as military alliances today guarantee security.

Political actions also need to recognize that initiatives are needed on all levels from the household (private), community (civil society), society (local and national governments and humanity (international organizations). Economies operate on all these different levels and there needs to be some barriers between these different levels. If not we are stuck with the increasing commodification of private life all the way into our kitchens. It is an interesting paradox that many things that are not well taken care of by either governments or markets (say the provision of shelters to the homeless) are addressed by civil society and communities. But when it comes to functions that the state is interested in controlling (e.g. city planning) or where the market sees an opportunity for profit (e.g. health care), then suddenly communities are seen as no longer up to the job.

The discussions about the food system cannot be decoupled from discussions about entitlement, power relations and ownership. In today's world, the 85 richest people own as much wealth as the poorest 3.5 billion, each one of them having the same wealth as 41 million fellow human-beings.[984] It is not acceptable that some people starve, are injured or poisoned while producing luxury items for richer. The food issue is closely related to equality. As Peter Kropotkin said: "the question of bread must take precedence over all other questions. If it is not settled in the interest of the people, the revolution will not be on the right road; for solving the question of bread we must accept the principle of equality".[985] Equitable sharing provides no guarantee that we can meet the combined challenge of a large population and limited natural resources, but it is a precondition for success. Political actions should be taken to roll back the huge inequalities,

nationally and internationally, through taxation and other redistribu-
tional efforts, such as land reforms. The concepts of individual
emission rights, ecological debt and ecological footprint could be a
starting point for a dialogue about how to share the planet's resources.
But ultimately I don't think any of them will form a sound basis for an
economic system. Even if the challenges are global, it is not evident
that one global system is the right response. Perhaps thousands of
regional systems are a better way. If for no other reasons that this
increases learning by doing, trial and error and diversity, all sound
principles for undertaking a massive social transformation.

Finally, political action is also about showing leadership and vision
and influencing people. When will we get leaders who make a new
food system a priority? Of course, some will say that we get the leaders
we deserve, and that the real challenge is to change people. This leads
us to the last part of my discussion, a discussion about values and
ethics.

29

Care and Share

"The land ethic simply enlarges the boundaries of the community to include soils, waters, plants, and animals, or collectively: the land".[986] In the beautiful essay on land ethics in the *Sand County Almanac*, conservationist and writer Aldo Leopold calls for a land ethic that puts the interest of this larger community ahead of the self-interest of the individual. This puts ethical and aesthetic considerations on par with economic ones. He says "We abuse land because we regard it as a commodity belonging to us. When we see land as a community to which we belong, we may begin to use it with love and respect."

Scientists now speak about the *Anthropcene*, the era in which Earth's huge hydrological, biological, climatic and even geological systems, are shaped by humans. The agricultural landscape is home to a significant part of the world's bio-diversity, it controls more than half of terrestrial primary production, it is the major consumer of freshwater, and it is involved in global scale manipulations of the nitrogen, carbon, methane and phosphorus cycles. As such farming is the most significant human management system of the planet and our future as humans on the planet will largely rest upon how we manage the farmscape. Food and agriculture are the main links between the human beings and the ecosystems of planet Earth. How and what we eat is therefore also linked to how we manage the planet.

The capitalist market economy has transformed everything involved in food production into commodities. Land, water, seeds livestock, labor, cheese, wine and bread are all treated as exchangeable commodities with monetary values assigned by the omnipresent and omnipotent market. It converts land, forest, humans, animals and food to real estate, ecosystem services, labor, McBurgers and calories. In the end everything is reduced to the universal measure of value – money, a process which also turns nature into a commodity to be consumed. This is also why the main function of the food market is to make us eat more and why it creates obesity. Even cooking and eating are increasingly commoditized and have long lost any relationship with the surrounding landscape. We don't *see* the landscape we eat anymore. We don't see the farmer or the animals, we don't see the hedgerow, or the hedgerow has already been taken down. This devoids the food we eat of meaning and leads to a neurotic relationship to food and eating. The act of eating, binding us together since we became humans, has rapidly become an individualized intake of prescribed diets.

We need to see food as something else than just 'products' or even worse 'commodities'. I once had a student, Phuntso from Bhutan, attend a course I was teaching. After a month in Sweden and visits to many farms, at the final evaluation of the course, he expressed his satisfaction. But he was sad that the farmers, advisors, and I, referred to cattle bred for the purpose of meat production as 'beef-cattle'. For me his reflection was a revelation. It is hard to see that one can combine animal welfare with the view of animals as commodities, which is by definition the prevailing view in a market based farming system. I believe we should instead see them as our symbionts, companions, for which we have responsibility. This perspective would provide a more stable foundation than the animal rights perspective for finding a compromise in how we manage animals, a compromise between veganism and ruthless exploitation. I am convinced that we need the partnership with our symbionts in order to manage the planet well, notwithstanding their importance for our diet. An ethics of care could form one of the pillars for how we maintain, continue and repair our world so that we can live in it as well as possible. This reemphasizes the relations that exist between all living things. A caring, regenerative farming system would also be the basis for regenerative foods, food that not only nourishes us with calories but also with the regenerative force of life, with meaning and connectedness.

As modern man lives so far from nature it might be easier to use food as the entry point for a new relationship with nature, our symbionts and ourselves. Reconnecting food with farming reconnects us with the landscape and therefore is also a process of reconnecting us to nature. For those of us who have the opportunity to grow our own food, or keep bees or laying hens it is a great experience. As long as we see eating as just a way of feeding the body with nutrients, we miss the point. Eating is what binds us together with each other and with nature, with food and farming. I have never been a believer in any religion, but I can see the value of saying grace before eating. It draws the attention to the act of eating and all the relationships that are embedded in it. Cooking and food preparation such as baking bread, brewing, making cheese and canning links eating with farming and is equally important. Through cooking we can become co-producers, break the division of producers and consumers and take more responsibility for our lives. We can swap the 'freedom' of the market, to buy a range of goods or services defined by others, commoditized for ease of production and marketing with a very different freedom: the freedom to be a whole human. 'Cooking for freedom': come to think about it that's quite a good slogan for transforming our world into a better place.

We also need to scrutinize our whole lifestyle and change from a consumption basis to a living basis. A movement for voluntary simplicity is part of this change. A new ethics of land and food and a new lifestyle need to be backed up and underscored by rules and systems. Only when there is harmony between the system in which we live in and the ethics we promote can they both come to fruition. The capitalist market-economy appeals to many human traits but not the ones we need to make a great transition. It is built on, and encourages, constant competition; it is built upon growth and increasing consumption and encourages the exploitation of natural resources. The values that are implicit and explicit in the capitalist market economy are not the ones we need to face up to the challenges ahead. Instead of seeing nature as some kind of sub-system or side-system, separate from the human economy, we need to see the human economy as part of nature's economy. As Wendell Berry says: 'The definitive relationships in the universe are thus not competitive but interdependent'.[987]

The principles for food production, the kind of social and economic system and the kind of nature stewardship will have to be mutually supportive and be built on similar foundations. A regenerative food system will have implications for the whole of society. For instance, one of the breeding grounds for regenerative production and consumption are systems whereby consumers and producers cooperate in the farm and food chain, a kind of co-production based on the land as a commons. We need to restore but also 'restory' both our food and our farming landscape, fill them with new meanings that build on traditions while bringing in new visions and energy. Grounding our food in the environment and in regenerative processes will not ensure we have good and wholesome food, but we will certainly be closer when we have embedded our food system in ecology rather than in the economy. Trade or exchange in food will also take place in such a future. But it will be oriented to ecological and nutritional needs, as was originally the case, and not based on bringing in food from somewhere else because it is five percent cheaper. If we go down the route of buying cheap we will just repeat the whole cycle over and again. Without making change based on this insight the global food chain will continue to be a social and environmental abomination.

A new land and food ethics has to include ourselves, human beings. The changes in our food system will have to be combined with a change in values and a situation where man's wealth neither results in nature's poverty nor the poverty of other people. How we accomplish that may be beyond the scope of this book. But, that said, I believe that food and farming provide an excellent starting point for any attempt to make a more just society and more just relations between humans. If we get food right, the rest will follow. Join the meal.

The digestive

Despite living in the information age, our knowledge of what is actually produced on the five hundred million farms in the world, and what is actually eaten by the earth's seven billion inhabitants is inadequate and inaccurate. When I worked with projects in Peru aimed at converting former coca growers to growing other income generating crops, they did plant these new crops, but they moved the coca bushes to new fields further away from NGOs and the police, who could then claim success for their coca reduction programs. I more recently did a job in Cambodia and realized that huge quantities of rice were being smuggled over the border to Vietnam as a result of failing government policies. Those quantities are lost in the statistics for Cambodia and perhaps added to the already record exports of Vietnam, unless the re-export also take place under the radar of authorities. These two examples illustrate the difficulty in getting accurate data of the production of half a billion farms, most of them living in a largely informal economy. Equally, I think most of us know that it is difficult to get data about what people actually eat. It is one thing to know what consumers buy – although it is already hard to get proper data on that in most places in the world – but much more difficult to know what they end up eating. And of course, if we look at historical data, the quality of data can be even poorer. The reader should keep in mind that there is no database with *complete and accurate* data for crop, animal and food production or consumption. So, there might be some errors in some details in my discussion. But by and large I think the data presented gives a reasonably comprehensive picture of pertinent aspects of our food system, and in particular about the direction in which it has and is moving.

I have made extensive calculations based on FAOSTAT, the USDA National Nutrient Database for Standard Reference, the FAO's Technical Conversion Factors (for rates of conversion e.g. from husked rice to milled rice), Feedipedia[a] and a few other sources. The case of beer made of barley, illustrates the complexities of the food system and calculations. According to the United States Department of Agriculture's *National Nutrient Database for Standard Reference* an average beer has 43 calories per hundred grams. From 1 kg of barley you can produce approximately 730 grams of malt. This malt is in turn converted to 4.7 liters of beer according to United Nations Food and Agriculture Organisation's *Technical Conversion Factors*. Based on FAOSTAT/categories of use, I estimate that 20% of barley produced in the world (132,886,519 tons) is used for brewing. Multiply this total by 20% and 4.7 and this gives 124,913,328,000 liters of beer, which equals 53,712,730,970,000 calories. This would be 21 calories per capita per day (assuming that infants also drink beer!), 1% of our total energy intake. If we compare this with directly using barley as food, 20% of the 132,886,519 tons of barley has 94,000,000,000,000 calories – which means we lose almost half of the energy of the barley by making beer out of it. But then we also have 'dregs' the residual product after brewing that is mainly used as animal feed, so some of this enters our food in another way. By and large this picture also applies to the process of grain-based biofuel production.

Vegetable oils, oilseeds and oilseed cakes or meal are another complicated group of crops. Together they are the most important categories (by volume) in international trade. Sometimes the oilseed is traded as such, but often the processing is done in the country where it is produced and the oil and/or the cake are exported. Calculating feed conversion rates in animals is also problematic especially as these differ a lot in different systems. There is, for instance, no reliable global statistic on the amount of grass converted to food by ruminants. So while the FAO statistics tell us that 1543 kcal per capita per day is used for animal feed and we get 510 kcal from livestock products we don't know how many of those 510 calories are directly from the feed used and how many come from grazing.

---

[a] An online feed database managed by *Institut National de la Recherche Agronomique, Centre de Coopération Internationale en Recherche Agronomique pour le Développement, Association Française de Zootechnie* and the FAO.

Table 6. Global crop areas 2012, 60 main crops

Crop	Area harvested (ha)	Percent of area	Production (tons)
Wheat	215,489,485	16.3%	670,875,110
Maize	177,379,507	13.4%	872,066,770
Rice, paddy	163,199,090	12.3%	719,738,273
Soybeans	104,997,253	7.9%	241,841,416
Barley	49,525,988	3.7%	132,886,519
Sorghum	38,161,647	2.9%	57,004,922
Seed cotton	34,700,133	2.6%	76,530,054
Rapeseed	34,085,066	2.6%	65,058,240
Millet	31,757,583	2.4%	29,866,016
Beans, dry	29,290,861	2.2%	23,598,102
Sugar cane	26,088,636	2.0%	1,832,541,194
Sunflower seed	24,843,104	1.9%	37,449,403
Groundnuts, with shell	24,709,458	1.9%	41,185,933
Cassava	20,385,206	1.5%	262,585,741
Potatoes	19,202,082	1.5%	364,808,768
Vegetables, fresh other	18,959,594	1.4%	269,852,343
Oil, palm fruit	17,243,830	1.3%	249,528,288
Chick peas	12,344,291	0.9%	11,625,545
Coconuts	12,114,141	0.9%	60,048,837
Cow peas, dry	11,294,193	0.9%	5,714,575
Olives	10,201,495	0.8%	16,555,375
Coffee, green	10,039,846	0.8%	8,826,903
Cocoa, beans	9,933,462	0.8%	5,003,211
Rubber, natural	9,864,054	0.7%	11,445,176
Oats	9,608,318	0.7%	21,062,972
Sweet potatoes	8,087,116	0.6%	103,145,500
Sesame seed	7,897,048	0.6%	4,036,289
Grapes	6,969,373	0.5%	67,067,129
Peas, dry	6,593,926	0.5%	9,830,016
Pulses, other	5,933,408	0.4%	5,169,161

Rye	5,564,996	0.4%	14,562,055
Plantains	5,407,361	0.4%	37,162,205
Pigeon peas	5,324,322	0.4%	4,237,122
Cashew nuts, with shell	5,313,415	0.4%	4,152,315
Mangoes, mangosteens, guavas	5,167,300	0.4%	42,139,837
Yams	5,036,905	0.4%	58,754,533
Bananas	4,953,315	0.4%	101,992,743
Sugar beet	4,900,845	0.4%	269,865,481
Fruit, fresh other	4,874,778	0.4%	31,447,977
Apples	4,842,822	0.4%	76,378,738
Tomatoes	4,803,680	0.4%	161,793,834
Tobacco, unmanufactured	4,291,014	0.3%	7,490,661
Lentils	4,206,024	0.3%	4,557,972
Onions, dry	4,203,648	0.3%	82,851,732
Cereals, other	3,954,285	0.3%	5,621,903
Oranges	3,816,692	0.3%	68,223,759
Triticale	3,691,578	0.3%	13,671,027
Watermelons	3,472,997	0.3%	105,372,341
Tea	3,275,991	0.2%	4,818,118
Fruit, tropical fresh other	2,788,155	0.2%	20,416,074
Plums and sloes	2,531,479	0.2%	10,702,774
Buckwheat	2,525,124	0.2%	2,275,005
Broad beans, horse beans, dry	2,513,439	0.2%	4,222,931
Linseed	2,485,810	0.2%	2,054,728
Cabbages and other brassicas	2,391,747	0.2%	70,104,972
Tangerines, mandarins, etc.	2,345,020	0.2%	27,060,756
Peas, green	2,266,369	0.2%	18,490,920
Cucumbers and gherkins	2,109,651	0.2%	65,134,078
Chillies and peppers, dry	1,989,664	0.2%	3,352,163
The rest	59,919,000	4.5%	
SUM	1,321,866,620	100.0%	

Source: FAOSTAT

Table 7. Main crops, area planted 2012, production and their share of global production of calories and protein. Descending order of share of calorific supply

Crop	Area harvested (ha)	Production (tons)	Protein %	kcal %	Million kcal/ha
Maize	177,379,507	872,066,770	19.6%	22.1%	17.9
Wheat	215,489,485	670,875,110	16.8%	15.8%	10.6
Rice, paddy	163,199,090	719,738,273	10.6%	14.2%	12.6
Soybeans	104,997,253	241,841,416	21.4%	7.5%	10.3
Sugar cane	26,088,636	1,832,541,194	0.0%	7.3%	40.3
Oil, palm fruit	17,243,830	249,528,288	0.3%	3.5%	30.1
Barley	49,525,988	132,886,519	3.3%	3.3%	9.5
Cassava	20,385,206	262,585,741	0.9%	2.9%	20.6
Rapeseed	34,085,066	65,058,240	3.0%	1.9%	7.9
Groundnuts, with shell	24,709,458	41,185,933	1.8%	1.6%	9.5
Sunflower seed	24,843,104	37,449,403	1.9%	1.5%	8.8
Potatoes	19,202,082	364,808,768	2.3%	1.5%	11.0
Sorghum	38,161,647	57,004,922	1.5%	1.3%	5.1
Sugar beet	4,900,845	269,865,481	1.0%	1.3%	37.3
Seed cotton	34,700,133	76,530,054	2.4%	1.0%	4.0
Millet	31,757,583	29,866,016	0.8%	0.8%	3.6
Vegetables, fresh other	18,959,594	269,852,343	1.5%	0.7%	5.7
Bananas	4,953,315	101,992,743	0.3%	0.6%	18.3
Sweet potatoes	8,087,116	103,145,500	0.4%	0.6%	11.0
Beans, dry	29,290,861	23,598,102	1.2%	0.6%	2.7
Yams	5,036,905	58,754,533	0.2%	0.5%	13.8
Oats	9,608,318	21,062,972	0.5%	0.4%	6.0
Rye	5,564,996	14,562,055	0.4%	0.3%	8.8
Grapes	6,969,373	67,067,129	0.1%	0.3%	6.6
Triticale	3,691,578	13,671,027	0.4%	0.3%	12.4
Plantains	5,407,361	37,162,205	0.1%	0.3%	8.4
Chick peas	12,344,291	11,625,545	0.5%	0.3%	3.4

Apples	4,842,822	76,378,738	0.1%	0.3%	8.2
Olives	10,201,495	16,555,375	0.0%	0.2%	3.3
Peas, dry	6,593,926	9,830,016	0.6%	0.2%	5.1
Onions, dry	4,203,648	82,851,732	0.2%	0.2%	7.9
Coconuts	12,114,141	60,048,837	0.1%	0.2%	2.7
Oranges	3,816,692	68,223,759	0.1%	0.2%	8.4
Watermelons	3,472,997	105,372,341	0.2%	0.2%	9.1
Tomatoes	4,803,680	161,793,834	0.3%	0.2%	6.1
Mangoes, guavas, etc	5,167,300	42,139,837	0.1%	0.2%	4.9
Cocoa, beans	9,933,462	5,003,211	0.0%	0.2%	2.5
Sesame seed	7,897,048	4,036,289	0.2%	0.2%	2.9
Cereals, other	3,954,285	5,621,903	0.2%	0.1%	5.0
Cow peas, dry	11,294,193	5,714,575	0.3%	0.1%	1.7
Fruit, fresh other	4,874,778	31,447,977	0.1%	0.1%	3.9
Pulses, other	5,933,408	5,169,161	0.3%	0.1%	3.0
Lentils	4,206,024	4,557,972	0.3%	0.1%	3.7
Pigeon peas	5,324,322	4,237,122	0.2%	0.1%	2.7
Cashew nuts,	5,313,415	4,152,315	0.1%	0.0%	1.3
Rubber, natural	9,864,054	11,445,176	0.0%	0.0%	0.0
Coffee, green	10,039,846	8,826,903	0.0%	0.0%	0.0
Tobacco, unmanufactured	4,291,014	7,490,661	0.0%	0.0%	0.0
Tea	3,275,991	4,818,118	0.0%	0.0%	0.0
Other	83,865,623	773,456,766	3.7%	4.3%	7.4

Source: Own calculations based on FAOSTAT, the USDA National Nutrient Database for Standard Reference, FAO Technical Conversion Factors, and Feedipedia.

Protein and calorie contents of the categories 'Other' 'Vegetables, other' and 'Fruit, other' are largely guesswork. The data is about production and not human consumption. Soybeans produce 21% of all protein, but human consumption of soybeans and processed soya is low, most soybeans are used as animal feed, and much of the protein is 'lost' in the conversion to milk, egg or meat.

Table 8. Global food trade 2011/12, 20 main food products by weight

Commodity	Quantity (tons)	Rank	Value (1000 $)	Rank
Wheat	147,205,956	1	51,184,264	2
Maize	108,067,148	2	36,342,489	5
Soybeans	90,813,977	3	51,403,325	1
Cake of soybeans	63,593,084	4	27,458,049	10
Palm oil	36,589,672	5	42,034,273	4
Sugar, raw centrifugal	33,838,303	6	22,649,899	15
Barley	24,260,294	7	7,339,628	42
Sugar refined	21,921,611	8	16,694,636	20
Waters, ice etc	20,309,400	9	3,190,496	81
Bananas	18,918,792	10	13,068,904	22
Rapeseed	18,029,793	11	11,789,984	26
Beverage non-alcoholic	14,941,618	12	14,911,417	21
Food prep various	13,416,474	13	49,892,030	3
Flour of wheat	12,893,516	14	5,915,524	49
Potatoes	12,243,448	15	4,936,529	58
Beer of barley	11,828,244	16	11,711,267	27
Chicken meat	11,391,477	17	21,792,056	18
Food wastes	10,540,514	18	8,956,976	34
Soybean oil	10,202,399	19	12,549,664	25
Wine	10,004,329	20	33,041,355	7

Source: FAOSTAT

Soya products have three positions in the table as soybeans, cake and oil. Taken together their weight is 164,609,460 tons and their value is US$91,411,038,000, making soybeans the most important traded crop in the world. Some processed products are high value per weight and don't appear in the list. For example rubber is the 6th most valuable product, but comes number 27 in weight; coffee is number 8 in value but number 34 in quantity; distilled beverages are number 9 in value and 56 in weight; cattle meat, cigarettes and cheese come in 11th, 12th and 13t[h] in value respectively. It is intriguing that the quantity of food waste that is traded is almost the same as the quantity of chicken meat or beer, and more than wine – more than ten million tons of food waste is traded globally. It is perhaps even more interesting that the value of the trade in food waste is nine billion dollars. This means that the waste is traded for almost a dollar per kg. I did not have the energy to investigate this further.

Table 9. Commodity imports, 20 main import streams 2011

Area	Commodity	Value (1000 $)
China, mainland	Soybeans	29,726,067
China, mainland	Cotton lint	9,466,067
China, mainland	Rubber, natural dry	8,572,961
United States of America	Coffee, green	7,081,860
India	Palm oil	6,765,572
China, mainland	Palm oil	6,634,042
United States of America	Distilled beverages	6,399,268
Japan	Cigarettes	5,758,924
Japan	Maize	5,347,247
Japan	Pork	5,205,930
United States of America	Wine	5,046,034
Germany	Coffee, green	4,902,386
United States of America	Rubber, natural dry	4,837,811
United Kingdom	Wine	4,781,924
Germany	Cheese of cow milk	3,997,915
United States of America	Beer of barley	3,795,971
Japan	Rubber, natural dry	3,783,464
Germany	Wine	3,252,589
Egypt	Wheat	3,199,207
United Kingdom	Prepared foods	3,111,616

Source: FAOSTAT

Table 10. Commodity exports, 20 main export streams 2011

Area	Commodity	Value (1000 $)
United States of America	Soybeans	17,563,868
Malaysia	Palm oil	17,452,177
Indonesia	Palm oil	17,261,248
Brazil	Soybeans	16,327,287
United States of America	Maize	13,982,404
Indonesia	Rubber, natural dry	11,735,105
Brazil	Sugar, raw centrifugal	11,548,786
United States of America	Wheat	11,134,659
Thailand	Rubber, natural dry	10,634,724
France	Wine	9,941,495
Argentina	Cake of soybeans	9,906,725
United States of America	Cotton lint	8,425,179
United Kingdom	Distilled alcoholic bev.	8,330,057
Brazil	Coffee, green	8,000,416
Brazil	Chicken meat	7,063,214
France	Wheat	6,738,299
Italy	Wine	6,075,404
Canada	Wheat	5,742,111
Australia	Wheat	5,709,036
Brazil	Cake of soybeans	5,697,860

Source: FAOSTAT

Table 11. Global average food supply per capita 2009

item	Energy (kcal/capita/day)	Protein (g/capita/day)	Fat (g/capita/day)
Grand Total + (Total)	**2831**	**79,3**	**81,81**
Vegetal Products + (Total)	2330	48,08	45,14
Animal Products + (Total)	501	31,2	36,7
Cereals - Excluding Beer + (Total)	*1292*	*32*	*5,9*
Wheat	532	16,2	2,4
Rice (Milled Equivalent)	536	10,1	1,5
Barley	7	0,2	0
Maize	141	3,4	1,2
Rye	6	0,2	0
Oats	3	0,1	0,1
Millet	27	0,7	0,3
Sorghum	32	1	0,3
Cereals, Other	7	0,2	0
Starchy Roots + (Total)	*136*	*2,2*	*0,3*
Cassava	37	0,2	0,1
Potatoes	61	1,4	0,1
Sweet Potatoes	22	0,2	0,1
Yams	11	0,2	0
Roots, Other	6	0,1	0
Sugar crops + (Total)	*4*	*0*	*0*
Sugar Cane	4	0	0
Sugar Beet	0	0	0
Sugar & Sweeteners + (Total)	*224*	*0*	*0*
Sugar, Non-Centrifugal	7	0	0
Sugar (Raw Equivalent)	194		
Sweeteners, Other	22	0	0
Honey	2	0	0

Pulses + (Total)	62	3,9	0,4
Beans	22	1,4	0,1
Peas	8	0,5	0
Pulses, Other	32	2	0,3
Tree nuts + (Total)	14	0,4	1,1
Oilcrops + (Total)	56	2,7	4,1
Soybeans	15	1,4	0,6
Groundnuts (Shelled Equivalent)	21	0,9	1,7
Sunflower seed	1	0	0
Rape and Mustard seed	2	0,1	0,1
Cottonseed	0	0	0
Coconuts - Including copra	12	0,1	1
Sesame seed	3	0,1	0,3
Palm kernels	0	0	0
Olives	2	0	0,2
Oilcrops, Other	1	0,1	0,1
Vegetable Oils + (Total)	277	0	31,3
Soybean Oil	80	0	9,1
Groundnut Oil	16	0	1,8
Sunflower seed Oil	33	0	3,7
Rape and Mustard Oil	35	0	4
Cottonseed Oil	13	0	1,5
Palmkernel Oil	7	0	0,8
Palm Oil	53	0	5,9
Coconut Oil	8	0	0,9
Sesame seed Oil	3	0	0,3
Olive Oil	11	0	1,2
Ricebran Oil	3	0	0,4
Maize Germ Oil	8	0	0,9
Oilcrops Oil, Other	7	0	0,8
Vegetables + (Total)	87	4,5	0,76

Tomatoes	10	0,54	0,13
Onions	10	0,4	0,1
Vegetables, Other	67	3,6	0,6
Fruits - Excluding Wine + (Total)	92	*1,1*	*0,6*
Oranges, Mandarines	9	0,2	0
Lemons, Limes	1	0	0
Grapefruit	1	0	0
Citrus, Other	1	0	0
Bananas	20	0,3	0,1
Plantains	9	0,1	0
Apples	11	0,1	0,1
Pineapples	3	0	0
Dates	4	0	0
Grapes	6	0,1	0
Fruits, Other	28	0,3	0,3
Stimulants + (Total)	7	*0,5*	*0,4*
Coffee	1	0,2	
Cocoa Beans	5	0,1	0,4
Tea	1	0,2	
Spices + (Total)	9	*0,3*	*0,3*
Pepper	0	0	0
Pimento	4	0,1	0,2
Cloves	0	0	0
Spices, Other	5	0,2	0,1
Alcoholic Beverages + (Total)	67	*0,3*	*0*
Wine	7	0	
Beer	31	0,3	
Beverages, Fermented	5	0	0
Beverages, Alcoholic	24	0	
Meat + (Total)	230	*14,1*	*18,8*
Bovine Meat	40	3,6	2,7

Mutton & Goat Meat	11	0,7	0,9
Pig meat	123	4,6	11,4
Poultry Meat	54	4,7	3,7
Meat, Other	3	0,4	0,1
Offal + (Total)	*7*	*1,1*	*0,2*
Animal Fats + (Total)	*60*	*0,1*	*6,7*
Butter, Ghee	28	0	3,2
Cream	2	0	0,2
Fats, Animals, Raw	30	0	3,3
Fish, Body Oil	0	0	0
Fish, Liver Oil	0	0	0
Eggs + (Total)	35	2,7	2,5
Milk - Excluding Butter + (Total)	134	8	7,3
Fish, Seafood + (Total)	*33*	*5,1*	*1,2*
Freshwater Fish	11	1,8	0,4
Demersal Fish	6	0,9	0,2
Pelagic Fish	9	1,3	0,4
Marine Fish, Other	2	0,4	0,1
Crustaceans	2	0,4	0
Cephalopods	1	0,2	0
Mollusks, Other	1	0,2	0
Aquatic Products, Other + (Total)	*2*	*0,2*	*0*
Meat, Aquatic Mammals	0	0	0
Aquatic Animals, Others	0	0	0
Aquatic Plants	2	0,1	0
Miscellaneous + (Total)	2	0,1	0

Source: FAOSTAT

Table 12. Global biofuel production 2011

	Biodiesel million liter/year	Ethanol million liter/year
Canada	139	1,393
United States	1,300	50,338
Brazil	2,386	28,203
Colombia	418	279
Austria	331	145
Belgium	493	290
Finland	325	17
France	2,147	1,045
Germany	2,843	754
Italy	841	116
Netherlands	435	116
Poland	406	232
Portugal	348	0
Spain	928	464
Sweden	232	203
United Kingdom	232	290
Australia	81	377
China	348	2,147
India	116	290
Indonesia	464	6
Korea, South	377	0
Thailand	638	435
Rest	3,768	1,506
World	19,600	88,648

Source: United States Energy Information Administration, International Energy Statistics, Biofuels production

For the calculations of how many calories are diverted to biofuel, I have calculated that all biodiesel is made from soybeans, even though some is made from rape seed or other sources. I have used the calorific content of the soybeans used to produce a quantity of soybean oil (with a 5.55 conversion rate) which is then converted to biodiesel with a 98% conversion factor. For ethanol I have calculated that a country uses either maize, wheat or sugar cane as feed stock, even if a few countries also use other sources, e.g. cassava. I used the same conversion figure for maize and wheat, 2.69 kg used for 1 liter ethanol produced. For cane, I have assumed that 1kg of sugar yields 0.684 liter of ethanol. This lead to the conclusion that the total calories per capita diverted to biofuels are oilcrops: 194, cereals: 215, cane: 71, giving a total of 480.

Acknowledgements

The book was written in a one year period, from August 2013 to July 2014. It benefits greatly from the many sources used, and from discussions with many over the years. Some people were interviewed specifically for this book and I made a few study visits as part of the research for the book. I thank all those who contributed their time. Many of the practical cases and examples I mention are from my work as a consultant over two decades. Some of them, such as the examples of the farmers Bob and Susan, originate from visits made in the process of writing the book *Jorden vi äter* ('the Earth we Eat'), commissioned by the Swedish Society for Nature Conservation, which I co-authored with Ann-Helen Meyer von Bremen. Some chapters are based on texts which have previously been published on my blog, Garden Earth.

I am grateful to René and Renétje Vossenaar who leant me their lovely house outside of Geneva to make some major progress with the book. I am also indebted to the excellent libraries of the city of Uppsala; the City Library but even more the libraries of the Swedish Agriculture University and the University of Uppsala. The manuscript was reviewed by Ann-Helen Meyer von Bremen, Joelle Katto-Andrighetto and Joe Clarkson all of whom gave me very valuable feed-back to the text. The English language editing was done by Nick Parrott at TextualHealing.nl who had to correct my many mistakes and also gave valuable feed back on the content.

A special thanks to Ugandan singer-songwriter Susanne Anique for letting me reproduce her poem *Making Luwombo*.

About the Author

Gunnar Rundgren has worked with most parts of the organic agriculture sector from farming to policy since 1977, starting on the pioneer organic farm, Torfolk. He is the founder and a senior consultant of Grolink (www.grolink.se), a consultancy company engaged in certification development, policy development, project development, marketing strategies and international training programmes – mainly targeting developing countries. He has been engaged as a consultant by NGOs, governments, private companies and intergovernmental organisations such as OECD, UNCTAD, UNEP, the World Bank and the FAO.

Rundgren is the initiator of several organisations for organic agriculture in Sweden, including its main eco-label KRAV (www.krav.se) where he was the director for the first eight years. He served as the first President of the Accreditation Programme Board of the International Federation of Organic Agriculture Movements (IFOAM) 1992-1997. He became an IFOAM World Board member in 1998 and the IFOAM President during the period 2000-2005. In 2002 he was a founding board member of the ISEAL Alliance.

He has published several books and reports related to organic farming. In 2010, he published a book about the major social and environmental challenges of our world: *Garden Earth: From hunter and gatherer to global capitalism and thereafter*. He also co-authored the book *Jorden vi Äter*, published in 2012, about the challenge of feeding the world's population in a sustainable way. His books have been translated to several languages.

Rundgren was awarded an honorary doctorate in Science at the Uganda Martyrs University 2009. The same year, he was appointed a Member of the Royal Swedish Academy of Agriculture and Forestry.

Internet: gardenearth.blogspot.com/
Contact: info@gardenearth.info

References

1   World Instant Noodles Association 2014 *'Expanding Markets'* http://instantnoodles.org.

2   Fabiosa, J. F. 2011. 'Globalization and food consumption' in J. L. Lusk, J. Roosen and J. Shogren (Eds) *The Oxford Handbook of The Economics of Food Consumption and Policy.* Oxford Handbooks in Economics.

3   Woody, T. 2010 *'Recycling Land for Green Energy Ideas'.* New York Times, www.nytimes.com.

4   Swedish Army Museum 2013 Exhibition at the Swedish Army Museum (visited 22 December 2013).

5   Honsberg C. and S. Bowden (undated) *'Average Solar Radiation'.* Photovoltaic Education Network, http://pveducation.org.

6   Bayliss-Smith, T. P. 1982 *The Ecology of Agricultural Systems* Cambridge University Press.

7   Uhlin, H. E. 1997 Energiflöden i livsmedelskedjan. Naturvårdsverket.

8   Richards, R.A. 2000 'Selectable traits to increase crop photosynthesis and yield of grain crops', *Journal of Experimental Botany,* Vol. 51, GMP special issue, pp 447-458.

9   Mann, C. C. 2005 *1491: New Revelations of the American before Columbus.* Alfred A. Knopf.

10   Frachetti, M. D. 2008 *Pastoralist Landscapes and Social Interaction in Bronze Age Eurasia.* University of California Press.

11   Higman, B.H. 2011 *How Food Made History* Wiley-Blackwell.

12   Kay, R. N. B. 1970 'Meat production from wild herbivores'. *Proceedings of the Nutrition Society* 29(2) (December): 271–278.

13   Livi-Bacci, M. 1992 *A Concise History of World Population,* translated by C. Ipsen. Blackwell Publishers.

14   Tansey, G. and T. Worsley 1995 *The Food System: A Guide* Earthscan.

15   Mann, C. C. 2005 *1491: New Revelations of the American before Columbus.* Alfred A. Knopf.

16   Higman, B.H. 2011 *How Food Made History* Wiley-Blackwell.

17   Bliege Bird, R., D. W. Bird, B. F. Codding, C. H. Parker and J. H. Jones 2008 'The "fire stick farming" hypothesis: Australian Aboriginal foraging strategies, biodiversity, and anthropogenic fire mosaics'. *Proceedings of the National Academy of Sciences of the United States of America.* 105 (39).

18   Bharucha, Z and J. Pretty. 2010. 'The roles and values of wild foods in agricultural systems'. *Philosphical Transactions of the Royal Society: Biological Sciences* 365, 2913–2926.

19   Rousseau, J. J. 1964 *The First and Second Discourses,* translated by R. D. Masters and J. R. Masters. New York: St Martin's Press.

20   Wikipedia 2014. *'Dog'* http://en.wikipedia.org/wiki/Dog.

21   Pelto, G. H. and P.J. Pelto 1983 'Diet and delocalization: Dietary changes since 1750'. *Journal of Interdisciplinary History,* vol 14 No 2, pp. 507-528.

22   Laudan, R. 2009 *'Bread, beer and agriculture',* 7 December 2009, www.rachellaudan.com.

23   Laudan, R. 2013 *Cuisine and Empire, Cooking in World History* California Studies in Food and Culture.
24   Fay, J. C. and J. A. Benavides 2005 'Evidence for domesticated and wild populations of Saccharomyces cerevisiae'. *Plos Genetics*.
25   Curtis, R. I. 2001 *Ancient Food Technology* Brill Academic Publishing.
26   Ibid.
27   Ibid.
28   Ibid.
29   Ibid.
30   Ibid.
31   Fieldhouse, P. 1998 *Food and Nutrition, Customs and Culture* Stanley Thornes Ltd.
32   Curtis, R. I. 2001 *Ancient Food Technology* Brill Academic Publishing.
33   Laudan, R. 2013 *Cuisine and Empire, Cooking in World History* California Studies in Food and Culture.
34   Higman, B.H. 2011 *How Food Made History* Wiley-Blackwell.
35   Laudan, R. 2013 *Cuisine and Empire, Cooking in World History* California Studies in Food and Culture.
36   Kiple, K. and K.C. Ornelas (editors) 2000 *Cambridge World History of Food*. Cambridge University Press.
37   Hughes, D. J. 2001 *An Environmental History of the World* Routledge.
38   Higman, B.H. 2011 *How Food Made History* Wiley-Blackwell.
39   Radkau, J. 2008 *Nature and Power: A Global History of Environment* Cambridge University Press.
40   Bath, B. S. van. 1976 *De agrarische geschiedenis van West-Europa (500–1850)*. Het Spectrum.
41   Columella. *De re rustica*. In Swedish translation 2009 *Tolv böcker om lantbruk* Royal Swedish Academy of Agriculture and Forestry.
42   Boserup, E 2005 The Conditions of Agriculture Growth: The economics of agrarian change under population pressure. Transaction Publishers.
43   Mazoyer, M. and L. Roudart 2006 *A History of World Agriculture: From the Neolithic Age to the Current Crisis* Monthly Review Press.
44   Sörlin, S. and P. Warde (editors) 2009 *Nature's End, History and Environment* Palgrave MacMillan.
45   Grantham, G. W. 1993 'Divisions of labour: agricultural productivity and occupational specialization in pre-industrial France'. *The Economic History Review* New Series, 46 (3) pp. 478-502.
46   Ernle, L. 1936 *English Farming Past and Present*. Fifth Edition. Longmans, Green & Co., Ltd.
47   Federico, G. 2005 *Feeding the World* Princeton.
48   Haines, M 2013 'Fertility and Mortality in the United States'. http://eh.net/encyclopedia.
49   Federico, G. 2005 *Feeding the World* Princeton.
50   Ibid.
51   Bath, B. S. van. 1976 *De agrarische geschiedenis van West-Europa (500–1850)*. Het Spectrum.
52   USDA Economic Research Service 2013 *Farm Size and the Organization of U.S. Crop Farming* Economic Resaerch Report 152 United States Department of Agriculture.
53   Federico, G. 2005 *Feeding the World* Princeton.
54   Liljewall, B. (editor) 1999 *Agrarian Systems in Early Modern Europe* Nordiska Museets Förlag.
55   Grigg, D. 1983 *The Dynamics of Agricultural Change* Palgrave Macmillan.
56   Living History Farm 2014 'Farming in the 1930s' www.livinghistoryfarm.org.

[57]   Lesney,M. 2014 Agriculture and Food Chemicals'. *Enterprise of the Chemical Science*

[58]   Living History Farm 2014 *'Farming in the 1940s' www.livinghistoryfarm.org*.

[59]   Bellamy Foster, J and B. Clark, 2004 'Ecological imperialism: the curse of capitalism'. *Socialist Register*.

[60]   Grigg, D. 1983 *The Dynamics of Agricultural Change* Palgrave Macmillan.

[61]   Federico, G. 2005 *Feeding the World* Princeton.

[62]   Grigg, D. 1983 *The Dynamics of Agricultural Change* Palgrave Macmillan.

[63]   Federico, G. 2005 *Feeding the World* Princeton.

[64]   Mazoyer, M. and L. Roudart 2006 *A History of World Agriculture: From the Neolithic Age to the Current Crisis* Monthly Review Press.

[65]   Federico, G. 2005 *Feeding the World* Princeton.

[66]   International Service for the Acquisition of Agri-Biotech Applications 2012 *'Global Status of Commercialized Biotech/GM Crops: 2012'*. Brief 44-2012. www.isaaa.org.

[67]   Prasad, A 2012 Like a virgin One World Publications.

[68]   USDA Economic Research Service 2013 *Farm Size and the Organization of U.S. Crop Farming* Economic Resaerch Report 152 United States Department of Agriculture.

[69]   Statistics Denmark 2014 http://www.dst.dk/

[70]   Schnepf, R. 2014 *US Farm Incomes* United States Congressional Research Service.

[71]   Federico, G. 2005 *Feeding the World* Princeton.

[72]   Livi-Bacci, M. 1992 *A Concise History of World Population*, translated by C. Ipsen. Blackwell Publishers

[73]   Radkau, J. 2008 *Nature and Power: A Global History of Environment* Cambridge University Press.

[74]   Federico, G. 2005 *Feeding the World* Princeton.

[75]   Mazoyer, M. and L. Roudart 2006 *A History of World Agriculture: From the Neolithic Age to the Current Crisis* Monthly Review Press.

[76]   Boserup, E. 2005 The Conditions of Agriculture Growth: The economics of agrarian change under population pressure. Transaction Publishers.

[77]   Federico, G. 2005 *Feeding the World* Princeton.

[78]   Radkau, J. 2008 *Nature and Power: A Global History of Environment* Cambridge University Press.

[79]   Mazoyer, M. and L. Roudart 2006 *A History of World Agriculture: From the Neolithic Age to the Current Crisis* Monthly Review Press.

[80]   UNFPA 2011 *State of World Population 2011–People and Possibilities in a World of 7 Billion* United Nations Population Fund.

[81]   McDonald. R. I., P.J. Marcotullio and B. Güneralp 2013 'Urbanization and global trends in biodiversity and ecosystem services' in Th. Elmqvist et al. 2013, *Urbanization, Biodiversity and Ecosystem Services: Challenges and opportunities,* Springer.

[82]   Satterthwaite, D., G. McGranahan and C. Tacoli 2010 'Urbanization and its implications for food and farming', *Philosophical Transactions of the Royal Society B-Biological Sciences* 365, 2809–2820.

[83]   Ibid.

[84]   Hughes, D. J. 2001 *An Environmental History of the World* Routledge.

[85]   Morley, N. 1996 *Metropolis and Hinterland* Cambridge University Press.

[86]   Steel, C. 2008 *Hungry City* Chatto&Windus.

[87]   Morley, N. 1996 *Metropolis and Hinterland* Cambridge University Press.

[88]   Ibid.

[89]   Ibid.

[90]   Ibid.

[91]   Satterthwaite, D, G. McGranahan and C. Tacoli 2010 'Urbanization and its implications for food and farming', *Philosophical Transactions of the Royal Society B-Biological Sciences B-Biological Sciences* (2010) 365, 2809–2820.

92   Wenzlau, S. 2014 *'Agricultural Population Growth Marginal as Nonagricultural Population Soars'* http://blogs.worldwatch.org

93   Pearce, F. 2014 *'Forget future land and water scarcity, will there be enough farmers?'* http://wle.cgiar.org.

94   Policy Link and the Food Trust 2010 *The Grocery Gap: Who has access to health food and why it matters.* http://thefoodtrust.org.

95   Vries, J. de 2008 *The Industrious Revolution* Cambridge University Press.

96   Mintz, S. 1985 *Sweetness and Power. The place of sugar in modern history* Viking Penguin.

97   Vries, J. de 2008 *The Industrious Revolution* Cambridge University Press.

98   Atkins, P. J., P. Lummel and D. J. Oddy (editors) 2007 *Food and the City in Europe since 1800.* Farnham, Ashgate.

99   Vries, J. de 2008 *The Industrious Revolution* Cambridge University Press.

100   Jones, O. R. 1993 'Commercial foods, 1740-1820'. *Historical Archaeology,* 1993, 27(2):25-41

101   Vries, J. de 2008 *The Industrious Revolution* Cambridge University Press.

102   Ibid.

103   Grigg, D. 1983 *The Dynamics of Agricultural Change* Palgrave Macmillan.

104   Regmi, A. and M. Gehlhar (editors) 2005 *'New Directions in Global Food Markets',* USDA Agriculture Information Bulletin Number 794.

105   Plunkett Research Ltd. 2013 *'Introduction to the Food & Beverage Industry'* www.plunkettresearch.com.

106   Larsson, R. 2009 Från stall till maskinhall Albinsson Sjögren bokförlag.

107   Plunkett Research Ltd. 2013 *'Introduction to the Food & Beverage Industry'* www.plunkettresearch.com.

108   Cutler, D. M. E.L. Glaeser and J.M. Shapiro 2003 'Why have Americans become more obese?' *Journal of Economic Perspectives.* 17 (3) pps 93–118.

109   Bryson, B. 2010 *At Home: A short history of private life* Doubleday.

110   FAO 2003 *World Agriculture: Towards 2015/2030. An FAO Perspective* Earthscan.

111   Mazoyer, M. and L. Roudart 2006 *A History of World Agriculture: From the Neolithic Age to the Current Crisis* Monthly Review Press.

112   Radkau, J. 2008 *Nature and Power: A Global History of Environment* Cambridge University Press.

113   Fieldhouse, P. 1998 *Food and Nutrition, Customs and Culture* Stanley Thornes Ltd.

114   Ibid.

115   Cohen, Y. A. 1968 'Food, Consumption Patterns' in *International Encyclopedia of the Social Sciences. Encyclopedia.com* www.encyclopedia.com.

116   Wilk, R. 2009 'Difference on the menu: neophilia, neophobia and globalization' in Inglis, D. and D. Giimlin (editors) *The Globalization of Food* Berg.

117   Inglis, D. and D. Giimlin (editors) 2009 *The Globalization of Food* Berg.

118   Hughes, D. J. 2001 *An Environmental History of the World* Routledge.

119   Polanyi, K. 1944 *The Great Transformation: The political and economic origins of our times* Farrar & Rinehart.

120   Steel, C. 2008 *Hungry City* Chatto &Windus.

121   Fernández-Armesto, F. 2001 *Food, a History* Macmillan.

122   Fraser, E. D.G. and A. Rimas 2010 *Empires of Food. Feast, famine and the rise and fall of civilizations* Free Press.

123   Morley, N. 1996 *Metropolis and Hinterland* Cambridge University Press.

124   Ibid.

125   Bardi, U. 2014 *'Power is nothing without control: how to lose an empire'* http://cassandralegacy.blogspot.se.

126   Ibid.

[127] Austen, R. A. 1987 *African Economic History* James Currey Ltd.
[128] Polanyi, K. 1944 *The Great Transformation: The political and economic origins of our times* Farrar & Rinehart.
[129] Persson, K. G. 2005 *Grain Markets in Europe, 1500-1900: Integration and Deregulation* Cambridge University Press.
[130] Steel, C. 2008 *Hungry City* Chatto&Windus.
[131] Persson, K. G. 2005 *Grain Markets in Europe, 1500-1900: Integration and Deregulation* Cambridge University Press.
[132] Atkins, P. J., P. Lummel and D. J. Oddy (editors) 2007 *Food and the City in Europe since 1800* Ashgate.
[133] Rioxson, D. 2010 *The History of Meat Trading* Nottingham University Press.
[134] Liljewall, B. (editor) 1999 *Agrarian Systems in Early Modern Europe* Nordiska Museets Förlag.
[135] Sörlin, S. and P. Warde (editors) 2009 *Nature's End, History and Environment* Palgrave MacMillan.
[136] Rioxson, D. 2010 *The History of Meat Trading* Nottingham University Press.
[137] Fordham University 2013 *'Medieval Sourcebook: The assizes of bread, beer, & lucrum pistoris'*, www.fordham.edu.
[138] Karlsson, G. and A. Sagnér (editors) 1953 *Boken om kött* B. Forsberg.
[139] Johnson, A., A. Brundin and E. Kroon 2012 *Kött och Blod* Informationsförlaget.
[140] Polanyi, K. 1944 *The Great Transformation: The political and economic origins of our times* Farrar & Rinehart.
[141] Persson, K. G. 2005 *Grain Markets in Europe, 1500-1900: Integration and Deregulation* Cambridge University Press.
[142] Atkins, P. J., P. Lummel and D. J. Oddy (editors) 2007 *Food and the City in Europe since 1800* Ashgate.
[143] Liljewall, B. (editor) 1999 *Agrarian Systems in Early Modern Europe* Nordiska Museets Förlag.
[144] Bath, B. S.van 1976 *De Agrarische Geschiedenis van West-Europa (500–1850)* Het Spectrum.
[145] Liljewall, B. (editor) 1999 *Agrarian Systems in Early Modern Europe* Nordiska Museets Förlag.
[146] Cochrane, W. W. 1993 *The Development of American Agriculture* University of Minnesota Press.
[147] Morley, N. 1996 *Metropolis and Hinterland* Cambridge University Press.
[148] Rioxson, D. 2010 *The History of Meat Trading* Nottingham University Press.
[149] Ibid.
[150] Mazoyer, M. and L. Roudart 2006 *A History of World Agriculture: From the Neolithic Age to the Current Crisis* Monthly Review Press.
[151] Gazeley, I. and A. Newell 2010 *'The first world war and working-class food consumption in Britain'* Forshungsinstitut zur Zukunft der Arbeit.
[152] Hughes, D. J. 2001 *An Environmental History of the World* Routledge.
[153] Mazoyer, M. and L. Roudart 2006 *A History of World Agriculture: From the Neolithic Age to the Current Crisis* Monthly Review Press.
[154] Clingingsmith, D. and J. G. Williamson 2005 *Mughal Decline, Climate Change, and Britain's Industrial Ascent: An integrated perspective on India's 18th and 19th Century deindustrialization* National Bureau of Economic Research.
[155] Inglis, D. and D. Giimlin (editors) 2009 *The Globalization of Food* Berg.
[156] Federico, G. 2005 *Feeding the World* Princeton.
[157] Linklater, A. 2013 *'When Pilgrims Privatized America'* Bloomberg.net.
[158] Federico, G. 2005 *Feeding the World.* Princeton.
[159] Hughes, D. J. 2001 *An Environmental History of the World* Routledge.
[160] Federico, G. 2005 *Feeding the World* Princeton.

161   Cochrane, W. W. 1993 *The Development of American Agriculture* University of Minnesota Press.

162   Xenophon. *The Economist* Kindle Edition.

163   Cochrane, W. W. 1993 *The Development of American Agriculture* University of Minnesota Press.

164   Federico, G. 2005 *Feeding the World* Princeton.

165   Tripp, R. 2003 *How to Cultivate a Commercial Seed Sector* Overseas Development Institute.

166   Ochieng L.A., P-W. Mathenge and R. Muasya. 2011 'A Survey Of On-Farm Seed Production Practices Of Sorghum (Sorghum bicolor L. Moench) In Bomet District Of Kenya', *African Journal of Food, Agriculture, Nutrition and Development* Vol. 11, Num. 5, 2011

167   Tripp, R. 2003 *How to Cultivate a Commercial Seed Sector* Overseas Development Institute.

168   Dillon, M. 'A brief history of the seed industry' http://seedstory.wordpress.com.

169   Federico, G. 2005 *Feeding the World* Princeton.

170   Ibid.

171   Maathai, W. M. 2006 *Unbowed: A Memoir* Alfred A. Knopf.

172   Maddison, A 2007 *Contours of the World Economy 1-2030 AD. Essays in macroeconomic history* Oxford University Press.

173   Atkins, P. J., P. Lummel and D. J. Oddy (editors) 2007 *Food and the City in Europe since 1800* Ashgate.

174   Federico, G. 2005 *Feeding the World* Princeton.

175   Ploeg, J. D. van der 2009 *The New Peasantries: Struggles for autonomy and sustainability in the era of empire and globalization* Earthscan.

176   Regmi, A. and M. Gehlhar (editors) 2005 'New Directions in Global Food Markets', USDA Agriculture Information Bulletin Number 794.

177   FAO 2007 *The State of Food and Agriculture 2007* Food and Agriculture Organization of the United Nations.

178   FAO 2012 *Statistical Yearbook 2012.* FAO Statistics Division Metalink: P2.HUN.FAO.TFS.SSCAL, p. 165

179   National Cotton Council of America 2013 *US and World Cotton Outlook September 2013* NCCA.

180   The Japan Times 2011 'Food self-sufficiency rate fell below 40% in 2010' 12 August 2011.

181   FAO 2012 *Statistical Yearbook 2012* FAO Statistics Division, Metalink: P2.HUN.FAO.TFS.SSCAL, p. 165

182   Ibid.

183   Brown, L. 2013 *Full Planet, Empty Plates: the new geopolitics of food scarcity* Earth Policy Institute.

184   World Shipping Council 2013 'About the Industry/Containers' www.worldshipping.org/about-the-industry/containers.

185   Fabiosa, J. F. 2011 'Globalization and food consumption' in J. L. Lusk, J. Roosen and J. Shogren (Eds) *The Oxford Handbook of The Economics of Food Consumption and Policy.* Oxford, Oxford Handbooks in Economics

186   Bernhofen, D. M., Z. El-Sahli, and R. Kneller 2013 'Estimating the Effects of the Container Revolution on World Trade' CESifo Working Paper Series No. 4136.

187   Daly, H. 1993 'The Perils of Free Trade' *Scientific American Magazine* November 1993.

188   Morley, N. 1996 *Metropolis and Hinterland* Cambridge University Press.

189   Wikipedia 2014 'Roman Campagna' http://en.wikipedia.org/wiki/Roman_Campagna.

190   Pelto, G. H. and P.J. Pelto 1983 'Diet and delocalization: Dietary changes since
       1750'. *Journal of Interdisciplinary History*, vol 14 No 2, pp. 507-528.
191   Rundgren, G. 2011 *Organic Agriculture, A step towards the green economy in the
       Eastern Europe. Caucasus and Central Asia region.* United Nations Environment
       Programme.
192   Higman, B.H. 2011 *How Food made History* Wiley-Blackwell.
193   Ibid.
194   Curtis, R. I. 2001 *Ancient Food Technology* Brill Academic Publishing.
195   Rioxson, D. 2010 *The History of Meat Trading* Nottingham University Press.
196   Higman, B.H. 2011 *How Food Made History* Wiley-Blackwell.
197   Rioxson, D. 2010 *The History of Meat Trading* Nottingham University Press.
198   Bryson, B. 2010 *At Home: A short history of private life* Doubleday.
199   Higman, B.H. 2011 *How Food Made History* Wiley-Blackwell.
200   Segers, Y., J. Bieleman and E. Buyst (editors) 2009 *Exploring the Food Chain. Food
       production and food processing in Western Europe 1850-1990* Brepols Publishers.
201   Welch R.W. and P.C. Mitchell 2000 'Food processing; a century of change' *British
       Medical Bulletin* 2000, 56.
202   Steel, C. 2008 *Hungry City* Chatto&Windus.
203   Higman, B.H. 2011 *How Food Made History* Wiley-Blackwell.
204   Rioxson, D. 2010 *The History of Meat Trading* Nottingham University Press.
205   Encyclopedia of Chicago. 2014. *'Meatpacking'*
       www.encyclopedia.chicagohistory.org.
206   Rioxson, D. 2010 *The History of Meat Trading* Nottingham University Press.
207   Wikipedia 2014 *'Irish famine'* http://en.wikipedia.org/wiki/Irish_famine.
208   Rioxson, D. 2010 *The History of Meat Trading* Nottingham University Press.
209   Sinclair, U. 1906 *The Jungle* Doubleday.
210   Segers, Y., J. Bieleman and E. Buyst (editors) 2009 *Exploring the Food Chain. Food
       production and food processing in Western Europe 1850-1990* Brepols Publishers.
211   Ibid.
212   American Public Works Association 2014 *'The Top Ten Public Works of the Century'*
       www2.apwa.net
213   Sinclair, U. 1906 *The Jungle* Doubleday.
214   Press in America 2014 *'Upton Sinclair'* http://pressinamerica.pbworks.com.
215   Segers, Y., J. Bieleman and E. Buyst (editors) 2009 *Exploring the Food Chain. Food
       production and food processing in Western Europe 1850-1990* Brepols Publishers.
216   Ibid.
217   Ibid.
218   Fernández-Armesto, F. 2001 *Food, a History* Macmillan.
219   Segers, Y., J. Bieleman and E. Buyst (editors) 2009 *Exploring the Food Chain. Food
       production and food processing in Western Europe 1850-1990* Brepols Publishers.
220   Ibid.
221   Ibid.
222   Lee, P. Y. (editor) 2008 *Meat, Modernity, and the Rise of the Slaughterhouse* University
       of New Hampshire Press
223   Ibid.
224   Ibid.
225   Segers, Y., J. Bieleman and E. Buyst (editors) 2009 *Exploring the Food Chain. Food
       production and food processing in Western Europe 1850-1990* Brepols Publishers.
226   Ibid.
227   Ibid.
228   Fieldhouse, P. 1998 *Food and Nutrition, Customs and Culture* Stanley Thornes Ltd.
229   Segers, Y., J. Bieleman and E. Buyst (editors) 2009 *Exploring the Food Chain. Food
       production and food processing in Western Europe 1850-1990* Brepols Publishers.

230   Ibid.
231   Kiple, K. and K.C. Ornelas (editors). 2000. *Cambridge World History of Food.* Cambridge University Press.
232   Gallo, A.E. 1999 'Food Advertising in the United States' in Frazão, E. *America's Eating Habits: Changes and consequences* USDA Agriculture Information Bulletin No. 750, May 1999.
233   Food & Water Watch 2013 *'Grocery Goliaths'* December 2013.
234   India Brand Equity Foundation 2013 *'Retail Industry in India';* www.ibef.org.
235   Associated Press 2013 *'Wal-Mart splits from India partner; stores on hold'* Wednesday Oct 09, 2013 www.newsdaily.com.
236   Stiegert, K. W. and V. Hovhannisyan 2009 'Food Retailing in the United States: History, Trends, Perspectives' in K.W. Stiegert and D.K. Hwan (editors) *Structural Changes in Food Retailing: Six country case studies* FSRG Publication, University of Wisconsin-Madison.
237   Fernández-Armesto, F. 2001 *Food, a History* Macmillan.
238   Stiegert, K. W. and V. Hovhannisyan 2009. 'Food Retailing in the United States: History, Trends, Perspectives' in K.W. Stiegert and D.K. Hwan (editors) *Structural Changes in Food Retailing: Six country case studies* FSRG Publication University of Wisconsin-Madison.
239   Ibid.
240   Ibid.
241   Wikipedia 2014 *'New South China Mall'* http://en.wikipedia.org/wiki/South_China_Mall
242   Regmi, A. and M. Gehlhar (editors) 2005 *'New Directions in Global Food Markets',* USDA Agriculture Information Bulletin Number 794.
243   World Bank 2007 *World Development Report 2007* World Bank.
244   Oliver, R. 2013 *'Should we Follow France in Cracking Down on Supermarkets?'* 24 May 2013, www.newstatesman.com.
245   Segers, Y., J. Bieleman and E. Buyst (editors) 2009 *Exploring the Food Chain. Food production and food processing in Western Europe 1850-1990* Brepols Publishers.
246   CPRE 2012 *'From Field to Fork: The value of England's local food webs'* Campaign to Protect Rural England.
247   Lantbrukarnas Riksförbund 2014 *'Matkronan, vem får konsumentens pengar?'* LRF.
248   USDA ERS 2014 *'The Food Dollars Series'* United States Department of Agriculture.
249   Lien, M. E. and B. Nerlich 2004 *The Politics of Food* Berg.
250   Cwiertka, K. J. 2002 'Popularizing a military diet in wartime and postwar Japan' In *Asian Anthropology* 1 (1) pps 1-30.
251   Wikipedia 2014 *'History of coffee'* http://en.wikipedia.org/wiki/History_of_coffee.
252   Wikipedia 2014 *'Rubber'* http://en.wikipedia.org/wiki/Rubber.
253   Bremzen, A. von 2013 *Mastering the Art of Soviet Cooking* Crown Publishers.
254   Gronow, J. 1997 *The Sociology of Taste* Routledge.
255   Bremzen, A. von 2013 *Mastering the Art of Soviet Cooking* Crown Publishers.
256   Coca Cola. 2014. *'History of Coca -Cola: 1941-1959'* www.coca-cola.co.uk.
257   Boisard, P. 2003 *'Camembert, a National Myth'* University of California Press.
258   Hook, D. H. and J. M. Norman. 1991. *The Haskell F. Norman Library of Science and Medicine* Historyofscience.com.
259   Cwiertka, K. J. 2007 *'War, Empire and the Making of Japanese National Cuisine':* An Asia Pacific e-journal 2007. www.japanfocus.org.
260   Myrdal, J. 2009 'Jordbrukets teknik hos Columella' in *Tolv böcker om lantbruk* Royal Swedish Academy of Agriculture and Forestry.
261   Cochrane, W. W. 1993 *The Development of American Agriculture* University of Minnesota Press.

262   Kaufman, F. 2012 'How to fight a food crisis' *Los Angles Times* 21 September 2012, http://articles.latimes.com.

263   Fraser, E. D.G. and A. Rimas 2010 *Empires of Food. Feast, famine and the rise and fall of civilizations* Free Press.

264   Kaufman, F. 2012 'How to fight a food crisis' *Los Angles Times* 21 September 2012, http://articles.latimes.com.

265   Ibid.

266   Vidal. J. 2012 'UN warns of looming worldwide food crisis in 2013' *The Guardian* 14 October 2012, www.theguardian.com.

267   Grant. G. 2012 'Why food security is not just a problem for the Third World'. *The Telegraph*, www.telegraph.co.uk.

268   Gazeley, I. and A. Newell 2010 'The first world war and working-class food consumption in Britain' *Forshungsinstitut zuk Zukunft der Arbeit* No 5297.

269   Ibid.

270   Cochrane, W. W. 1993 *The Development of American Agriculture* University of Minnesota Press.

271   Royal Swedish Academy of Agriculture and Forestry 2013 'Global Outlook, future competition for land and water' *KSLA tidskrift 5/2013*.

272   Federico, G. 2005 *Feeding the World* Princeton.

273   European Union 2014 *'European School Milk Scheme'* http://ec.europa.eu.

274   Royal Swedish Academy of Agriculture and Forestry 2013 'Global Outlook, future competition for land and water' *KSLA tidskrift 5/2013*.

275   Environmental Working Group 2012 *Environmental Working Group Database on Farm Subsidies 1995-2012*. http://farm.ewg.org.

276   Government of Switzerland 2004 *Swiss Agriculture Policy*. Government of Switzerland.

277   Jarrett, P. and C. Moeser 2013 *'The Agri-food Situation and Policies in Switzerland'* OECD.

278   Tehelka 2009 *'The Double Bind Principle'*, 20 February www.tehelka.com.

279   Rundgren, G. 2013 *Garden Earth - from hunter and gatherers to global capitalism and thereafter* Regeneration.

280   Federico, G. 2005 *Feeding the World* Princeton.

281   Mazoyer, M. and L. Roudart 2006 *A History of World Agriculture: From the Neolithic Age to the Current Crisis* Monthly Review Press.

282   Lee, P. Y. (editor) 2008 *Meat, Modernity, and the Rise of the Slaughterhouse* University of New Hampshire Press.

283   Atkins, P. J., P. Lummel and D. J. Oddy (editors) 2007 *Food and the City in Europe since 1800* Ashgate.

284   Ibid.

285   Lee, P. Y. (editor) 2008 *Meat, Modernity, and the Rise of the Slaughterhouse* University of New Hampshire Press,

286   Wikipedia 2014 *'Bovine Spongiform Encephalopathy'* http://en.wikipedia.org/wiki/Bovine_spongiform_encephalopathy.

287   Inglis, D. and D. Giimlin (editors) 2009 *The Globalization of Food* Berg.

288   Shiva, V. 2005 *Earth Democracy: Justice, Sustainability and Peace* South End Press.

289   Forbes 2013 *'Why Are Mexico And Mike Bloomberg Battling Coca-Cola?'* www.forbes.com.

290   Higman, B.H. 2011 *How Food Made History* Wiley-Blackwell.

291   Ibid.

292   Etilé, F. 2011 'Food consumption and health' In Roosen, J., J.L. Lusk and J.F. Shogren (editors) *The Oxford Handbook of The Economics of Food Consumption and Policy* Oxford Handbooks.

293 Fogel, R. W. 2004 *The Escape from hunger and premature death, 1700-2100. Europe, America and the third world* Cambridge Studies in Population, Economy and Societies in Past Times.

294 Pelto, G. H. and P.J. Pelto 1983 'Diet and delocalization: Dietary changes since 1750'. *Journal of Interdisciplinary History*, vol 14 No 2, pp. 507-528.

295 Fogel, R. W. 2004 *The Escape from hunger and premature death, 1700-2100. Europe, America and the third world* Cambridge Studies in Population, Economy and Societies in Past Times.

296 Pelto, G. H. and P.J. Pelto 1983 'Diet and delocalization: Dietary changes since 1750'. *Journal of Interdisciplinary History*, vol 14 No 2, pp. 507-528.

297 Fabiosa, J. F. 2011 'Globalization and food consumption' in J. L. Lusk, J. Roosen and J. Shogren (Eds) *The Oxford Handbook of The Economics of Food Consumption and Policy*. Oxford Handbooks in Economics.

298 World Instant Noodles Association 2014 *'Expanding Markets'* http://instantnoodles.org.

299 Jakarta Post *'Indonesia caught in wheat trap'*, July 11 2013.

300 Etilé, F. 2011 'Food consumption and health' In Roosen, J., J.L. Lusk and J.F. Shogren (editors) *The Oxford Handbook of The Economics of Food Consumption and Policy* Cambridge Studies in Population, Economy and Societies in Past Times.

301 World Health Oorganization 2014. *'Obesity and Overweight'* www.who.int.

302 Kaushik, P. 2013 'America and the War on Obesity' *Huffington Post*; www.huffingtonpost.com.

303 Cochrane, W. W. 1993 *The Development of American Agriculture* University of Minnesota Press.

304 Stiegert, K. W. and D.K. Hwan (editors) 2009 *Structural Changes in Food Retailing: Six country case studies* FSRG Publication University of Wisconsin-Madison.

305 Drewnowski, A. and S.E. Specter 2004 'Poverty and obesity: the role of energy density', *American Journal of Clinical Nutrition* 79 6–16.

306 Cutler, D. M., E. L. Glaeser and J. M. Shapiro 2003 'Why have Americans become more obese?' *Journal of Economic Perspectives* 17 (3) pp. 93–118.

307 Gronow, J. 1997 *The Sociology of Taste* Routledge.

308 Cutler, D. M., E. L. Glaeser and J. M. Shapiro. 2003 'Why have Americans become more obese?' *Journal of Economic Perspectives* 17 (3) pp. 93–118.

309 Hawkes, C. 2008 'Dietary implications of supermarket development: A global perspective', *Development Policy Review* 26 (6) pp. 657-692.

310 Plunkett Research Ltd. 2013. *'Introduction to the Food & Beverage Industry'* www.plunkettresearch.com/food-beverage-grocery-market-research/industry-and-business-data.

311 FAO 2013. *The State of Food and Agriculture* 2013 Food and Agriculture Organization of the United Nations.

312 Ibid.

313 Kneafsey, M. et al. 2008 *Reconnecting Consumers and Producers and Food* Berg.

314 Inglis, D. and D. Giimlin (editors) 2009 *The Globalization of Food* Berg.

315 Fieldhouse, P. 1998 *Food and Nutrition, Customs and Culture* Stanley Thornes Ltd.

316 Atkins, P. J., P. Lummel and D. J. Oddy (editors) 2007 *Food and the City in Europe since 1800*. Ashgate.

317 Wikipedia 2014 *'Scurvy'*; http://en.wikipedia.org/wiki/Scurvy.

318 Carpenter, K. J. 1994 'The life and times of W.O. Atwater' *The Journal of Nutrition* 124 (9 Suppl) 1707S-1714S.

319 Atkins, P. J., P. Lummel and D. J. Oddy (editors) 2007 *Food and the City in Europe since 1800* Ashgate.

320 Ibid.

321   Cullather, N. 2007 'The Foreign Policy of the Calorie' *American History Review* April 2007

322   Carpenter, K. J. 1994 'The life and times of W.O. Atwater' *The Journal of Nutrition* 124 (9 Suppl) 1707S-1714S.

323   Ibid.

324   Ibid.

325   Ibid.

326   Ibid.

327   Scrimshaw, N. S. 1968 'Food' in *International Encyclopedia of the Social Sciences* www.encyclopedia.com.

328   Gronow, J. 1997 *The Sociology of Taste* Routledge.

329   Pollan, M. 2008 *In Defense of Food: An Eater's Manifesto* Penguin.

330   FAO 2013 *The State of Food and Agriculture 2013* Food and Agriculture Organization of the United Nations.

331   Cutler, D. M., E. L. Glaeser and J. M. Shapiro. 2003. 'Why have Americans become more obese?' *Journal of Economic Perspectives* 17 (3) pp. 93–118.

332   IMAP 2010 'Food and Beverage Industry Global Report 2010'. IMAP inc.

333   Higman, B.H. 2011 *How Food Made History* Wiley-Blackwell.

334   Pollan, M. 2008 *In Defense of Food: An Eater's Manifesto* Penguin.

335   United States National Academy of Science 1989 'Recommended Daily Allowances, 1989'

336   Inglis, D. and D. Giimlin (editors) 2009 *The Globalization of Food* Berg.

337   LeGout 2014 'Qu'est-ce que la Semaine du Goût ?' www.legout.com.

338   Miller, D. 2014 'The surprising healing qualities of dirt' *Yes Magazine.*

339   Dhiman T.R., Anand G.R., Satter L.D. and Pariza M.W. 1999 'Conjugated linoleic acid content of milk from cows fed different diets' *Journal of Dairy Science* 82 (10) 2146-56.

340   Davis, Donald R., Melvin D. Epp and Hugh D. Riordan. 2004 'Changes in USDA food composition data for 43 garden crops, 1950 to 1999'. *Journal of the American College of Nutrition* 23(6): 669–682.

341   QLIF 2009 'Effects of production methods' QLIF subproject 2 *Quantifying the Effect of Organic and Low Input Production Methods on Food Quality and Safety and Human Health* Quality Low Input Food.

342   Pollan, M. 2008 *In Defense of Food: An Eater's Manifesto* Penguin.

343   Steel, C. 2008 *Hungry City* Chatto & Windus.

344   Mazoyer, M. and L. Roudart 2006 *A History of World Agriculture: From the Neolithic Age to the Current Crisis* Monthly Review Press.

345   Oregon State University 2013 *World Food Crops/ Classification of Crops and Their Role in Human Nutrition* http://oregonstate.edu/instruct/css/330/two/index2.htm.

346   Laudan, R. 2013 *Cuisine and Empire, Cooking in World History* California Studies in Food and Culture.

347   Morley, N. 1996 *Metropolis and Hinterland* Cambridge University Press.

348   Wojtan, L.S. 1993 'Rice is more than just food' *Japan Digest,* November 1993

349   Smith, C.W. et al. 2004 *Corn* John Wiley & Sons Inc.

350   Pollan, M. 2008 *In Defense of Food: An Eater's Manifesto* Penguin.

351   Molina, J.M. et al. 2011 'Molecular evidence for a single evolutionary origin of domesticated rice' *Proccedings of the National Academy of Sciences of the USA* 108 (20) pp 8351-8356.

352   Linares, O. F. 2002 'African rice (Oryza glaberrima): History and future potential' *Proccedings of the National Academy of Sciences of the USA* 99 (25) pps. 16360-16365.

353   FAO 2004 'Rice is Life' *FAO factsheet* Food and Agriculture Organization of the United Nations.

354   Kush, G. S. 2005 'What it will take to feed 5 billion rice consumers in 2030' *Plant Molecular Biology* 59 1–6.
355   Linares, O. F. 2002 'African rice (Oryza glaberrima): History and future potential' *Proccedings of the National Academy of Sciences of the USA* 99 (25) pps 16360-16365.
356   Ibid.
357   Kerkar, P.J. 2009 'Traditional agriculture declines sharply in state' *The Times of India*, Jul 10, 2009
358   Fernández, A. T., T. A. Wise and E. Garvey 2012 'Achieving Mexico's maize potential', *Global Development And Environment Institute Working Paper* NO. 12-03.
359   Ibid.
360   FAOSTAT.
361   Ibid.
362   National Corn Growers Association 2013 *The World of Corn 2013* National Corn Growers Association.
363   Edge Magazine 2008 '*King Corn: Documentary film reveals how subsidized corn is driving the fast-food industry*' www.edgemagazine.net.
364   Smith, C.W.et al. 2004 *Corn* John Wiley & Sons Inc.
365   Boguea, A. G. 1983 '*Changes in Mechanical and Plant Technology: The Corn Belt, 1910–1940*' Journal of Economic History, 43, pp. 1-25.
366   Smith, C. W. et al. 2004 *Corn* John Wiley & Sons Inc.
367   Ibid.
368   Ibid.
369   Ibid.
370   EMSI 2012 '*Industry Report: Wet Corn Milling*' www.economicmodeling.com.
371   OECD 2013 Environmental Working Group Database on Farm Subsidies 1995-2012.
372   Werner M.S. (editor) 1997 *The Encyclopedia of Mexico: History, culture and society* Fitzroy Dearborn Publishers.
373   Shewry P. R. 2009 'Wheat' *Journal of Experimental Botany* 60 (6) pp. 1537–1553.
374   Ibid.
375   Wikimedia 2014 '*Oldest_ship_biscuit-Kronborg-DK.JPG*' http://commons.wikimedia.org.
376   Fernández-Armesto, F. 2001 *Food, a History* Macmillan.
377   Wikipedia 2014 '*Baker's yeast*' www.wikipedia.org/wiki/Baker's_yeast.
378   Pollan, M. 2008 *In Defense of Food: An Eater's Manifesto* Penguin.
379   Welch, R.W. and P.C. Mitchel 2000 'Food processing: a century of change' *British Medical Bulletin* 2000, 56 (No 1) 1-17.
380   Shewry P. R. 2009 'Wheat' *Journal of Experimental Botany* 60 (6) pp 1537–1553.
381   Flour Fortification Initiative 2008 Global Update 2008 Flour Fortification Initiative.
382   Wilkinson, P.A. et al. 2012 'CerealsDB 2.0: an integrated resource for plant breeders and scientists' *BMC Bioinformatics* 13 219.
383   Mülenchemie 2013 '*Products for flour improvement*' www.muehlenchemie.de
384   Wikipedia 2014 '*Wheat production in the United States*' http://en.wikipedia.org/wiki/Wheat_production_in_the_United_States.
385   Shewry P. R. 2009 'Wheat' *Journal of Experimental Botany* 60 (6) pp 1537–1553.
386   Ibid.
387   Ibid.
388   Leshnik, S. L. and G-D Sontheimer 1975 *Pastoralists and nomads in South Asia.* Harrassowitz.
389   Milkproduction.com 2014 '*Digestive physiology of the cow*' www.milkproduction.com.

390   McTavish, E. J. et al. 2013 'New World cattle show ancestry from multiple independent domestication events' *Proccedings of the National Academy of Sciences of the USA* 2013 110 (15) E1398-E1406.

391   Evershed, R. P. et al. 2008 'Earliest date for milk use in the Near East and southeastern Europe linked to cattle herding' *Nature* 455, 528-531.

392   Homewood, K. 2008 *Ecology of African Pastoralist Societies* James Currey.

393   Zhen, L. et al. 2010 'Comparing patterns of ecosystem service consumption and perception of range management between ethnic herders in Mongolia and Inner Mongolia' *Environmental Research Letters*, 5 015001.

394   Mathias, E. 2012 *Livestock out of Balance, from Asset to Liability in the Course of the Livestock Revolution* League for Pastoral Peoples and Endogenous Livestock Development.

395   Blench, R. 2001 *Pastoralists in the New Millennium*. Overseas Development Institute.

396   Ibid.

397   Zhen, L. et al. 2010 'Comparing patterns of ecosystem service consumption and perception of range management between ethnic herders in Mongolia and Inner Mongolia' *Environmental Research Letters*, 5 015001.

398   Mathias, E. 2012 *Livestock out of Balance, from Asset to Liability in the Course of the Livestock Revolution* League for Pastoral Peoples and Endogenous Livestock Development.

399   Homewood, K. 2008 *Ecology of African Pastoralist Societies* James Currey.

400   Mathias, E. 2012 *Livestock out of Balance, from Asset to Liability in the Course of the Livestock Revolution* League for Pastoral Peoples and Endogenous Livestock Development.

401   FAOSTAT, figures from 2011.

402   Gerosa, S. and J. Skoet 2012 'Milk availability, trends in production and demand and medium-term outlook' *FAO, ESA Working paper* No. 12-01.

403   Falvey L. and Chantalakhana C. (editors) 1999 *Smallholder Dairying in the Tropics* International Livestock Research Institute.

404   Karlsson, G. and A. Sagnér (editors) 1953 *Boken om kött* B. Forsberg.

405   Fairlie, S. 2008 'Can Britain feed itself?' *The Land* 4 Winter 2008-8.

406   Grigg, D. 1983 *The Dynamics of Agricultural Change* Palgrave Macmillan.

407   Sainsbury's 2014 'Milk'; http://sainsburys.lgfl.org.uk.

408   Atkins, P. J. 1980 'The retail milk trade in London, c.1790-1914' *Economic History Review New Series*, 33 (4) pp. 522-537.

409   Steel, C. 2008 *Hungry City* Chatto&Windus.

410   Sainsbury's 2014 'Milk' http://sainsburys.lgfl.org.uk/milk.htm.

411   Atkins, P. J. 1980 'The retail milk trade in London, c.1790-1914' *Economic History Review New Series*, 33 (4) pp 522-537.

412   Ibid.

413   Atkins, P. J., P. Lummel and D. J. Oddy (editors) 2007 *Food and the City in Europe since 1800* Ashgate.

414   Ibid.

415   FAOSTAT. Data for 2009-2011.

416   Fonterra 2013 www.fonterra.com.

417   New Zealand Ministry of Primary Industries 'Dairy' www.mpi.govt.nz

418   Dairy Companies Association of New Zealand 2013 'Dairying today, www.dcanz.com.

419   Fonterra 2014 'Farmgate Milk Price' www.fonterra.com.

420   Forest and Bird 2014 'One Conclusion from Water Report - Dairy Conversions Need Moderating' www.forestandbird.org.nz.

421   Pelto, G. H. and P.J. Pelto 1983 'Diet and delocalization: Dietary changes since 1750'. *Journal of Interdisciplinary History*, vol 14 No 2, pp. 507-528.

422   Hummel, S. 2013 'Argentina's beef industry: A fall from grace' *Argentina Independent* 30 May 2013 www.argentinaindependent.com.
423   Queck, P. 2013 'Argentina provides a lesson in how to ruin a beef industry' *Beef Magazine* 26 September 2013 http://beefmagazine.com.
424   Heinrich Böll Foundation 2014 *Meat Atlas* Heinrich Böll Foundation.
425   Wikipedia 2014 *'Sugar'* http://en.wikipedia.org/wiki/Sugar.
426   Jensen, H. H. 2011 'Changing nutritional content of food' in *The Oxford Handbook of the Economics of Food Consumption and Policy.*
427   USDA Economic Research Service. 2013 *Sugar and Sweeteners Yearbook Tables* www.ers.usda.gov. United States Department of Agriculture.
428   Mintz, S. 1985 *Sweetness and power. The place of sugar in modern history* Viking Penguin.
429   Kiple, K. and K.C. Ornelas 2000 'Sugar' in *Cambridge World History of Food* Cambridge University Press.
430   Galloway, J.H. 1989 *The Sugar Cane Industry. A historical geography from its origins to 1914* Cambridge University Press.
431   Kiple, K. and K.C. Ornelas 2000 'Sugar' in *Cambridge World History of Food* Cambridge University Press.
432   Mintz, S. 1985 *Sweetness and Power. The place of sugar in modern history* Viking Penguin.
433   Economist, The 2011 *'The sugar trade, sweet and rich'*, 13 August 2011 www.economist.com.
434   Mintz, S. 1985 *Sweetness and Power. The place of sugar in modern history* Viking Penguin.
435   Ibid.
436   Ibid.
437   Kiple, K. and K.C. Ornelas 2000 'Sugar' in *Cambridge World History of Food* Cambridge University Press.
438   Ibid.
439   Ibid.
440   Galloway, J.H. 1989 *The Sugar Cane Industry. A historical geography from its origins to 1914* Cambridge University Press.
441   Raizen. www.raizen.com.br.
442   Galloway, J.H. 1989 *The Sugar Cane Industry. A historical geography from its origins to 1914* Cambridge University Press.
443   Ibid.
444   European Union *'Sugar'* http://ec.europa.eu/agriculture/sugar/
445   Wikipedia 2014 *'Sugar'* http://en.wikipedia.org/wiki/Sugar.
446   BBC Research 2013 *'The Market For High-Intensity Sweeteners Is Expected To Reach Nearly $1.9 Billion In 2017'* 3 March 2013 www.bccresearch.com.
447   FAOSTAT.
448   Crédit Suisse 2013 *'Sugar Consumption at a Crossroads'.*
449   Pollan, M. 2006 *An Omnivore's Dilemma. A natural history of four meals* Penguin.
450   Crédit Suisse 2013 *'Sugar Consumption at a Crossroads'.*
451   Canadian Sugar Institute 2014 *'The Canadian Sugar Market'* www.sugar.ca.
452   Galloway, J.H. 1989 *The Sugar Cane Industry. A historical geography from its origins to 1914* Cambridge University Press.
453   Crédit Suisse 2013 *'Sugar Consumption at a Crossroads'.*
454   Mintz, S. 1985 *Sweetness and Power. The place of sugar in modern history* Viking Penguin.
455   Crédit Suisse 2013 *'Sugar Consumption at a Crossroads'.*

456   FAO Statistical Division 2014 'Dietary Protein Consumption, Country groups 1990-92 1995-97 2000-02 2005-07'.

457   Fabiosa, J. F. 2011 'Globalization and food consumption' in J. L. Lusk, J. Roosen and J. Shogren (Eds) The Oxford Handbook of The Economics of Food Consumption and Policy. Oxford, Oxford Handbooks in Economics.

458   Own calculations based on USDA calorie tables and prices from Index Mundi www.indexmundi.com.

459   International Margarine Association of the Countries of Europe 2013 'The Role of Fats in the Diet' 2 December 2013 www.imace.org.

460   Curtis, R. I. 2001 Ancient Food Technology Brill.

461   Wikipedia 2014 'Ghee' http://en.wikipedia.org/wiki/Ghee.

462   Vries, J. de 2008 The Industrious Revolution Cambridge University Press.

463   Wikipedia 2014 'Whale' http://en.wikipedia.org/wiki/Whale.

464   National Park Service 2014 'New Bedford Whaling' www.nps.gov.

465   Wikipedia 2014 'Whale'; http://en.wikipedia.org/wiki/Whale.

466   Lai, O-M. T, C-P. Akoh and C. Casimir 2012 Palm Oil - Production, Processing, Characterization, and Uses. AOCS Press.

467   Hartley, C.W.S. 1988 'The Oil Palm' in The Cambridge World History of Food Cambridge University Press.

468   Obidzinski, K., R. Andriani, H. Komarudin and A. Andrianto 2012 'Environmental and social impacts of oil palm plantations and their implications for biofuel production in Indonesia'. Ecology and Society 17 (1) 25.

469   FAOSTAT.

470   Lai, O-M. T, C-P. Akoh and C. Casimir 2012 Palm Oil - Production, Processing, Characterization, and Uses. AOCS Press.

471   Gaworecki, M. and L. Moyer 2013 'How palm oil in everything from food to fuel is killing orangutans and exacerbating climate change' Alternet www.alternet.org.

472   Obidzinski, K., R. Andriani, H. Komarudin and A. Andrianto 2012 'Environmental and social impacts of oil palm plantations and their implications for biofuel production in Indonesia'. Ecology and Society 17 (1) 25.

473   Norway-Indonesia REDD+ fact sheet 2010 Norwegian Embassy in Indonesia.

474   National Soybean Research Laboratory 2014 'Soy Benefits' www.nsrl.illinois.edu.

475   Gibson, L. and G. Benson 2005 'Origin, History, and Uses of Soybean' Iowa State University Department of Agronomy 1 January 2014 www.agron.iastate.edu.

476   Shurtleff, W. and A. Aoyagi 2013 'History of Soy Flour 1100 B.C. to the 1980s', Soyinfo Center, www.soyinfocenter.com.

477   Ibid.

478   Gibson, L. and G. Benson 2005 'Origin, History, and Uses of Soybean' Iowa State University Department of Agronomy 1 January 2014 www.agron.iastate.edu.

479   Shurtleff, W. and A. Aoyagi 2007 'History of Soybeans and Soyfoods: 1100 B.C. to the 1980s', Soyinfo Center, www.soyinfocenter.com.

480   Ibid.

481   Brown, L. 2013 Full Planet, Empty Plates: The new geopolitics of food scarcity Earth Policy Institute

482   Shurtleff, W. and A. Aoyagi 2007 'History of Soybeans and Soyfoods: 1100 B.C. to the 1980s', Soyinfo Center, www.soyinfocenter.com.

483   USDA Foreign Agriculture Serevice 2014 'Major Vegetable Oils: World Supply and Distribution' United States Department of Agriculture.

484   USDA Foreign Agriculture Serevice 2014 'Butter Production and Consumption: Summary for selected countries'. United States Department of Agriculture.

485   Gerosa, S. and J. Skoet 2012 'Milk availability, trends in production and demand and medium-term outlook' FAO, ESA Working paper No. 12-01.

486   USDA Foreign Agriculture Serevice 2014 *'Major Vegetable Oils: World Supply and Distribution'* United States Department of Agriculture.
487   FAOSTAT.
488   Wikipedia 2014 *'Margarine'* http://fr.wikipedia.org/wiki/Margarine.
489   Ibid.
490   Fernández-Armesto, F. 2001 *Food, a History* Macmillan.
491   Wikipedia 2014 *'Margarine'* http://fr.wikipedia.org/wiki/Margarine.
492   Fairlie, S. 2008 'Can Britain feed itself?' *The Land* 4 winter 2008-8.
493   Fabiosa, J. F. 2011 'Globalization and food consumption' in J. L. Lusk, J. Roosen and J. Shogren (Eds) *The Oxford Handbook of The Economics of Food Consumption and Policy.* Oxford, Oxford Handbooks in Economics.
494   Adler, J. and A. Lawler 2012 'How the chicken conquered the world' *Smithsonian Magazine* June 2012 www.smithsonianmag.com.
495   Wikipedia 2014 *'KFC '* http://en.wikipedia.org/wiki/KFC.
496   Idel, A. 2013 'Livestock production and food security in a context of climate change and environmental and health challenges' *Trade and Environment Review 2013* UNCTAD.
497   Mail Online, the 2010 *'The disturbing conveyor belt of death where male chicks are picked off and killed so you can have fresh eggs'*, 4 November 2010 www.dailymail.co.uk.
498   Chong J-R. 2003 'Wood-chipped chickens fuel outrage' *Los Angeles Times* 22 November 2003.
499   Feedstufffoodlink 2014 *'Poultry'* http://feedstuffsfoodlink.com.
500   Ibid.
501   Sprows, A. 2014 *'Delmarva and its Poultry Industry'* http://faculty.salisbury.edu.
502   Feedstufffoodlink 2014 *'Poultry'* http://feedstuffsfoodlink.com.
503   Ibid.
504   PEW Environment Group 2011 *Big Chicken* PEW Environment Group.
505   USDA Economic Research Service 2013 *Farm Size and the Organization of U.S. Crop Farming* Economic Resaerch Report 152 United States Department of Agriculture.
506   PEW Environment Group 2011 *Big Chicken* PEW Environment Group.
507   Feedstufffoodlink 2014 *'Poultry'* http://feedstuffsfoodlink.com.
508   Cederberg, C. 2013 *'Kycklingproduktionen kan inte enbart vara beroende av GM-soja'* Extrakt.se.
509   Mathias, E. 2012 *Livestock out of Balance, from Asset to Liability in the Course of the Livestock Revolution* League for Pastoral Peoples and Endogenous Livestock Development.
510   Farm Aid. 2013 *'The Crutchfields: Life Under Contract'* www.farmaid.org.
511   Sprows, A. 2014 *'Delmarva and its Poultry Industry'* http://faculty.salisbury.edu.
512   Compassion in World Farming 2014 *'About Chickens'* www.ciwf.org.uk.
513   USDA Foreign Agriculture Service 2014 *'Livestock and Poultry: World markets and trends'* United States Department of Agriculture.
514   Ostendorrf, F. 2013 'Excessive industrialization of livestock production: the need for a new agricultural paradigm' *Trade and Environment Review 2013.* UNCTAD.
515   Mercopress 2013 *'Brazil JBS becomes largest chicken producer; purchases main tannery in Uruguay'* 10 June 2013 http://en.mercopress.com.
516   Poultry News 2011 *'WTO and US chicken exports: China puts its case'* www.thepoultrysite.com.
517   Adler, J. and A. Lawler 2012 'How the chicken conquered the world' *Smithsonian Magazine* June 2012.
518   Yum! 2014 *'About Yum! Brands'* 10 May 2014 www.yum.com.

519   Elfick, D 2013 'A Brief History of Broiler Selection: How chicken became a global food phenomenon in ift years' http://cn.aviagen.com.

520   Cobb-Vantress 2013 'Our History' www.cobb-vantress.com.

521   Heinrich Böll Foundation 2014 Meat Atlas Heinrich Böll Foundation.

522   Leenstra, F. 2013 'Raising cockerels as part of free range egg production' Low Input Breeds Technical Note 4.6.

523   Higman, B.H. 2011 How Food Made History Wiley-Blackwell.

524   New York Times 2011 'A Century of Meat' 15 March 2011 www.nytimes.com.

525   Economist, The 2013 'Henmania, Chicken is set to rule the roost in the global meat market' 14 September 2013 www.economist.com.

526   Columella De re rustica. In Swedish translation 2009, Tolv böcker om lantbruk Royal Swedish Academy of Agriculture and Forestry.

527   Economist, The 2011 'Counting chickens' 27 July 2011, www.economist.com.

528   United States Congressional Budget Office 2009 The Impact of Ethanol Use on Food Prices and Greenhouse-Gas Emissions United States Congress.

529   Masters, W. A. 2011 'Economic development, government policies and food consumption' in The Oxford Handbook of the Economics of Food Consumption and Policy Oxford Economic Handbooks

530   FAOSTAT.

531   Ababouch, L. 2009 'Fish utilization and trade' in P. Wrammer, H. Ackefors and M. Cullberg (editors) Fisheries, Sustainability and Development: Fifty-two authors on coexistence and development of fisheries and aquaculture in developing and developed countries Royal Swedish Academy of Agriculture and Forestry.

532   FAO 2013 Food Outlook November 2013. Food and Agriculture Organization of the United Nations.

533   Pollan, M. 2006 An Omnivore's Dilemma. A natural history of four meals Penguin.

534   Laudan, R. 2001 'A plea for culinary modernism. Why we should love new, fast, processed, food Journal of Critical Food Studies 1 (1) pp 36-44.

535   Fieldhouse, P. 1998 Food and Nutrition, Customs and Culture Stanley Thornes Ltd.

536   Wilk, R. 2009 'Difference on the menu: Neophilia, neophobia and globalization' in D. Inglis and D. Giimlin (editors) The Globalization of Food Berg.

537   Inglis, D. and D. Giimlin (editors) 2009 The Globalization of Food Berg.

538   Ibid.

539   Fox News 2003 'Americans Just Say 'Non' to French Products'. Fox News Channel. February 19, 2003.

540   Laudan, R. 2013 Cuisine and Empire, Cooking in World History California Studies in Food and Culture.

541   Kuhnlein, H. V. et al. 2009 Indigenous Peoples' Food Systems. Food and Agriculture Organization of the United Nations, Centre for Indigenous Peoples' Nutrition and Environment.

542   Kiple, K. and K.C. Ornelas (editors) 2000 Cambridge World History of Food. Cambridge University Press.

543   Fernández-Armesto, F. 2001 Food, a History Macmillan.

544   Ibid.

545   Ibid.

546   Steel, C. 2008 Hungry City Chatto & Windus.

547   Ibid.

548   Schneir, M. 1996 'Women and economics, Charlotte Perkins Gilman' in M. Schneir (editor) The Vintage Book Of Historical Feminism Vintage.

549   Higman, B.H. 2011 How Food Made History Wiley-Blackwell.

550   Fabiosa, J. F. 2011 'Globalization and food consumption' in J. L. Lusk, J. Roosen and J. Shogren (Eds) The Oxford Handbook of The Economics of Food Consumption and Policy. Oxford, Oxford Handbooks in Economics.

551   Hochschild, A. R. 2012 *The Outsourced Self. Intimate life in market times* Metropolitan Books.
552   Ackerman-Leist, P. 2013 *Rebuilding the Foodshed* Chelsea Green Publishing.
553   United States Bureau of Labor Statistics 2012 'How do US expenditures compares with those of other countries?' *US BLS* March 2012, 2 (16).
554   Fabiosa, J. F. 2011 'Globalization and food consumption' in J. L. Lusk, J. Roosen and J. Shogren (Eds) *The Oxford Handbook of The Economics of Food Consumption and Policy*. Oxford, Oxford Handbooks in Economics.
555   Stewart, H. 2011 'Food away from home', in *The Oxford Handbook of The Economics of Food Consumption and Policy* Oxford Economic Handbooks.
556   General Mills 2014 *'Boosting profit and market share in our food away-from-home business'* www.blog.generalmills.com.
557   Higman, B.H. 2011 *How Food Made History* Wiley-Blackwell.
558   Inglis, D. and D. Giimlin (editors) 2009 *The Globalization of Food* Berg.
559   World Bank 2007 *World Development Report 2007* World Bank.
560   Regmi, A. and M. Gehlhar 2005 'Processed food trade pressured by evolving global supply chains' *Amber Waves* 3(1): 12–19.
561   Heinrich Böll Foundation 2014 *Meat Atlas* Heinrich Böll Foundation.
562   Inglis, D. and D. Giimlin (editors) 2009 *The Globalization of Food* Berg.
563   Food & Water Watch 2013 *Grocery Goliaths* Food & Water Watch.
564   Ibid.
565   Stiegert, K. W. and D.K. Hwan (editors) 2009 *Structural Changes in Food Retailing: Six country case studies* FSRG Publication, University of Wisconsin-Madison.
566   Dagens Nyheter 2013 *'Ica drar ifrån Coop i kampen om kunderna'* 28 May 2013 www.dn.se.
567   CPRE 2012 *'From Field to Fork: The value of England's local food webs'* Campaign to Protect Rural England.
568   Steel, C. 2008 *Hungry City* Chatto & Windus.
569   Food & Water Watch 2013 *Grocery Goliaths.* Food & Water Watch.
570   Regmi, A. and M. Gehlhar (editors) 2005 *'New Directions in Global Food Markets'*, USDA Agriculture Information Bulletin Number 794.
571   ATL 2013 *'Arla tror på emv-varor'* 19 August 2013 www.atl.nu.
572   Tesco 2014 *Our Brands* http://realfood.tesco.com.
573   Hernandez, M. A. and M. Torrero undated *Market Concentration and Pricing Behavior in The Fertilizer Industry: A Global Approach.* International Food Policy Research Institute.
574   Wikiinvest 2013 *'Fertilizer Companies'* www.wikinvest.com.
575   Leland, G. 2003 'Farm crisis or agricultural system crisis?, Defining National Problems in a Global Economy' *International Journal of Sociology of Agriculture and Food* 11 pp15-30.
576   ETC 2011 'Who will control the Green Economy?' *ETC Communiqué* no. 107 ETC.
577   Mamana, I. 2014 *'Concentration of Market Power in the EU Seed Market'*, Study commissioned by the Greens/EFA Group in The European Parliament.
578   Hubbard, K. 2009 *'Out of Hand: Farmers face the consequences of a consolidated seed industry'* National Family Farm Coalition.
579   ETC 2011 'Who will control the Green Economy?' *ETC Communiqué* no. 107 ETC.
580   Hubbard, K. 2009 *'Out of Hand: Farmers face the consequences of a consolidated seed industry'* National Family Farm Coalition.
581   Ibid.
582   Schnepf, R. 2014 *US Farm Incomes* United States Congressional Research Service.
583   Müller, D 2013 'A critical analysis of commodity and food price speculation' in *Trade and Environment Review 2013* UNCTAD.

584 Visit and interview Chicago Board of Trade May 2012.
585 Vargas, M. and O. Chantry 2011 *'Ploughing Through the Meanders in Food Speculation'*. Mundobat
586 UTNE Reader 2013 *'Bet the farm: spinning wheat into gold'* UTNE Reader January/February 2013 www.utne.com.
587 Visit and interview Chicago Board of Trade May 2012.
588 UNCTAD 2011 *Price Formation in Financialized Commodity Markets: The role of information* UNCTAD.
589 Government of Canada 2010 *'Consumer Trend Report –Convenience'* *Market Analysis Report* June 2010. Government of Canada.
590 Steel, C. 2008 *Hungry City* Chatto & Windus.
591 Carey, J. 2011 *Who Feeds Bristol?* Bristol City Council.
592 IMAP 2010. *Food and Beverage Industry Global Report 2010.*
593 Greencore 2014 www.greencore.ie.
594 F. Lawrence, P. Allen and P. Scruton 2013 'The complex food supply chain that led to the horsemeat scandal' *The Guardian* 22 October 2013 www.theguardian.com.
595 Seth, A. and G. Randall 2001 *The Grocers: The rise and rise of the supermarket chains.* Kogan Page Publishers.
596 Pollan, M. 2013 *Cooked, a Natural History of Transformation* Allen Lane.
597 Aftonbladet 2001 *'Hemmafrun är utrotningshotad'*, 5 September 2001 www.aftonbladet.se.
598 Bremzen, A. von 2013 *Mastering the Art of Soviet Cooking* Crown Publishers.
599 Pollan, M. 2013 *Cooked, a Natural History of Transformation* Allen Lane.
600 Inglis, D. and D. Giimlin (editors) 2009 *The Globalization of Food* Berg.
601 Ritzer, G. 2009 *The McDonaldization of Society* Pine Forge Press.
602 Fernández-Armesto, F. 2001 *Food, a History* Macmillan.
603 Hamermesh, D. S. 2006 'Time To eat: household production under increasing income inequality', *NBER Working Paper* 12002 National Bureau of Economic Research.
604 John Hopkins Center 2014 *'Teaching the Food System'* www.jhsph.edu.
605 ACNielsen 2006 *'Asians are the World's Greatest Recreational Shoppers'* 19 July 2006 http://sg.nielsen.com.
606 Hochschild, A. R. 2012 *The Outsourced Self. Intimate life in market times* Metropolitan Books.
607 Kneafsey, M. et al. 2008 *Reconnecting Consumers and Producers and Food* Berg.
608 Fernández-Armesto, F. 2001 *Food, a History* Macmillan.
609 Ibid.
610 Millenium Ecosystem Assessment 2005 *Millennium Ecosystem Assessment: Ecosystems and human well-being–synthesis* World Resource Institute.
611 OECD 2001 *Environmental Indicators for Agriculture, Volume 3: Methods and results.* Organisation for Economic Co-operation and Development.
612 IAASTD 2009 *Agriculture at a Crossroads: Global Report* International Assessment of Agricultural Knowledge, Science and Technology for Development.
613 Chen, X-P. 2011 'Integrated soil–crop system management for food security', *Proceedings of the National Academy of Sciences* April 19, 2011 108 (16).
614 European Science Foundation 2013 'Nitrogen in Europe, Current problems and future solutions' part of *The European Nitrogen Assessment* www.nine-esf.org.
615 Ibid.
616 Ayres, R. U. (editor) 1998 *Eco-Restructuring: Implications for sustainable development* United Nations University Press.
617 Millenium Ecosystem Assessment 2005 *Millennium Ecosystem Assessment: Ecosystems and human well-being–synthesis* World Resource Institute.
618 Ibid.

619   USDA 2013 *Fertilizer Use and Price* www.ers.usda.gov.
620   Murphy J. C., R. M. Hirsch and L. A. Sprague 2013 *Nitrate in the Mississippi River and its tributaries, 1980 to 2010: Are we making progress?* United States Geological Survey Scientific Investigations Report 2013–5169.
621   UNEP 2010 *UNEP Year Book 2010: New science and developments in our changing environments* United Nations Environment Programme.
622   Millenium Ecosystem Assessment 2005 *Millennium Ecosystem Assessment: Ecosystems and human well-being–synthesis* World Resource Institute.
623   Cordell, D., J-O. Drangert and S. White 2009 'The story of phosphorus: Global food security and food for thought' *Global Environmental Change* 19 (2) pp292-305.
624   Ackerman-Leist, P. 2013 *Rebuilding the Foodshed* Chelsea Green Publishing.
625   Liebieg, J. von. 1865 *Agrikulturchemie.*
626   PAN Germany 2012 *Pesticides and health hazards, facts and figures* www.pan-germany.org.
627   President's Cancer Panel 2010 *Reducing Environmental Cancer Risk: What we can do now? 2008–2009 Annual Report* United States Department of Health and Human Services.
628   World Bank 2007 *World Development Report 2007* World Bank.
629   PAN Germany 2012 *Pesticides and health hazards, facts and figures* www.pan-germany.org.
630   President's Cancer Panel 2010 *Reducing Environmental Cancer Risk: What we can do now? 2008–2009 Annual Report* United States Department of Health and Human Services.
631   Brändli D. and S. Reinacher 2012 'Herbicides found in human urine' *Ithaka Journal* 1 2012 pp 270–272.
632   NPIC 2014 *Glyphosate Technical Fact Sheet* 30 March 2014 National Pesticide Information Centre.
633   OECD 2001 *Environmental Indicators for Agriculture, Volume 3: Methods and results.* Organisation for Economic Co-operation and Development.
634   Donald, D. B. et al. 2007 'Pesticides in surface drinking-water supplies of the northern great plains', *Environmental Health Perspectives* August 2007 115 (8) pp 1183–1191.
635   Pesticide Action Network. 2014 *'Neonicotinoids'* http://bees.pan-uk.org
636   Gallai, N. et al. 2009 'Economic valuation of the vulnerability of world agriculture confronted with pollinator decline' *Ecological Economics* 68(3) pp 810–821.
637   UNEP 2012 *The Cost of Inaction Report* United Nations Environmental Programme.
638   UNEP United Nations Environmental Programme 2012 *Global Chemicals Outlook: Towards sound management of chemicals* United Nations Environmental Programme.
639   European Centre for Disease Prevention and Control/European Medicines Agency 2009 *Joint Technical Report: The bacterial challenge: time to react* ECDC.
640   EU–US Summit 2009 *EU–U.S. Summit Declaration* 3 November 2009 http://eeas.europa.eu.
641   Levitt, T. 2011 'Overuse of drugs in animal farming linked to growing antibiotic-resistance in humans' *The Ecologist* www.theecologist.org.
642   Heinrich Böll Foundation 2014 *Meat Atlas* Heinrich Böll Foundation.
643   Ibid.
644   Levitt, T. 2011 'Overuse of drugs in animal farming linked to growing antibiotic-resistance in humans' *The Ecologist* www.theecologist.org.
645   Sapkota, A. R. et al. 2011 'Lower prevalence of antibiotic-resistant enterococci on U.S. conventional poultry farms that transitioned to organic practices' *Environmental Health Perspectives* 2011 November; 119 (11) pp 1622–1628.
646   Heinrich Böll Foundation 2014 *Meat Atlas* Heinrich Böll Foundation.

647 Daxenberger, A., H. Meyer, K. Meyer and B. Schiffer 2011 'The fate of trenbolone acetate and melengestrol acetate after application as growth promoters in cattle: Environmental studies.' *Environmental Health Perspectives*, 109 (11) 1145-51.

648 Heong, K.L. A. Manza, J. Catindig, S. Villareal and T. Jacobsen. 'Changes in pesticide use and arthropod biodiversity in the IRRI research farm' *Outlooks on Pest Management* October 2007, p 1-5.

649 Millenium Ecosystem Assessment 2005 *Millennium Ecosystem Assessment: Ecosystems and human well-being–synthesis* World Resource Institute.

650 Constanza, R. et. al. 1997 'The value of the world's ecosystem services and natural capital' *Nature* 387 15 May 1997.

651 Ellis, E. C. and N. Ramankutty. 2008. 'Putting people in the map: Anthropogenic biomes of the world' *Frontiers in Ecology and the Environment* 6(8): 439–447.

652 Stolton, S. 2002 *Organic Agriculture and Biodiversity* International Federation of Organic Agriculture Movement.

653 CPRE 2012 *'From Field to Fork: The value of England's local food webs'* Campaign to Protect Rural England.

654 FAO 2014 *'Use Them Or Lose Them'* www.fao.org.

655 FAO 2011 *Save and Grow, a policymaker's guide to the sustainable intensification of smallholder crop production* United Nations Food and Agriculture Organization.

656 Stolton, S. 2002 *Organic Agriculture and Biodiversity* International Federation of Organic Agriculture Movement.

657 FAO 2014 *'A Safety Net for the Future'* www.fao.org.

658 Redman, M. and M. Hemmami 2008 *Developing a National Agri-environment Programme for Turkey* Institute for European Environmental Policy.

659 FAO 2014 *'A Safety Net for the Future'* www.fao.org.

660 World Bank 2007 *World Development Report 2007* World Bank.

661 Neely, C., S. Bunning and A. Wilkes (editors) 2009 *Review of Evidence on Dryland Pastoral Systems and Climate Change.* United Nations Food and Agriculture Organization.

662 Ursu, A., A. Overenco, I. Marcov. and S. Curcubat 2014 'Chernozem: Soil of the steppe', in D. Dent (editor) *Soil as World Heritage* Springer.

663 ClimSoil 2008 *Review of Existing Information on the Interrelations between Soil and Climate Change* European Commission.

664 Montgomery, D. R. 2007 *Dirt: The Erosion of Civilizations* University of California Press.

665 FAO 2003 *World Agriculture: Towards 2015/2030. An FAO Perspective* Earthscan.

666 Chapman, J. L. and M. J. Reiss 1999 *Ecology: Principles and applications, 2nd edition* Cambridge University Press.

667 Neely, C., S. Bunning and A. Wilkes (editors) 2009 *Review of Evidence on Dryland Pastoral Systems and Climate Change.* United Nations Food and Agriculture Organization.

668 FAO 2007 *The State of Food and Agriculture 2007* United Nations Food and Agriculture Organization.

669 USDA Conservation Reserve Program 2011 *Annual Summary 2011.* United States Department of Agriculture.

670 World Bank 2007 *World Development Report 2007* World Bank.

671 Neely, C., S. Bunning and A. Wilkes (editors) 2009 *Review of Evidence on Dryland Pastoral Systems and Climate Change.* FAO.

672 FAO 2007 *The State of Food and Agriculture 2007* United Nations Food and Agriculture Organization.

673 IUCN 2010 'TEEB, public goods and forests'. *Arborvitae: The IUCN Conservation Programme Newsletter* (41): 8–9.

674 European Commission 2011 *Overview of best practices for limiting soil sealing or mitigating its effects in EU-27* European Union.

675 Pretty, J. et al. 2005 'Farm costs and food miles: An assessment of the full cost of the UK weekly food basket' *Food Policy* 30 pp 1–19.

676 Ibid.

677 Dobbs, T. L. and J. Pretty 2008 'Case study of agri-environmental payments: The United Kingdom' *Ecological Economics* 65 pp 765–775.

678 Global Energy Initiative 2014 'Briefs' *Global Energy Affairs* January 2014.

679 Rundgren, G. 2012 *'Paying Farmers for Environmental Services in Japan'* 30 October 2012 http://gardenearth.blogspot.se.

680 Daly H. 2013 *'Growth and Laissez-Faire'* 23 September 2013 http://steadystate.org.

681 Kraatz, S., D.J. Reinemann and W.E. Berg 2008 'Energy Inputs for Corn Production in Wisconsin and Germany', presentation at the *2008 American Society of Agricultural and Biological Engineers Annual International Meeting.*

682 Rundgren, G. 2013 *Garden Earth -from hunter and gatherers to global capitalism and thereafter* Regeneration.

683 UNIDO 2008 *Energy, Development and Security: Energy Issues in the current macroeconomic context* United Nations Industrial Development Organization.

684 Tittonell, P. A. 2013 *Farming Systems Ecology: Towards ecological intensification of world agriculture* Inaugural Lecture, Wageningen University.

685 Rundgren, G. 2013 *Garden Earth - from hunter and gatherers to global capitalism and thereafter* Regeneration.

686 Ibid.

687 Rundgren, G. 2013 *'Energy-efficient Food Production? Sure but within reason'* 19 March 2013 http://gardenearth.blogspot.se.

688 International Forum for Rural Transport and Development 2009 *'Animal Traction'* www.ifrtd.org.

689 FAO 2000 'The energy and agriculture nexus' *Environment and Natural Resources Working Paper* No. 4. United Nations Food and Agriculture Organization.

690 Rundgren, G. 2013 *Garden Earth - from hunter and gatherers to global capitalism and thereafter* Regeneration.

691 USDA- Agriculture Marketing Service 2011 *'Brazil Soybean Transportation'* www.ams.usda.gov.

692 United States Congressional Research Services 2004 *Energy Use in Agriculture: Background and issues* United States Congressional Research Services.

693 Baky, A. et al. 2013 *Sveriges primärproduktion och försörjning av livsmedel - möjliga konsekvenser vid en brist på fossil energi.* Jordbrukstekniska Institutet.

694 Canning P. et al. 2010 *Energy Use in the U.S Food System* Economic Research Report No 94. USDA Economic Research Service.

695 Ibid.

696 Ibid.

697 Ibid.

698 Rundgren, G. 2013 *'Energy-efficient Food Production? Sure but within reason'* 19 March 2013 http://gardenearth.blogspot.se

699 Rundgren, G. 2013 *Garden Earth - from hunter and gatherers to global capitalism and thereafter* Regeneration.

700 Ibid.

701 Bardi, U. et al. 2103 'Turning electricity into food: the role of renewable energy on the future of agriculture' *Journal of Cleaner Production* 53 pp 224-231

702 Howard, J. K. 2003 *Montana: High, wide, and handsome.* Bison Books.

703 Montgomery, D. R. 2007 *Dirt: The Erosion of Civilizations* University of California Press.

704   Ibid.
705   World Bank 2007 *World Development Report 2007* World Bank.
706   FAO 2003 *World Agriculture: Towards 2015/2030. An FAO Perspective* Earthscan.
707   MINAGRI 2009 *Strategic Plan for the Transformation of Agriculture in Rwanda–Phase II (PSTA II)* Final Report of the Republic of Rwanda's Ministry of Agriculture and Animal Resources.
708   Montgomery, D. R. 2007 *Dirt: The Erosion of Civilizations* University of California Press.
709   Ibid.
710   MINAGRI 2009 *Strategic Plan for the Transformation of Agriculture in Rwanda–Phase II (PSTA II).* Final Report Republic of Rwanda: Ministry of Agriculture and Animal Resources.
711   Montgomery, D. R. 2007 *Dirt: The Erosion of Civilizations* University of California Press.
712   Ibid.
713   Hughes, D. J. 2001 *An Environmental History of the World* Routledge.
714   Cunfer, G. 2005 *On the Great Plains: Agriculture and environment* Texas A&M University Press.
715   Cochrane, W. W. 1993 *The Development of American Agriculture* University of Minnesota Press.
716   Montgomery, D. R. 2007 *Dirt: The Erosion of Civilizations* University of California Press.
717   FAO 2003 *World Agriculture: Towards 2015/2030. An FAO Perspective* Earthscan.
718   Federico, G. 2005. *Feeding the World* Princeton.
719   FAOSTAT.
720   Federico, G. 2005 *Feeding the World* Princeton.
721   Danish Ministry of the Environment 2005 *Nature and Environment 2004. Theme: Nature in Denmark.* Danish Environmental Protection Agency, Ministry of Environment.
722   United States Geological Survey 2013 '*Nitrate in the Mississippi River and its Tributaries, 1980 to 2010: Are we making progress?*' http://pubs.usgs.gov.
723   Federico, G. 2005 *Feeding the World* Princeton.
724   FAO 2003 *World Agriculture: Towards 2015/2030. An FAO Perspective* Earthscan.
725   United States Sugar Corporation 2014 '*Environmental Stewardship*' www.ussugar.com.
726   American Farmland Trust 2014 '*Farmland by the Numbers*' www.farmland.org.
727   John Heinz III Center 2008 *The State of the Nation's Ecosystems 2008: Measuring the lands, waters, and living resources of the United States* Island Press.
728   SCB 2004 'Pressmeddelande nr 2004:172' Statistiska Centralbyrån.
729   Danish Ministry of Environment 2005 *Nature and Environment 2004. Theme: Nature in Denmark* Danish Environmental Protection Agency, Ministry of Environment.
730   Farmdoc 2010 'Farmland Price Outlook: Are farmland prices too high relative to returns and interest rates?' 18 October,2010 University of Illinois.
731   Land Matrix 2014 www.landmatrix.org.
732   Valoral Advisors 2014 *Global Agribusiness Investment Outlook 2014* Valoral Advisors.
733   Mail Online 2010 '*Look who owns Britain*', 10 November 2010.
734   Land Report 2013 '*2013 Land Report 100*' www.landreport.com.
735   Kirschenmann, F. 1995 Preface to G. Gershuny, and J. Smillie *The Soul of Soil* third edition. Agaccess.
736   Meyer von Bremen, A-H and G. Rundgren 2012 *Jorden vi äter*, Swedish Society for Nature Conservation.
737   FAO 2003 *World Agriculture: Towards 2015/2030. An FAO Perspective* Earthscan.

738   Brown, L. 2013 *Full Planet, Empty Plates: the new geopolitics of food scarcity* Earth Policy Institute

739   Leflaive, X. 2012 'Water Outlook to 2050: The OECD calls for early and strategic action' *OECD Discussion Paper* 1219.

740   Australian Government 2008 *Restoring the Balance in the Murray-Darling Basin* Department of Environment, Heritage and the Arts.

741   Tansey, G. and T. Worsley 1995 *The Food System: A Guide* Earthscan.

742   United Nations 2013 *Millennium Development Goals Report 2012* United Nations.

743   Millenium Ecosystem Assessment 2005 *Millennium Ecosystem Assessment: Ecosystems and human well-being–synthesis* World Resource Institute.

744   Vitousek, P. M., H. A. Mooney, J. Lubchenco and J. M. Melillo 1997 'Human domination of the earth's ecosystems' *Science* 277: 494–99.

745   World Bank 2007 *World Development Report 2007* World Bank.

746   Worldwatch Institute 2000 *State of the World 2000* W. W. Norton & Company, Inc.

747   OECD 2001 *Environmental Indicators for Agriculture, Volume 3: Methods and results.* Organisation for Economic Co-operation and Development.

748   Worldwatch Institute 2013 'Reforming Energy Subsidies Could Curb India's Water Stress' www.worldwatch.org.

749   Research Councils UK India 2013 *Report: Roundtable on Applying Energy Water Food Nexus Thinking* Research Councils UK India.

750   USDA 2002 *GAIN Report #SA2022* Global Agricultural Information Network Online United States Department of Agriculture.

751   Arab News 2013 'Kingdom to halt wheat production by 2016' 14 April 2013 www.arabnews.com.

752   UNEP 2009 *A Global Green New Deal. First draft report* (February 2009) United Nations Environment Programme.

753   Earth Institute 2010 'California's Water Rights Controversy: Should farmers be allowed to transfer water to developers?' 20 November 2010 http://blogs.ei.columbia.edu.

754   Bloomberg Businessweek 2008 'There will be water' www.businessweek.com.

755   Vivero Pol, J.L. 2013 *Food as a Commons: Reframing the narrative of the food system* 23 April 2013 Centre for Philosophy of Law, Université Catholique de Louvain.

756   Stanton, T., M. Echavarria, K. Hamilton and C. Ott 2010 *State of Watershed Payments: An emerging marketplace.* Forest Trends.

757   Reuters 2013 'Don't mess with Texas water, frackers warned, www.reuters.com.

758   IEA 2012 'Water for energy, Is energy becoming a thirstier resource?' *World Energy Outlook 2012* IEA.

759   Research Councils UK India 2013 'Report: Roundtable on Applying Energy Water Food Nexus Thinking'. Research Councils UK India.

760   Ibid.

761   Bloomberg 2011 'World's Biggest Dam Opens Sluices to Refill China's Parched Yangtze, Lake' 24 May 2011 www.bloomberg.com.

762   IEA 2012 'Water for energy, Is energy becoming a thirstier resource?' *World Energy Outlook 2012.* IEA.

763   New York Times 2010 'Recycling land for green energy ideas' 11 August 2010 www.nytimes.com.

764   Rundgren, G. 2013 *Garden Earth - from hunter and gatherers to global capitalism and thereafter* Regeneration.

765   Millenium Ecosystem Assessment 2005 *Millennium Ecosystem Assessment: Ecosystems and human well-being–synthesis* World Resource Institute.

766   Grigg, D. 1983 *The Dynamics of Agricultural Change* Palgrave Macmillan.

767   Linklater, A 2013 'When Pilgrims Privatized America' Bloomberg.net.

768 Rundgren, G. 2013 *Garden Earth - from hunter and gatherers to global capitalism and thereafter* Regeneration.

769 Millenium Ecosystem Assessment 2005 *Millennium Ecosystem Assessment: Ecosystems and human well-being–synthesis* World Resource Institute.

770 Bayliss-Smith, T. P. 1982 *The Ecology of Agricultural Systems* Cambridge University Press.

771 FAO 2000 'The Energy and Agriculture Nexus' Environment and Natural Resources Working Paper No. 4. United Nations Food and Agriculture Organization.

772 Malmaeus, M. 2013 *Tillväxt Till Varje Pris?* Notis.

773 Schnepf, R. 2014 *US Farm Income* United States Congressional Research Service.

774 Ploeg, J. D. van der 2009 *The New Peasantries: Struggles for autonomy and sustainability in the era of empire and globalization* Earthscan.

775 Farmdoc 2010 'Farmland Price Outlook: Are farmland prices too high relative to returns and interest rates?' 18 October 2010, University of Illinois.

776 Ploeg, J. D. van der 2009 *The New Peasantries: struggles for autonomy and sustainability in the era of empire and globalization* Earthscan.

777 Capreform.eu 2013 'CAP Reform Uncertainty and the Market for Entitlements' April 3, 2013 http://capreform.eu.

778 Rundgren, G. 2013 *Garden Earth - from hunter and gatherers to global capitalism and thereafter* Regeneration.

779 Kijne, J. et al. 2009 *Opportunities to Increase Water Productivity in Agriculture with Special Reference to Africa and South Asia* Stockholm Environment Institute.

780 Grace Communications 2013 *Food, Water and Energy, Know the Nexus.* Grace Communications.

781 Meyer von Bremen, A-H. and G. Rundgren 2012 *Jorden vi äter,* Swedish Society for Nature Conservation.

782 Mekonnen, M.M. and Hoekstra A.Y. 2012 'A global assessment of the water footprint of farm animal products' *Ecosystems* (2012) 15: 401–415.

783 Rundgren, G. 2013 *Garden Earth - from hunter and gatherers to global capitalism and thereafter* Regeneration.

784 Renault, D. 2002 *Value of Virtual Water in Food: Principles and virtues* United Nations Food and Agriculture Organization.

785 Kijne, J. et al. 2009 *Opportunities to Increase Water Productivity in Agriculture with Special Reference to Africa and South Asia* Stockholm Environment Institute.

786 Sauber, M. 2010 'Low agricultural productivity in a monetary economy' paper *to the 12th Annual conference of the AHE* Association for Heterodox Economics.

787 Schmidhuber J., J. Bruinsma and G. Boedeker 2009 'Capital requirements for agriculture in developing countries to 2050', *Paper to Expert Meeting on How to Feed the World in 2050* United Nations Food and Agriculture Organization.

788 Gerosa, S. and J. Skoet 2012 'Milk availability, trends in production and demand and medium-term outlook' *FAO, ESA Working paper* No. 12-01.

789 Rundgren, G. 2013 *Garden Earth - from hunter and gatherers to global capitalism and thereafter* Regeneration.

790 Israelson, C. 2006 'Klasskillnader även bland kor på 1800-talets torp och herrgårdar' *SLU fakta nr 7,* 2006 Swedish Agriculture University.

791 Herrmann, Michael. 2009 *Food security and agricultural development in times of high commodity prices,* Discussion paper of the United Nations Conference on Trade and Development, No. 196, November 2009, UNCTAD.

792 Vivero Pol, J.L. 2013 *Food as a Commons: Reframing the narrative of the food system* 23 April 2013 Centre for Philosophy of Law, Université Catholique de Louvain.

793 Feyder, J. 2013 Agriculture: A unique sector in economic, ecological and social terms in *Trade and Environment Review 2013* UNCTAD.

794 Guardian, The 2001 'Food for thought', 31 March 2001 www.theguardian.com.

795   KSLA 2012 *The Global Need for Food, Fibre and Fuel* Royal Swedish Academy of Agriculture and Forestry.

796   FAOSTAT.

797   Rundgren, G. 2011 *Organic Agriculture, A step towards the green economy in the Eastern Europe. Caucasus and Central Asia region* United Nations Environmental Programme.

798   Trewavas, A. J. 2001 'The Population/Biodiversity Paradox. *Plant Physiology January 2001 vol. 125 no. 1 174-179.*

799   Rundgren, G. 2013 *Garden Earth - from hunter and gatherers to global capitalism and thereafter* Regeneration.

800   World Bank 2007 *World Development Report 2007* World Bank.

801   Rundgren, G. 2013 *Garden Earth - from hunter and gatherers to global capitalism and thereafter* Regeneration.

802   Auberbach, R, G. Rundgren and N. El-Hage Scialabba 2013 *Organic Agriculture: African experiences in resilience and sustainability* United Nations Food and Agriculture Organization.

803   Jaggard, K. W. A. Qi and E.S. Ober 2010 'Possible changes to arable crop yields by 2050' *Philosophical Transactions of the Royal Society.*

804   Brown, L. 2013 *Full Planet, Empty Plates: the new geopolitics of food scarcity* Earth Policy Institute

805   Grassini, P., K.M. Eskridge and K.G. Cassman 2013 'Distinguishing between yield advances and yield plateaus in historical crop production trends' *Nature Communications,* 17 December 2013.

806   Heisey, P. W. 2009 'Science, technology, and prospects for growth in US corn yields' *Amber Waves* 7 (4). USDA/ERS.

807   Meyer von Bremen, A-H. and G. Rundgren 2012, *Jorden vi äter,* Swedish Society for Nature Conservation.

808   Agro News 2012 'GM crops push up pesticide sales in Brazil' 13 August 2012 http://news.agropages.com.

809   Brown, D. 2013 '2,4-D and dicamba-resistant crops and their implications for susceptible non-target crops', 7 November 7 2013 http://msue.anr.msu.edu.

810   Centers for Disease Control and Prevention 2014 'Facts About Paraquat' 20 June 2014 http://emergency.cdc.gov.

811   Wu, M. et al. 2010 'Still Poisoning the Well' Natural Resources Defense Council.

812   Bengtson, J 2013 'In which ways could modern biotechnlogy be part of sustainable agriculture?' *Sveriges Utsädesförenings Tidskrift* 1-2013.

813   Marketwatch 2013 'BASF, Monsanto to launch new GM corn in U.S.' www.marketwatch.com.

814   Monsanto 2103 'Corporate Profile' www.monsanto.com.

815   Hoffmann, U. 2011 'Assuring Food Security in Developing Countries Under the Challenges of Climate Change: Key trade and development issues of a fundamental transformation of agriculture', *Discussion Paper of the United Nations Conference on Trade and Development,* No. 201, February 2011 UNCTAD.

816   Tomatina 2013 www.latomatina.org.

817   FAO 2011 *Global Food Losses and Food Waste* Food and Agriculture Organization of the United Nations.

818   Rundgren, G. 2013 *Garden Earth - from hunter and gatherers to global capitalism and thereafter* Regeneration.

819   Buzby, J. C. et al. 2014 *The Estimated Amount, Value and Calories of Postharvest Food Loss at the Retail and Consumer Levels in the United States.* USDA/ERS.

820   Gunders, D 2012 *Wasted: How America is losing up to 40% of its food from farm to fork to landfill* Natural Resources Defense Council.

821   Sinclair, U. 1906 *The Jungle* Doubleday, Jabber & Company.
822   Hughes, D. J. 2001 *An Environmental History of the World* Routledge.
823   Schneider, F. 2011 'The history of food wastage', *Proceedings of the 3rd International Conference on Waste*. Edmonton Waste Management Centre of Excellence.
824   Reuters 2011 *'South Carolina scientist works to grow meat in lab'* 30 January 2011 www.reuters.com.
825   BBC 1986 'The Proteen Plant' *Doomsday Reloaded* www.bbc.co.uk/history/domesday.
826   Russia and India Report 2013 *'Which 3D organ will be bioprinted in Moscow first?'* http://indrus.in.
827   Algae Industry Magazine 2012 *'Low-cost algae production–is it finally with us?'* 13 May 2012 AlgaeIndustryMagazine.com.
828   Timmons, M., and P.W. Aho 1998 'Comparison of aquaculture and broiler production systems' *Proceedings of the Second International Conference on Recirculating Aquaculture*. G.S. Libey. M.B. Timmons (editors) Roanoke, Virginia.
829   Teisl, M. F. 2011. 'Environment and food consumption' in *The Oxford Handbook of the Economics of Food Consumption and Policy*. Oxford Economic Handbooks.
830   Zareen B and J. Pretty 2010 'The roles and values of wild foods in agricultural systems' (2010) *Philosophical Transactions of the Royal Society* 365, 2913–2926.
831   Economist, The 2013 *'Bowhunting in America'* 21 December 2013
832   United States Fish and Wildlife services 2013 *'Hunting'* 27 December 2013 www.fws.gov.
833   University of Michigan's Global Change 2014 *'The Flow of Energy: Primary production to higher trophic levels'* 25 March 2014 www.globalchange.umich.edu.
834   FAO 2014 *The Contribution of Insects to Food Security, Llivelihoods and the Environment* 20 April 2014. www.fao.org.
835   Ibid.
836   Ibid.
837   Gericke, W. F. 1940 *The Complete Guide to Soilless Gardening* Putnam.
838   Time 1938 *'Science: Hydroponics to wake'* Monday, 23 May 1938 http://content.time.com.
839   Time 2010 *'Vertical Farming - The 50 Best Inventions of 2009'* http://content.time.com.
840   Atkins, P. J., P. Lummel and D. J. Oddy (editors) 2007 *Food and the City in Europe since 1800* Ashgate.
841   Björklund, A. 2010 *Historical Urban Agriculture* Acta Universitatis Stockholmiensis.
842   Steel, C. 2008 *Hungry City*. Chatto & Windus.
843   Hughes, D. J. 2001 *An Environmental History of the World* Routledge.
844   Steel, C. 2008 *Hungry City* Chatto & Windus.
845   Guardian, The 2009 *'Allotment demand leads to 40-year waiting lists'* 2 June 2009.
846   Acton, L. 2011 'Allotment gardens: a reflection of history, heritage, community and self'. *Papers from the Institute of Archaeology* 21:46-58.
847   Ackerman-Leist, P. 2013 *Rebuilding the Foodshed* Chelsea Green Publishing.
848   Carey, J. 2011 *Who Feeds Bristol?* Bristol City Council.
849   Vivero Pol, J.L. 2013 *Food as a Commons: Reframing the narrative of the food system* 23 April 2013 Centre for Philosophy of Law, Université Catholique de Louvain.
850   Kennedy, J. F. 1963 *'Remarks to World Food Congress Delegates'* 4 June 1963; www.jfklibrary.org.
851   ETC 2011 Who will control the Green Economy? *ETC Communiqué* no. 107 ETC.
852   USDA Economic Research Service 2013 *Farm Size and the Organization of U.S. Crop Farming* Economic Resaerch Report 152 United States Department of Agriculture.
853   National Corn Growers Association 2013 *The World of Corn 2013* National Corn Growers Association.

854 US-EIA 2014 *'International Energy Statistics/Biofuels Production'* www.eia.gov.

855 US-EIA 2013 *Tracking Clean Energy Progress 2013* U.S. Energy Information Administration.

856 Makar, H. P. S. (editor) 2012 *Biofuel Co-Products As Livestock Feed: Opportunities and challenges.* Food and Agriculture Organization of the United Nations.

857 Pimentel, D. and T. W. Patzek 2005 'Ethanol production using corn, switchgrass, and wood; biodiesel production using soybean and sunflower' *Natural Resources Research,* 14 (1).

858 Makar, H. P.S. (editor) 2012 *Biofuel Co-Products As Livestock Feed: Opportunities and challenges.* United Nations Food and Agriculture Organization.

859 Ibid.

860 FAO 2008 *'The World Only Needs 30 Billion Dollars a Year to Eradicate the Scourge of Hunger'* Press release 3 June 2008 www.fao.org.

861 Erb, K-H. et al. 2009 *Eating the Planet: Feeding and fuelling the world sustainably, fairly and humanely–a scoping study* Institute of Social Ecology and Potsdam Institute for Climate Impact Research.

862 Johansson, K. et.al. 2010 'Agriculture as provider of both food and fuel' *Ambio* 39(2): 91–99.

863 Brown, L. 2013 *Full Planet, Empty Plates: The new geopolitics of food scarcity* Earth Policy Institute.

864 Rundgren, G. 2013 *Garden Earth - from hunter and gatherers to global capitalism and thereafter* Regeneration.

865 Gibbs, H. K. et al. 2008 'Carbon payback times for crop-based biofuel expansion in the tropics: The effects of changing yield and technology' *Environmental Research. Letters.* 3 034001.

866 United States Congressional Budget Office 2009 *The Impact of Ethanol Use on Food Prices and Greenhouse-Gas Emissions* United States Congress.

867 Ibid.

868 Sundberg, C. M. et al. 'Organic farming without fossil fuels – life cycle assessment of two Swedish cases' in *Organic Farming Systems as a Driver for Change,* Bredsten, Denmark, 21-23 August 2013 Nordic Association of Agricultural Scientist.

869 Johansson, S. and K. Belfrage. 'Self-sufficiency of fuels for tractive power in small-scale organic agriculture' in *Organic Farming Systems as a Driver for Change* Bredsten, Denmark, 21-23 August 2013 Nordic Association of Agricultural Scientist.

870 FAO 2006 *Livestock's Long Shadow* Food and Agriculture Organization of the United Nations

871 Mathias, E. 2012 *Livestock out of Balance, from Asset to Liability in the Course of the Livestock Revolution* League for Pastoral Peoples and Endogenous Livestock Development.

872 FAO 2006 *Livestock's Long Shadow* Food and Agriculture Organization of the United Nations.

873 Pettersson, R. (editor) 2008 Bekvämlighetsrevolutionen. Stockholmia Förlag.

874 Ibid.

875 Mathias, E. 2012 *Livestock out of Balance, from Asset to Liability in the Course of the Livestock Revolution* League for Pastoral Peoples and Endogenous Livestock Development.

876 Cassidy, E. S. et al. 2013 'Redefining agriculture yields: from tonnes to people nourished per hectare' *Environmental Research Letters* 8 (2013) 030415.

877 USDA 2012 *Agricultural Statistics 2012* United States Department of Agriculture.

878 Cassidy, E. S. et al. 2013 'Redefining agriculture yields: from tonnes tp people nourished per hectare' *Environmental Research Letters* 8 (2013) 030415.

879   Ibid.

880   Fairlie, S. 2008 'Can Britain feed itself?' *The Land* 4 Winter 2008-8.

881   Worldwatch Institute 2006 *State of the World 2006. Special focus: China and India.* W. W. Norton & Company, Inc.

882   FAO 2007 *The State of Food and Agriculture* Food and Agriculture Organization of the United Nations.

883   Erb, K-H. et al. 2009. *Eating the Planet: Feeding and fuelling the world sustainably, fairly and humanely–a scoping study* Institute of Social Ecology and Potsdam Institute for Climate Impact Research.

884   FAO 2006 *Livestock's Long Shadow* Food and Agriculture Organization of the United Nations.

885   Worldwatch Institute 2006 *State of the World 2006. Special focus: China and India.* W. W. Norton & Company, Inc.

886   FAO 2007 *The State of Food and Agriculture* Food and Agriculture Organization of the United Nations.

887   OECD 2011 *Industrial Biotechnology and Climate Change* Organization for Economic Cooperation and Development.

888   Coca-Cola Company 2013 *'Plantbottle'* www.coca-colacompany.com.

889   OECD 2011 *Industrial Biotechnology and Climate Change* Organization for Economic Cooperation and Development.

890   American Horse Council 2014 *'National Economic Impact of the U.S. Horse Industry'* www.horsecouncil.org.

891   Macklean 2013 Mat eller motor *Macklean Insikter*

892   Gasson and Errington 1993 quoted in Farnworth, C. R. (editor), *Creating Food Futures : trade, ethics and the environment.* Gower Publishing.

893   USDA Economic Research Service 2013 *Farm Size and the Organization of U.S. Crop Farming* Economic Resaerch Report 152 United States Department of Agriculture.

894   SCB 2012 *Hållbarhet issvenskt Jordbruk 2012* Statistiska Centralbyrån.

895   Canning, P. et al. 2010 *Energy Use in the U.S Food System,*. USDA-ERS Economic Research Report No 94.

896   Mathias, E. 2012 *Livestock out of Balance, from Asset to Liability in the Course of the Livestock Revolution* League for Pastoral Peoples and Endogenous Livestock Development.

897   Ibid.

898   Cochrane, W. W. 1993 *The Development of American Agriculture* University of Minnesota Press.

899   Mazoyer, M. and L. Roudart 2006 *A History of World Agriculture: From the Neolithic Age to the Current Crisis* Monthly Review Press.

900   Ibid.

901   Ibid.

902   Deutsch, L., R. Dyball and W. Steffen 2013 'Feeding cities: Food security and ecosystem support in an urbanizing world', in Elmqvist et al. (editors) *Urbanization, Biodiversity and Ecosystem Services: Challenges and opportunities* Springer.

903   Food Research and Action Center 2013 *Food Hardship in America 2012.*

904   Ackerman-Leist, P. 2013 *Rebuilding the Foodshed* Chelsea Green Publishing.

905   Ibid.

906   Allegretto, S.et al. 2013 *Fast Food, Poverty Wages: The public cost of low-wage jobs in the fast-food industry* University of California Berkley Labor Center.

907   Kneafsey, M. et al. 2008 *Reconnecting Consumers and Producers and Food* Berg.

908   Anglade, J., G. Billen and J. Garnier 2013 'Agronomical and environmental performances of organic farming', in *Organic Farming Systems as a Driver for Change*, Bredsten, Denmark, 21-23 August 2013.

909   Organic Standard, The 2014 'Danish statistic for organic dairy', *The Organic Standard* 151, February 2014.

910   Pollan, M. 2006 *The Omnivore's Dilemma: A Natural History of Four Meals* Penguin.

911   Noe, E. et al. 2013 'Barriers for developing more robust organic arable farming systems in practice', in *Organic Farming Systems as a Driver for Change*, Bredsten, Denmark, 21-23 August 2013. Nordic Association of Agricultural Scientist.

912   Interview with Knud Erik Sörensen, October 2013.

913   Schäfer, M. 2008 'Beyond Profit Making: Combining economic and social goals in the German organic agriculture and food sector', in Farnworth, C. R. (editor), *Creating Food Futures : trade, ethics and the environment*. Gower Publishing.

914   Pollan, M. 2013 *Cooked, a Natural History of Transformation* Allen Lane.

915   Ackerman-Leist, P. 2013 *Rebuilding the Foodshed* Chelsea Green Publishing.

916   Kirschenmann, F. 1995 Preface to G. Gershuny, and J. Smillie *The Soul of Soil* third edition. Agaccess.

917   El Pilar Forest Garden Network 2013 www.mayaforestgardeners.org.

918   WWF/MEDPO 2006 'Cork screwed?, the environmental and economic impacts of the cork stoppers market'. WWF.

919   Glover J.D. 2010 'Harvested perennial grasslands: Ecological models for farming's perennial future', *Agriculture, Ecosystems and Environment* 137 (2010) 1–2.

920   Heinrich Böll Foundation 2014 *Meat Atlas* Heinrich Böll Foundation.

921   Bengtson, J. 2013 'In which ways could modern biotechnlogy be part of sustainable agriculture', *Sveriges Utsädesförenings Tidskrift* 1.

922   Jackson, W. 2010 *Consulting the Genius of the Place* Counterpoint

923   Kremen, C. and Miles, A. 2013 'Ecosystem services in biologically diversified versus conventional farming systems: benefits, externalities and trade-offs' *Ecology and Society* 17(4):40.

924   Interview with Anders Lunneryd, December 2013.

925   Ibid.

926   Youl, R., S. Marriot and T. Nabben 2006 *Landcare in Australia, founded on local action*. SILC and Rob Youl Consulting Pty Ltd.

927   CPRE 2012 '*From Field to Fork: The value of England's local food webs*' Campaign to Protect Rural England.

928   Harper, A. et al. 2009 *Food Policy Councils: Lessons Learned* Food First.

929   Campbell, B. 2013 'Close to home'*Home Magazine*.

930   Born, B. and M. Purcell 2009 'Food systems and the local trap' in D. Inglis and D. Giimlin (editors) *The Globalization of Food* Berg.

931   Haase, D. 2013 'Shrinking cities, biodiversity and ecosystem services' in Elmqvist et al. *Urbanization, Biodiversity and Ecosystem Services: Challenges and opportunities*, Springer.

932   Food Justice Certified 2013 http://agriculturaljusticeproject.org.

933   Interview with Knud Erik Sörensen, October 2013.

934   Wright, C. 2009 'Fairtrade food: connecting producers and consumers', in D. Inglis and D. Giimlin (editors) *The Globalization of Food* Berg.

935   National Resource Institute 2013 *Final Technical Report: Assessing the poverty impact of sustainability standards*. National Resource Institute.

936   Karlsson, J. 2013 'The impossibilty of an ethical consumer' in H. Röcklingsberg (editor) *The Ethics of Consumption*, proceedings from EurSafe.

937   Pirscher, F. 2013 'Animal welfare labelling: is the market the right governance structure to meet people's moral concerns?' in H. Röcklingsberg (editor) *The Ethics of Consumption*, proceedings from EurSafe.

938 Aerts, S. 2013 'The consumer does not exist: overcoming the consumer/citizen paradox by shifting focus' in Röcklingsberg, H. (editor) The Ethics of Consumption: The Citizen, the Market and the Law (2013) Wageningen Academic Publishers.

939 Ekomatcentrum 2013 *Ekologiskt i Offentlig Storhushåll* 2012 Ekomatcentrum.

940 Ploeg, J. D. van der 2009 *The New Peasantries: Struggles for autonomy and sustainability in the era of empire and globalization* Earthscan.

941 USDA 2014 *'Farmers Markets and Direct-to-Consumer Marketing'* www.ams.usda.gov.

942 Kneafsey, M. et al. 2008 *Reconnecting Consumers and Producers and Food* Berg.

943 Bashford, J. et al. 2013 *European Handbook on Community Supported Agriculture Sharing Experiences*, Urgenci.

944 Canning et al. 2010 *Energy Use in the U.S Food System* Economic Research Report No 94. USDA Economic Research Service.

945 Hashimoto, S. 2014 *'The Teikei System in Japan'* http://blog.urgenci.net.

946 Fullton Center for Sustainable Living 2014 *Robyn Van En Biography*. www.wilson.edu/about-wilson-college/fulton/robyn-van-en-center/robyn-van-en-biography/index.aspx. 20 June 2014.

947 Peacework 2014 www.gvocsa.org.

948 Interview with Elizabeth Henderson, April 2014.

949 Ibid.

950 Ibid.

951 Ibid.

952 Kneafsey, M. et al. 2008 *Reconnecting Consumers and Producers and Food* Berg.

953 Ibid.

954 Ibid.

955 Canning P. et al. 2010 *Energy Use in the U.S Food System* Economic Research Report No 94. USDA Economic Research Service.

956 Ibid.

957 Interview with Rob Hopkins 3 February 2014

958 Transition Town Totnes 2012 *Economic Blueprint for Totnes & District: Our local food economy.* Transition Town Totnes.

959 Interview with Rob Hopkins 3 February 2014

960 Ibid.

961 Hopkins, R. and P. Lipman 2009 *'Who We Are and What We Do'* Transition Network.

962 Interview with Rob Hopkins 3 February 2014

963 Ibid.

964 Tiffen, H. 2013 *Crop Gaps Research, an exploration of how agricultural practices of the past can assist re-localising the totnes food system for the future.* Food Link Totnes.

965 Deane, T. 'The Last Field Vegetable- reflections at the end of a rotation', *The Organic Grower* #24, Autumn 2013

966 Canning P. et al. 2010 *Energy Use in the U.S Food System* Economic Research Report No 94. USDA Economic Research Service.

967 Ooooby 2014 www.ooooby.org.

968 Tiffen, H. 2013 *Crop Gaps Research, an exploration of how agricultural practices of the past can assist re-localising the totnes food system for the future.* Food Link Totnes.

969 Food Commons 2011 *The Food Commons 2.0*, October 2011.

970 Pretty, J. 2002 *Agri-culture: Reconnecting people, land and nature* Earthscan.

971 United Nations General Assembly 2013 *The Right to Food, Interim report of the Special Rapporteur on the Right to Food*, 7 August 2013, A/68/288

972 Ibid.

973 Ibid.
974 Sanchez-Montero, M. and N. S. Ubach 2010 *Undernutrition, What Works?'* ACF International Network.
975 Vivero Pol, J.L. 2013 *Food as a Commons: Reframing the narrative of the food system* 23 April 2013 Centre for Philosophy of Law, Université Catholique de Louvain.
976 Walker, J. 2014 *'Food Nullification'* http://reason.com.
977 GMO-free Europe 2014 www.gmo-free-regions.org.
978 Harper, A. et al. 2009 'Food Policy Councils: Lessons Learned' Food First.
979 Shiva, V. 2005 *Earth Democracy: Justice, sustainability, and peace* South End Press.
980 IFOAM 2005 *'First Legal Defeat of a Biopiracy Patent: The Neem case.'* International Federation of Organic Agriculture Movements.
981 No Patents on Seed 2014 www.no-patents-on-seeds.org.
982 Helfrich, S. 2009 *'Strengthen the Commons–Now!'* translated by M. Thorne, S. Helfrich and D. Bollier Heinrich Böll Foundation.
983 Oksana M. et al. 2013 *Lessons from Nordic Council of Ministers' Study "Improving Nordic policymaking by dispelling myths on sustainable consumption"* Nordic Working Papers 2013:915, Nordic Council of Ministers.
984 Oxfam 2014 *Working for the Few* Briefing Paper 178 Oxfam.
985 Kropotkin, P. 2007 *The Conquest of Bread*. Project Gutenberg EBook.
986 Leopold, A. 1966 *A Sand County Almanac: With other essays on conservation from Round River*. Kindle Edition.
987 Berry, W. 1977 *The Unsettling of America: Culture and agriculture* Sierra Club Books.

37079068R00242

Made in the USA
Charleston, SC
26 December 2014